AMERICA'S
AFFLUENT AGE

Other Books by Floyd and Marion Rinhart:

American Daguerreian Art
American Miniature Case Art

AMERICA'S AFFLUENT AGE

Floyd and Marion Rinhart

South Brunswick and New York: A. S. Barnes and Company
London: Thomas Yoseloff Ltd

A. S. Barnes and Co., Inc.
Cranbury, New Jersey 08512

Thomas Yoseloff Ltd
108 New Bond Street
London W1Y OQX, England

SBN 498 07335 1
Printed in the United States of America

Contents

America's Affluent Age
Section IV
THE PEOPLE OF AMERICA

Acknowledgments and Picture Credits

To Miss Josephine Cobb, specialist of iconography, National Archives, Washington, D. C., we are deeply grateful not only for her encouragement over many years of research but for her expert help and suggestions for avenues of research. She has also been generous in making available early daguerreotypes from her own collection for use in this volume. Also, special acknowledgment should be given the Still Pictures Branch of the National Archives, Miss Josephine Motylewski, Joe Thomas, and Harry Bauda.

We are grateful for the generous help given by the Smithsonian Institution. A very special debt is owed to Dr. Philip W. Bishop, chairman, Arts and Manufactures, for his time, knowledge, and encouragement. Also offering expert help were: Mrs. Anne Murray, costumes; Dr. S. Bedini, industrial arts; Dr. D. H. Johnson, mammalogy; Edgar Howell and Donald E. Kloster, uniforms; Dr. Sturtevant and Margaret C. Blaker, American ethnology; and Eugene Ostroff, photography.

For his valuable help in locating needed historical prints, we give warm thanks to Milton Kaplan, specialist in Historical Prints, Library of Congress; special thanks are also due Hirst Milhollen, former specialist in photographs, and Miss Virginia Daiker. We are grateful to the other members of the library staff who were always helpful and courteous during the long period of research in the library.

We are indebted to Miss Stella Scheckter, Reference Librarian of the New Hampshire State Library, Concord, for helping to check state registers that provided a clue for identifying a daguerreotype scene, Timothy Kenrick's store, as located in Lebanon, New Hampshire. Mr. Sam Stevens, Lebanon, New Hampshire, helped to identify another daguerreotype scene. Among Mr. Stevens' collection of old newspapers, he recalled one with a reprint of a painting of the old Town Hall of Lebanon. The artist's rendition in the 1890 newspaper proved the identification. Mr. Stevens also allowed his copy of an early map of the town to be photographed for use in the book. To James de T. Abajian, former Librarian of The California Historical Society, we are grateful for providing a clue to the identification of the daguerreotype of gold mining in Jamestown, California. Mrs. Ruth Ann Newport, former curator of Tuolumne County Museum, Sonora, California, researched records and provided factual help by proving that Byron Woodworth had his carpenter shop in Jamestown during the early 1850s. We are grateful to Gerald J. Parsons, Syracuse Public Library, Syracuse, New York, who searched for records that proved the final step in identifying the Oneida Conference Seminary daguerreotype. Also in helping to identify some of the rare daguerreotypes used throughout the book, our son George, a scholar of history, was very helpful.

Special thanks should be given to Norman Mintz and his associate Morris Weiss of Time-Out Antiques, New York City, for generously sending rare scenes and portraits to be photographed for use in this work. We are indebted to Robert A. Weinstein, Los Angeles, California, for making available his rare gold-mining scene.

Our deep appreciation is expressed for the help given by the late Dorothy Ross of Deerfield Beach, Florida—for her many hours of manuscript reading and critical appraisal of the material and for her general editing, and to George G. Hutchinson, chairman, division of English, Mills College of Education, New York City, for his many valuable suggestions and for editing parts of the volume. Also, warm thanks go to Henri Davis, a veteran photographer, who made suggestions as to equipment needed, the principles of lighting, and the many other details necessary to know for the photographing of original daguerreotypes for use in this book.

Other individuals and institutions helpful during our research and study or having provided pictorial materials, are the following:

Ansco Company, Binghamton, New York. Philip Mikoda, Joseph Guderian.

Boatman's National Bank, St. Louis, Missouri.

Howard I. Chapelle, Smithsonian Institution, Washington, D. C.

Chicago Historical Society.

Columbia Historical Society, Washington, D. C.

D.A.R. Library, Washington, D. C.

Alfred V. Frankenstein, San Francisco, California.

Frick Art Reference Library, New York City. Mrs. Henry W. Howell, Jr., Miss H. Sanger.

Introduction

The fame of Mathew B. Brady and his associates, whose dramatic and realistic photographs of the Civil War have received wide acclaim, has obscured the fact that the recording of American social history in photographs began some twenty years before the outbreak of the war. In reality, the camera began capturing the exact image of America in the fall of 1839. The invention of the Frenchman Louis Daguerre, who discovered that a photographic likeness could be recorded on the highly polished silvered surface of a copper plate, was introduced to America by Samuel F. B. Morse. Yankee ingenuity rapidly developed improvements on Daguerre's techniques, and by the winter of 1840 a clear photographic image, particularly in the field of portraiture, was an established fact.

The daguerreotype—a photograph—was unique. Nothing quite like it had appeared before. It marked the first time an exact image could be fixed in a mirrored reflection. It excited the entire world and can be likened to Christopher Columbus's discovery of a new world. Illustrated history prior to this had to depend on lithographs, paintings, and line drawings, which were often idealized and inaccurate representations of persons or events. Now the discerning eye of the camera could capture realistically the pageant of history, especially the life of the common man, in the important years preceding the Civil War.

From the fall of 1839 to early 1841, photography had expanded into a substantial commercial industry. Faces and scenes were photographed in ever-increasing numbers. The range of subjects was wide, taking in views of towns and cities, mountain views and urban streets, people at work in fields and factories. Many possibilities presented themselves. However, the early photographic process was complicated and depended greatly on weather conditions and on the ingenuity of the daguerreotypist. Taking pictures out of doors was difficult, so that studio pictures far outnumbered outdoor scenes. Few scenes are extant; those remaining are to be found scattered throughout the country in museums, in private collections, and in the collections of historical societies.

Early photographers seemed serious in their efforts to record the faces and the scenes of America. More than they perhaps realized, their efforts exerted an undeniable influence on American society. Daguerreotype photography encouraged a new feeling of national closeness. Prominent men of the day were photographed and their pictures displayed in daguerreian parlors. In an age of lithographic illustration, the exact image mirrored in the daguerreotype plate impressed and stirred considerable interest among the people. Exhibitions were held in the large cities as well as in the smaller ones; excited sightseers came from far and near. Scenes of distant American locales stimulated a desire for travel. The daguerreotype made it possible for a society in the process of national expansion, a society on the move, to send pictures back home. Special events and proud accomplishments and portraits of dear ones could now be recorded. A customer could enter a daguerreian parlor, have his photograph taken, and walk out of the establishment a few minutes later with his image, enclosed, as a jewel would be, in a handsome case.

The daguerreotypes chosen and copied for the present volume represent a cross section of middle-class America. They were selected from all parts of the country, and the faces and scenes reflect the small towns in America as well as the larger cities. Many of the photographs throughout the book (copied from daguerreotypes) are used as a vehicle to point out the prototype of persons or events. To illustrate a void left when photographs were not available in the coverage of a particular event or subject of the era, copies of contemporary engravings, sketches, and paintings are used. Dates of the photographs are determined whenever possible by study of physical characteristics of the originals and are fairly accurate within a two- or three-year period. All photographs used to illustrate the book are copies of daguerreotypes or ambrotypes; the few exceptions are so noted in the captions.

In order that the reader may gain a more comprehensive view of this age and its many facets, the text has been dealt with topically rather than as a series of chronological events. By consulting contemporary books and periodicals of the era, the authors have steeped themselves in the feelings of the people and their attitudes. Hence these have often been given precedence over the better-known attitudes of the era's contemporary political figures or historians, for they are equally representative of those times.

The purpose of this volume is to bring into clearer focus the era of 1840–1860, and perhaps it may help to overcome the many erroneous notions that have grown up over the years surrounding and beclouding an era of great social change in America. For this purpose the daguerreotype has great documentary value for the study of the emerging national character in this period. These early photographs have an almost breath-of-life quality, an intensity, and a directness; studying them offers a fresh new insight into the era.

As the study and writing of the book progressed, the people of the era emerged as so warmly human, so hu-merous, so serious, and so broad in outlook, that many of the old "truisms" prevalent in modern education melted away. It was found that this was a society completely divorced from the later nineteenth century. Although mid-nineteenth century America is often referred to as the Victorian Age, the mere fact that Victoria was Queen of England from 1837–1901 can hardly justify the grouping of an American society into one category for the balance of the century.

In general, the society of 1840–1860 has a definite Anglo-Saxon heritage . (the daguerreotype tends to prove this contention) , and it was not subjected to the mixed-European caste of the latter part of the century. The mid-nineteenth century had little affinity in outlook for, and lacked the claustrophobic feeling so evident in, the latter society. The society of 1840–1860 was a distinctive one in American history.

AMERICA'S
AFFLUENT AGE

Section I

THE IMAGE OF AMERICA

1

The World Image of America

The infant republic had matured and come of age; he stood like a lusty giant, much larger and greater than his European sire. It might be said that "the Young Bull had challenged the Old Bull!" John Bull and La Belle France emitted large volumes of criticisms and advice. Other nations joined in to a lesser degree.

The Europeans boiled, fumed, and ranted at these United States that now challenged their leadership. And, like the proverbial offspring, the Americans bragged to high heaven and promptly produced what they boasted about.

Ever since the War of 1812, the Americans had steadily severed, one by one, the colonial type of political influences of Europe that were evident in the period before 1812. The tremendous growth of the population was more than matched by the economic growth, and by the 1840s there had been established, especially in the expanding cities, a well-rounded American society. The basic background of this society was a well-fed, affluent, middle class of American. Also, census records for rural areas show the farmer having a net worth of $10,000 or more, to be commonplace.[1]

In the early 1840s a cultural explosion caused a tremendous growth of libraries, learned societies, clubs, and museums, all dedicated to intellectual improvement and advancement. This atmosphere of lively social ferment created a period highly favorable to greater achievements in literature and the arts. For example, the established American native school of artists felt that art should not serve a cultural elite exclusively, but, to summarize their attitude, that they should "paint not for the few but for the many." This attitude is best reflected in cold statistical figures of art attendance; a New York City exhibition devoted to displaying the native school of art attracted 57½ percent of the city's population for the years 1839 to 1851. Pride in American art achievements, as in other fields, shines out in the era's efforts to afford better living for the entire population.

In the 1840s and 1850s the Americans went abroad in large numbers—"the original American tourist." Their bragging and opulence must have been convincing to the European poor, for in the one year of 1854 there were more than 300,000 people crossing the sea to make a permanent home in the United States. What the less wealthy European saw in the typical American tourist was "a poor man grown rich," an opportunist with opportunity.

"Hard work with just compensation" seemed a very desirable creed to the European living in almost feudal circumstances. The American tourist was dressed as richly as European statesmen and leaders, and, above all, he said what he thought and said it loudly, much to the chagrin of European traditional wise men.

In the field of military endeavor the Europeans were casting a wary eye in America's direction. The year 1838 saw the United States with a small, well-balanced fleet of warships, consisting of 15 ships of the line, 35 frigates, and 16 war steamers. Comparably, Britain had 90 ships of the line, 93 frigates, and 12 war steamers. In number of ships America rated fourth after Britain, France, and Russia, in that order. Analytically, much of European sea power consisted of obsolete ships left over from the Napoleonic wars. By 1840 the United

ca. 1853   *Courtesy Time-Out Antiques, N.Y.C.*
An Unknown Waterfront Community
*America's growth in this period was reflected in its many well-
ordered towns and cities.*

States had the most modern navy in the world. An American innovation changed the naval rating of a ship's effectiveness from a rating by the number of guns she carried to a rating by the efficiency of the armament —revolutionary in 1840. The new American steamers were huge ships with few guns of very heavy caliber. The decade beginning in 1840 was one of the greatest periods of advancement in the art and science of marine architecture and engineering that had yet been seen. The years 1840–1845 saw the Americans mounting an 8-inch bore, shell-firing cannon on their warships.[2] This radical change had been proposed by John Dahlgren, U.S.N. No other nation was this advanced in naval conception.

In 1842 the U. S. Naval Department was greatly enlarged to five separate bureaus. The U.S.S. *Princeton*

was launched in 1844, thus being the first warship in the world equipped with a screw-driven propeller, which utilized John Ericsson's invention. Britain followed with a screw-driven warship in 1845. The Naval Academy at Annapolis opened this same year of 1845. These and other challenges caused Great Britain to wake up from the nostalgic dreams of Trafalgar and she now looked to the future. The great black American fleet of the 1850s stood unchallenged. With Matthew Perry's opening of the Japanese treaty ports to world trade, a new view of the American navy was given to the world.

Ever since the days of 1812 the American sailor had been rated the best in the world. In the 1840s the merchant marine was the largest, fastest afloat. In 1840 the United States had 2,180,764 tons of documented mer-

1841

. . . he stood like a lusty giant, much larger and greater than his European sire.

1842

. . . The basic background of this society was a well fed, affluent, middle-class American.

An outdoor photograph.

1849

In the 1840s and 1850s the Americans went abroad in large numbers. They dressed expensively and traveled first class. It is not surprising that the European, seeing this prosperous image, migrated to America in the hope of becoming rich.

1844

. . . John Bull and La Belle France emitted large volumes of criticisms and advice. . . . The European commented that America had cold bedrooms, tiring dinners, drank cold water, and had poor manners.—An English daguerreotype.

Courtesy Columbia Historical Society
U.S.S. Princeton *from an old lithograph*
Launched in 1844, the Princeton *was the first warship to use*
the screw driver propeller, invented by John Ericsson.

chant marine, which represented an almost 83 percent increase over 1830 and, in 1850, 3,535,454 tons, a 62.1 percent increase over 1840.

Beginning in 1841 with the development of the American Clipper Ship, the English boat builders were taught a lesson. It took the English almost ten years to duplicate this fast sailing ship, and not until then did they again share in the lucrative China trade.

The winter of 1840 saw the United States lay claim to the discovery of the Antarctic Continent. Lieutenant Charles Wilkes commanded a fleet of five vessels, organized and authorized by the Congress for the express purpose of exploring the south polar regions. Wilkes claimed the land for the United States, and although apparently none of his party landed on terra firma, there were repeated reports by his men of sighting land.

The French and British were afloat for the same purpose in that year, and while the United States' claim was generally recognized, it became the center of a controversy that lasted well into the twentieth century.

The Europeans complained in 1840 that the Americans could, with ease, pick their best locks, thus implying that perhaps if recognition were due, it would be on the shady side. In the early 1840s, a visiting Italian gentleman touring the United States published in New York City a book "Why a National Literature Cannot Flourish in the United States of North America." Not abashed at this criticism, The Franklin Press published Mr. Rocchietti's work in 1845. It sold to the public for 25¢.

Another similar testimony to the American future was written by an English tourist under the pseudonym

"Uncle Sam." Entitled *Uncle Sam's Peculiarities,* it appeared in 1844.

From 1845 to 1855 the Americans were recognized as the world leaders in the art of daguerreotyping. From the very beginning of photography in 1839, the Americans, unlike their European counterparts, had sought to photograph the entire population rather than just the prominent people. The Americans' broad scope resulted in the establishing of "American Daguerreian Parlors" in many cities of Europe.[3] Promoter John Plumbe had established an outlet in Paris by 1846. John Mayall of Philadelphia opened his London studio that same year. He soon became the most fashionable portraitist in London; his daguerreotypes were the finest portraits of Queen Victoria.

The first World's Fair, London 1851, saw the Ameri-

Courtesy National Archives
Busy United States Navy dockyards along the Eastern Seaboard reflected America's growing might. By 1840, all American navy yards were using steam to saw timbers. The use of iron-working equipment was being introduced at a steady pace to meet the demands of the iron steamer. A view taken in 1847 of Drydock No. 1 of the New York Navy Yard at Brooklyn (above).

Courtesy Howard I. Chapelle from
The History of the American Sailing Navy
The sailing warship was fast disappearing in 1840. A view of the stern of the U.S.S. Pennsylvania, *120 guns, largest sailing man-of-war ever built for the United States. She burned at Norfolk Navy Yard on April 20, 1861.*

A View of Boston Harbor, 1840
Photography had come to stay. It ushered in an era where, for the first time, the camera's eye would record history in its exactness. The rare daguerretotype above shows one of the first exact images of America—an early steamboat and the unfinished Bunker Hill Monument may be seen in the far background. Photographs, as the one above, were taken on rooftops in the bright sunshine because of the long time exposure required.

cans display their art of daguerreotyping. The Americans won most of the honors, including three of the top five first-place awards.

Photography had come to stay. It ushered in an era where for the first time the camera's eye would record history in its exactness. The pioneer photographers, many unknown and forgotten, recorded with the daguerreotype method of photography a treasure of the American past.

The daguerreotypists, from a few pioneers in 1840, would expand in ever-increasing numbers, all eager to record the life and faces of America. The photographer-artists would meet the challenge of technical difficulties with the same inventiveness and ingenuity that typified the expanded America of this era.

In the 1840–1850 era, it has been estimated, every fourth American male had a ready-made scheme for becoming rich. This fourth male was busy discovering inventions, devising improvements, and dreaming theories. In short, this age should rightly be called the "Age of Invention." Inventions in this era could not be confined to mechanical advancements but were extended to the many fields of literature, arts, education, and better daily living for the masses. Edgar Allan Poe's *Murders in the Rue Morgue*, the first modern detective story, was an example of literary invention in 1841.

Somehow contemporary America of the period realized the vast, expanding, unlimited horizon of invention. Men were not limited to a narrow field of thought. Typically, Samuel Morse—artist, inventor, business man

Courtesy Library of Congress
The sloop of war, U.S.S. Vincennes, *eighteen guns, led the Wilkes expedition to the Antarctic Continent and also explored the South Seas and the Pacific Coast of the North American Continent. The sketch above, from the Wilkes's Report of 1844, shows the* Vincennes *disabled off San Francisco.*

1840

1843

1843

—would stand out as a man of multiple thoughts and talents. There were many others in this unique era.

To Dr. John W. Draper may well go the honor of being the first American to capture the elusive "Sun Beam" image in exact form. In the early 1830s Professor Draper, then a professor of medicine at the University of Pennsylvania, began the quest for, in simple terms, a photograph. In 1837 he was elected Professor of Chemistry at the University of the City of New York. During the same year he published in the Journal of Franklin Institute the results of a successful experiment made in 1835. In that published report, he stated that he had "determined the chemical effects of light on a plate."

Thus it was that Samuel Morse, after his return from France in 1839, and with the arrival of Daguerre's process of photography, immediately contacted Dr. Draper. In collaboration, they quickly devised the first photographic improvement, which enabled them to take a portrait clearly. This improvement may be credited to Draper, who had, prior to this, realized the importance of chemicals, focus, lens, and length of camera box in relation to one another.

So it was that this natural joining of great talents—Morse the artist-inventor, Draper the chemist-photographer—resulted in a series of experiments conducted on a rooftop of New York University in the early part

1841

1841

1848
Recorded with the daguerreotype, a treasure of the past. Picking berries and wildflowers was a pleasant outdoor pastime for children in this era.

1841
. . . In many respects this society was the end product of the Revolutionary War.
An outdoor photograph by John Plumbe, Jr.

1845
The Civil War and a new industrial age would bring to an end a leisurely way of life. The girl's necklace was believed to ward off disease. In the 1840s it was difficult sometimes to distinguish small boys from girls, as they wore dresses over pantaloons.

1845
The Americans, unlike their European counterparts, sought to photograph the entire population rather than just the prominent people. Yankee ingenuity brought the price of a portrait down from $5.00, in the early 1840s, to twenty-five cents for a small picture by 1856.

of 1840. Progressively, they built a studio of glass on the roof. By 1841, as the result of their experiments, rooftop and open-sunlight photographs gave way to indoor portraits, using the skylight as a source of light.

There were other pioneers at the same time, experimenting and improving the photograph. Some dabbled with color, some were striving to reduce the length of exposure time, and still others were overcoming the technical difficulties encountered in early photography.

The American way of life in this era was leisurely yet energetic, expanding yet solid, laying the groundwork for later America. The westward surge, the California gold rush, and the most successful war the United States ever fought were all part of this era. In many respects this society was the end product of the Revolutionary War.

The Civil War would bring to an end this way of life and never again for the next forty years would America have a well-to-do middle class as the stabilizing influence.

With the end of the Civil War the United States would enter the "Age of industrial pirates." There would be the rich and the poor, with the middle class oppressed.

In sum, the era was marked by many extremes: extremes in national pride; extremes in personal independence—yet with the contradiction of slavery; extremes in achievements—in arts, literature, and invention; extremes in national expansion; extremes in fads and social reforms—altogether a wonderful and interesting era. The United States had earned, for a brief period, the title of the leading nation in the world.

2
A Glimpse of the Rural East

America was still an agrarian society in 1840. One quarter of its seventeen million population farmed the land. Thousands of towns and villages stood as yet remote and isolated in their untamed settings of pastoral beauty and rugged grandeur.

Far from transportation and communication, the rural community had to be entirely self-sustaining. Three factors blended the rural community into a self-sufficient and democratic unit—the experience derived from the traditional tilling of the soil, the sympathetic and charitable attitude of the people toward each other, and the prevalence of independent and resourceful leaders. These factors, combined with the working guideposts of the church and the town hall, spelled the making of a successful community.

Travelers found the hardy country folk hospitable and friendly, and full of inquisitive leading questions. In the general store one might be given a sales talk and offered a friendly drink of whiskey even if the sale was lost. No nonsense was tolerated in regard to chivalry toward women. Unless a woman was obviously for sale she was given every consideration. In 1847 a self-important traveling Englishman secured first place in a coach. He was told by the proprietor, "Here are some ladies. Will you be good enough to take a seat on the other side. Very sorry, sir, but the best place is always for the ladies." Then spoke John Bull "Sir, I took my place at Cumberland and paid for it. It is mine, and all America shall not take it from me." Then with a volley of oaths he fell back in his place. "As you please, sir," said the proprietor. "You may keep it if you like to all eternity," and he closed the door. In about ten minutes John Bull opened the door and looked out. They had very quietly harnessed the horses to another coach, which was now a quarter of a mile up the road.

The farm, following a traditional pattern since colonial days, was a complete unit in itself, the layout of the buildings and land having been planned for the utmost in convenience with regard to both work and weather. It had the completeness and the efficiency of a well-run factory or business enterprise. Everything possible was raised on the farm—livestock and poultry, vegetables, and fruits. Flocks of sheep provided wool for clothing that could be woven by the womenfolk. Many a farmer's son went to college dressed in homespun. Bartering was resorted to for other needs. A satisfactory swap could usually be worked out with a nearby neighbor or merchant at the county seat.

The farm woman was a lady of many talents. She could sew a fine seam, bake, make butter and cheese, preserve, and make her own soap and candles. Her formal education was scanty but her earthy knowledge was vast. Higher education was not considered necessary for women but men were as well educated as circumstances would permit. In the 1840s a new surge of interest was taking place in education and literature and its influence was being felt in the rural areas as well as in the cities.

On the surface it appeared as though the traditional picture of rural America still existed, but beneath this placid cover changes were in motion by 1840 that would revolutionize the farm industry in America. Restless and ambitious, many would leave the farm to try out a new idea, seek a new, richer territory, and many would

1843
. . . *The hardy country folk were both hospitable and friendly.*

battered craft. A cart might rattle by with recently landed whalesmen, unkempt and unshaven, a motley and savage-looking group already in tow by a "land shark." The men would soon be rid of their hard-earned wages after visiting the local taverns and would have to sign up for another long four-year cruise. The lower town of New Bedford could boast of the greatest variety of humans to be found anywhere: Europeans of every country, native Yankees, Negroes, Portuguese, and a sprinkling of Chinese, Australians, and Polynesians. Here nationality, color of skin, religion, or ancestry meant nothing. A man was judged by his seamanship alone.

Whaling was a big, highly competitive business, an industry that was tough and cruel, fraught with danger. New Bedford was established in 1765 and would reach its peak of production in the 1840s and 1850s. By 1857 it had 329 registered whaling ships and employed 10,000 people in its industry. From then on the widespread use of petroleum as an illuminant would spell the doom of whaling as a big industry and the Civil War would

migrate to the city to engage in a new trade. Within 20 years, from 1840–1860, a completely different concept of farm life and the industrialization of food supply would emerge. McCormick's reaper, already gaining popularity in the West, would be far reaching in scope and the fast new railroads and steam travel would speed up the process that would make rural America, as history knew it, a thing of the past.

Many small towns had already taken on an industrial look. The coastal towns built ships and engaged in seafaring industries. One of these busy ports was New Bedford, Massachusetts, a large whaling center. A handsome town, it was built principally of wood, with long streets and ornamental cottages surrounded by attractive shrubberies and flower gardens, reflecting the affluence and good taste of its citizens. Down at the wharves one would stumble on the spoils of the sea—shells from Madagascar, coral from a far-away reef, and war clubs from the man-eating New Zealanders. The busy wharves were covered with anchors, rusty cables, hoops and lances, staves and empty oil casks. Gangs of caulkers and riggers would be busy refitting a storm-

1849
Farmers were advised to furnish their sons with small tools as play-toys.

1851
On the surface it appeared as though the traditional picture of rural America still existed, but, beneath this placid cover, by 1840 changes were in motion that would revolutionize the farm industry in America. McCormick's reaper, fast new railroads, and steam travel would all speed up the process of making traditional rural America a thing of the past.

almost completely bring to a close this adventuresome bit of American history.

The inland towns carried on small industries and built tiny factories, making an endless variety of small products. If a town did not have enough water power there were always nearby brooks, streams, and rivers to be utilized. In Hampton, Connecticut, as early as 1800, a stream no more than 15 feet wide contained eight dams and ten mills. Three of these were within one half mile of each other. Dry spells caused many a controversy among the mill owners!

These rural mills and small factories stemmed from the pioneering efforts of Samuel Slater, "Father of American Manufacturers." Slater, a young Englishman, came to America in 1789. He was able to re-create cotton-spinning machinery from memory, which he used in his first small factory started in 1790. The first yarn automatically turned out in America was produced in December of that year. After a succession of frustrating problems, a pattern of success began developing. Over the years many of the men who had worked for Slater started their own mills and the industry began to mushroom.

The pioneering of Samuel Slater, combined with the

Many of the small coastal towns were busy building ships and engaged in a variety of seafaring industries. Gangs of caulkers and riggers could always be seen at these ports, repairing storm battered crafts.

1857
This boy, propped against pillows, is possibly a whaler's son holding a toy harpoon.

1843
. . . New England sea captains linked America with foreign
lands. . . . From 1812 onward, American seamen were considered the best in the world.
Above, ship's mast in background; an outdoor daguerreotype
by L. C. Champney.

invention of the cotton gin by Eli Whitney, made certain the phenomenal future of American cotton manufacturing and laid the groundwork for all factory systems to come.

The first real effort to manufacture cotton cloth in America was made in Lowell, Massachusetts. The town was founded by Patrick Jackson, Nathan Appleton, and Paul Moody of Boston. Need for adequate water power led them to a site by Pawtucket Falls on the Merrimack River, in the village of East Chelmsford. They bought the Pawtucket Canal and in 1822 incorporated the Merrimack Manufacturing Company. The first cotton cloth was produced in 1823. Results were a miserable failure; texture was very coarse and color poor. Calico figured with white dots proved even worse, hardly worth the price of 30 cents a yard. The spots washed out, leaving gaping holes the sizes of bullets. English dyers and printers were imported and the problems were resolved.

1851
Numerous small factories were built in the East, which made an endless variety of products. Nearby streams were utilized for power. Mechanized industry was in its infancy before 1836; almost every article was made by hand with few exceptions. Many rural households made shoes, nails, and pencils. Factories in the southern New England area and Middle States were mostly small, and were run by individuals rather than corporations. By 1860 many of the wooden machines used, gave way to iron ones and water power yielded to steam.

In 1826 a separate township was formed from part of Chelmsford and was named in honor of Francis Cabot Lowell, who with his brother-in-law, Patrick Jackson, had improved the Cartwright power looms.

After improving the quality of their cloth the corporation looked around for a labor force for the expanding mill. Eyes were fastened on the energetic, independent farm girl, but how to entice her to factory labor? Here was a problem. Visionaries dreamed an ideal town, pleasant working conditions, moral safeguards, above all an aura of respectability. A cultural atmosphere would be encouraged, with lectures, and a program of literature and arts. In addition, a rule of mandatory church attendance and a night curfew of 10 P. M. would be inaugurated. Backed by this idealistic picture, agents were sent out to the farms. The farmer was assured by the agents that his daughters would be in safe hands, and after getting his approval, the girls and their belongings were deposited in the waiting coach. Then on to the next farmhouse. When the coach

1846
The New England farm girl was attracted to factory work at Lowell, Massachusetts, by a free cultural program of arts, literature, and lectures.

1849
"They are very pretty women, by the eternal!" said President Jackson when he made a tour of the Lowell cotton mills in the 1830s.

was filled with laughing girls they headed toward Lowell, the girls eager and ready for the new adventure away from home.

Turnover at the factory was heavy. Most of the female operatives had no idea of staying on indefinitely, as most came to earn money for marriage, business, or home. A certificate of honorable discharge was given to them on leaving, and instead of being downgraded by factory labor many went on to better jobs.

Of the eleven corporations subsequently formed in Lowell, Merrimack Company remained the queen of the cotton mill industry. The great canal was owned by them, the water power, and all land below the falls. In 1844, the combined mills manufactured 100,000,000 yards of printed cloth and 15,000,000 yards of dyed cloth, thus showing the tremendous growth of the industry. In this same year the mills used one-eighth part of all raw cotton grown in America.[1]

In 1843 one half of all the bank deposits in Lowell were made by the mill girls. The accumulated savings of the female operatives averaged, according to the

1845 records, $1,250 per girl. A few averaged $2,000. The interest rate paid on savings was 7 percent.[2]

Average weekly earnings ranged from $2.50 to as high as six to ten dollars. Wages were paid monthly, out of which a $1.25 weekly board and room fee was deducted. Wages, although seemingly small, were three times higher than for comparable work in Europe.

The mill worker society was divided into four categories. In the top echelon were the agents or "aristocrats" who lived in large houses with beautiful gardens. The "overseers" lived in company tenements. The female operatives lived in boarding houses, each usually housing 20 girls, three to a room. A room for callers was provided, nicely furnished, including a piano. On the lowest rung of the ladder was a group called "Lords of spade and shovel" who lived on the "acre" in shanties.

Rules for ages of workers varied with the corporations. A few employed children under 14 with the stipulation that school must be attended three months a year. Most workers were not hired until they were 15 years old. Children employed changed bobbins and worked 15 minutes out of the hour, the rest of the time being their own. Hours at the mill were tailored after the farm—5 A. M. until 7 P. M.—with half-hour breaks.

The girls joined in wholeheartedly with the literature and art programs. A literary magazine, "The Lowell Offering," was written and published by them from 1840–1845. Local lectures were attended, based not only on literature and arts but on topics of the day —anti-slavery and the like. Fads and reformers came to Lowell. Amelia Bloomer, pioneer dress reformer, paraded the streets of Lowell on July 4, 1850, with her bloomer girls. Statesmen and visitors from other countries came. President Jackson said in 1833, when he visited Lowell, as the operatives paraded to meet him dressed in white and carrying green-fringed parasols, "They are very pretty women, by the Eternal!" Another tribute to the fairness of the Lowell girls was a court decision handed down following two breach-of-promise suits in 1845. The two fair plaintiffs received $2,000 and $2,500, respectively, five hundred more than was asked for.[3]

The town was a source of delight to visitors. The streets were clean and straight. One sensed an air of health and contentment. Schools were numerous, and the poorest were able to send their children to primary school. There were thirty schools in all, including eight "upper seminaries" for the wealthy, and even the local workmen founded a "laboring man's hall," where reading, writing, and languages were taught. Somehow the town had combined industry with culture, a difficult task. It was not until the 1850s that the evils began creeping in. By 1857 machinery had been improved, but the girls were pushed and now had no leisure time. Prices rose and wages remained the same. Immigrants poured into Lowell, and leisure hours were spent in beer drinking instead of literary pursuits. The farm girls drifted back to their homesteads. The bright example of a model factory town dimmed.

In the "town meeting country," as inland rural New England was called, towns and villages were expanding and growing, reflecting the pulse of the country. These towns took care of their local problems and were also keenly interested in state and national affairs.

A typical example of such a town in the 1850s was Lebanon, New Hampshire. An early daguerreotypist recorded for history scenes of this small town. Few towns would be so fortunate in having their proud heritage photographed, because outdoor photographs in this period required bulky equipment. Weather conditions, too, were a factor in successful outdoor photography.

The town hall or "The Old Meeting House," as it was called in Lebanon, back in 1826, had a two story pulpit and galleries on three sides. The upper story was made into a Universalist Church, the lower story, the town hall. In 1841 the building was repaired and renovated, and in 1842 a new duty was imposed on the town clerk, Timothy Kenrick, to take charge of the meetinghouse and to see that it was kept in proper repair. The people were proud of their town hall and contributed from their own pockets to buy a new clock for the belfry tower. Children were welcome in the building; their shouting and laughter were frequently heard as they romped and played within. The women used the hall for town suppers and other social events; the men conducted their business meetings and town affairs in the building. Any man interested in pursuing a scientific venture was invited to use the premises free of charge.

The meetinghouse was moved from its original site in 1851 and repairs and some changes were then made under the supervision of the town selectmen. The hall continued as a focal point of activity for the community until 1887, when the great fire of Lebanon destroyed it and much of the town.

Typical of a leading citizen in a small town of America in this era was Timothy Kenrick of Lebanon. Kenrick, town clerk and merchant, had been born in Amesbury, Massachusetts, in 1793. Two years after his father was killed in a shipyard fall, sixteen-year-old Timothy had come to Lebanon, and except for a year spent in Enfield, New Hampshire, he made his home there until his death.

In 1819 Kenrick was elected town clerk, succeeding

1851

The Town Hall and part of the village square, Lebanon, New Hampshire, is shown above. The daguerreotype pictured was taken shortly after the hall was moved from its original site in 1851.

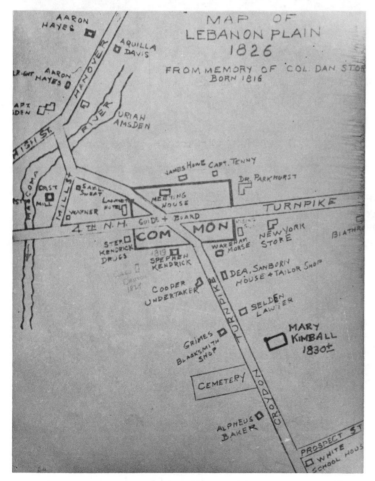

1848
In New England children were welcome in the town halls.

The map left shows the town of Lebanon, New Hampshire, in 1826. All of the elements that made a town self-sustaining were present. The town had a doctor, lawyer, wheelwright, tailor, undertaker, blacksmith. It also had a gristmill, general store, school, and cemetery. Directly in the center of town, on the village common, stood the meeting-house, where all of the town's affairs were held.

1851
The general store, shown above, faced the village square and
was owned by Timothy Kenrick, town clerk of Lebanon,
New Hampshire. The Congregational Church, rear above,
was built in about 1829.

his uncle, Stephen Kenrick, who had been the town clerk from 1812. Timothy Kenrick held the office until his death, although his political party was for many years in the minority. Meanwhile, he had married Sarah Cook, a local girl, and had become a prominent citizen and had gained the reputation of being a friendly, kind man, one with good judgment. He represented the town several times at the State Legislature and had gained the friendship and esteem of many of the leading men of the state; it was through Kenrick's influence that Lebanon was able to get its first bank charter, this being quite a feat, because the leading political party in power at the time was opposed to banks in general. During his lifetime Kenrick was a director of the bank. Espousing the temperance crusade, Kenrick and his uncle were the first to give up the sale of liquor. As a dealer in general merchandise, this meant losing many of his best customers. At the age of 63, Timothy Kenrick died on December 27, 1856, and the town mourned the passing of its good citizen.

Many talented men like Kenrick devoted many a spare hour during their lifetimes helping the community and their fellow man. Individuality was a quality admired and honored, a quality evidenced in many of the reformers and intellectuals of the day. Leisure hours were few for these people. The church was a mainstay for social events. Village gossip was readily exchanged and religion and politics were favorite topics. Visitors were welcomed and questioned endlessly; relatives came, many from great distances, all bringing new stories and ideas with them.

The idea of culture had penetrated every household in New England, and no matter how modest a home, it usually had a few well-chosen books. Lecture courses were sponsored in every town and village on such subjects as chemistry, botany, history, literature, and philosophy. A season ticket to the lectures, consisting of ten to fifteen courses, cost two dollars. Lectures also supplied social contact for the young, as boys would invite the girls to the lectures, and in turn were invited by the girls to supper after the event. Almost every prominent man in New England joined in the effort to further knowledge and offered his services to that end.

For hardier recreation, there were the winter sports of ice-skating for all ages and moonlight sleigh rides, followed by dancing for the romantic young couples. The daring enjoyed sleigh racing.

Come summer there was the Fourth of July to celebrate, with picnics spiced with long orations given by the prominent citizens.

The big event of the year would come in August, the County Fair. This annual event, although long a tradition in America, would gain new widespread popularity during the 1850s. The Fair gave an opportunity for all of the town and country people to show off their talents and abilities to their neighbors. Livestock was brought in to be exhibited and judged, horses to be exhibited and raced. Handiwork and food were featured. These were usually housed in separate tents or buildings. There was much competition among the women, as

1856

The Country Fair
This annual event gave an opportunity for all of the town and country folk to show off their talents and abilities to their neighbors. The fairs were usually held in August and lasted three days. On the first day exhibits were arranged and harness racing was featured in the afternoon. The next day was the big one with the cattle exhibited and judged. On the third day horses were shown and the feature of the day was horse racing. The main tent (above) featured "celebrated Utopia." The American flag flies above all.

Flocks of sheep in rural areas often provided wool for home-spun clothing for the farm family. The first merino sheep (4,000) were imported to America in 1808–1810. By 1840 sheep had become a major farm animal. In 1841 a standard health recommendation for sheep was: "a gill of tar for every 20 sheep during the grazing season" and "Indian tobacco" was suggested for certain diseases.

1858

The favorite pastime of aged ladies was knitting wool socks for the family.

prizes were awarded for the best in the various categories of food and handiwork. Most fairs had lectures on the various fads of the day and the larger fairs had

acrobats or side shows, minstrels and other music. This was a big day for the children with so much excitement in the air, and even the stingiest father would loosen his purse strings for the special occasion.

The fairs were usually held for three days. The first day the exhibits were arranged and harness racing was featured in the afternoon. At some of the fairs, rural America's favorite, Hiram Woodruff, was present, a sulky driver who could handle a horse as no other man could. Betting was heavy on any horse he drove. The second day of the fair was the biggest, with the cattle exhibited and judged, and ribbons awarded. On the third and final day of the event, the horses were shown and horse racing went on all day. The country fair reflected the great interest in horse flesh and horse racing, so popular in America of this era.

Horticulturists strove to see who could raise the largest vegetable. It was reported in a scientific journal that a beet 20 inches in circumference was said to have been grown, and a carrot 3 feet in diameter and 4 feet long, and turnips 30 inches in diameter. One fancier had high hopes; he wanted to grow a cabbage head 17 feet in circumference for the next exhibition![4]

All of these reflections, and more, of rural America in the twenty-year span of 1840–1860 were faithfully recorded by the great story-tellers and poets of American literature. The unspoiled landscape was captured in realism by eminent American landscape artists of the mid-nineteenth century, and the interesting, expressive faces of these people who were experiencing great social and economic change would be recorded by the early pioneer photographers on the silvered plate of the daguerreotype.

THE BATTERY.

3
Life in the City

A large number of travel books were written by visitors from abroad during the 1840s. The most vivid recollections of this group centered on the often curious customs and social life observed in America's rapidly growing cities, especially those of the East and Midwest. Whereas the traveler from across the sea wrote usually in a humorous vein, often decrying the American way, native editors of magazines and newspapers were more serious and explicit in their examination of city social life, and its problems and impact on society in general. Of all cities in America, New York was the most praised, criticized, and rebuked; its unique geographical position and active port, used as a heavy immigration dumping ground, provided a likely target for the perceptive eye of a critic.

Despite the fact that New York was the hub of America, it still had a provincial look in 1840. The streets in the older, lower part of the city were narrow and crooked, and many were badly in need of drains and repairs. In contrast, the newer streets were wide and straight, and the footwalks free of the usual blocking of crates, boxes, and other clutter in front of buildings that caused extreme annoyance to the city visitor. New York streets were said by tourists to be lighted in all areas, although in some quarters the only illumination was a ghostly flicker from a lone oil lamp.[1]

It was a common sight to see pigs of assorted shapes and sizes wandering aimlessly about, poking at the litter and garbage on the pavement. Many of these creatures demanded and got the right of way over the pedestrian. Sanitation and safe drinking water were as yet at a pre-

mium, but help was on the way; the huge Croton Aqueduct Reservoir, the engineering feat of the mid-nineteenth century, was under construction and due for completion July, 1842. This would bring to the city for the first time an adequate water supply. Other sanitary measures would soon follow. In 1844 Mayor Harper had the streets kept clean despite complaints that hose boys often flooded the sidewalks under the thin shoes of lady pedestrians. In 1846 a new construction law was added to the books that health wardens must inspect and approve every sink, privy, or cesspool south of 14th Street before a roof could be put on.

A few wooden buildings were still seen along Broadway in the 1840s; some were painted a gay bright red with seams of crisp white, others were painted in a clear yellow. However, because of frequent fires in this era, wood was outlawed, so that most of the structures were made of brick. The panorama of life seen on this narrow street called Broadway was perhaps best described by the famous journalist N. P. Willis, who had watched humanity in action at various hours of the day from his office window in the year 1844. At eight o'clock in the morning he noted that the sidewalk was rather deserted. Clerks had already gone by. The orange-women were now setting up their corner tables. Seamstresses and schoolmistresses with veils down hurried by. Omnibuses were returning empty from Wall street. Gravediggers in St. Paul's churchyard were making ready for the day's funeral. At nine o'clock and after, a throng of well-dressed men walked swiftly to their business establishments. Mr. Willis likened the sidewalk at

Arriving warships were a thrilling sight for New York visitors. The "Hudson" was built in 1826 and was broken up in 1844. The above engraving was the last work of William J. Bennett, who was also a marine painter.

this hour to "a swarm of black beetles running races across it." The museum people at Barnum's were now on top of the building; flags were being drawn across Broadway and Ann by pulleys fastened to trees and chimneys. At the noon hour and after, discount-seekers crowded into the Chemical Bank with "hats over their eyes." Flower-merchants now began setting out pots of roses and geraniums along an iron fence. A blind beggar arrived and sat down with his back against the churchgate. Ladies clad in exclusive gowns promenaded by. The gravediggers, having finished their job, went home to dinner. A woman was run over at Fulton crossing.

At one o'clock and after, school boys were out and the Tomb's bell was ringing fire in the third district. Ornaments were now abroad—a high-priced canary bird was hung on the fence and drew a crowd. Mr. Willis observed that well-dressed women on the streets were noticed mainly by other females, because it was the first week for spring dresses. One had on a charming straw hat and primrose shawl. At half-past three the sidewalk was in the shade. The orange-man sat on a lemon-box listening to band music coming from Barnum's balcony playing "Ole Dan Tucker." Three being the uni-

versal dinner hour for "bosses," a migration now began toward the many city restaurants. From four to five, the hotel boarders lounged along the crowded sidewalk with toothpicks. The crowd was interrupted by the funeral at St. Paul's while the coffin was moved across the sidewalk.

From the hour of five and after, Broadway became gay. Men were in couples and women in couples—not many ladies were accompanied by gentlemen. Dandies strolled along. No private carriages were out now except those headed for the ferries and a drive into the country. The women were lovely. At half past six and after, the flower-seller began loading his wagon. Gas lamps were lighted here and there. The museum band added two more musicians and became noisier. Business men were bound for home. Streetwalkers commenced to ply their trade, their vulgarity showing through their silks and feathers. Gentlemen paid them no attention; sailors, rowdies, country people, and strangers were the ones attracted to them. The omnibuses were heavy-laden and carriages made their way to the Park Theatre.

On warm summer days, the avenues in New York were clogged with ice vans, portable lemonade foun-

Courtesy Library of Congress
A view of Broadway photographed from Barnum's Museum
about 1855—a stereograph by Langenheim Brothers of Phil-
adelphia. Hacking cabs, waiting for fares, may be seen stand-
ing in front of the city park.

1843

"Broadway one gay procession. Few ladies accompanied by gentlemen—fewer than in the promenades of any other country. Men in couples and women in couples." A description by Nathaniel P. Willis of the hour five and after on the famous avenue in 1844.

1850

tains, portable beer wagons, and a score of fruit peddlers pushing cartloads of pineapples, melons, and peaches. Vendors of all kinds roamed the thoroughfares crying their wares. Oystermen blew their horns and dispensed oysters (ready to eat) from street stands. Ragmen pushed along rickety carts. Bell hangers strolled along looking for bells and locks to repair.

In the winter months the street scene abruptly changed. Crowds now gathered at theatres and the popular ten-pin alleys (nine-pins had been outlawed). With the arrival of snow, Broadway presented a lively appearance. Some of the sleighs abroad were magnificent, drawn by sixteen horses, gorgeously attired and crowded to overflowing with passengers, at six cents a head, on their way to the business sections of the city. Strange sights and sounds of tinkling bells abounded as various sleigh contraptions, which before had been quietly resting in cellars or other storage places, joined the gay scene. One was formed of two rude poles for runners, on which was nailed an old crate. The proud owner attached to this a car-horse, and his outfit moved at a swift pace. The sleighs were of all imaginable forms, in strange contrast to each other, and presented a constantly changing picture in motion. Moonlight sleighing parties, snow permitting, were a popular sport, and at the hour of seven immense sleighs, drawn by six horses, were seen filled with young couples. A merry ride lasting for about five miles usually ended at a tavern for "something warm" and dancing. Later, at

eleven, the party-makers stopped somewhere for supper. Two in the morning was a likely homing hour.

Public cabs had come into use in March, 1840, when a man named Brigham Eaton placed three in front of the Astor House. In a few weeks the number multiplied many times over. Fare for hacking coaches and cabs was reported in 1846 to be twenty-five cents for the first mile plus twenty-five cents for each additional mile, or a flat rental rate of five dollars a day.[2] Cab drivers were invariably called "Jehu." Along Third Avenue about every mile was a stopping post where horses could be rubbed down and watered. One city visitor noted that while the horses were being tended the driver went inside the station to see his cronies—a group of off-duty clerks, bartenders, and loafing gentry, who were usually occupied playing a game of "rounce" or dominoes. After a drink, a cigar, and a bit of conversation, the driver left to go on to the next stopover. This routine went on day after day all year round, driving, drinking, smoking, bragging, betting, and swearing on Third Avenue. Drinking places were open all night as well as all day, with bartenders working in two or three shifts around the clock. The habits of the city cab drivers perhaps influenced the passing of a law in 1846 that outlawed racing of horses and betting. The driver of a horse was not allowed to exceed a speed of five miles an hour.

The thrifty out-of-town or foreign visitor complained loudly of a scarcity of private rooms in the city. This condition had come about because boardinghouses were an institution in New York. There were all kinds for all pocketbooks, many very fashionable. Whole families piled into the big old residences until the rooms bulged with humanity—the old, the young, and the squalling infant all housed within the walls. The land-

THE SLEIGH RIDE.

A popular winter sport in the city. Sketch from Godey's
Lady's Book, *1849.*

ca. 1856
. . . Cab drivers were invariably called "Jehu." . . . Standard
fee for one-day cab rental was five dollars in 1846.

lord, counting heads and seeing dollar signs, packed as many people into each room as possible, usually starting with eight in one room and so on down the scale, leaving only one or two private rooms available.

Families that did not want the responsibility of running a household chose the boardinghouse way of life; others hoped to avoid the high rents and shortage of household help. This way of living appeared an easy existence on the surface, but its shortcomings soon became apparent to the unwary patron. The roomer soon learned that it took plenty of ingenuity, diplomacy, and a quick sleight of hand to manage a good square meal, and a deaf ear was a blessing to get a good night's sleep. A bell signaled the warlike meals, 2 P.M. for dinner and 7 P.M. for supper. An average of thirty or forty people sat down together for meals with only one servant in attendance. Here at the dining table, democracy must of necessity be at work to insure fair distribution of food. As a general rule, the food was good and plain; some disgruntled roomers, however, decried the serving of raccoon, small tortoises, tough fowl, mush, undone corn, and mutton.

To those who could afford it, life at a hotel was preferred. The appointments were better, the food tastier. Room and board in 1846 at an ordinary New York Hotel averaged between $1.25 and $2 a day.[3] The most luxurious and fashionable ones appealed to the plush visitor and local social climber. Often the "climber" trying to make the inner circle of society would reserve a table at the best hotel, possibly the "Union Palace" or the "New York," which had introduced the private bath in 1844. Some of these society hopefuls were willing

Many prominent New York families chose life at a hotel, thus avoiding the responsibility of running a household. The Lafarge Hotel, illustrated above, was designed by James Renwick and built in 1853 at a cost of $200,000. The building contained 228 separate apartments.

to pay as high as $10,000 a year for gourmet dining, just to be seen by society's favorites. This same pattern held true in popular watering places such as Niagara Falls or Saratoga. The fervent wish of all society was to reach the financial and social heights of A. T. Stewart, millionaire owner of America's pioneer department store.

Foods were wonderful and plentiful in New York. Seventy to eighty varieties of seafood were available, with beef, fowl, grouse, and turkey in abundance. Ices of all descriptions were a big business and were kept cool in metal refrigerator boxes. Pies were universal favorites. Some of the preferred breakfast dishes were melon and radishes, and buckwheat cakes with sugarcane molasses. The favored Sunday breakfast was baked pork and beans with brown bread. Differing from the boardinghouses, the main meal at hotels and homes was usually served at 1 P.M., supper at 5 or 6 P.M.

A man planning to break the New York society barrier would have a real estate broker take him about the city, looking over lot locations for a home site. The broker would then tell the prospective buyer that Mr. Fish of the United States Senate, or some other notable, had just settled in the desired neighborhood. This would most likely settle the real estate transaction. Homes ranged in price in these fashionable areas from $10,000 to $200,000, most of them being mortgaged. The architecture was mostly Gothic style, some houses showing a Greek influence. These residences usually featured high windows, "airy" French wallpapers, curtains of silk and muslin, large showy mirrors, elaborate

sofas and chairs, and fine imported art objects as decorative accessories.

If the wealthy lived like kings, the merchants and professional men imitated their "betters" and lived in adjoining two-and-a-half-story dwellings. The half story was below street level, the two stories above. Rents were from $300 to $500 a year (as compared to a cottage advertised on West 13th Street in the New York *Daily Tribune* in 1843, at a yearly rental of $140). Each of these residences had its own roof and separate yard, and contained six rooms besides offices and servants' quarters. They were finely finished, featuring mahogany for inside doors, stairs, and railings. Furnishings were elegant and mostly imported, accessories often being imitations. Clocks and other ornamental objects were imported from France, carpets from England or Brussels. Marble was available in the United States.

The upper- and some of the middle-class society often sent their young people abroad for study for a two- or three-year period. It was not unusual for the family en masse to go on a "grand tour of Europe," sometimes staying abroad for several years, the idea being to absorb culture and European manners. The trip was also a sign to the world that the family had "arrived," financially and socially. Touring Europe was especially popular during the 1850s.

1856
In the 1850s it was not unusual for the family to go on a "grand tour of Europe." The trip was a sign to the world that they had "arrived," financially and socially.

Homes in the fashionable areas of New York City ranged in price from $10,000 to $200,000. Architecture was mostly Gothic.

The wealthy young scion in this era prided himself on feats of daring such as "backing down a police officer" or driving the fastest team on Third Avenue. He

young ladies went to parties with arms and shoulders bare and thinly clad.

The most ambitious feat of New York society was the Valentine Boz Ball, February 14, 1842. The affair, held at the Park Theatre, was put on as a public reception for Charles Dickens, who was in America for a visit. The 3,000 tickets for the event at $5.00 each (some were reported for sale as high as $40.00) sold out immediately. All of the important celebrities were present. Pantomime scenes from Dickens's novels were given at intervals on stage between dances. Food delicacies included oysters, ham, candies; liquids served were champagne, tea, or chocolate. On the days following the af-

1856
Opera and a midnight snack at a fashionable restaurant were expected of a young man about town.

ca. 1855
A social life in the city for men required a large wardrobe. Parties, operas, and elaborate balls were commonplace.

kept absolute track of the latest in fashion and etiquette. He sported a goatee, wore loud vests and trousers, and, when it came to foods, considered himself a gourmet. He rose at the respectable hour of eleven and later dined promptly at 5 P.M. After the supper hour he drove about town for an hour or two, then he might attend the opera (to keep up with culture), and, to complete the evening, have a midnight snack at Florence's, a restaurant out at McComb's Dam on the Harlem River.

Well-to-do young ladies could be seen any hour of the day downtown in the shops, looking over the latest in silks and patterns and displaying a haughty air with other customers. Much time was spent on fashion and preening; attending of parties, opera, and even elaborate balls was commonplace. A sure sign of social success at a ball or party was to be the last one to leave. A journal of 1848 noted that it could not understand young ladies: they were unable to run up and down stairs because they were delicate, but they could outdance a man even until 5 A.M. Others complained that

fair, newspapers moralized on the evils of gay living.

New York in 1846 had 200 churches, 25 banks, six theatres, and two opera houses, also an amphitheatre.[4] Theatres in the city offered the public a wide range of entertainment. The kind of amusement that filled the coffers of enterprising theatre managers was not very often of an intellectual nature. Drama for its own sake

ca. 1855
City belles spent much time on fashion and preening.

was not always a money-maker. Tableaux, burlesques, thrilling melodramas, ballets, spectacles, dwarfs, giants, rope-dancers—all of these formed a continuing attraction to the theatre. During the 1840s and 1850s many interesting performances were given by touring foreign artists, although there were also a number of American entertainers. Plays were given at the Park, Bowery, Niblo's, and National theatres; some put on in the 1840s were: "The Virginian," "Jack Sheppard," "Don Caesar de Bazan," "His Latest Legs," "London Assurance," and "Revenge." The Olympic Theatre featured farce, burlesque, ballet, and opera.

The Bowery theatre, the oldest in New York, adapted well to spectacles. Boisterous representatives of the city's first families had tastes well suited to themes of patriotic sentiment, terrific combats with thrilling effects, and they especially enjoyed seeing virtue triumph over villainy. It was in the Bowery that New York saw the beginning of the vaudeville act by a circus performer, which included a wild animal, on April 3, 1837. The performance was the Greek role of Constantine in a piece called "The Lion Lord." Another stage role, "Blue Beard," followed at the National Theatre in 1838. The versatile star of these roles was America's foremost animal trainer, Isaac Van Amburgh, who began his career working as an animal keeper at the age of ten. In 1834 at the Zoological Institute in New York, he boldly entered a cage of wild beasts. This was shocking because no man had attempted, as yet, to train the "man-eating animals" of the cat family.

Van Amburgh's way with animals was unheard of in any country. He obtained command, with obedience from the cats, and they seemed to regard him as a friend and protector; as he played with and fondled the animals, their ferocity faded away. He had the distinction

The lithograph above illustrates the fifth "Bowery Theatre." The original theatre, oldest in New York, had been destroyed by fire, as were the others.

A sketch of the inside of a Broadway theatre of the era.

crushed it. She died shortly after being removed from the cage. Thereafter, women were barred from this field. Other tragedies resulted as whips, sticks, pitchforks, guns, red-hot bars, and incessant noise from at-

of being the first man to perform with a mixed group of animals, among which was a "melanic" tiger, the first seen in this country. In England at Astley's in 1847 he did a spectacular role in a scene from Eugene Sue's "Wandering Jew," entitled "Morok the Beast Tamer." Also in 1847 in England he did a sensational "black tiger" act exhibited at the Royal Academy. During this year Sir Edwin Landseer painted the popular performer, showing him with a group of wild beasts; the painting was exhibited at the Royal Academy. Van Amburgh was in America again in 1848, but was sent to England in that year to purchase arena horses and engage arena talent from a Mr. Batty in London. The horses purchased had been used in an English spectacle, "Battle of Waterloo." The Americans, in turn, were planning a spectacle, with the procured horses and talent, for a proposed piece depicting a battle scene, "Battle of Mexico."[5]

Isaac Van Amburgh had introduced a new thrill in public entertainment and was copied everywhere. Every circus now had a wild animal act that was performed almost anywhere—in a wagon, cage, or arena. This new idea in circus acts led to tragedy for future performers and to evils in connection with working with wild animals. At the close of the 1840s, "Hilton's Show" staged a "Lion Queen," performed by Hilton's daughter. Another show, not to be outdone, hired a young woman named Nellie Chapman, and she became the "Lion Queen" of the day. Later, an adventuresome girl named Helen Bright succeeded her and tragedy struck. After repeated warnings from the management, she flicked her whip once too often in a tiger's face, and at a performance given in Chatham Theatre, January, 1850, a tiger sprang, seized the girl's head in his jaws and

1850
Isaac Van Amburgh was America's foremost circus performer. Popular in England as well as America, he gave command performances before Queen Victoria. Van Amburgh had a way with wild beasts unheard of in any country; the "cats" seemed to regard him as a friend and protector. It was Van Amburgh who inspired the greatest of all circus songs, "The Menagerie," by C. T. Miller.

1850
Van Amburgh used wild animals in his many spectacular stage roles. He introduced a new thrill in public entertainment and was copied everywhere.

tendants were used to incite the animals during performances. The resulting spectacle was not only revolting but cruel and dangerous.

Van Amburgh, talented and popular, held his reputation as having "the nerve of a thousand men" and continued to perform both in America and England. He died a wealthy man in 1865.

Another event that shocked the theatrical world took place at the Astor Place Opera House, May 19, 1849. The great English actor, William Macready appeared there in the role of "Macbeth." A mob of anti-English gathered at the theatre. Tension had built to the boiling point against the English. America's popular actor, Edwin Forrest, had made two tours of England, one in 1836, the other in 1845. English audiences and critics had disliked the actor and, according to reports, treated him poorly. The ensuing resentment toward the English was probably stimulated further by local city radicals. The theatre was set on fire and twenty-three persons were killed and twenty-three wounded in the three-day riot following the event. The crowd would not disperse until the Seventh Regiment was called out.

Along Broadway were museums that offered fantastic sights and fancies. Peale's New York museum and picture gallery, opposite City Hall, advertised in the November 7, 1843, New York *Tribune*: "Capper Houser, half man and one half monkey, yet has the power of speech." Phineas T. Barnum purchased Scudder's American Museum in 1841. The museum, founded in 1810 and featuring stuffed birds from all over the world, also preserved animals and reptiles. In 1842 Barnum exhibited Charles Stratton (General Tom Thumb), the dwarf, and this won him instant fame at home and abroad. Barnum offered a continuous line of outlandish inducements, in the form of advertising, to the public to visit his museum. His greatest achievement for fame in this period was the engaging of the "Swedish Nightingale," Jenny Lind, in 1850.

New York had clubs for "fast people." They catered to all sorts of "fast livers" and men about town. A fa-

1856
Many museums along Broadway featured oddities of the human race. The man above has an extra finger on each hand.

1850
Phineas T. Barnum's Museum on Broadway offered the public fantastic sights. He had bought Scudder's American Museum in 1841, which featured stuffed birds, animals, and reptiles. The above is a mutation of a calf, which had been stuffed.

mous one was the Abbey, located seven miles outside the city, near the banks of the Hudson River, far from prying eyes. The "fast" men arrived at the club in brown linen coats, to ward off the dust from the long drive from the city. The establishment appealed to lovers of vice. There were pistol galleries, billiard tables, card rooms, ten-pin alleys, dancing rooms, eating and sleeping rooms, and parlors. Smoke filled the air, whiskey and wine ran like water, women were plentiful. The gambling rooms held forth with a well-rounded group of characters—Yankees, Southerners, out-of-towners, and young bucks who were out on the town. It was whispered that the Yankee gambler bet

higher than the southern gentleman. The Northern fellow was out to make money, but the Southerner liked the entertainment of the game. On losing, the Southern gambler, it was said, got fighting drunk and the winning Yankee nonchalantly folded up his money and walked out, probably taking the lady of his choice with him. Few disturbances were heard of at these Northern gaming tables.

The romantics and lovers in the city flocked to Taylor's Ice Cream Saloon. Champagne, ices, candies, and tropical fruits were served in a lavish setting. A young man fashionably dressed with fancy vest, striped pants, elegant patent-leather footgear, and hat and

1847

Romantics and lovers in New York flocked to Taylor's Ice Cream Saloon for champagne, ices, and tropical fruits.

stick in hand would be seen entering with a beautifully gowned young woman, lovely in her bright colored silk, her bonnet trimmed with ribbon, net, and flowers, and carrying an exquisite parasol. The saloon appealed not only to romantics but tired shoppers and visitors. It was said to have cleared several hundred dollars' profit daily.

Another romantic and popular place for amusement was Niblo's Garden, corner of Broadway and Prince Street. It was burned in 1846, and rebuilt in 1849. It included a theatre, garden, and refreshment pavilion. The American Institute held its annual fairs there to promote agriculture, commerce, manufacturing, and the arts. Exhibits were brought in from all over the country. Another elaborate garden, famous for music and fun, and patronized by the large German population of the city, was the German Winter Garden at 45 Bowery. The Germans also favored Jones Park in Harlem, a rural resort, where they could sit in booths and summerhouses in a picturesque setting and look out on the river and sip their favorite lager beer, dreaming of their homeland.

The interior of the new Taylor's Restaurant and Hotel was furnished in a décor of gold and crimson. The high ceilings were ornamented with gilded scroll works. The highlight of the establishment was a cut glass fountain—17 feet high.

The Germans favored Jones Park in Harlem, a rural resort, where they could sit in a picturesque setting and sip their favorite lager beer.

By the close of the 1850s there were a large number of restaurants in New York, and they ranged from very modest to very expensive, prices varying according to location and lavishness; however, all prices had risen "since the gold went up." At the exclusive restaurants uptown, the waiters resembled clergymen and were paid handsome salaries for their impressive appearance and demeanor. In these establishments the chairs were soft, cut glass was in evidence, and views of waterfalls were seen. Quail served was estimated by some partakers to be worth its weight in silver. Champagne cost six dollars a bottle, red wine two dollars, toothpicks ten cents each. Bills presented were not itemized—just a series of dashes; the lame excuse was that patrons would not find it worthwhile to read the figures. Most restaurants were à la carte and did itemize the bill. Many of the wealthy not taken in by pretentious display patronized some of the excellent restaurants near Wall Street that served good wholesome food and comforting beverages.

Along Broadway, above Bleecker Street, restaurants catered to artisans—sign painters, house decorators, piano-key makers, coach varnishers, music professors, and gamblers. Here, dinner was served with a bottle of red wine in a Bohemian atmosphere. On William Street a modest restaurant served a complete meal including beverage for sixty cents. A comparable price at a restaurant in a more exclusive location at Union Square would be two dollars. German eating places, noisy and smoky, were plentiful along Broadway. The lager beer served there was said to exhilarate, not intoxicate, at the first stage; after that came a stupor and "tangled hair." Bread and coffee were said to be excellent, and the price for a meal was fifty cents plus beverage.

An English Chop House was located over on Houston and Bleeker streets. Here, the bill of fare featured stewed tripe, liver and bacon, mutton chops, porterhouse steak, and cuts from "joints." The menu was posted over the bar. Broiled chops and steaks were a specialty, unusual in this land of fried foods. "Arf an' arf" was the standard drink. Poached eggs and Welsh rarebits served were said to give a sporting, noisy tone to the house. The big-muscled landlord maintained good order and was well able to fight his own battles. The customers were noisy and given to swearing. A visitor noted that the man at the next table swore at the rate of $22\frac{1}{2}$ oaths per minute, or an estimated 1,350 per hour. Another man, thought to be a horse dealer, was also profane, but vicious in his profanity, and was rebuked by the landlord. Gamblers who came to dine were noted to be quiet and civil. The restaurant also won considerable fame from having "gentlemen of the ring" visit the premises.

The sport of prize fighting was a barbarous contest in this day, and because it was against the law in America, it attracted, for the most part, the dregs of society. A common practice was for the contestants and spectators to leave the city by boat and travel to some remote spot, where they would build a crude ring out of materials on hand, always keeping a wary eye out for the law. The first professional bouts in America had been

There were many fashionable gourmet restaurants in New York for the wealthy, where champagne could be served for six dollars a bottle. The working man could also find excellent dining places at modest prices, some as low as sixty cents for a complete meal.

fought between slaves. Rules were few and the bouts lasted from forty to fifty rounds, with kicking, biting, and gouging fair game. Spectators usually came from the low strata of society and the boxers themselves were undesirables if not criminals.

In 1841 James Sullivan (Yankee Sullivan) came to America after a twenty-year stay in a British penal colony in Australia. His nickname "Yankee" came from the fact that he always wore an American flag in his

Sullivan resumed the title of champion until defeated by a well-trained fighter, John Morrisey, in 1853. Sullivan made money in the ring and later became involved in Tammany politics in New York City.

The most notable ring bout of this period was the match between the English champion Tom Sayers and the American John C. Heean. It was a two-hour battle, fought in Farnsborough, England, April 17, 1860. The American weighed 190 lbs. and the Englishman 150. The bout was declared a draw but was considered outstanding because of the pluck and courage exhibited by the smaller man, Sayers. He had pulled a tendon in his right arm, yet continued to fight with his left. This boxing match created great disapproval, and prize fighting was eclipsed for another twenty years until John L. Sullivan emerged on the boxing scene in 1881.

Another sport higher on the social scale had its first real beginning in New York in 1842. A group of "respectable" men met Sunday afternoons on a vacant lot in lower Manhattan, their purpose being to play a game called baseball for fun and exercise. Keeping the body fit and muscles in tone was considered in this era necessary for good health, and there were many large well-equipped gymnasiums throughout the city. The baseball amateurs called themselves "New York Knickerbockers" and made their own rules in 1845, which by 1850 were adopted everywhere by various clubs.

Social problems increased steadily in the city during the 1840 decade. Poverty and crime had existed in 1840, but it was not until the vast tide of immigration swept into New York during the 1840s that a definite problem was created. In 1844 the city had about 100,000 Irish, 20,000 French, and 60,000 German residents. Native New Yorkers numbered only about one-fourth of the city's total population. The Irish immigrant, unlike the German who had a skill or craft and some money, came prepared with a will to work and little else. The continuing great immigration swelled the city's poor districts to the bursting point. Unfortunately, many of these immigrants who brought poverty with them, also brought vice of every description. The *Scientific American* reported in 1847 that New York had 594 houses of prostitution (2,673 prostitutes), 11 mock auction houses, and 115 second-hand clothing stores—the latter all receivers of stolen goods. Police officers numbered 160 on duty in this year.

New York did not have a municipal police until 1844, when one was formed by Mayor Harper without regard to state law. This effort proved unsuccessful, and in 1845 it was abandoned. One under state law was then put into effect, and with the new ordinance the mayor was empowered to appoint up to 800 men a day for duty

1850

The Champion

The man pictured above was the victor of the first bona fide prize-fighting championship match held in the U.S. The stakes were also the highest, $10,000. Tom Hyer held the advantage, as he outweighed his opponent, Yankee Sullivan, who was an escaped criminal from an Australian penal colony, by 30 pounds. Both men were considered the best America had to offer. The match took place in an isolated spot, Rock Point, Maryland, which was picked to evade pursuing lawmen, as boxing was against the law. The fight was bare knuckle, with wrestling holds permitted above the waist only. A round lasted until one of the men went down. London rules were used. The fight lasted 16 rounds before the unconscious Sullivan was carried off to a Baltimore hospital. Tom Hyer, although considered America's first champion, never fought again.

girdle whenever he fought. On February 7, 1849, at a remote spot in Rock Point, Maryland, Sullivan lost to a fighter named Tom Hyer in the largest-stake battle ($10,000) fought in America. The bare-knuckle bout ended in the unconscious Sullivan's being brought to a Baltimore hospital. Tom Hyer never fought again, so

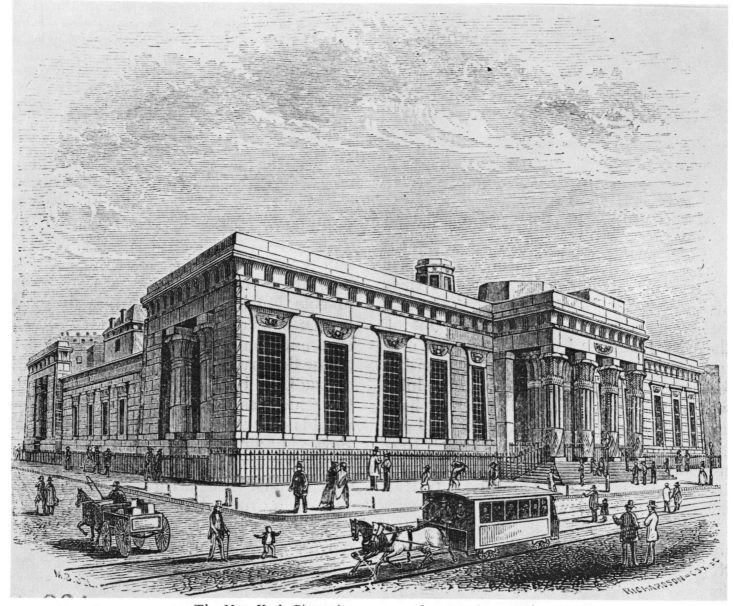

The New York City prison, commonly referred to as the
"Tombs," was a subject of controversy in the early 1840s.

if needed. The police continued the duties of the former watchmen and, in addition to keeping the peace, made reports on all disorderly houses and gambling dens. One law passed in 1846 for citizens' protection prohibited the firing of firearms or firecrackers.

Charles Dickens, during his tour of America, had visited in 1842 the gloomy city prison, the Tombs. In his "American Notes," he made a stinging criticism of conditions found there. Journalist N. P. Willis gives a rather different account in 1844. Although the Tombs was dark, dreary, and dingy, he found the prison doors "all open." The prisoners who were working in the kitchen wore no prison-dress and seemed very little like prisoners. In the inner part of the prison, the cells all opened on a quadrangle, and around each of the four stories ran a light gallery. The turnkey's desk and a stove were in the center of the quadrangle. The cell doors had been thrown open at the time of Mr. Willis's visit, and the inmates were mostly outside, "hanging over the railings," smoking, and chatting with each other and the keepers. One old gentleman was described as "very worthy looking"; he was a celebrated passer of counterfeit money. Another prisoner was a "studious looking" young man who had been a successful swindler. Friends were permitted to bring the prisoners any luxury. In the female prison most of the cells were double-bedded. Of the 19 or 20 women observed, two-thirds had scratched faces![6]

In a slum area called Five Points, a short distance from New York's city hall, fires, murders, and drunkennes were a common occurrence.

Just a short distance from City Hall was the blight of the city, and the shock and shame of the country—a slum area called "Five Points." The lower story of every second house in the area was a barroom, and every bench in them had a sleeper. Conditions there were beyond description, with the malaria-ridden filthy cellars, the blank-looking drunken females lounging on doorsteps, the pitiful half-naked children foraging for food along the streets like hungry animals. The population here was evenly divided between Negro and white. The Negro controlled the district, because he owned and kept most of the drinking and dance places. It was a common sight to see bestial-looking men with delirium tremens who looked barely human. Sometimes five or six men shared a room, completely devoid of furniture except for crude straw pallets.

The champions of the needed social reforms were from the ranks of high society. The older "grand dames" made philanthropic and benevolent societies their pet ventures and would contribute huge sums to welfare, particularly if the names and amounts of the contributions were published. Already by 1840 there were over thirty-five relief agencies in New York. An investigating committee in 1842–1843 condemned them all for lack of working together. After the committee hearings, an "Association for Improving the Condition of the Poor

in New York City" was formed in 1843.

In addition to the relief agencies already established, by 1850 New York City now had added an asylum for the relief of "Respectable Aged and Indigent Females," a home for poor widows and small children, and several orphans' homes. By 1853 the list grew long, the grand total now showing 90 charities of benevolent associations, 22 asylums, 8 hospitals, 7 dispensaries, and 75 fraternal societies with aid programs. With these facilities growing at such a rapid pace, social reform was off to a fine start. After the financial panic of 1857, New York City started a public works program to offset unemployment. One of the projects was work on the new Central Park.

Until New York was brought under the general state school system in 1842, an association called the "Public School Society" ran the public education in the city. Even after the state school system went into effect, the society was still allowed to retain its control over its own schools. In 1843 the newly formed Board of Education, under state control, opened its first schools. Gradually the authority of the Public School Society diminished, for by 1848 its right to erect new buildings was withdrawn. In 1853 the society voluntarily withdrew, and turned its 17 schools and property over to the city.

Art was receiving some attention in New York. The National Academy of Design, already established (1826), was active in this era, with the leading artists of the day as members, participating in art exhibits that attracted national attention. The American Art Union, which would play a great part in promoting art in America, was founded in 1840 as the Apollo Association. Also, the New York Gallery of Art came into being in 1844, but it was short-lived, because in 1848, for lack of a display room, the pictures were put in storage.

Contributing greatly to the arts in New York, and for all America, were the early pioneer Broadway photographer-artists. The most famous of these were John Plumbe, Mathew Brady, Martin Lawrence, and Jeremiah Gurney. Broadway was considered the best location to "net" a customer because of the popularity of this avenue with promenaders. As the 1840s progressed, daguerreian galleries were clustered like bunches of grapes along the avenue. By 1850 competition was intense among the Broadway photographers; many were making preparation to submit their finest daguerreotypes to the first World's Fair exhibition that would be held at the Crystal Palace in London in 1851. Photographers sought interesting subjects, often advertising for "any man or woman over 100 years old."

ca. 1855

Ambrotype by Brady
Mathew B. Brady, early Broadway photographer, contributed greatly to the arts in New York City. Brady won a medal at the first World's Fair exhibition at the Crystal Palace in London in 1851 for the excellence of his collection.

1854

Daguerreotype by Lawrence
Martin M. Lawrence, Broadway photographer competitor of Brady, won honors for America in the World's Fair exhibition in 1851 for his "Past, Present, and Future" daguerreotype.

Others looked for Revolutionary War veterans or twins eighty years old. Two New Yorkers won two out of the five medals awarded for photography at the London exhibition. Mathew Brady won for the excellence of his submitted collection; Martin Lawrence, competitor of Brady, won for his "Past, Present, and Future" daguerreotype of three young ladies, facing to left, front, and right.

Industrially, New York was on the move. Between 1840 and 1858 the tonnage cleared at New York had nearly quadrupled—from 408,768 in 1840 to a stupendous gain of 1,460,998 by 1858. This was because of the predominance of the Erie Canal as a freight carrier. New York City had the monopoly of the Erie and the canals of Ohio, which gave it the trade of the Upper Mississippi basin during this period.

New York in 1860 still had a sizable number of animals wandering the streets. The city's Inspection Department, the Bureau of Sanitary Inspection, reported for one week ending September 22, 1860, the removal

of 50 dead horses, nine cows, and 135 other small animals, besides nine dogs. These were removed to the waiting "offal" boat at the 34th Street wharf.

All American cities in this twenty-year span had the same basic social structures, similar internal problems, and all were struggling to develop their own culture, which evidenced itself in the distinctive flavor of the various cities. Boston, for instance, was known for its intellectual capacity, Charleston for its gaiety and color. The city made the perfect balance for the rural area, each needing and complementing the other, not only as exchange depots for goods but for new ideas and concepts for progress, social and otherwise.

The tremendous swing of population to these humming American cities by 1860 pointed out, as nothing else could do, that a new industrial America had arrived and would usher in a busy, highly competitive way of life.

4

The South

"The pen is mightier than the sword" could symbolically be applied to Harriet Beecher Stowe's *Uncle Tom's Cabin,* but in the final analysis it took the sword to settle the slavery dispute. Unfortunately for later historical records, this inflamed picture, and many more pieces of emotional writing, so colored and distorted the true facts of the ante-bellum South that it was not until the twentieth century that any sort of impartial story could be read. The passions aroused by *Uncle Tom's Cabin* alone would last well over a hundred years. This book became the apex of a fanaticism that reached a white heat of unreasonableness in the period following the death of Lincoln. The Reconstruction Act passed by Congress in 1867 was forced upon the South. Led by the fanatic Thaddeus Stevens of Pennsylvania, this atrocious legislation might never have been enacted into law without the abiding influence of Mrs. Stowe's book. It is not surprising that later generations of well-meaning historians also wrote an erroneous picture of the South in the period of 1840–1860.

Of the 8,000,000 white people living in the South in 1860, about 400,000 owned slaves. There were 2,700 planters who owned 100 or more slaves each. The thinking men of the South had, in a practical manner, long realized that despite its being upheld by law, the slavery system was not able to compete with private enterprise based on the endeavors of free men. Many a slave owner, in his last will and testament, gave his slaves freedom and a passage to Africa. Planters in Virginia, Maryland and North Carolina had early in the nineteenth century set the fashion of releasing slaves and granting them their freedom, so that by 1860 more than 200,000 free Negroes were living in these three states. The other slave states had only 50,000, thus making a total of 250,000 free Negroes for all the South. This was a slow beginning in the year of 1860, when, by contrast, there were 3,800,000 still in bondage.[1] Slavery, hindsight reveals, certainly had no justification; but to the slave owners of this era it was an accepted way of life.

Many historians compare, on a limited basis, the planter aristocracy of the South with feudal Europe. The planter aristocracy may be defined as made up of growers owning one or more plantations and employing more than 100 slaves. Less than ten percent of the total southern population was involved with, or was supported by, this group of landed estates. It was a numerically small group of people who wielded influence, both political and financial, far beyond their properly proportioned place. The great estate owners had the leisure to pursue the values in life that they considered necessary for their happiness—generally politics, sports, and society. They by necessity instituted the plantation overseer system, in which the physical operation of a plantation was left to a hired supervisor. Oftentimes this overseer class, in reality professional plantation managers, worked on a quota or percentage of the profits derived from a plantation's production. With such a system, its malfunction became the South's weakest link in supporting the institution of slavery. The brutality of some overseers in handling of slave problems appalled and shocked many people both North and South. To the abolitionist, the larger estates employing managers were a ready-made rallying point for their crusade. The many lithographs portraying the raised whip in the hand of the overseer, with its implied cruelty and suggested evil, became the image of the Southerner conveyed so well by the pens of the abolitionist writers of the era. In a surprisingly short time "all" southerners except a few "mean whites" were planters, living in great pillared mansions, drinking intemperately, cavorting with female slaves and selling "down the river" their own blood without a trace of a civilized blush.[2] Thus through the writers of the period, fiction became fact, distorting the statistical records of the era beyond recognition. In the South,

ca. 1855   Courtesy Time-Out Antiques, N.Y.C.
Richmond, often referred to as the leading city of the South, had contributed much to the history of the republic. As a political seat it had heard the patriotic utterances of Patrick Henry, and in 1807, the trial of Aaron Burr. The capitol, completed in 1792, (above center, right), was modeled from the Maison Carrée, Nimes, France. Plans were supplied by Thomas Jefferson when he was minister to France. In 1855 the population was about 33,000.

1857   *Courtesy Time-Out Antiques, N.Y.C.*
A dry goods store, Richmond, Virginia.

THE OVERSEER.

. . . the malfunction of the overseer system became the South's
weakest link in support of the slavery institution.

1855

Unknown children
of
Augusta, Georgia
The boy's clothing is a replica of the United States army
uniform of the 1850s. The tiny eagle shown just below the
boy's chin was the patriotic symbol of the era.

writers defending slavery were busily painting the northerner as rich, cold-hearted and a money-grubber. So it was that the two societies drifted apart without hope of compromise.

The aristocratic, well dressed, perfectly mannered plantation owner who spent most of his time toying with politics, gambling, and attending the Charlestown winter races or the traditional "Posey" dance of St. Augustine, was to become the prototype of a southern gentleman to future historians. However, the real backbone of the plantation system was the owner-grower who owned only one operation, had 100 to 200 slaves and supervised his own estate. Such a man was Bennett H. Barrow, whose 1,500 acres lay on the Mississippi River just above Baton Rouge, Louisiana. The name he gave his estate was "Highland." Cotton was his top crop, but he also grew oats, hay, fodder, corn and peas for the market. A slave crew tilled a communal truck garden and maintained an orchard of peach, plum and apple trees. Working livestock ran between 70 to 80 horses and mules, plus oxen for heavy work. Food livestock used to help feed the plantation ran to 200 head of cattle and in addition uncounted hogs, chickens and sheep. Barrow, as the era passed, slowly converted to steam mechanism his cotton gin, sawmills and grinding mills. Profit income from cotton brought from $7,000 in a low poor year to $25,000 in the best years. To expand his acres required Mr. Barrow to pay one-third down and the balance in three years; during his lifetime he increased his land by about 5,000 acres, more than three times his original land holdings. His neighbors described Barrow as a "human man." He employed no overseers and made his slaves foremen with rewards. To quote his view, "I hope the time will come when every Overseer in the country will be compelled to adopt some other mode of making a living. . . . I make better crops than those Who employ them." He supervised his slaves closely, studied their work habits and instructed them in doing a better job. The Negroes on the Highland plantation were well fed and adequately clothed. At Christmas time they received money and apparel as presents, more or less as a bonus. He had divided his field hands into rival crews. The losers would give the winning crew a dinner and the winners would receive awards from Barrow. Whether because the slaves were his most valuable possession or from a humanitarian urge, he instituted improvements: frequently new wells were dug, cabins were repaired each year, a dance hall was constructed, and the Highland jail was kept clean. Yearly, his slaves received two suits or dresses, two pairs of shoes, and one new blanket every third year. Every Black over four years old re-

1850

Jefferson Davis—impressively handsome in the years before the Civil War. In 1835 he became a cotton planter in Warren County, Mississippi, after serving in the army. It was as a planter that he became interested in political philosophy. During the Mexican War he distinguished himself for gallantry at Buena Vista. In late 1847, Davis was appointed to fill a vacancy in the U.S. Senate. In this office he became the leader of the southern Democrats.

ceived five pounds of good meat a week and, in addition, hogs, sheep and cattle on holidays. High moral standards were set, with marriage encouraged among the slaves and religion taught. Runaway slaves were punished severely. Occasional entries in the plantation record read of "whippings for rule infringements." Barrow deplored cruelty and in his judgments tried to judge fairly, so he said. His children studied with private tutors and also took music and dancing lessons. All in all, Bennett H. Barrow was a moderately successful and typical planter in the era of slavery.[3]

Virginia planters worked along similar lines but were

production, and only through the freed and independent Black could the South escape from the never-ending burden of the slavery system. In 1850 one old southern gentleman was asked "why the South did not have all of the conveniences of New York City?" He replied, "Because, while the people here have been working for themselves, old fogy Virginia has been working for the negroes. The people of the North were shrewd enough, years ago, to sell all of theirs to the South." Two planters, one in Florida and one in Georgia, had established Negro schools with the intention of preparing these people to be good and free human beings. In the 1850s cries were heard in the southern newspapers that the safety of the South lay in her workingmen and in the independence of her small man![5]

In many parts of the South financial pressure from wasted lands, failing markets and unsatisfactory political conditions in the eastern states was never so great. The South prior to 1840 had been a series of frontiers, drawing the population of Virginia, North and South Carolina and Tennessee ever south and westward. By 1840 the mass movements of the restless ones were over and

1856

A portrait of a Belle. Southern women were renowned for their beauty and gentle manners in this era.

possibly more progressive, with the knowledge that the end of slavery must someday come to America. Statistics for that state show there were 15 whites and seven blacks per square mile. The custom in Virginia allowed slaves to earn extra money in their traditional vacation period—Christmas through New Year's Day. Other money could be earned by raising vegetables on the small plot of ground assigned to each slave family. Some Virginia plantations taught their slaves to read and write, each cabin possessing a Bible. Neat rows of white cabins resounded with banjo music on festive occasions. In some parts of the South competitive prizes were awarded to the plantation having the best slave quarters.[4]

The more perceptive Southerner viewed slavery as a burden. The theory was that the North could improve its production through revising and improving its machinery; the South could not improve its Negro slave

1851

Often, Negro babies were pampered on the plantation.

After 1856
Many early Virginia "great houses" were built in the 1700s
and before—an English gambrel roof was a distinctive feature
of the above dwelling. The growing of tobacco created great
Virginia plantations that stretched along the James River
between Jamestown Island and Richmond.

the South had settled down to a more stable population. An overwhelming number of yeoman-farmers did exist in the South—a class that did not differ in any fundamental or essential way from the prosperous farming class of the northwest. These yeoman-farmers had steadily increased their acreage and ownership throughout the 1840–1860 period. In comparison, throughout the period the planters were shifting southward. Many Virginia planters growing wheat and tobacco were maintaining their prosperity through the sale of their surplus Negroes. The Deep South was becoming the center of activity of slavery. Cotton production in 1850 was 1,000 million pounds and by 1860 it had increased to 2,300 million pounds. Of this cotton crop about one half was

grown by small farmers owning from one to six slaves.

Many southern yeoman-farmers still lived in log cabins. The crude frontier appearance of North Carolina was described by a visiting Englishman, who estimated that 66% of the population lived in log cabins. Lack of skilled craftsmen and of an established widespread group of store-keepers kept the towns very small in population. Often these towns consisted of only a blacksmith's shop, a courthouse and a jail. Farmers dressed in homespun—often blue trousers and orange-brown coats—gathered in these town centers for legal affairs and repairs to equipment rather than for social activities. In some sections, people of the communities did gather in their towns for their annual competitive

1850

Virginia gentlemen, like the one pictured above, were often educated in the North.

1849

The wealthy southern planter often had private tutors for his children.

horse-racing, which usually lasted for three days. Their social centers were usually the churches; for example, in Surry County, North Carolina, there were thirty churches, all but three being Methodist or Baptist. A statistical breakdown of the South shows that there were 901,102 men classified as yeoman-farmers who owned their own land. Added to this figure, there were 228,407 who labored at farming on the land of others, plus 228,-407 men who were classed in this group but pursued rural outdoor occupations other than tilling the soil. Combined into one group, they represented a population of more than 6,000,000 white people—men, women and children.[6] They were the sinews and backbone of the South.

The more prosperous farmer owned, in some cases, from one to six slaves although by and large three-quarters of the land and slaves were owned by the planter class. Often the white farmer labored shoulder to shoulder with his black slave in a friendly rivalry, which was sometimes no greater than over who could cut the widest swath of wheat. This peculiar relationship, in reality friendly but strictly segregated, would

last more than a hundred years after the slave had gained his freedom through the Emancipation Proclamation. This relationship had often been a source of puzzlement to the white northern fanatic, who could not understand why many southern Negoes did not hate the southern white. They, the southern white and Negro, were interdependent in a long tradition of mutual relationship.

For the most part the yeoman-farmers lived remote from the great thoroughfares and were seldom seen by the traveler. They had settled in the "up country" and "backwoods" and led industrious and plodding lives. Calhoun, Clay, Alexander H. Stephens, Andrew Johnson, and even Abraham Lincoln had sprung from this populous southern middle-class log-cabin society. However, all would not rise above their heritage; such a man was William J. (Bible) Smith who, on the day he became of age, was led to the barn of his father, blessed and given a "Mule-brute" as his legacy. "Bible" wandered and finally "squatted" on a promising piece of land. Fortune smiled on Smith as the result of hard work at clearing and planting, helped by his "Mule-brute." His next move was to hire a Negro slave, one Jake by name, whom he soon bought outright. Bible

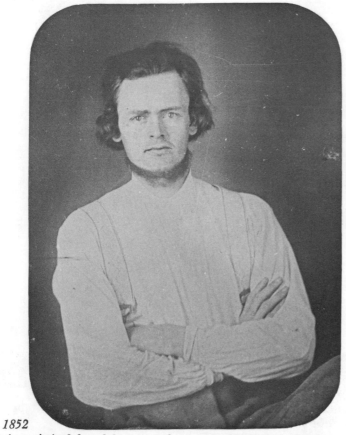

1852
A statistical breakdown of the South shows that there were 901,102 men classified as yeoman farmers.

1855
Statistics show that very few southern families were able to afford hired help in the rearing of children.

1860
One or more dogs were usually kept at country homes in the South.

1848
The South in this period had a remarkable middle class of free Negroes, and it was estimated that by 1860 Negroes owned $15,000,000 worth of property in New Orleans alone.

1847

The Golden Portrait

Many early photographers were also artists or had studied the art principles of posing, lighting, and proportion. Some daguerreians experimented in bringing color to the portrait by emulating miniature paintings and often created beautiful portraits like the one shown above. Daguerreotype by the daguerreian-artist Lorenzo G. Chase, Boston.

1847

Daguerreotypists advertised that they would take portraits of the deceased in the studio or at home. Occasionally, as in the case of a child, the body was held upright to give a natural effect. See above.

ca. 1851　　　　　　　　*Courtesy Miss Josephine Cobb*

The "long tom" method of gold mining (below) came out in 1850 and was considered the ne plus ultra *of mining machinery. It replaced the "cradle" and could wash ten times more earth using the same manpower. The miner with the shovel stationed at the end cleared away the tailings and also stirred up the earth accumulated in the tom.*

ROCKSTON.

For the most part the yeoman-farmers lived remote from the great thoroughfares. They had settled in the "up country" and backwoods, where they led industrious and plodding lives.

and Jake worked back to back, acquiring larger crops and livestock possessions and sharing a common shelter. As the years passed Smith prospered; he acquired a wife and family, also a whitewashed log-cabin home, nicely chinked and with an open front porch. Two enormous brick chimney-stacks protruded at either end of the home. Inside there was a tidy rag carpet and plastered walls ornamented with half a dozen neatly framed engravings and a gilded looking glass festooned with sprigs of evergreen. A huge mahogany piece stood nearby—half sideboard, half bureau. Chairs were six in number, all rustic and covered with untanned deerskin. There was a large pine table, oftentimes the center of family life, which stood sturdy and unyielding, occupying the center of the main room. Food, for Bible, had lost its scarcity. Now that it was plentiful, he could load the table on a festive occasion with bacon, venison, wild-fowl, hominy, corn-pone, fritters, tea, cider and apple jack, all in promiscuous confusion. Furthermore he had acquired books—the Bible, *Pilgrim's Progress,* and *Doddridge's Expositor.* His wife was literate and was passing on to his children this precious heritage. The public school had not generally made its appearance in the rural South. In the village, some ten miles away, Mr. Smith could not yet afford the pretentious "Female College" or the "Institute of Learning for Young Men" where "a little Latin and less Greek" were dispensed for a fee of four to five hundred dollars per session.

Times were changing. The old idea that education was an accomplishment and not a necessity was slowly giving way. Still, to the William Smiths of this era, the church, and not the school, was the center of their social life. Thus they left leadership in education as well as in politics to the ruling class of planters. The 1850 census shows that only two-thirds of the males and less than one-half of the females of the middle-class group could read or write, this despite the fact that the 1,000,000 population of this group included those engaged in trades, manufactures and the professions. Unlike his northern counterpart, the southern farmer might employ his daughter to follow the plow, gather corn, pick cotton, chop wood and sell his products in the public market, but he would not allow her to be employed as a housemaid, nurse or cook. In the South, these occupations were traditionally reserved for the Negro female.

In the newly settled counties of the South, log rollings, corn shuckings and quiltings were the pleasant necessities of a sparse population. In Georgia, the "quiltings," more than. any other social activity, were popular, because in the evening there could be a dance. Such a gathering was not only a dance, but included

1844
Unlike his northern counterpart, the southern farmer might employ his daughter to follow the plow.

for the nondancers such amusements as wrestling, playing "Old Sledge" or perhaps drinking an unreasonable quantity of whiskey. Excess energy, as always, was expended in fights, but they never, through some odd code of honor, ended in a permanent feud. These events were highlighted by a pine-knot fire.[7]

One northerner traveling through backwoods North Carolina illustrated in his record the thought of the rural farmer in this era. He wrote that he came upon one white farmer and four Negroes busily engaged in making "plow-lines." When asked how many they could make in a day, "four" was the reply. The stranger pointed out that plow-lines could be purchased much cheaper and of better quality, so why didn't the Carolinian buy them? The southerner answered, "Dad did it this way!"[8]

Most remarkable, in the South of this period there was a middle-class of free Negroes. Many enterprising Negroes had risen to substantial wealth; William Johnson of Natchez was one. His father had been a white man, his mother a mulatto woman. Johnson began his career as a barber who loaned money on the side to spendthrift white men. Expanding, he bought three

While quilting parties were on the wane in the North, the South held to the old tradition of a quilting bee, followed by a dance and socializing. A sketch from Godey's Lady's Book, *1849.*

1845

Robert Adger, above, was a prominent cotton merchant and banker of Charleston.

barber shops and became a planter and slaveowner. In his diary he tells of renting out slaves and whipping slaves; he finally describes the poor morality of the times with, for example, "Mr. Jenkins was caught in bed with Mr. Parker's old big black woman." Natchez, in this era, set up a "Court of Inquisition," a vigilante committee that ran out of the state any free Negro suspected of abolitionist activity.[9] Often a petition had to be signed by leading white citizens for a free Negro to remain in the state. Charleston, South Carolina, which in this period supported the most polished circle of white society in the United States, had its most popular hotels owned by a Negro, John Jones, owner of some $40,000 worth of real estate. Nearby, a Negro in St. Paul's Parish, South Carolina, owned 200 slaves, a white wife and a white son-in-law in 1857. These Negroes and others had developed a social caste system similar to the white society of the day. In the South a Negro with a craft or trade was welcomed and allowed to work unmolested. By contrast, in the North white craftsmen

often resorted to violence against the skilled Negro with a trade. In Baltimore there were several colored grocers and druggists. At Atlanta, Georgia, Rodney Badger was a Negro dentist. Soloman Humphries, grocery store proprietor of Macon, Georgia, was worth $20,000 in slaves and property. In North Carolina, a successful Negro cabinetmaker employed white helpers. But nowhere in the South—or North, for that matter—were the Negroes becoming so prominent as in the state of Louisiana. In New Orleans there were many Negroes engaged in the professions of architecture and lithographing. It was estimated that by 1860 Negroes owned $15,000,000 worth of property in that city alone.[10] One, Victor Sejour, became the literary idol of Paris and a friend of Alexander Dumas and Louis Napoleon. Between 1844 and his death in 1874, twenty-one of his plays were produced in Paris theatres. In science, Norbert Rillieux, educated in France, became chief engineer of the Louisiana Sugar Refining Company. He also made an important advancement in sugar refining by inventing an evaporat-

1852
The South in this period had a remarkable middle class of
free Negroes, and it was estimated that by 1860 Negroes
owned $15,000,000 worth of property in New Orleans alone.

ing pan. On the sea, Paul Coffee owned several sailships. Thomy Lafon was said to be worth a half million dollars at his death.

White New Orleans, the code of Duello, the Creole Society—so proud and sensitive, so brave, so hyprocritical—were all part of the ante-bellum South. New Orleans was the capital of the cotton kingdom and, in a measure, also of sugar and rice. In this era, the rough Anglo-Saxon met the cosmopolitan French Creole in a competitive race that would eventually blend the two into one, but in the period of 1840–1860 the line of demarcation was sharp and definite. Opera, the theatre, horse racing and gambling were all publicly subscribed to by the wealthy. Amid this setting there grew, by 1840, a unique custom among the wealthy Creole gentlemen of New Orleans. Their code of pretentiousness included a fashion that decreed the keeping of a mistress, sometimes referred to as "The system of the Octoroon"—a tradition of mistresses based on the color of the woman's flesh, but never pure Caucasian. The cost of maintain-

ing a mistress would vary from $1,500 to $2,000 per year. All negotiations were transacted between the "gentleman" and the mother of the young lady. In many cases the bargain would include an old-age pension for the girl's mother. In the proper manner of a contract, other similar details were worked out before establishing the mistress in a cozy home of her own. The light color of the woman's skin played a large part in the prestige of the gentleman in relation to the other wealthy dandies of the city. An "octoroon" (offspring of a quadroon and a white) brought the highest price. The "quadroon" (offspring of a mulatto and a white) followed closely in prestige value and price tag. Next came the mulatto, the lowest mistress in the system being the "griffe" (offspring of a mulatto woman and a Negro). Social life abounded for the fortunate Creole mistress. There were "Quadroon Balls," which lavishly testified to the high standing of the Octoroon. A literary wit of the day remarked of the ball, "No virtuous woman to be seen." There were carriages of fashion for these mistresses to parade in and be seen—a society within a society, all part of the South.

In his book *Slave Power,* written in this period, Professor Cairnes of Dublin, Ireland, describes a population group in the South: "Combining the restlessness and contempt for regular industry peculiar to the savage, with the vices of the "prolétaire" of civilized communities, these people make up a class at once degraded and dangerous; constantly reinforced, as they are, by all that is idle, worthless, and lawless among the population of the neighboring States, [they] form an inexhaustible preserve of ruffianism, ready at hand for all the worst purposes of southern ambition." This was a European's academic view of the "mean white" or "poor white trash" group in the South, who numbered about a half-million people. A traveling Englishman summed

(*Courtesy The New York Public Library
The I. N. Phelps Stokes Collection of American Historical Prints*)
The halcyon period of Mississippi River steamer traffic, 1840–1860, made New Orleans the leading port of the South. The aquatint of New Orleans (above) was done by W. J. Bennett in 1840.

1857
The Creole of New Orleans society was of colonial descent of French and Spanish blood (no Negro). Favorite pastimes of the society were Opera, horse-racing, theatre, and gambling.

1858
In New Orleans society a light skin played an important part in "the system of the octoroon."

A sketch of a northern traveler's conception of a southern "mean white."

1848

1849

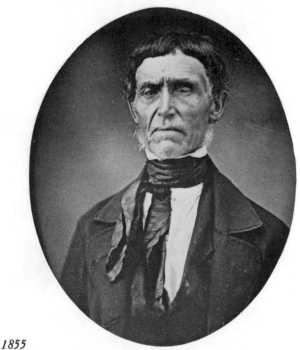

1855

Men of the era, particularly in the South, where the duello was still in use, often settled their differences through violence.

up this group's fighting creed as "regular kick and biting system—fair play, Kentucky style with gouging one eye when you can get your opponent down—a Ring-Tailed Roarer." A northerner writing of this class of southerner gave a more detailed description in 1864 when he wrote: "They are given to whiskey-drinking, snuff-dipping, clay-eating, and all manner of social vices!"

Always with bare head and feet, the "mean white" woman had for her only garment a coarse "cottonade" dress, falling straight from the neck to just below the knee. The men wore slouched hats, linsey trousers and

1854

hunting shirts so begrimed with filth and so torn and patched that scarcely a vestige of the original was left. The northern writer of 1864 described them: "Many of them—owing no doubt, to their custom of intermarrying—are deformed and apparently idiotic, they all have stunted, ague-distorted frames, dull heavy eyes, saffron-hued skin, small bullet-shaped heads and coarse, wiry hair which looks like oakum shreds bound into mops and dyed with lampblack." This was written during the Civil War, with some artist's license used by the author!

For the most part, the "white trash" of the South lived in rough, one-room huts, with the bare ground as the floor. There would be a few rickety chairs, several low beds with corn shuck mattresses and a few cast-offs as cooking utensils. Without ambition they dwelled where they could best eke out a minimum subsistence; many were found near the Mississippi River. They were compared on a favorable descriptive basis with the "scum" of northern cities. Eschewing shaving and cleanliness, their place in the South was, as in other societies, on the lowest rung of the human ladder.

Thus in the South of the 1840–1860 era, there was both a cultural and an economic lag. If a simplified reason could be found, it would be in the failure of the bulk of the southern population, as represented by the yeoman-farmer, to assert its proper right and place in a democratic society. Had these men raised their voices in moderation, perhaps they would have been heard by their northern counterparts and possibly have avoided political control by fanatical groups in both North and South.

5
The West

The landing of the Pilgrims at Plymouth Rock established the elastic word "west." To them the word was definable as the wilds of western Massachusetts. So, too, in the many years that followed, "west" was just a little farther west than the boundary of law and order.

The westward push of the Americans by 1840, had reached, roughly, a geographical boundary line just a little west of the Mississippi River. In that year, the great territory of Iowa had a population of 43,000 people.[1] This territory, combined with the Missouri and Arkansas territories, was the far western frontier of the United States of that day.

The pioneer settlers were pouring into the frontier states of Indiana, Michigan, Illinois, and, to an extent, Wisconsin. Later, the discovery of lead ore in Wisconsin caused that state to boom, and claim stakes would cover the entire state. Michigan's population doubled between 1840 and 1850.[2] The other sister states were experiencing similar population explosions. The pioneers were also overflowing into the far western frontier. Future historians would call this area "The Middlewest" or "Midwest." The settling pioneers streaming to this area in the early forties were, for the most part, native-born Americans who were seeking escape from the established eastern and southern society. These pioneers were independent of mind and spirit. They would, for future generations, fix a pattern of the "Typical American" and set a profile of America. Also merging in with the native stock, beginning in the late forties, were the immigrating Germans. By 1850 there were 83,000 Germans living in the Midwest frontier.[3] They had left Europe for political reasons rather than economic ones. These incoming Germans were not poor, either in money or skills; many were skilled craftsmen with a limited amount of personal capital.

If the pioneering spirit was heading west, so, too, were the railroads, canals, turnpikes, and river transportation. The northern route to the west, for the migrating easterner, began at Albany, New York. There were seven railroads, all connecting short lines, running from Albany to Buffalo, New York. Thus Buffalo, in the forties, was the center of the northern depot point for the westward-bound settler. The streets of Buffalo were piled high and sometimes choked with household goods when in 1845 some 95,000 people passed through the city.[4] Journeying on from Buffalo, they went by boat to Detroit, by rail from Detroit to New Buffalo and then transferred back to boat for the remainder of the journey to Chicago. Pioneers were settling along this route, so that by the time Chicago had been reached only a handful of the more hardy souls would have made the entire journey, plus, of course, a few travelers whose destination would be St. Louis via the downstream Mississippi.

The independent pioneers from the Middle Atlantic States were streaming westward along "The Old Cumberland Road." This road, the original turnpike, was the first straight through road for interstate travel. Along the highway were accommodations for the travelers. Inns, taverns, hotels, and camping areas were dotted along the turnpike. The states along its path would object to the conception of a straight line's being the shortest distance between two points, thus bypassing nearby towns and cities. The Federal government, tir-

Punca Indians encamped on the Banks of the Missouri
The engraving above was taken from a painting by Charles Bodmer, who made an expedition in 1833. The Missouri River was one of the most important factors in the development of the Northwest. The American Fur Company began to use steamers on the Missouri in 1830, and from then onward until the advent of the railroad, it was a main artery for transportation. Traffic on the river was at its height in 1858, when it had no fewer than 60 regular packets. The following year traffic declined with the completion of the Hannibal and St. Joseph Railway to St. Joseph, Missouri.

1847
Dressed in gingham and calico, the eastern emigrants sought new homes and fortunes in the ever-expanding West.

ing of the turnpike's upkeep, finally turned the road over to the states in its path. The several states involved, upon obtaining the road, promptly converted this first turnpike to a toll road. Cincinnati was to this route what Buffalo was to the northern path, a gateway to the West and to St. Louis.

Migrating pioneers from the South came by boat. Seeking new worlds, they sailed up the Mississippi River. St. Louis, the focal western town of America in 1840, had its first daguerreotype parlor, "Moore and Ward's," open there in 1841.[5] A Mr. Garlick opened his studio in Cleveland, Ohio, that same year.[6] Photographers, like the other pioneers, were spreading over the West.

Some Americans were settling beyond the Mississippi

in this period, in some cases far beyond—all the way to the Pacific Ocean. A new breed of frontiersmen, in the decade of 1840s, would organize exploring expedition after expedition, some official, some unofficial, all intent on recording knowledge of the terrain for the benefit of the pioneers heading to the far western land. In their explorations they were aided by the remnants of the fast-disappearing American fur trappers. Over the thirty some odd years prior to 1840, these fur trappers, who bore the picturesque name of "mountain men," had depleted the fur-bearing animals of the Rocky Mountain areas. The mountain men had left their mark on the area by ruthlessly exterminating the creatures of the forests by their quest for furs.

Outdoing the Indian in his natural habitation, this

City of Columbus, Ohio
The engraving shown was drawn by J. Smillie from a sketch
by T. Addison Richards and was made especially for Gra-
ham's Magazine, 1844. The Borough of Columbus became a
city in 1834; by the close of the decade, the National Road,
which passes through Columbus, was completed.

the adventuresome. If the tales told by traveling merchants, explorers, and empire builders could be believed, a great future awaited the frontier pioneer. Besides, the settling pioneers from the East and South were pouring into the Mississippi valley in great numbers. Industry and law and order were being quickly established in the old frontier.

The Oregon country, in 1840, was in the open competitive market as to whether it would belong to the United States or to Great Britain. The American visionary saw a country from sea to sea settled by the Americans. The rivalry for the unclaimed areas in North America, which began on the village green of Lexington, would end, for the British and the Americans, on the shores of the Pacific Ocean in the territory of Oregon. The Oregon story for the people of the United States began with the discovery of the Columbia River by the American, Robert Gray, in 1792. Prior to Gray's voyage, noted English explorers had long sought this river without success. Gray's discovery gave to the United States a claim to the whole great territory drained by this river. In 1805–1806, under presidential orders, the Lewis and Clark expedition went west to the Columbia River and reached the Pacific Ocean. In the period following 1806, the Americans established a number of fur-trading posts in the vicinity of Astoria, their main base at the mouth of the Columbia River.

The War of 1812 saw all of the American fur traders driven out of the Oregon area. The Treaty of Ghent at the end of the war stipulated that all of the western territory captured from the Americans should be restored, but no definite boundary had been determined. The "Oregon Question," or, as it was often called, "The Northwestern Boundary Dispute" would develop into a point of agitation between England and America in the years following the War of 1812. The border dispute would last over a period of thirty years and at times bring the two nations close to war. In 1818, the two major contestants signed a treaty agreeing to joint occupation of the territory for the next ten years. In 1828 it was renewed for an indefinite period. Meanwhile, both Russia and Spain were minor claimants for the area, but in 1821 Spain publicly renounced its claim (in favor of the United States) to all territory north of the 42° parallel. And in the same year, Russia, faced with an odd combination of American and British solidarity, ceded all of its claims to territory south of the 50° 40′ line. The English Hudson's Bay Company, backed by British sanction, ruled and dominated the Oregon picture until the end of the 1830s. During this period there mutually developed an unwritten agreement that the Americans would settle south of the Columbia River and the English to the north.

1858   *Courtesy Time-Out Antiques, N.Y.C.*
The eastern theatre often provided its own view of the West. Above, probably an actor portraying a young Indian warrior.

fur-trapping breed of sometimes very uncivilized white man had managed to intermarry or interbreed with the various Indian tribes of the far west. The legacy they left the Indians was one of alcohol, disease, and often an implacable hatred for the white man. By 1860 pure-breed tribes of Indians, even the mighty Sioux, were making treaties with the half-breed descendants of these "legendary" men.[7] So it was that the remaining handful of mountain men would gain a new page in history by serving as guides for the emigrating American pushing into the far west in the 1840s.

The financial panic of 1837 had left the people, particularly in the Mississippi valley, restless and discontented. The opportunities of an "El Dorado" beckoned them westward for a new start in the rich lands of the far west, or so they dreamed. Tales of riches to be found in California and Oregon were eagerly listened to by

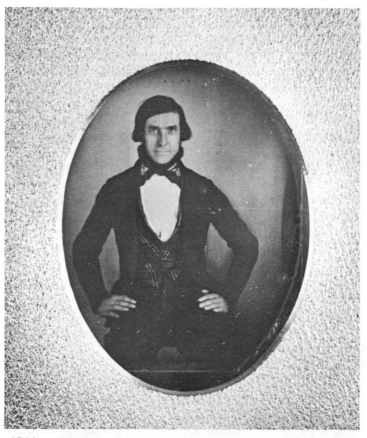

1844

"FIFTY-FOUR FORTY OR FIGHT"
War between the United States and England seemed the only solution to the northwestern boundary question in 1844. A major campaign slogan used by the Democratic Party in the presidential election that year was "Fifty-four forty or fight." The dispute was settled by peaceful compromise in 1846 and the forty-ninth parallel became the permanent boundary between Canada and the United States.

Beginning in 1837 with the first group of pioneer settlers, the Americans would come to Oregon in ever-increasing numbers. Before 1841 the settlers had come to the territory by boat. Back in the Mississippi valley, about 1837, in town after town, there were organizations either formed or forming for the purpose of gaining information on the various land routes, equipment needed, and conditions to be met in making an overland journey to both California and Oregon. Sometimes these "California Societies" or "Oregon Societies" would publish their complete knowledge and information as an aid to other societies. In 1841 the first organized group of pioneers, called the "Western Emigration Society," elected John Bartleson their leader, and with a motley assortment of equipment left Sapling Grove, Missouri, on May 19th, California bound. Luck

floated their way at the very start of the trip when a group of mountain men joined the party to serve as guides. They suffered hardship and misery in the nearly six-month journey and finally reached their destination in early November. The first caravan with "Oregon Fever" made the trip in 1842. Both of the two small first parties could be considered pilot trips for the massive far-west movements occurring in 1843, Oregon territory as the destination. Early in 1843, a very large caravan of emigrants made rendezvous at Independence, Missouri. Wagon after wagon gathered near the town until over one thousand hardy souls had massed for this first large overland trip. In all, more than 3,000 Americans made the trip overland to Oregon in that year.

In Oregon as early as 1841, the permanent American settlers felt the need to establish a civil government. They, in effect, did not care for the law as administered by the Hudson's Bay Company. The Americans established a provisional government in 1845 and elected a governor. This newly formed Oregon government looked north for even more territory to control. Meanwhile, back East increased American feeling caused the Democratic National Convention of 1844 to declare "that the whole of the Oregon territory should belong to the United States." One of the campaign slogans growing out of that convention was "Fifty-four forty or fight." The Democrats won the election and for a while

1857
Frontier living called for sturdy, practical clothing.

the war clouds looked dark. However, in 1846 a compromise with England was reached and a permanent boundary was set at the 49° parallel, thus ending the Oregon dispute.

If the lure of Oregon was being painted with a flourishing brush, so too were the incredible tales of instant riches being extolled by the advocates of California. In the early forties many glowing accounts of Oregon and California were flooding the publishing world in the East. The fad was set—"Go west." "Manifest Destiny" was on the march. With the close of the Oregon controversy, the Hudson's Bay Company reverted to its role of supplying Europe with furs. Its fur offerings and exports set the style in dress among European royalty. For example, in 1849, the Company exported to Hungary 8,807 white wolf skins worth about 30 shillings each. The Hungarian nobles used these skins for trimming their pelisses and Hussar jackets, the fashion of the day in Hungary.

Nothing in the history of the world's people can be compared to the explosive effects and the after-effects of one magic word uttered in 1848. The word was GOLD. The location was California. The word was out, the rush was on! Americans, English, French, Chinese, Polynesians, Negroes, merchants, mechanics, anybody, all, flocked to a new occupation—that of the miner; all had a singleness of purpose—overnight wealth. The sleepy California of ten years before had disappeared even before the discovery of gold. The Californians were completely absorbed in their native way of life in 1838. Their largest problem, politically, was to outwit, and to keep on the path of honesty, the ever-changing territorial governors sent by Mexico to rule their relatively quiet life. A few Americans had

. . . If the tales told by traveling merchants, explorers, and empire builders could be believed, a great future awaited the frontier pioneer.

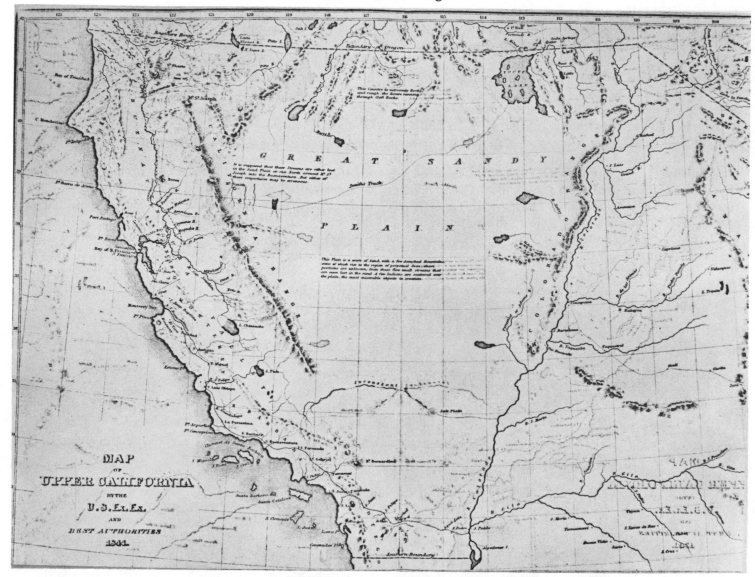

In 1841 Charles Wilkes, commanding a naval squadron, explored the Pacific Coast of the North American Continent, including the Columbia River, San Francisco Bay, and the Sacramento River. The above map was drawn in 1844 as a part of Wilkes's report of the expedition.

settled permanently to the life of a ranchero. This small cadre of Americans for the most part kept a steady stream of written propaganda flowing back to the United States, extolling the riches to be had and the easy way of life in the beautiful California climate. Yankee ships had a long-flourishing history in the trade of hides and tallow with the West Coast. American whalers had long made San Francisco a port of call and sometimes a ship or two bound for the Orient would make California a refitting point. But these contacts were minor until Richard H. Dana wrote his master-

piece, "Two Years Before the Mast," in 1840. His interesting description of the California coastline painted a picture for "Mr. Every American," who perhaps could now see himself pioneering in this beautiful land.

The old Oregon Trail would see more and more wagon trains turning south at Bear River and heading southwestward for the Sacramento valley as the decade progressed. By 1845 mass wagon trains were moving out, California bound. Back home in Washington the government seemed to realize that one large prize in the darkening clouds of an imminent war with Mexico would be California. The United States dispatched the Pacific fleet in 1845 on a secret and confidential mission. Commodore John Sloat's instructions stated that, in case of war, he would seize or blockade all California ports. If formal war did not occur, he would be prepared to assist, on further instructions, and take advantage of, any native revolutionary movement that might take place. Also, other instructions were dispatched to Brevet Captain John C. Frémont, appointing him to head an expedition (his third) to explore the Cascade and the Sierra Nevada Mountains. This would place Frémont and his sixty armed men very close to, or in, California at about the same time the Pacific fleet was scheduled to appear off the coast. Simultaneously, Colonel Stephen W. Kearny's force, headed by five regiments of United States Dragoons, would march toward his first goal of Santa Fé and then on to California. A dual purpose could be served, so Washington felt: a show of military might would awe the increasingly belligerent Indians, and also a need felt by the army would be satisfied, that of a trail to transport armies westward if need be, particularly since the Oregon question had reached a fevered heat and had not yet been settled.

Frémont and his party reached the vicinity of Sutter's Fort, California, in December of 1845. Slowly, he drifted down the coast to Monterey and sojourned there for much of the winter. The Mexican government inquired as to why an armed party from the United States had decided to pay so protracted a visit. "Merely peaceful exploring" had been Frémont's reply. The Captain had received, originally, orders meant for the public's consumption, instructing him to explore northward toward Oregon after reaching California. Whatever private orders, if any, he received have never been found. With orders to head northward, his actions are interesting. He did linger on in the California scene through one pretense or another, sometimes engaging with the Mexican authorities in blunt, open hostilities just short of warfare. Quite a few of the eight hundred Americans then living in California offered Frémont their rifles and services. However, the boiling point was soon to be reached. "The Bear Flag Revolt" crystallized the situation and destiny was again on the march! If the great waves of migration of 1843 and 1845 made Oregon truly American despite anything Washington or London could do, so too did the great deluge of migration that was about to break on the golden shores of California. Thus in June 1846, the stage was set; Frémont was on the stage, Kearny in the wings, and the Navy en route. The Bear Flag hostilities commenced with the capture of a Mexican military party by Ezekiel Merritt and a small group of American settlers. The settlers, at Frémont's prompting, moved quickly and captured Sonoma. The revolting group then raised the Bear Flag and proclaimed the "Republic of California" a reality. Frémont then cast aside his cloak of peaceful explorer, organized a small army of settlers and native Californians, and began operations against the Mexican government. At this point he had no knowledge that war had been declared with Mexico. Frémont's gamble had paid off—luck was smiling and word was received in July that the war was real. Also with the war news from Mexico was word that Monterey had been captured by the fleet and that the fleet was underway, heading for San Francisco, Frémont's headquarters.

From then on events moved rapidly. Commodore Stockton proclaimed California as a United States territory. Kearny arrived on the scene. Fighting was brief and decisive. California was won for America by the end of 1846. John Charles Frémont would be elected the first United States Senator from California in 1850 and in that same year, by then internationally famous, he received a medal of honor from the Royal Geographical Society of London, England, for his services in promoting the knowledge of geography. Back in 1842 on his first exploring expedition. Frémont had brought along a camera. He was the first explorer to realize the value of photographs to illustrate the wild country he was exploring. History does not tell us .if the camera was used on his first trip, but on his fifth exploring expedition in 1853 and 1854, he did take two professional photographers with him. One of the photographers was a daguerreotypist, the other took ambrotypes (photographs on glass) . Frémont's theory was that if the daguerreotype method failed to capture a scene, perhaps the ambrotype might succeed. Thus the two competing methods of photography would be in open competition with one another. Solomon Carvalho, the daguerreotypist with the expedition, later published his recollections in a book called "Incidents of Travel and Adventure in the Far West." In this book he recounts his attempts to capture the exact image in the camera's lens. He complains of the effects of low temperatures, high altitudes, and other difficulties encountered in taking the daguerreotypes. Carvalho brought back scenes of landscapes and portraits of Indians, but somehow these photographs were lost or destroyed in later history. The ambrotypist, Bomar by name, apparently encountered similar troubles; he probably brought back ambrotype examples of the Far West, but they too were lost in later history.

The year 1847 saw the overland wagon trains of emigrants heading for the new land of California in large numbers. More routes were being used. The Mormons discovered the Salt Lake City site and founded a new land to escape the persecution that had plagued them

1845
The internationally famous Frémont received a medal of
honor from the Royal Geographical Society, London, for his
services in promoting the knowledge of geography. Also,
Frémont was the first explorer to realize the value of photo-
graphs to illustrate the wild country he was exploring. John
C. Frémont and Jessie Benton, above (attributed), were
married in 1841. In 1856, Frémont became the Republican
Party's first presidential candidate.

Solomon Carvalho in his book "Incidents of Travel and Adventures in the Far West," *complained of the effects of low temperatures, high altitudes, and other difficulties encountered in taking daguerreotypes. Carvalho had accompanied the Frémont expedition in 1853–1854.*

for so long. Salt Lake City had a population of 5,000 by the end of 1848. In these years a new danger had been added to western travel. By 1846 the Indians had turned from being semi-friendly to becoming downright belligerent. They started attacking wagon trains freely, and often wiped out an entire party. The earlier white settlers and the mountain men had shown the Indians an iron fist and the Indians, now thoroughly alarmed at the heavy influx of pioneers, had begun a sporadic warfare that would not end until the end of the century. The United States and Mexico signed the Treaty of Guadalupe Hidalgo in 1848. This brought the war with Mexico to a successful conclusion and restored peace to the Far West except for Indian warfare. California had been made secure for the incoming American pioneer.

The projected settlement of California along the lines of the Oregon emigration was suddenly diverted from its course. The reason—the magic word GOLD; the place—Sutter's Fort, California; the year—1848. No more peaceful settlers coming in droves, no, but 80,000 adventurers and fortune-seekers in the one year of 1849 alone would come to California. Of that number, half came by the overland routes, the other half by boat from the eastern United States. Those who came by water either sailed the long voyage around Cape Horn

1858
Brandy Legs, a southwestern Indian of the era.

or used the newly popular route of boat to Panama, over the Isthmus by land, and reembarkation for the sea voyage to San Francisco. Bad relations between the Panamanians and the Americans using this route might be best shown by a quotation from the news in *Harper's Monthly,* first volume, in 1850. The report said that a group of emigrants crossing the Isthmus clashed with the natives in which two or three on each side were killed. The clash "grew out of the arrest of a Negro boy on a charge of theft and a supposition on the part of the natives that the Americans intended to hang him."[8] These disorders grew more frequent as more and more Americans used this route. Of the many routes from eastern United States, the story of the Central American route is perhaps the most obscure, and yet this area would play a large part in future American history.

The story begins for the 1840–1860 era, with the British operating a steamship service between Valparaiso, Chile, and Panama on a regular schedule. For this service the Pacific Steam Navigation Company operated two 800-ton sidewheelers in 1840. To complete its link to England, the Royal Mail Steam Packet Company inaugurated regular monthly service to the West Indies by 1846. The English used a makeshift system of canoe and mule transport across the Isthmus in the link between the two ship services. The year 1846 saw the Americans begin to drift into the picture when the United States and New Granada signed a treaty in which, in return for certain commercial privileges, the United States guaranteed the neutrality of the Isthmus of Panama.

In early 1847 Congress passed two separate acts designed to improve communications with the west coast. One act was to provide a mail service between Panama and Oregon; the other would provide for carrying mail between New York, New Orleans, and Panama. The steamship "California" left New York in October 1848 to assume her obligation to carry mail between Panama and the west coast. When she left New York she had not one passenger aboard, but by the time she had made a passage around Cape Horn and back to the Pacific side of Panama, "Gold Fever" had struck eastern America. Waiting in Panama City for the "California's" arrival were more than 500 eager prospectors. They had caught up with her by sailing from New York and upon reaching the Atlantic side of the Isthmus had rushed across to Panama City. When the "California" left Panama she carried 365 passengers—more than half again as many as she was designed to carry. After a voyage of trials and tribulations, she finally dropped anchor in San Francisco harbor on February 28, 1849, whereupon all members of the crew, except the captain, promptly deserted and joined the ranks of gold seekers. She was the first of the gold-rush steamers to arrive at San Francisco.

The Pacific Mail Steamship Company, owner of the "California," quickly added two more steamers to the Panama-San Francisco run. By 1850 other lines had entered competition to the Mail Steamships on both the Pacific and Atlantic side of Panama. The Pacific Mail Company added the steamship "Golden Gate" in 1851. She was capable of carrying 850 passengers without crowding. The next year this same company added a large ship which even boasted of having a bathroom. The original price for first-class passage from New York to San Francisco was $450, but with ticket speculators operating in the eastern cities, the price was often boosted to more than $1,000. In 1850, the Americans began constructing a railroad across the Isthmus. It took the private company five years to complete the 48 miles of track and in 1855 the railroad was running trains from ocean to ocean across the Isthmus. The price to ride the newly completed route was 50¢ per mile or about $25.00 for the six-hour trip from the Atlantic to the Pacific.

For a gold miner in 1848 the outlook was bright. It was not unusual for a miner to take $500 to $700 worth of gold per day and those in possession of a rich

1858

The original price for first-class passage by boat from New York to San Francisco was $450, but with ticket speculators operating in the eastern cities the price often went up and over $1,000.

Milk—5 shillings per quart.
Eggs—$4 to $6 per dozen.
Beef—1 to 2 shillings per pound.
Raisins—$12 per box.
Flour—$16 to $20 per barrel.
Pork—$25 to $30 per barrel.
Potatoes—10¢ per pound.[9]

Restaurant price for a beefsteak and coffee meal was a reasonable $1.50, but if an egg was added the price would be $2.50. These food prices can be compared with the price of $2.00 per day for lodging in a good New York hotel with meals included. The wage for a carpenter that 30th of June was $16.00 per day, and his helper's wage was $10.00 per day. The houses they built were usually 12′ x 14′, made of rough common boards, which, when completed, brought in a rental income of about $75.00 per month. On the same date, the *Scientific American* in an editorial prophesied the fate of the miners when it wrote "More than two-thirds will lay down their bones before gaining fortune."[10] Their observation was not without foundation, for the price of a doctor's services, without comforts of any kind, ranged from $600 to $1,000 per month.[11]

Daguerreotypists were among the early fortune seekers in those mad days. They recorded many scenes of the gold mining landscapes and preserved the exact image of the miners. William Shew, pioneer daguerreotypist and casemaker, closed his Boston Gallery and moved permanently to San Francisco. In 1852 he took his famous five-piece panorama of San Francisco, showing the rotting and abandoned ships in the harbor, thus preserving for posterity exactly how the city looked in that year—one of the great scenes of early photography. Robert Vance, who specialized in scenes of gold-mining activities, put on display more than 300 daguerreotypes of them in New York City in 1851.[12] They showed the true picture of life in the gold fields and their eventual disappearance presents a mystery in early photographic history.

Most of the early gold discoveries were confined to the Upper Sacramento Valley and along the Klamath River. Town sites dotted the valley by 1850. Of the shifting, ever-moving population of California in 1850, the United States attempted to take a census. Compared with the well-organized census-counting back East, the first California census was rather wild, but despite the difficulties encountered, it proved rather accurate. Sometimes the methods of counting were not in the usual pattern of the formal census but were picturesque and sketchy. To quote from one of the census takers, the note on the bottom of a census page read: "This day

strike might even make $1,000 to $5,000 per day. Many large nuggets were found, ranging in value from $1,000 to $20,000. San Francisco became the supply center for the gold activity in the early days of the rush. With the very first cry of gold, realty values in the city fell sharply. The exodus of native gold seekers left it virtually deserted. However, this was short-lived. Ships from all over the world began arriving through the Golden Gate in ever-increasing numbers. The population increased from 2,000 in February 1848 to 20,000 by the end of the year. This gateway city to the gold fields became a city of tents and shanties by 1849, with real estate prices increasing tenfold. In early 1850 more than 500 ships of all types were rotting away in the bay, most of them deserted by their crews. Merchandise and goods clogged the streets. Speculators were swarming everywhere. Prices listed in San Francisco as of June 30, 1849 were as follows:

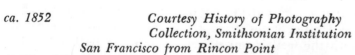

ca. 1852   *Courtesy History of Photography*
                             Collection, Smithsonian Institution
             San Francisco from Rincon Point
*William Shew, pioneer daguerreian and casemaker of Boston,
became a permanent resident of San Francisco in 1850.
With a sense of history, he recorded on five whole-plate da-
guerreotype plates a panorama of San Francisco from Rincon
Point, one of the most dramatic scenes of the gold-rush days.
Shew went on using his camera to capture the portraits of
many early pioneers of San Francisco.*

1849

Bakers were found in all mining camps in California. The man's hat (far right) was made from a flour sack. In 1849 flour brought sixteen to twenty dollars per barrel in San Francisco.

1852

Prosperity and San Francisco were an unbeatable combination in the gold rush days. Daguerreotype by William Shew, San Francisco.

1855

Many who settled in California were ill prepared for the rigorous life encountered there.

I came upon eighty Chinese camped on a river bank, mostly engaged in mining although a few appeared to be cooks." Half way up the page at the sign of the asterisk he had entered the count of "Eighty Chinese—miners." Other census takers must have been chagrined to learn that the majority of the Chinese, when asked their name, answered "Ah Choo." The United States head-counters faithfully and meticulously recorded each

"Ah Choo" and his occupation. Never before or after have so many men subscribed to the occupation of "miner" as in this census. Other occupations listed, in the obscure department, were "Catching wild horses" and "Chinese prostitute." Law and order were almost nonexistent in this year of 1850. Personal disputes were quickly settled with violence; crimes against "society" went unpunished. The census proved that eight percent

1851

... Nothing in the history of the world's people can be compared to the explosive effects and after-effects of one magic word uttered in 1848. The word was GOLD. The location was California. The word was out; the rush was on! ...
Main Street, Jamestown, California (above). A typical mining camp showing the sluicing method of gold mining, center foreground.

1855
A note with the original photograph tells of "wonderful California gold."

1851 (or before)   Courtesy Robert Weinstein, Los Angeles, California
"Panning" for gold was the only method used in the first days of the gold rush. The unidentified scene above is possibly one of the earliest taken of gold miners at work; it may have been daguerreotyped on one of the many bars along the South Fork of the American River.

of the population were females, but only two percent of the women lived in mining territory.

Mining could not exist without a ready, nearby supply of water. Many of the future cities of California would develop from the early mining sites. Many picturesque names like "Frenchman's Gulch," "Chinese Ditch," and "Peppermint Creek" were used by the miners. Jamestown, California, is a typical city formed from small mining camps. It held its first elections in 1850, put together its first mining laws in 1853, and by 1855 it boasted of about thirty stores and shops, and had one church and a Masonic Hall. The fall elections in the year 1855 drew 299 voters to the polls; only five years before gold had been dug where its main street now ran. Many towns, like Jamestown, would eventually bring permanency to California. However, by 1855 there were still many dangers existing. The Indians had not become reconciled to the white influx and had banded together in a great league to resist the encroachments of the pioneers and the miners. This spelled "Indian Warfare." Other perils were the frenzy and mad rumors of gold to be found here or there. This caused thousands of excitable miners to rush to a site where a supposedly rich new find of gold had been discovered. The "Kern River Fever" of 1855 and the even greater "Frazer River Rush" up in British Columbia in the year 1858 were examples of mad gold searches. The latter fevered rush took perhaps 20,000 men northward out of the States and caused a tremendous amount of physical suffering. Many interior towns lost half of their population to these rushes, and even San Francisco suffered a real estate crash in 1858.

ca. 1851   *Courtesy Miss Josephine Cobb*
The "long tom" method of gold mining (above) came out in 1850 and was considered the ne plus ultra *of mining machinery. It replaced the "cradle" and could wash ten times more earth using the same manpower. The miner with the shovel stationed at the end cleared away the tailings and also stirred up the earth accumulated in the tom.*

1852

A Typical Miner
$81,294,270 of gold was mined in California for the year 1852.

1858

A Western Scene
In the center of the below ambrotype may be seen a railroad locomotive and three cars. It had just crossed over a trussed bridge spanning the river. A very large mountain can be seen in the far background. Exact location is unknown.

Toward the end of the 1850s, the solitary miner with his washing pan had long since given way to more productive methods. First came the cradle method, which was quickly replaced with the "Long Tom." By 1855 hydraulic mining was the last word. Big companies were coming along, buying everything in sight. The day of the lone gold seeker was over. His heyday had been reached back in 1850 when he had mined almost fifty million dollars worth of gold and oftentimes paid forty dollars for a shirt.

The pioneers of the nation, by the latter part of the fifties, were looking back to the land they had forgotten —the land where the Mormons had sought refuge—east of the Sierra Nevada and west of the Missouri River, a land of wilderness and Indians. In the spring of 1860 the House of Representatives passed a law prohibiting the practice of polygamy so that the gentile had again caught up with the Mormon. Other events were occurring to help fill the last great wilderness. In 1859, by every conservative estimate, the "Pikes Peak Gold Rush" had swept more than one hundred thousand eager Gold Seekers from hearth and home. Not more than forty thousand of these ever reached Cherry Creek; many settled along the way or turned back. The Dakotas and Montana were being eyed. The expedition "To Red River and Beyond" was being read by the subscribers of *Harper's Monthly* in 1860. Bands of fashionable English hunters were roving in Montana in search of big game.[13]

Thus, in the period of 1840 to 1860, the United States grew to a nation spanning the continent from the Atlantic to the Pacific, a nation peopled with Americans.

Section II

INSTITUTIONS OF AMERICA

6
Politics

The age of Jackson was dead! It had slowly died during the four years of President Van Buren's leadership. The last vestige of Andrew Jackson's political stability melted away in the fiery presidential campaign of 1840. A new spirit was abroad in the land and it was reflected in a new type of political campaign. The new pattern for wooing voters would become standard procedure for politicians in the years to come. Catchy slogans, night rallies under torchlight, mass meetings, and marching men singing popular songs were evidence of a new tempo. Torchlight parades became the fad after Jeremiah Martin of Boston patented a portable oil torch in 1837.[1]

The political arena of 1840 was dominated by the great triumvirate of American statesmen—Clay in the center, with Webster and Calhoun in the opposite wings of opinion. Other men like Thomas Benton and Lewis Cass were nearing their political greatness. The old adage "politics make strange bedfellows" was true in 1840. The now-consolidated Whig Party named William Henry Harrison as its presidential candidate when it met at Harrisburg, Pennsylvania, on December 4, 1839; and in the following May, the Democrats renominated Van Buren as its standard-bearer. President Van Buren would be the last incumbent to be chosen by his own party as a presidential candidate in the era of 1840–1860.

Two catchy Whig slogans emerged by the summer and fall of 1840: "Tippecanoe and Tyler, too" (referring to Harrison's military deeds in defeating the British and Indians in the War of 1812) and "Log Cabin and Hard Cider," which pictured Harrison as a humble friend of the people. These, along with the image of Harrison created by his enthusiastic Whig followers, proved an unbeatable combination, and Van Buren was soundly defeated by a margin of 174 electoral votes. Looking back, Van Buren had done little to gain popularity in the term he had served as president, for in 1837, with a financial panic in full rage, he had adopted a hands-off policy. In addition, he had riled the professional political waters by dealing firmly with the spoils system of political appointments.

A challenge to the checks and balances of the original government was occurring in 1840 and a new era was emerging—that of a strong Congress. For the next two decades, many of the undecided questions of the American experience in democracy would be debated and oftentimes resolved.

On March 4, 1841, William Henry Harrison, the ninth American president, took his oath of office. The day was a nasty one, cold and damp, for the traditional outdoor ceremony. One month later, on April 4, Harrison died of pneumonia, probably caused by his long exposure to the weather on Inauguration Day. His father had been one of the signers of the Declaration of Independence. Much of Harrison's life had been spent in public service as an executive, and he was probably well equipped to handle the office of the presidency. In his brief month in office, his one noteworthy deed had been the appointment of Daniel Webster to his cabinet.

One of the first major questions of the era to be decided was a constitutional one—one that had to be quickly solved, one that had not been specifically set

1839

In the first few years following the advent of photography, many prominent daguerreians opened "parlors" in Washington. Political figures were among the first to have their portraits taken. Above, one of the first daguerreotypes made in Washington City; probably taken in the late fall of 1839.

forth by the founders. The problems caused by the death of a president in office, with emphasis on the status of the vice-presidential chair, had to be settled. John Tyler, when informed of Harrison's death, moved decisively; he was sworn in as the President of the United States on April 6. The nation had been without a chief of state for a two-day period. The office of vice-president was vacant; a precedent had been set.

"The doomed victim of disarrangement," was the opinion of the editor of the *New-Mirror* in 1844, and it referred to Tyler's original cabinet. This editor, Nathaniel P. Willis, was simply stating that the Whigs had elected a president in 1840 but had failed to explore the political philosophy of the vice-president. The Whigs had assumed that Tyler would follow party policies. Disillusionment came quickly when he became President, for within a short time Harrison's cab-

inet, with the exception of Webster, all resigned. Tyler's new appointees did not follow the party line.

It was in this new atmosphere of political change that a popular and often-quoted speech was made before the Atheneum Institute of Philadelphia in 1841. The highlights of the oration outlined the aims, tribulations, and guidelines for a political office-seeker. In opening, the speaker said: "The halls of legislation are open to all . . . and if you do run for office . . . acquit yourself with honor and usefulness . . . But it may seek you . . . under circumstances when, as good citizens, you cannot decline it." The oration went on to tell of the pitfalls of politics, a path beset with difficulties and dangers. "Of all occupations to which pride or

1844

John Tyler, Tenth President
The political animosity between John Tyler and former President John Quincy Adams was highlighted when they both met at a daguerreian studio on April 12, 1844. Adams wrote in his diary, for that day, "While I was there President Tyler and his son John came in; but I did not notice them."

idleness can drive a man, the most degrading is that of a begging politician, a regular place-hunter." In closing, the orator said: "Serve your country, when your country wants you, but seek not popular favour at the expense of your honor, independence and self-respect."[2] The oration became a guide to those of political bent in the 1840s.

In 1843, many politicians were promoting an image of the national character that had gradually emerged, extolling from the platform, "the right of some to spit and whittle, some to eat eggs from wine glasses, some to eat peas with their knives, and others to pour tea into saucers." Many voters, in terms of national politics, had the feeling of being "overgoverned." "It might be

Courtesy Library of Congress

One of the first daguerreotype views taken of Washington, D.C. (above). It shows Pennsylvania Avenue looking west from the capitol toward the White House. The nation's capital had gradually become the center for America's political affairs, and in the period of 1840–1860 a national focus would intensify on the city with the problems of preserving the Union. By the end of the era many new government service departments were established; the Smithsonian Institution, the Independent Treasury, and other bureaus had become part of the Washington scene.

1845

Julia Tyler (above) wrote her mother on March 6, 1845: "Saturday, then the President approved the Texas Treaty, and I have now suspended from my neck the immortal golden pen, given expressly for the occasion."

well to convene Congress for the first three months of each administration," was suggested as a means of curtailing national legislation. The more outspoken compared Congress with a fester, with Congress the "national pustule—the offensive head and vent of all the purulent secretions of the body politic." It was urged: "Let the worst issue of our national shame be aired on the floor of Congress, better so than to pent it up." And then there were those demanding and fault-finding voters who would visit Washington to assert their "fifteenth million part" of privilege. Such a visitor, in 1843, would make the Capitol his palace, make its grounds his grounds, and use the library as a lounging place.

Political freethinking to the American public in 1843 meant many things to the separate sections of the country. A horizontal cross section showed the many variations of rural thought as opposed to the city bloc-voter. For example, the powerful clan of "Round Rim-

mers" of East Bowery, New York City, "a fraternity of gentlemen, who in round crape bound hats, metal mounted blue coats, tallow smooth locks, and, with the terrible device of a pyramid, wrought on the brassy buttons on their waistcoats, carry terror and dismay where they move, manage to sway voters with intimidations." A thoughtful author who was concerned for democracy wrote, suggesting that "a newspaper be edited by each citizen for the free exchange of ideas and an opportunity for a close examination of one to another."[3]

The old gentlemen of the year 1843, with the wisdom of the ages, railed by the hour and condemned Congress for its long speeches and its philanthropic outlook on law and order. The old ones agreed that "a murderer before the bar of justice was called 'an unfortunate man' lest we hurt the culprit's fine feelings." "And those congressmen, those advocates of progress, progress to the dark ages," was one old man's version of those who would loosen the security of property and the safety of the person. Other opinions about Congress expressed by the aged were: "The truth is, it owes more than it can pay, the sooner it winds up its concern, the better."

Nathaniel P. Willis, America's counterpart of Charles Dickens, made a concise political analysis of America in 1844. He said: "One of the pleasures of living in a free country is the unceasing satisfaction one feels at not having died last week . . . another peculiarity of our country,—good or bad as you chance to feel about it—is the necessity to talk a great deal about yourself." He also went on to illustrate the basic differences in the municipal governments of Boston and New York City. Of New York, he said that it was, "unfortunately, in some measure, a political tool and compelled to shape its administration with a view to politics." In his comparison he said of Boston: "that they would act at the first sign of license and would use harsh measures without fearing that the party out of power would use such perversion, as a counter-current of sympathy and resentment." Willis went on to illustrate the political differences in a practical manner. For example, it was the custom of the Germans in New York City, some 20,000 each Sunday, to use the ferry to Hoboken for a day's outing in the fields. Had the "Puritans" in Boston been faced with the same situation, Sunday being a day of rest, the ferry would have been suppressed without hesitation. Willis also described the reform mayor of New York picturesquely, as a man who "peers through the official eye-glasses in a manner that portends trouble to all municipal delinquents."

Over the years, the National Postal System, under

1851
Babies were often dressed in dark fabrics. Above, an unusual daguerreotype of a diapered baby.

1851
Head coverings were often worn in hot weather to shade the face and shoulders from the sun. Parasols were small and dainty in this period.

1852
A country boy photographed in color by Levi L. Hill.

1852
Samuel Morse wrote of "the beauty of the flesh tints . . ." when describing a hillotype of Hill's daughter. Mary Hill, seated on an oval trunk, above.

1853
"Invisible goblins of the new photogenic process"; so said Hill when describing his efforts to reproduce the colors of nature. Color failures, as shown above, must have been frequent.

1855
Plaids of the gayest colors were worn by little girls, and short sleeves and full skirts were popular in this year.

The White House was usually called "The President's House" in this era. A winter view (above), from a carte de visite taken about 1865.

A view of the rear of the White House (above), from a carte de visite of about 1865.

1859

1859

The Village Post Office
After fighting private competition in 1848, the United States
Post Office Department put into effect a uniform rate for the
entire country. The village Post Office became the meeting
place of rural America.

the central direction of Washington's successive politically minded postmasters general, had built an unrivaled system of abuses, and by 1844 the crusade to correct the inequities of the United States Post Office was at its height. It was termed "the spoils system at its worst." For the unscrupulous postmaster officeholders, the collection of postal fees became a golden method of advancing individual fortunes. Many of the postal abuses were centered in the smaller towns and villages where, because the mailing fee was paid by the receiver, the postmaster could set the rate, almost at will, depending only on his interpretation of a fee. Journalists of monthly magazines like *Graham's Magazine, Godey's Lady's Book, The New-Mirror,* and others, purveyors, they said, of "higher cultural readings," were busy pointing out the inequities of the postal rates—and they

in the same manner as in the 1840 election year. Only the name had changed—the Democrats were the aggressors—they had enthusiasm and popular catchy slogans: "Manifest Destiny," "Re-annexation of Texas," "Fifty-four forty or fight," and "Polk, Dallas and the Tariff of 1842." And they had a new face in national politics, the first dark horse candidate, James K. Polk. John Quincy Adams, admittedly prejudiced, described Polk's failings as an orator when he said: "He has no wit, no literature, no point of argument, no gracefulness of

Courtesy Library of Congress
James Knox Polk, 1795–1849
The Eleventh President of the United States
The historian Bancroft (Secretary of the Navy under Polk) held the opinion that Polk was "prudent, far-sighted, bold, exceeding any Democrat of his day in his undeviating correct exposition of Democratic principles."

Courtesy Library of Congress
Henry Clay, 1777–1852
For more than a half century and until his death, Henry Clay was often the focal point of American politics. He was called the "father of the Compromise of 1850," which was a series of measures designed to heal the widening rift of sectionalism. He had often been a candidate for president, and yet it was he who said: ". . . I would rather be right than president." In a just self-judgment, he wrote "If anyone desires to know the leading and paramount object of my public life, the preservation of this Union will furnish him the key."

proved their points with facts. They gave examples: A daily newspaper could be mailed to a place in Massachusetts for one and one-half cents, while a monthly paper, usually smaller in size and less weight, cost a varying five to fifteen cents; a monthly magazine mailed to a receiver in St. Louis would cost five cents, while the same issue mailed to Mt. Vernon, New York, would cost fourteen cents. Editors of periodicals wrote the postmaster general, "Why should literary papers of the same weight be more taxed than newspapers"? The resulting outcry accused the Post Office of suppressing public welfare and general education. Congress in 1846, beset by the need of reform, began a shaping of a national uniform postal service with a passage of the first act in that year. Additional acts were passed in the years following until 1863, when a uniform postal service became a reality.

In 1844 the people reacted to political showmanship

delivery, no elegance of language, no philosophy, no pathos, no felicitous impromptus; nothing that can constitute an orator, but confidence, fluency and labor." Meanwhile, the Whig factions had united behind a strong presidential candidate—Henry Clay, the foremost political orator and idol of the era. His oratorical utterances held universal esteem; his political experience was vast; his friends were legion. His backers ranged from Horace Greeley, with his powerful pen, to a rural politician, Abraham Lincoln of Illinois, who would deliver for Clay a majority in his district. Despite Clay's prominence and abilities, the American voters gave James K. Polk a victory by a margin of 65 electoral votes in the fall of 1844.

President Tyler, politically unpopular to the end, signed, on the last day of his term in 1845, the necessary papers toward making Texas part of the Union—an honor that had long been denied him.

The eleventh president, Polk, had presented a well-balanced platform while campaigning; it was a program that he intended to carry out when elected. Upon assuming office it became clear that his policies would be followed. His cabinet appointments highlighted his talent as an able administrator. "Young Hickory," as he was called by the friendly, promptly declared that he would be a one-term president and he dispelled any idea that his acts would be based on political expediency. By 1846, Polk and his administration had passed a bill establishing an independent treasury system, had reduced tariff through the Walker bill, and had settled the Oregon border dispute with Great Britain; all had been a part of his platform.

Polk generally followed the line of Manifest Destiny in policy. He was an owner of a Mississippi plantation, a native of Tennessee, but despite this background he showed no inclination to further the interests of the South. He was primarily a Unionist; sectionalism he deplored. His bitter opposition to the Wilmot Proviso and his differences with both Calhoun on the one hand and Van Buren on the other showed his impartiality. Polk was backed wholeheartedly by Congress in the war with Mexico. As Commander-in-Chief, his relations with the victorious generals, Taylor and Scott, strained as they were at times, were above politics, and he showed no inclination to replace them with other military men. Polk's ability to recognize and use new talent was illustrated by his selection of Nicholas P. Trist, a clerk in the Department of State, to negotiate peace with Mexico.

Despite the president's efforts, sectionalism had grown during his term of office. Its growth had not been confined to the South but to other sections as well.

"Before the Election," from an 1849 sketch.

Jefferson Davis, a young congressman in 1845, had pointed out the dual view of the North when it opposed the admittance of Texas as a state, while it looked forward eagerly to the conquest of Canada. To Davis, this seemed a convenient opinion in the light of the fact that the southern coastline was inadequately protected.

The Whigs had gained control in the off-year elections of 1846. The tide of popular fancy was on the upsurge for them and by 1848, they had not one but two national heroes to nominate for a presidential standard-bearer, Taylor and Scott. In addition, they had Henry Clay. Horace Greeley, always loyal to Clay, loudly opposed the selection of a military man for a presidential nominee. The Whigs, meeting in Philadelphia in 1848 to select their ticket, were not long in making a decision—it was Zachary Taylor on the fourth ballot. As a concession to the Clay faction, Millard Fillmore would be his running mate. On the fourth ballot, like the Whigs, the Democrats, now without strong leadership, nominated Lewis Cass of Michigan. At the start of the campaign, Cass, hoping to please all factions, came out in favor of the Wilmot Proviso; then, in an effort to gain votes in the South, he sent a contradictory letter supporting the southern viewpoint. The Whigs were quick to capitalize on the Democratic nominee's mistake when the contents of the letter became known. Meanwhile, the Whigs had adopted a catchy slogan "Rough and Ready" to build into the national image of Taylor. In the following November Taylor's slim margin of victory was 36 electoral votes.

One of the more colorful figures of the era was Orson Squire Fowler. Fowler, or "Professor Fowler" as he liked to be called, was recognized as one of the great "Fad Promoters" of all time. Although his fame rested primarily on phrenology and octagon houses, he was also an author and philosopher. Fowler often mixed his subjects and in his *Phrenological Journal* of 1848 he devoted considerable space to current politics. His insight into the political situation, although from a layman's eye, was astute when he wrote: "How long should we allow ourselves to be thus cheated? As long as we vote party tickets! . . monstrous abuses . . . all this the fruits of blind adherence to Party!" Fowler foresaw the break up of the major political parties in the decade to come. His political denouncements were many; he wrote of office-seekers whose qualifications were judged by a sole reference, their electioneering influence, and it was no secret, he said, that many votes were bought for money, especially the votes of foreigners. His observa-

A sketch a few months later in 1849, titled "After the Election."

tion on Fourth of July celebrations was: "I would that my fellow freeman might be persuaded to expend in the improvement of our government the interest and enthusiasm now wasted in shouts and fireworks." He questioned the awarding of so much patronage to the president: "Does he know who, in all our towns and villages, are the most qualified to receive and deliver our letters, better than we do? They are wanted to serve us, not him. Then why not we elect our own postmasters and appoint their salaries?" Rounding out his subject, he said that recent reforms had reduced the mail service fees by forty percent, which had been "paid by poltroons to knaves."

In 1848 the United States was in the process of conducting a geodetic survey of rivers and harbors. Fowler set down his facts and figures on how that could be improved. He suggested how to reduce the amount of money paid to private contractors and gave as an example the cost of six charts that had been recently completed. The government had paid $14,500 for them; the artist-lithographers had received only $780 of that amount. He also recommended smaller charts because they ranged from seven to fifteen feet in length and could hardly be spread out in the cabins of common vessels.[4]

Fowler, veering to the field of political theories, held the opinion that "when men pay money directly for a given object, they always watch its disbursement." Warming to his subject he wrote, "A direct tax would make economy and integrity with the public moneys a political hobby."

Fowler breathed patriotism—he loved the word "republicanism." He extolled the unrivaled national prosperity of 1848 and gave as an illustration the real estate values in America as compared with Europe. One citation read: ". . . a house and lot be bought in Prince-Regent-street—the royal street of the first empire of the world—for $10,000, which in Broadway could not be bought for $50,000?"

Fowler was not afraid to predict the future and he felt certain that whoever lived to see 1900 would behold a new order of things and a new race of beings; through republicanism and its companion liberty, a new life would be in store not only for Americans but for all the world.

The Inaugural Address of President Taylor in 1849 had been redolent with old-fashioned patriotism and it breathed the very spirit of George Washington. From the very outset, the problem of sectional strife plagued the new administration. The difficulties surrounding the slavery question had increased formidably since the annexation of Texas and the Mexican War.

Zachary Taylor, 1784–1850
The Twelfth President
*It had been Taylor's ambition to be President of the whole
people. He was the second president to die in office (July 9,
1850), after a brief term in which he had opposed sectionalism.*

In 1850 the *Edinburgh Review* (founded in 1802),
in a comprehensive article that analyzed American
thought and institutions, observed: "But we are hopeful of American civilization and of American democracy, which two must stand or fall together; and we
would not willingly believe the slavery schism so fundamental as to sever all the natural and habitual ties
which bind the southern states to the common interests
and glory of the Union. . . . A republican league upon
the basis of slavery, or a war of independence for such
a cause, could not prosper in the modern world. The
north would not hold its own, and the south would fall
a prey to civil discord and servile war. This, we think,
must be so clear to reflecting men on both sides, that
in the last extremity it will save the Union." This
prophetic vision of history came from the thoughts and
observations of Sir Charles Lyell after his second visit

to the United States in 1845. There were others in
Europe who held that the "American democracy had
outlived the virtues of its founders and had become
corrupt, acquisitive, envious, factitious and insensible
to honor."

In 1850 many of the body politic were men of good
will bent, as a paramount necessity, on preserving the
Union. In the midst of the mediators was Henry Clay;
standing with him and often differing in opinion were
Webster, Benton, Cass, Calhoun, and Foote (Benton
and Foote clashed physically) . In this year men of good
will would unite for the last time for the common cause
of the Union.

Daniel Webster (1782–1852)
*Webster, an exponent for a strong central government, was
one of the great orators of all times. He, with Clay and Calhoun, formed the famous triumvirate of American statesmen.
The death of Webster in 1852 brought to an end the powerful influence that they had exerted for a forty-year period in
American politics.*

Daniel Webster, referring to the increasingly violent and belligerent newspaper editors of the era, could still honor a difference of opinion when he said: "Again, sir, the violence of the press is complained of. The press violent! Why, sir, the press is violent everywhere. There are outrageous reproaches in the north against the south and there are reproaches no better in the south against the north. The extremists in both parts of this country are violent; they mistake loud and violent talk for eloquence and for reason. . . . And this we must expect, when the press is free, as it is here, and I trust always will be; . . . the entire and absolute freedom of the press is essential to the preservation of the government on the basis of a free constitution." And Webster again rose to his full height as an orator and statesman in defining the duties of the members of Congress,

Courtesy Library of Congress
In 1850 Henry Clay spoke eloquently in favor of the compromise he proposed to reconcile the drift in the country toward sectionalism. His oratory convinced both Daniel Webster and John C. Calhoun that his view must prevail if the Union were to be preserved.

when he said: ". . . If there was a government on earth, it is this government . . . which should consider itself as composed by agreement of all: each member appointed by some, but organized by the general consent of all—sitting here, under solemn obligations of oath and conscience, to do that which they think to be best for the good of the whole."

On February 5, 1850, Senator Henry Clay, feeble and aging, but still the grand master of eloquence, began a two-day oration in which he introduced a series of measures designed to reconcile the now-widening rift in opinion between the North and South. He pictured a coming war in which no one would win. He pleaded for unity. He brought forth "The Compromise of 1850." His proposition included two favorable measures for the North, two favoring the South, and one that deferred the settlement of differences to the future.

Courtesy Library of Congress
Millard Fillmore, 1800–1874
The Thirteenth President
Fillmore, like Tyler, assumed the presidency through the death of the elected president. As vice-president, he had presided over the exciting Senate debates on the "Compromise Measures of 1850." And as president he signed the measures into law. It was under Fillmore that Commodore Matthew C. Perry made his successful voyage to Japan.

Courtesy Library of Congress
John Caldwell Calhoun, 1782–1850
Calhoun, a believer in "states' rights," often held the opposite view of Daniel Webster's. He had held the office of vice-president under two presidents, John Quincy Adams and Andrew Jackson, and had resigned from that office in 1832. He was reelected to the Senate for the last time in 1845. He was a strong believer in the Union of the United States, but he also held that the minority must be protected from "the tyranny of the majority."

A month later, Senator John C. Calhoun, fearing for the Union but too weak to stand, had his speech read for him. In it, he conceded that the North had outstripped the South in material progress—and pleaded for understanding of the South's problems. In closing, he pointed out that each state, each with a measure of sovereignty, should maintain the Union uninterrupted. Calhoun died just a few days later on March 31.

Despite the eloquent plea (Webster spoke on March 7) of the famous trio of statesman and others favoring reconciliation, it appeared in the months following that the measures were doomed to failure. Zachary Taylor, the second president to die in office, passed away July 9, 1850. The new President, Millard Fillmore, and his administration favored the compromise bills, and in September all five separate measures were made into law. The men of ill will, radicals from both North and South—Seward, Chase, and Davis—had lost their battle to reason; Senator Robert Rhett of South Carolina resigned his Senate seat in disgust and retired to his plantation. A temper of the people was reflected in a measure, when the southern radicals' meeting in Nashville at a convention in the summer of 1850 had been poorly attended. The time was not yet ripe when "Events may occur which may catch the multitudes in an unthinking humor, and carry it away with them; or may blind the judgement by flattering appeals to the passions of the populace."

Voices in the South were loud for continuing the Union, and many leading spokesmen spoke out clearly supporting the compromise measures: General Thompson of South Carolina, Governors Brown of Florida and Collier of Alabama, Senator Downs and Soule of Louisiana. Georgia brought the issue to the ballot box, and those favoring continuation of the Union were in the majority by more than 30,000 votes. North Carolina legislators defeated all efforts to promote the scheme of disunion. Only in South Carolina did the seeds of disunion continue to thrive. General Sam Houston wrote a strong letter to the governor of Virginia condemning the efforts of South Carolina for separation.

In the North general compliance with the newly passed compromise laws was gaining acceptance. Governor Fort of New Jersey urged full support and so did the Delaware House of Representatives. By January, 1851, the governors of New York, Indiana, Illinois, and Pennsylvania had all gone on record as supporting the Fugitive Slave Law, although a few of the governors had reservations. Pro-Union meetings were being held in both the North and South in December, 1850, and January, 1851: in Boston, Nashville, Staunton (Virginia), and other places. Of the northern states, only in Vermont was the spirit of the compromise lacking. In November, 1850, the Vermont legislature passed a bill designed to circumvent the fugitive slave measure. It charged Vermont's state attorney "to use all lawful means to protect, defend and cause to be discharged every person arrested or claimed as a fugitive slave."

President Fillmore in his message to the thirty-first Congress said that he would be guided by the Constitution as interpreted by the courts. A national furor was caused in Boston by the seizure of a suspected fugitive

1851

With political tempers flaring, many new flags and patriotic emblems were being designed in the era.

slave under the new law. A mob, consisting mostly of colored men, had overpowered the arresting officer and released the fugitive, who escaped to Canada. Fillmore immediately issued a proclamation commanding obedience to the law. Many incidents took place. A British Member of Parliament was heckled when he made an anti-slavery speech in Boston, given under the auspices of William Lloyd Garrison. By April 1851, a general political acceptance of the Fugitive Slave Law was a fact.

Meanwhile, feelings in the South were of conciliation. In the spring of 1851, Virginia's General Assembly passed a series of resolutions: one condemned interference of northern states in the domestic affairs of the South; another appealed to South Carolina "to desist from mediated secession on her part." The *Richmond Enquirer* pronounced the resolutions as being the sentiment of the South, with but rare exceptions. The cause to continue the Union was on the rise; in Mississippi, where strong secession sentiments were to be found, Jefferson Davis, candidate for governor in 1851, was defeated. The spirit of conciliation was evident also in the new state of California. The state legislature in May 1851, in an effort to resolve a three-way tie for the seat of United States Senator, rejected John Frémont. Frémont's views on slavery were too positive for the temper of the Californians.

California had been one of the "bargains" of the

"Compromise Measures of 1850." And to celebrate the state's entrance into the Union, the people of San Francisco held a mammoth parade on December 29, 1850. Some spectators described the parade as "an array in a tournament from the pages of *Ivanhoe*." The parade was led by the chief marshal, who was dressed in white and gold. Following the leader were his assistants picturesquely clothed in sky blue and silver, and white satin fringed with gold. Other marching groups of settlers followed, one by one, in a riot of colorful uniforms —the politicians, the English, the Germans, the Spanish,

and others. And bringing up the rear of the settlers' division was a group from the Celestial Empire, who were attired in the rich brocades of the East. They carried a banner of crimson satin, which bore an inscription of great length in elaborate calligraphy. When translated it meant "China boys."

Led by the "Triumphal Car," the wheeled vehicles followed the marchers. The "car" was the central float of the parade. It carried thirty young boys who were dressed in white shirts, black pants, and liberty caps, and in their midst stood a beautiful little girl who

1848   *Courtesy Time-Out Antiques, N.Y.C.*
The Franklin

Volunteer fire companies were a very strong political factor in the mid-nineteenth century. Firemen annual balls, parades, chowder parties, and picnics were all used as a stepping-stone for the politically minded. Success in a fire company was a sure path to success in politics.

wore white satin and held a wreath of roses. Young Miss California represented the thirty-first state to enter the Union.

The last section of the parade displayed many fire companies; engines and equipment were gayly decorated in bright colors. The crowds were delighted and amazed at one hook and ladder engine, which had a live eagle perched on top of a pyramid of ladders.[5]

The second half of the nineteenth century began on January 1, 1851—the date and the event were well marked by the written material of the era. America was turning outward toward Europe and a close examination was taking place of its peoples and their political situations. One of the nation's weekly periodicals, making an analysis of the world, country by country, concluded: "The American republic is a great power in the world."

Congress adjourned on March 4, 1851, as required by the Constitution, but not before it had passed a joint resolution authorizing the President to grant the use of a Navy ship to bring Louis Kossuth, the Hungarian patriot, and his companions to America. The American crusade to help the Europeans establish democracy in Europe was exemplified by the cause of Kossuth in Hungary. Kossuth's efforts to liberate his country had excited the popular fancy of Americans during the 1840s. His cause had collapsed in 1849, and he had fled to Turkey. Kossuth was widely acclaimed when he came to the United States in 1851.

Only in America was democracy successful—a solitary world example of self-government. By 1850 Europe's traditional rulers were again in control—Spain and its king, Germany and the King of Prussia, Vienna and the Hapsburgs, and France at the mercy of a prince. The unrest in Europe was reflected in the tide of immigration to America. This in turn had caused a change in American voting patterns. In the 1840 decade 1,965,518 foreign-born citizens had settled in the free states, while only 245,310 had settled in the slave states. Primarily the bulk of the immigrants in the 1840s had come from the British Isles (sixty-six percent) and Germany (twenty-five percent). Ireland had provided about two-thirds of the immigrants from the British Isles.[6] The Irish had brought with them the intense religious overtones that would mark the bloc-voting techniques during the 1850s. This problem had been further intensified by an additional 2,589,214 immigrants, many Irish, during the 1850 decade. With regard to immigration, many of the northern free states had gradually loosened voting requirements; for example, Ohio in 1851 had simplified a voter's eligibility to "a free white male adult."

1860

The ever-increasing tide of immigration from Europe was causing the voting pattern to change. In the cities, where many of the new Americans settled, the office seeker was busily wooing their support.

The passage from Liverpool to New York in 1850 was £4 for steerage accommodations and £6 to £7 for second-class cabins. The average vessel catering to the immigrant trade carried 400 passengers each trip over. Many American seaboard cities had passed stringent regulation to control immigration by 1850. If an immigrant proved incapable of self support or had a contagious disease, a ship's captain was liable for a fine of $75 and support for the immigrant for a three-year period. In New York City a tax of $1.50 per head was levied on each immigrant; the proceeds went to the maintenance of the city's hospitals.[7]

A point was reached in the early 1850s when the population of growing America overtook that of Great Britain, excluding Ireland. The fear that had long plagued the British political body had now been realized, and the energetic nation across the sea was now a world power to be reckoned with. No record exists of the number of secret informers placed in America, but many English aristocrats openly aided and abetted the northern anti-slavery agitators. The prince consort, Albert, had set the pace with his pronounced anti-slavery views in the early 1840s. English money had often provided training and education for the young American agitators. The American abolitionists were feted and made welcome during their visits to England.

An editorial in *Putnam's Magazine* (1854) pointed a finger of suspicion at England in a blunt statement:

> the blatant zeal of the English aristocracy against Southern slavery, . . . to engender a suspicion that they are quite as much moved in their energies by a hatred of the democracy of this country as they are by a hatred of its slavery. We should esteem it a strange sight if Nicholas or Louis Napoleon should be smitten with a sudden anti-Southern-slavery impulse, but a moment's reflection would convince us that their pretended philanthropy was, in all likelihood, a *ruse* to hide some enormity of their own. In the same way, when we see the English nobles active against the slavery of the United States, we can hardly refrain from imputing to them a sinister motive.

Again, on the same theme, *Putnam's* commented in a book review (*A Voice to America*) in 1855: "But, is it not remarkable that a work, intended to teach Americans their rights and duties, should have been edited by one Englishman and published by another?"

Only a few ripples marred the serenity of America's body politic in 1852. Politically, the "Compromise of 1850" was an established and accepted fact for the more peaceful citizen of the republic. The campaign for the office of President, that year, offered the voter two choices. The Democrat's nominee, Franklin Pierce, presented a picture of continued tranquility based on the pact of 1850. The Whigs, not so content with the 1850 solution, felt that they had the answer for a successful presidential candidate in the war hero, General Winfield Scott. The Whigs were wrong; Pierce won overwhelmingly. The cohesiveness of the Whig Party and its great political leaders of other years was gone. The Liberty Party and the Know-Nothing Party, and the differing view of the Southern Whig and the Northern Whig, all contributed their share to Scott's defeat.

The new President's cabinet was devoid of sectionalism—able men filled each chair. An old friend, Jefferson Davis of Mississippi, was appointed Secretary of War. And almost immediately after assuming office, Pierce's status was enhanced by Commodore Perry's voyage to Japan. The American public was thrilled when he returned with many mysterious and wondrous curios, the visible results of his expedition.

Meanwhile, moderate editors in the North were pin-pointing William H. Seward of New York as the leading agitator on the political scene. They had long decried the southern hotheads and had often focused the wrath of the pen on South Carolina. Seward, the editors had come to realize, was a statesman who could lead the cause for disunion in the North. One editor wrote: "The characteristics of Mr. Seward's mind are clearness, activity and cunning; to use the term in its best sense . . . and Mr. Seward therefore, who has long been active in pushing projects of one-sided benefit, should not complain if the public, in spite of his nobler and liberal performances, in the cause of universal human freedom, should confound his motives with those of his sordid clients."[8] In short, Mr. Seward's actions had been

Courtesy Library of Congress
Franklin Pierce, 1804–1869
The Fourteenth President
No president since James Monroe had received such a plurality of votes as did Franklin Pierce in 1852. His courtly manners, personal magnetism, and ability to make friends served him well during his term of office.

viewed with suspicion and uneasiness despite his adherence to high political ideals.

Outpourings from the Know-Nothing or American Party had grown to a torrential outcry of public feeling against immigration and the new citizen by the end of 1854. And in the background were the darkening clouds over Kansas. In the North, the abolitionists, Garrison, Parker, Phillips, Weld, Grimké, and others, were all sowing their seeds of unrest and all with a measure of political influence. On the other hand, in the South the "Fire-eaters" had been busy, not with as much oratorical ability, perhaps, but steadily preaching fanatical doctrines in support of slavery.

Back in 1852, a new political party had had its be-

Courtesy Boatmen's National Bank of St. Louis
From village to village, rural America was being wooed by the politician. The painting above, "Stump Speaking," was done by George Caleb Bingham in 1854.

ginnings—The American Party, popularly called the Know-Nothing Party. It had grown rapidly in membership, picking up its backbone strength from the tired old Whig Party. It had expanded by 1854 to a potent political organization. The party had come together as a native American fraternity—the basic creed was anti-immigration with some pro-slavery overtones, a point of dissension within the ranks. Its creeds and platforms embraced many controversial issues, both popular and unpopular. For example, it endorsed the exclusion of Bible-reading in the public schools and would deny the use of public funds for denominational schools.

The situation in Kansas was best summed up by the *St. Louis Intelligencer* in August, 1855 when it stated: "Emigrants from the northern or free states have ceased to go to Kansas, because they can find as good land elsewhere, not cursed by mob law nor ruled by non-resident bullies. Emigrants from the southern states do not go to Kansas, because they will not put their slave property in peril. . . ." The repeal of the Missouri Compromise restrictions had given license for the plunder of Kansas by hotheaded troublemakers from all sections of the country. In the East, "Emigrant Aid Societies" were formed: Often they were composed of well-meaning legitimate settlers led by professional abolitionists—destination Kansas. From the South came the "hirelings," who supported "the ascendance of the bowie-knife and the rifle over the ballot-box and the law." The southerner, in the race to seize Kansas for a slave state, had gained control of the legal machinery through the Kansas legislature and had passed laws to curtail "rights which are the very essence of a free commonwealth. . . . Those precious defenses of the citizen—

A cartoon of the era depicting violence at a voting place.

speech, the press, the bar, the jury—alike were invaded with inquisitorial zeal." In addition the death penalty was instituted for those who aided a slave to escape. The high-handed behavior of the southern hothead in Kansas was exposed and proclaimed all over the North.

By 1855 the peaceable Northerner was being slowly convinced that the only result he had derived from the " '50 compromise" was to make him a slave-catcher—a role he found little liking for and one he would evade at every opportunity. The fact that California had come into the Union as a free state and part of the pact of 1850 had now been forgotten by the northerner. Politically the pro-slavery men had been active—"the bill for the organization of the Nebraska Territories" had put the free states on the defensive. The northern voter had come to think in terms that were repugnant to him five years earlier. He now tended to favor: The Repeal of the Fugitive Slave Law; The Restoration of the Missouri Compromise; No More Slave States; The Homestead for Free Men on Public Lands.

Further grist for the abolitionists' mill occurred in the spring of 1856 with the "caning of the United States Senator Charles Sumner of Massachusetts." It was magnified in the North far beyond its true proportions and it enabled the agitators to picture how determined was the man of the South to impose the society of slavery at all costs!

The story, as it unfolded, began on May 20, when Mr. Sumner had concluded a long and elaborate speech denouncing the affairs in Kansas. In his anti-slavery harangue, he had focused his wrath on the aged Senator Butler of South Carolina. Sumner had likened Butler to "Don Quixote, whose mistress is slavery . . . Heroic Knight . . . Exalted Senator . . . a second Moses for Exodus . . . the tyrannical sectionalism of which the Senator from South Carolina is one of the maddest zealots." Sumner's speech was denounced at once by many of his fellow senators as exceeding right use of freedom of political speech. The reaction of Senator Cass of Michigan, a moderate, was that it was "the most un-American and unpatriotic speech" he ever "heard of this floor." The *New York Times* quoted Douglas of Illinois as charging Sumner with "having taken an oath to support the constitution and then violated it." Senator Mason publicly called Sumner "a liar."

Senator Sumner was a massive man, six feet four; the image he presented was that of a formidable physical opponent. Whether Sumner, after the ensuing emotional reactions to his speech, had been "called out," in the manner of the day, during the time lapse between May 20, and May 22, is not known. However, on the morning of May 22, against his usual custom, he

Two doctors had examined Sumner soon after the beating and made a diagnosis that while the wounds were serious, he would recover. The second version on the front page of the *Times* gave an emotional account of the incident, telling of blood and bones oozing from Sumner's head and his close proximity to death.

The only spectator was a man in the balcony and the two silent friends of Brooks. Brooks, after the beating, had reported to a magistrate and had been released on bail. For the offence he was later fined $300.00.[9]

But the deed had been done—violence in the Congress—and even the vast numbers of moderates North or South could hardly condone or defend violence as a form of government!

The massacre of five pro-slavery men at Pottowatomie Creek in Kansas, two days later on May 24, gave the hot-headed southerner a rebuttal to the caning of Sumner.

In the spring of 1856, about 5,100,000 citizens were eligible to cast a ballot; only about 3,100,000 exercised

Courtesy The Metropolitan Museum of Art, Gift of I. N. Phelps Stokes, Edward S. Hawes, Alice Mary Hawes, Marion Augusta Hawes, 1937
Charles Sumner (1811–1874)
After graduating from Harvard College, Sumner was eagerly sought after as an orator. He supported public education, prison reforms, and peace among nations. He first entered politics in 1851, and became a leading figure for the abolitionist cause in the years following.

1855   *Courtesy Time-Out Antiques, N.Y.C.*
Many political speakers were heralded by the drum and the fife.

arrived at the Senate in a carriage and entered the building through the rear door. Preston Brooks, a Congressman from South Carolina and a nephew of Senator Butler, had loitered with two friends outside the front entrance to the Senate Chamber from early morning hoping to meet Senator Sumner. The Senate met and adjourned early that day; however, Sumner remained at his desk working after the other Senators had departed. Of the events that followed, the *New York Times* carried on its front page two versions of the "Caning of Senator Sumner." The factual version reported that Brooks had approached Sumner at work and had beat him about the head until Brook's gutta percha cane broke and Sumner had fallen to the floor.

their voting privilege. The percentage of the apathetic non-voter varied by states and sections, with Massachusetts having the poorest record for voter turnout. A political observer noted: "It was not an uncommon thing to hear people say—that one party was as good as another. . . . Others, again, disgusted by the low tone of political life—the abuse and vulgarity in which it abounds . . . do not so much as cast their ballots."

It was said of the presidential election of 1856, that it ruined one party (Know-Nothing), it temporarily checked another (Republican), and there was a doubtful ascendancy of another (Democrats). It was also ac-knowledged that the tone of the campaign had been conducted on a higher level than before. The style of speaking had been better, the character of the audiences improved, and the political rallies had been held away from the vicinity of low and filthy grog shops, the patrons of which had usually attended meetings while reeking of rum and tobacco.

The results of the 1856 presidential election gave James Buchanan 174 electoral votes. His closest competitor, John C. Frémont, received 114 electoral votes. Ex-President Millard Fillmore, running on the American Party's ticket, did badly, carrying only the state of Maryland. However, the Republican Party had come to stay, with the anti-slavery groups uniting for the most part under one banner.

Politics and religion often walked hand in hand during this era. A southern religious periodical held a view about the slavery issue, "until modern Abolitionism made its appearance, introduced here, no doubt, by emissaries from Europe, with a special view to produc-

The habitués of nearby grog shops often provided an audience for political rallies. The upright citizen complained of the reek of rum and tobacco.

ing a rupture between the Northern and Southern States. These professed benefactors, instead of going to the slaveholders and declaring to them their sin, began to preach in the North against slavery, and to organize societies for putting it down. The evils of the institution were exaggerated with shocking falsehoods. . . . The war was carried into the pulpits . . . and sentenced to everlasting perdition all who held slaves."[10] The southern Christian periodicals often portrayed "the cunning Yankee" and told of scattered groups of "Freemen" and "Turners" (Germans) throughout the northern states, all breaking down Sunday laws through their mastery of the municipal politician in the year 1856.

The incoming president in 1857, Buchanan, had chosen for his cabinet pro-Union men—a fact not pleasing to the radicals of both North and South. Two days after his inauguration, the Supreme Court handed down a decision on the "Dred Scott v. Sanford" court action. Its ruling placed the court as a target for abuse from the anti-slavery agitators. The abolitionists felt that the court had joined hands with the South to perpetuate slavery.

The financial panic of 1857 began spreading over the northern states a few weeks later, making more trouble for the Buchanan administration. When the national credit structure collapsed, the slavery issue was temporarily put aside—the people, rich or poor, were involved with personal financial survival. Almost everywhere banks stopped specie payments; factories were closed and farmers could find no market for their products. Politicians did little to alleviate the situation.

The make-up of the Democratic Party was changing in 1857. Disagreement between two old-line party adherents occurred. Senator Stephen Douglas of Illinois, strong in national politics, and President Buchanan, titular head of the Party, parted and went their separate ways. When Douglas and his followers left the "Administration" Democrats, it brought a new alignment for the northern moderates. Much of Douglas's prestige in the South was lost by his move and thus, like the Whigs before them, the Democrats turned to sectionalism. The people of the North could now choose between the moderate Democrats under Douglas or the more radical Republicans under Seward.

The first test of the new political alignment for the North came in 1858. It was in the contest for the United States Senate seat in Illinois that the new political philosophies would be expounded. The Republicans nominated the ex-Whig, Abraham Lincoln, to oppose Stephen Douglas. The issue, simply, was the present and future of slavery as a national concern.

Lincoln made his stand in his acceptance speech for

Stephen Douglas (1813–1861)
Douglas began his political career as a Jackson Democrat in 1834 and was first elected to Congress in 1843. He quickly gained national recognition as a resourceful political leader; as an adroit debater he advocated national territorial expansion. Hardly five feet high, strong-voiced and barrel-chested, he was called "The Little Giant"—a marked contrast to his ofttimes political opponent, the tall, rangy Abraham Lincoln.

continued relentlessly, until the one or the other shall be subdued, and all the states shall either become free or become slave."[11] In reply to the Douglas accusations, Lincoln was forced to clarify many of the points made in his original speech.

Such were the opening moves of a contest on which the eyes of the nation would become fixed. Throughout the campaign that followed, speech by speech, Lincoln slowly became the aggressor, and even in the series of debates that were the highlight of the campaign, Lincoln maintained the attack.

Election day gave Lincoln a popular plurality of 4,085 votes, but because of the apportionment of the legislative districts of Illinois that favored the Democrats, Senator Douglas was returned to Congress.

Lincoln, the loser, had campaigned against a master politician, an orator and figure of national note, and had emerged from an Illinois politician to a figure of national status. One result of the campaign, from a southern viewpoint, was that the image of Lincoln had changed from a Republican to a Black Republican and that he was hardly a figure to breach the widening rift of sectionalism. And at the same time, Douglas had said nothing to increase his popularity in the South.

Meanwhile, in 1858, William L. Yancy of Alabama had been busy promoting sectionalism. He had issued a letter advocating, in the South's behalf, the appointment of committees of safety, the formation of a League of United Southerners, and the repeal of laws making the African slave trade a piracy. The southern viewpoint for continuing the Union was slowly weakening under the cry for a united South to face the mounting political pressure from the North.

In May of 1859, at Chatham, Canada, a meeting was held by John Brown, and those who thought like him, to determine a plan to establish a Provisional Government of the United States. It was worked out that Brown would be Commander-in-Chief, with almost dictatorial powers, while his followers would be appointed to the important posts within the proposed government. Much of Brown's support had come from the Massachusetts-Kansas Committee (Boston) in the form of funds and arms for his anti-slavery activities.

After the Canada meeting, Brown later rented a farm in Maryland near Harpers Ferry, Virginia, as a base of operations. He and his "army of 22 men" attacked and captured the United States Arsenal at Harpers Ferry on the night of October 16, 1859. Brown had hoped to gain manpower support through a revolt of Negro slaves after he had occupied his objective—the arsenal.

Brown's dream for a new government was dead when he was captured two days later by a United States mili-

nomination when he said, in part: "I believe this government cannot endure, permanently half slave and half free. I do not expect the Union to be dissolved—I do not expect the house to fall—but I do expect it will cease to be divided. It will become all one thing, or all the other." In his first speech, Lincoln had set the tone of a campaign in national character instead of state issues, but he had also put Douglas in a position to attack his statements. Douglas quickly answered, "Mr. Lincoln advocates boldly and clearly a war of sections, a war of the North against the South, of free states against the slave states, a war of extermination, to be

Courtesy Library of Congress
Legal justice moved swiftly in the case of John Brown. He was captured on October 18, convicted October 31, and hanged until dead (above) on December 2, 1859. Bells tolled his passing in many northern communities, thus adding insult to an already affronted South. The event occurred in a stubble field, near Charleston, Virginia.

tary force. He was quickly convicted by the end of October and hanged by the neck on December 2, 1859.

Governor Wise of Virginia, in his comments on the Brown affair, said: "One of the most irritating features of the predatory war against the South . . . is that it has its seat in the British provinces, which furnish asylums for fugitives, and send them and their hired outlaws from rendezvous in the neighboring States."[12]

Meanwhile in October, the dominant American Party in the city of Baltimore had organized bands of ruffians to surround the voting polls to prevent the op-position from casting their ballots; several people were killed and a number injured.

The thirty-sixth Congress convened on December 5, 1859. Only 48 of the 66 members were present in the Senate. The House had a better record with 230 of its 237 members present. In the Senate, Mr. Mason offered a resolution to investigate the recent seizure of Harpers Ferry by a band of armed men. The business of electing a speaker in the House did poorly, although Mr. Sherman, Republican, was within three votes of the chair.

President Buchanan delivered his message to Congress on December 27, and, on the Harpers Ferry episode he commented that it derived its chief importance from the apprehension excited in the public mind but he entertained no apprehensions as to the possible peril to our institutions.

Throughout January, 1860, the House continued in its effort to elect a speaker, but it was not until February 1, and after 44 ballots, that it succeeded. The year 1860 was a presidential election year, and, not without tradition, the House in February appointed certain committees to investigate charges of corruption and bribery made against the administration.

Meanwhile, the Senate was very active. Mr. Davis of Mississippi introduced a series of seven resolutions. The ones accented were those dealing with States' rights and the relation of slavery to the national Union. Mr. Seward presented a memorial asking that Kansas be admitted to the Union (Kansas after its blood bath had gradually become a free state). Senator Seward, now the outstanding Republican in the country, was often the Party's spokesman. He condemned the Harpers Ferry affair and disclaimed any apprehensions or disunion or the overthrow of the government. Senator Douglas, as might be expected, launched an attack on Mr. Seward and the Republicans.

By April the House of Representatives had lost whatever good will it might have had and became almost an armed camp. The abolitionist's propaganda had done its work well—Representative Van Wyck of New York said: "One gentleman spoke of Massachusetts burning witches in ancient times. Does he not know that your own people [of the South] burn slaves at the stake, and it seems to waken no horror in your minds?" Congressman Davis of Mississippi (no relation of Jefferson Davis) branded Van Wyck "a liar and a scoundrel" and issued a challenge to settle the matter "outside the District of Columbia."[13] A few days later the House was

Washington City, in the era 1840–1860, had become a powerful seat of national government. Many magnificent new buildings had been constructed and no longer did the members of Congress have to wade through the mud on a journey from the White House to the Capitol. A lithograph of the city in 1859.

William H. Seward (1801–1872)

Seward was a native of Florida, New York, and as a young lawyer, still in his twenties, he began a career in politics. He was elected governor of New York in 1838 and again in 1840. Seward was an early national political opponent of slavery, a pioneer member of the Republican Party, and, in the years following, the Party spokesman. His ambition to become a presidential candidate was twice thwarted: by Frémont in 1856 and Lincoln in 1860.

again in turmoil. A member from Illinois made a violent speech against slavery; his manner of gesticulating aroused the ire of the southerners to a fighting pitch and to such an extent that it was necessary for the Sergeant-at-Arms to restore order. The business of the House was slowed down considerably.

By the middle of April the Senate Committee investigating the Harpers Ferry incident had made little progress, but it had sent Mr. Thaddeus Hyatt to prison for not answering their questions. Further, the committee had been unable to bring F. B. Sanborn of Massachusetts to Washington. He had been the man who handled much of the money that financed John Brown.

The violence exhibited in Congress by the men of ill will became the national spectacle of 1860.

Meanwhile, House tempers had improved very little. At one point, a duel with bowie knives appeared a certainty, to settle a disagreement between two members of the House.

The first political convention in 1860 was held by the Democratic National Party in Charleston on April 23, to nominate a candidate for the presidency. After eight days a platform was adopted that proved unacceptable to many southern delegates. A total of seven southern states, led by Alabama, walked out of the convention. Further proceedings by the convention to nominate a presidential candidate proved futile, and after 57 ballots it was decided to adjourn and meet again in Baltimore on June 18.

A new political group, The Constitutional Union Party, held its convention in Baltimore on May 10. It quickly nominated John Bell of Tennessee for president and Edward Everett as his running mate. The group declared other political parties to have sectionalism in their platforms but that only they stood for a united America under the Constitution.

The Republican National Convention met on May 16, in a huge building called "The Wigwam" in Chicago. The city was crowded with an additional 25,000 people to watch the proceedings. It was estimated that the Tremont House had put up at least 1,500 guests. In the opening days of the convention a moderate platform, much on the line of the old Whig Party, was adopted, adding only a mild resolution concerning the slavery dispute. Of the hopeful presidential aspirants, it was believed that Seward would win, although Lin-

ca. 1860
John Bell, *right*, ex-Whig and a conservative, was the Constitutional Union Party's candidate for the presidency in 1860. His only campaign crusade was to preserve the Union. He received over a half-million votes, mostly from the South. An ambrotype copy of a lithograph.

The Republic Wigwam Convention Hall in Chicago (daguerreotype above) was the scene of Lincoln's nomination in the spring of 1860.

coln, Cameron, and Chase were also likely candidates for the nomination. Each had his respective delegations and political camps. On the third ballot, Abraham Lincoln was nominated as the Republican's candidate for president; to share his banner, Hannibal Hamlin of Maine would run for vice-president.

The "Divided Democrats" reassembled in Baltimore on June 18 to make another attempt to agree on a platform and a presidential candidate. However, their division was now a cleavage—Mr. Douglas was nominated only after delegates from the Southern States, Oregon, and California withdrew from the convention. The dissenting Democrats went on to form a Democratic (Southern) Party and nominated John C. Breckinridge of Kentucky for their presidential candidate.

Congress adjourned on June 23, but not before it had heard the reports of several committees. The committee investigating the John Brown affair had found no evidence that Brown had been a part of a widespread conspiracy, although they did censor "The Massachusetts-Kansas Committee" for negligence, for supplying arms and money to Brown.

A portrait of the Prince of Wales, Edward Albert, eldest son of Queen Victoria and heir apparent to the throne of England, from a paper photograph ca. 1859. He visited Canada and the United States in 1860.

Courtesy Chicago Historical Society
"Abraham Lincoln of Illinois" as he looked in 1860.

Another investigating committee, looking into corruption in high places in the executive branch of the government, reported that while they had found an immense amount of evidence to support the charges, they would not make formal charges or censure any member of the administration

The summer election campaign began with President Buchanan's announcement that there was no regular Democratic nomination for the presidency and any Democrat could feel free to vote for either Douglas or Breckinridge. All presidential candidates expressed confidence of victory for their respective campaigns.

In addition to the excitement of a presidential campaign, the average American felt flattered in the summer of 1860. Queen Victoria of England was sending her eldest son, Albert, Prince of Wales, to America. He would come as a guest of President Buchanan and would arrive by early fall. Oddly, his title while touring the United States would be "Baron Renfrew" to disguise his nobility. He arrived in Detroit on September 21, after an extended tour of Canada. He made his way southward, stopping at Chicago, St. Louis, Cincinnati, and Baltimore, and arrived in Washington on October 3, accompanied by his large entourage. After a four day stay in the capital, the Prince and his party went on to Richmond, then back to Philadelphia and New York. To mark his visit to New York, a grand ball was held in his honor. The royal party inspected West Point on their way to Albany. From Albany they traveled to Boston, and then on to the port of embarkation, Portland, Maine, arriving there on October 20. The Prince of Wales's tour through America had been a success, and he had been readily accepted as a belated honor due the great democracy, although a few Americans, with a native suspicion of things foreign, attached a sinister motive to the visit.

As September approached and the election drew nearer, the activity of the presidential campaign increased. An effort was made in several states, but mainly centered in New York, to unite the various Democratic groups in face of the Republican onslaught. Nationally, Douglas was conducting a vigorous campaign in his own behalf. Mr. Seward proved to be an indefatigable worker for Lincoln and the Republican Party.

As election approached, it became evident among the

1860
The "Wide Awakes" were a semi-military organization composed of Lincoln boosters, who numbered from 200,000 to 400,000 men. The group played a colorful part in Lincoln's campaign for the presidency in 1860. The "Wide Awakes" paraded at night to the lights of tar barrels and fireworks; each man carried an oil torch. The campaigners marched in a zigzag formation, simulating a split-rail fence, row upon row, singing "Old Abe Lincoln came out of the wilderness." The cost of the uniform, shown above, ranged from seventy-five cents to one dollar and fifteen cents, including the oil torch.

Courtesy Library of Congress
To Portland, Maine, fell the honor of bidding farewell to the touring Prince of Wales and his party. His visit had been the highlight for America's social leaders in 1860. The Prince and Mayor Howard (of Portland) are seated in the rear of the carriage (above). A stereoscopic view.

many political forecasters that the Republicans would win the presidential chair. Throughout the South, many political leaders were openly planning secession, but only in Alabama had the legislature gone on record instructing the Governor to call a convention in the event that Lincoln was victorious. Amid the loud cry of southern voices for secession was heard the quiet voice of Alexander H. Stephens of Georgia cautioning the South to first consider the certainty of a Civil War and the folly of bloodshed if their present policy of disunion was carried out.

But more and more southerners were examining the picture portrayed to them with foreboding. The Republicans had a dominant fringe of fanatical abolitionists, the large semi-military organization of "Wide Awakes," Mr. Lincoln's ardent boosters, who paraded in uniforms often to the tune of firework and firearm displays. A Negro "Wide Awake" club in Boston did little to dispel southern fears. All must have given dread to the people and support to the southern politician advocating secession.

The result of the November, 1860, election was as

Courtesy Library of Congress
James Buchanan, 1791–1868
The Fifteenth President and his Cabinet
James Buchanan began his active political career in 1814. His background marked him well for the presidency in 1856. He had sat in both houses of Congress and had represented the United States in Russia. Later, he was minister to Great Britain and had been active as a Democrat on the national scene.

the forecasters had predicted. Abraham Lincoln, Republican, was elected President. He had received 180 electoral votes to his combined opponents' 123, but in the popular vote he was clearly "a minority President."

The reaction to the election was almost immediate in the South. Feeling in favor of secession had mounted to a proportion not hitherto recognized in the North. South Carolina took an active lead toward the day of secession and other southern states were now veering to this opinion. However, the secession movement was slowed by the problems of operating an autonomous government. Clearly, if a new government was formed, the seceding states would need time to put their houses in order.

Congress met on December 3, 1860, with the foremost political officeholders present; of statesmen in the tradition of Clay, Webster, and Calhoun, there were none.

President Buchanan's message to Congress on the state of the nation was transmitted on the 4th of December. He stated that the long and continued intemperate interference of the northern people had at length produced its natural consequence—the different sections of the country were now arrayed against each other. He suggested that the American people might settle the slavery question and restore peace and harmony simply by leaving the southern states to manage their domestic institutions in their own way. He pointed out that the election of any person to the office of President did not, of itself, afford just cause for dissolving the Union, and that the late election had been held in strict conformity with the Constitution. He went on to state that the "Fugitive Slave Law" was the law of the nation—it had been properly declared legal by the Supreme Court and it was his duty to uphold the law. On the other hand, he noted that the doctrine of secession was hardly a Constitutional remedy for any wrongs and that the government derived its power directly from the people—that the Constitution of the United States was in effect the constitution of each state. He flatly urged looking danger fairly in the face. Secession, the President's message continued, was neither more nor less than revolution and while it was his duty to uphold the law, in the case of South Carolina there was no judicial authority to issue process and no marshal to enforce it. President Buchanan brought up the point of whether Congress had the power to coerce a state withdrawing from the Union. He concluded that "so far from this power having been delegated to Congress, it was expressly refused by the convention which framed the Constitution." He advised that even if Congress had this power it would be unwise to exercise it. At the same time he cautioned the hotheads in South Carolina that any attempt by that state to forcibly seize any United States property would be met with equal force, but he felt that an arrangement for its purchase could be made and that Congress had that power.

Politically, the affluence America had enjoyed in the eyes of the world was coming to a close. The dissolution of the Republic began on December 20, 1860, when South Carolina seceded from the Union.

7

Religion

Religion was so closely woven into the fabric of American life before the Civil War that it touched firmly on all of the important institutions—education, politics, the arts. It had been consistently the thread that held the sectional areas of the country together since it was first colonized. However, many factors were at work during the first half of the nineteenth century that would weaken the existing religious pattern. The tremendous movement of peoples to the western frontiers resulted in the establishment of churches either loosely connected with the churches back East or independent ones fitting into the needs of frontier life. Also, the surging influx of the foreign-born to the West was destined to transplant old world ideas and traditions that would mingle with American thought. The "experimenters," those groups that often sprang from nonconformists who sought self-expression, started new religious sects or new adaptations of old religious doctrines. Large numbers of rural Americans lured by industry migrated to the cities, leaving old values behind. Another potent factor destined to cut deep rifts into existing churches was the slowly intensifying slavery issue.

All of these influences caused strong sectional feeling in the country; the Americans on the move had caused a social and economic upheaval. The once-strong thread of existing religion, now weakening, showed splits in many places and a mending operation had to be undertaken by the church and its organization. Conversely, although a weakening was present in the overall fabric of religion, churches experienced a tremendous growth in the ante-bellum era and a whole new religious pattern was in the making.

It was natural for liberal theologies to take root among a self-reliant American people, and it was just as natural for old-line conservatives to fight the disrupting influences. The liberal seed had been planted long before the nineteenth century; religious leaders and intellectuals had reshaped many of the religious ideas and teachings. Doctrines had been adapted to the times. New religious leaders, notably from New England, had wrenched many followers away from old Puritan beliefs, which had included predestination and infant damnation. The wrench was painful and caused sharp severings from the main bodies of established religious sects. The new liberal thought evolving from its basic foundation of Puritanism, and also, later, Deism and Unitarianism, had led to a more rational and optimistic view for man—an important change from the idea of God as an angry father to one of a loving father.

New England had long led the way in religious theology and ideas. Unitarianism, which embraced a non-Christian idea of God alone in that it did not believe in the Trinity, had started in America in the eighteenth century. With one exception at the beginning of the nineteenth century, all of the Boston churches were filled by Unitarian preachers. In mid-eighteenth century, Harvard College, had represented the most advanced thought of the time, and a score of clery throughout New England were advocating Unitarianism.

In the first decades of the nineteenth century, William Ellery Channing (1780–1842), whose maternal grandfather William Ellery had been one of the signers of the Declaration of Independence, was the leader and the interpreter of this theology. Religious periodicals and organizations contributed further to the spread

After 1853
Nineteenth-century leaders, especially from New England, had gradually, with persuasive teachings, weaned many followers away from old Puritan beliefs. There were still, however, many who clung to the old Puritan ways in New England. The above Ambrotype shows a New England village gathering. A woman in the background, seated on a pedestal, is in Puritan dress. The time of year the photograph was taken suggests a possible Thanksgiving ceremony.

The spacious old house and garden illustrated was the residence of America's poet and essayist Ralph Waldo Emerson. In the 1830s a small group of intellectuals met at Emerson's home as a discussion group. From the group discussions a new religious line of thought emerged—Transcendentalism. An engraving from a daguerreotype, 1853.

of Unitarianism, all of which resulted in a growing division in the early established and primarily New England Congregational churches.

As the nineteenth century began unfolding, Unitarianism was not warmly accepted by the oncoming "Romantic Age." Instead of rationalism in religion, people preferred a more spiritual and abstract approach. In the 1830s a small group of intellectuals around Concord, Massachusetts, met at the home of former Unitarian minister Ralph Waldo Emerson as a discussion group. Many well-known men joined in the religious and philosophical exchanges, including Theodore Parker, James Freeman Clark, Amos Bronson Alcott, Nathaniel Hawthorne, Orestes Brown-

son, George Ripley, Henry David Thoreau, and two talented women, Margaret Fuller and Elizabeth Peabody. From the discussions of this interesting group a transcendental line of thought developed that would cause a further upheaval in religious thinking. Many of the group's ideas were taken from prominent European thinkers and were modified by these intellectuals. Here again in the transcendental theology basic religion was being modified, and now by the Romanticism of this age. A trace of mysticism and a touch of Quakerism were evident in the new thought that man could transcend himself above just pure reasoning. Transcendental thought offered new hope for man. However, Transcendentalism was too radical a change

1854   *Courtesy Time-Out Antiques, N.Y.C.*
An octagon church of the era. The cost to support religion in America in the mid-1850s was estimated at about $25,000,- 000 annually. About 1,000 new churches were being built each year.

for the many conservatives who fought new ideas, or for most Americans. They continued being Congregationalists, Presbyterians, Baptists, and Methodists.

By mid-nineteenth century great changes had taken place in American religion; a rapid growth of churches, and new, interesting religious groups had been formed and colorful religious personalities had emerged.

The Christian church itself had undergone a vast change in the one-hundred-year period before the Civil War. The comfortable, spacious, modernized, heated city church was a far cry from the days of the church of the banging and noisy door, the huge, roaring iron stove, and the vapor curling from the mouths of the pew occupants. No more lunching in the pews or corners! The city church now had a neat vestibule, carpeted aisles, commodious pews stuffed all around with elbow bolsters and plump red cushions. Colors used in the church were harmonious, as was the music,

The lithograph above is titled "The Way to Church." The rural church in mid-nineteenth century formed a great part of community life in America. In the West and South the church drew far-flung towns together and was an important binding factor in the social, economic, and political make-up of these regions.

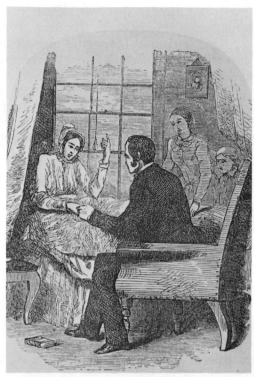

One of the minister's many duties was the visitation of the sick. A sketch from a religious tract of the era.

and all—even the ushers—were decorous and appropriate. The keynote of the whole affair seemed to be the huge fat cushion upon the pulpit desk. Sunday morning church attendance in the city held firmly, but the hundred-year-old custom of afternoon church service was now slipping badly; the few stragglers who came were far outnumbered by the red cushions on the empty seats.

In the 1840–1860 period, and before, religion and politics were the great powers in the land, church attendance was heavy and widespread, for it was both fashionable and respectable to be a church member, and in this ante-bellum society it was certainly a political and social asset. Social activities, radiating from the church, formed a great part of rural community life; in the western and the southern states the church became the impetus for far-flung towns to draw closer together, thus helping them economically, socially, and politically.

The clergy, despite their prestige, were said to be the hardest working and poorest paid of the professions, with some exceptions. The Episcopalians for one, since colonial days had, in the prosperous South, kept their clergy in comfort. In South Carolina in the mid-nineteenth century some Episcopal ministers were paid $1,200 per year and were often provided with both

a summer and a winter house and nearly all of their food.[1]

Ministers were at the mercy of the public quite as much as were editors of the day. They had to maintain a style of living equally as good as their parishioners, and were expected to have an overall knowledge of current affairs, literature, arts, and the sciences. Besides the preparation of two weekly sermons, their duties were many—innumerable meetings of all kinds during the week, visiting the sick, and helping the poor.[2]

Many preachers had impressive backgrounds; it was common practice for theological students to go to Germany in order to keep up with the latest scholarship in theology. The ambitious young student was often attracted to the ministry as a stepping stone to success. After graduating from school, he made his first persuasive orations from the pulpit, then later turned to professorship or, as frequently happened, entered politics. In later years, he might become a scholar and well-known historian.

Revivalism, rampant in the first half of the nineteenth century, brought many bright young men into the ministry. Revivals were held regularly on college campuses and many students like Theodore Weld, the famous abolitionist, were first converted by Charles Grandison Finney, the great evangelist. Finney was raised in Oneida County, New York, and began his famed revivals in 1826. Traveling about through the big cities in the next few years, he made an unusually strong impact on the "city" man. Thousands were influenced by his timely logic, which was scholarly in its New England approach, but his plain speaking also appealed to the hard-working frontier man.

In the same evangelistic fervor, great camp meetings were formed, in which thousands were converted to the Gospel. Notices of the meetings and the area in which they would be held were posted two or three months in advance. On the great day, roads near the designated site became jammed with coaches, wagons, and carts of all kinds. People also arrived on horseback and on foot; but whatever their mode of travel, they brought all sorts of provisions—mattresses, tents, utensils, and food, usually enough to last for a week's stay. (If a camp meeting was held anywhere near a main railroad line, platforms were crowded along the stops for miles.) People of all ages, wealthy and poor, Negro and white, came to the meetings.[3] Some comers were merely curious, others had politics in mind, but all anticipated great excitement.

A host of preachers of different denominations arrived on the scene; many would get their first training

The first camp meetings were instituted in 1799 under the joint auspices of the Presbyterians and the Methodists in the Kentucky-Tennessee area. They spread to other Protestant groups and by 1840 onward, their large, noisy meetings were attended by as many as 20,000 fervent religious followers. The meetings, which were held during the summer months, were sometimes held around the clock—early morning, afternoon services, and "the midnight cry" were all part of the camp life. Large divided tents were generally shared by families from the same area.

In the early 1840s it was said "under revivalism it is the sinner who gets religion, not religion that gets the sinner." From a sketch of the era.

in evangelistic techniques at these great mass meetings. Tents were pitched near a handy stream; lanterns were hung on convenient trees or shrubs; and in a few hours, a religious city was stirring with life. Cooking fires sprang up and the pleasant aroma of family cooking filled the air. A cup of coffee and a meal were often shared with a neighbor. Sometimes an unexpected disaster struck, such as the storm that tore down tents and played general havoc at an Eastern Shore Maryland meeting in September 1846, but usually there was little to dampen the enthusiasm of these affairs.

There is no doubt that the extensive use of the evangelistic camp meeting helped to cut down the earlier popularity of Deism and Unitarianism. It made a big impact also on the current religious publications and Bible Societies. By 1840, the number of religious publications stood at 850, one half of which were put out by the Presbyterians and Universalists, although the Methodists had originally led the way.[4] Orestes Brownson, author and clergyman, complained that, "Matters have come to such a pass, that a peaceable man can hardly venture to eat or drink, to go to bed or get up, to correct his children or kiss his wife" without the permission of some society.

Different sects seemed to congregate in certain areas of the country. In 1830 Congregationalists had nine-tenths of their churches in New England. Universalists had a heavy concentration there also in 1850, with almost half of their 529 churches located in that region.

In 1850 the Methodists and Baptists had ninety percent of all churches in Georgia, while the Catholics settled along the Mississippi Valley in great numbers.

Congregationalism came to America in 1620 with the immigration of a church elder, William Brewster, to New England. Most of the early settlers adopted a Calvinistic theology and from it there developed through the years two schools of thought—"The New England Theology" and the "Liberal School." The Congregational church, whose members were largely anti-slavery in sentiment, took an important part in the theological controversy that raged during the first half of the nineteenth century, and, because of its general academic interest, also furthered education. During the 1840s Congregationalists were active in missionary conversion work among the Negroes, including those of the South. They also worked among the Indians of the West and later with Chinese along the Pacific coast. In 1850 their churches banded together for the purpose of westward expansion. In 1853 the "American Congregational Union" was formed with its expressed aim to build in the West new churches and missions and to bring to them scholarly New England theology.

1851

The Presbyterians, who were considered the richest and most influential denomination of the period, also stemmed from one of the earliest settlements in America. Their church in the new land stood half way between Episcopalianism and Congregationalism. Great revivals increased their membership and resulted in the establishment of theological seminaries, many of which were in the South. In the 1830s a great deal of ill feeling on doctrines and other policies beset the church, and the festering slave question aroused old differences. The ensuing squabbles resulted in the churches lining up on the "Old Side" or the "New Side." The majority of the southern states joined the

"Old Side." Later in this decade two General Assemblies were organized, the "Old" and the "New School." Several years of confusion followed, but by 1840 a safe comparison could be drawn up—the Old School had 1,308 ministers, 1,898 churches, and 126,583 communicants. The New School had 1,234 ministers, 1,375 churches, and 102,060 communicants. The New School assembly declared in 1850 that slave holding was a cause for church discipline. This resolution became a cause of irritation so that by 1858 a United Synod was organized from withdrawal groups comprised of 15,000 communicants. The Old School still held a membership lead in 1860. (In 1861 the southern Presbyters of

1856

In 1855, about twenty-one million people were under some form of religious instruction, and by 1857 it was estimated that there was one clergyman for every 810 souls.

the Old School Assembly withdrew and organized the General Assembly of the Presbyterian Church in the Confederate States of America.)

The Baptists started in America about March 1639, in Narragansett Bay Province, when Roger Williams and eleven others decided to form a church of baptized believers (he later withdrew). The Baptists became outstanding in missionary work and from 1817 on stormed the frontier and worked on foreign soil. Harsh words were spoken between northern and southern church members in early sessions of their Triennial Conventions. Fearing that the ever-increasing slave controversy would injure their missionary work, it was peaceably agreed to a separation of the North and South church after a dispute over an appointment of a slave-holding missionary. In 1845, at Augusta, Georgia,

1854

A Presbyterian religious tract pictured a missionary converting the heathen Africans. The practical missionary used a covered ox-drawn wagon as his living quarters. A lithograph, 1852.

the Southern Baptist Convention was organized, giving the members the control of their own Home and Foreign Missionary Boards. Later, Sunday School Boards were formed. By mid-century the Baptists were a powerful group in America.

The Anglican Church, which held its first church service in Jamestown, Virginia, in 1607, was not accepted by the colonial settlers; except for Maryland and Virginia, there were few early Episcopal churches or clergy. The Puritans condemned all that was Anglican. However, in 1686, when the Massachusetts Colonial Charter was revoked, the Church of England took root in America.

It was not until 1789, after the Revolution, that an American church with its own Episcopacy came into being and was called the Protestant Episcopal Church. The church, under the able leadership and work of its bishops, increased its growth so that by the 1820s seminaries and colleges were started and a missionary program both domestic and foreign was inaugurated. The church expanded in the growing western sections of New York and Pennsylvania, besides gaining strength in the South, in New Jersey, and in Ohio, but it missed out on much of the new western growth because of lack of resources.

A church controversy that had started in England in

1833 reached America in the 1840s. It was known as Anglo-Catholicism, and was a throwback to the old "High Church" party, having many of the pre-Reformation doctrines that tended toward Roman Catholicism. When Bishop Levi Silliman of Ives, North Carolina, was converted to the Roman Catholic Church in 1853, that gave credence to the suspicions that there was a trend toward Roman Catholicism. This continuing controversy was probably the reason the Episcopal Church did not become embroiled in politics or the slave question during the era. It remained neutral.

The Methodists had a later beginning in America than some of the other denominations, making their appearance with the immigration of a "local preacher," Philip Embury, to America in 1760. Another Irish immigrant, Robert Strawbridge, settled in Maryland about the same time. A "circuit rider system" of evangelism was introduced by the Methodists, and doctrines were simplified and adapted to the new land. In December, 1784, a special conference was held to organize the Methodist Episcopal Church. Over the years changes of church policy were many, and again the big issue was slavery.

Matters came to a head at the 1844 conference when Bishop James Osgood Andrew, a southerner who had inherited slaves (his wife also a slave holder), was

1851
The Reverend William F. F. D. Morgan, of Hartford, Connecticut, became famous as the rector of St. Thomas Episcopal Church in New York City. In 1857, Columbia University awarded him the degree of Doctor of Sacred Theology.

asked to "desist from the exercise of the office of Bishop while this impediment remained." Bishop Andrew could not under Georgia law free his slaves. The southern members of the conference felt that such a stigma placed on their beloved Bishop Andrew would weaken the church's influence in the South. A tentative plan for separation was then adopted by almost unanimous vote which bisected the Methodist Episcopal Church. The representatives of the thirteen conferences in the slave states met in 1845 at Louisville, Kentucky, and organized with the help of Bishop Andrew the Methodist Episcopal Church South, making the separation complete. When the general Methodist conference was held in 1848, a loss to the church was represented of 780 traveling preachers and 532,290 members.

The splintering of church sects had even reached the Quakers, or Society of Friends. A division among their ranks resulted in a separation in 1827–1828 of a group of followers called "Hicksites" who were led by Elias Hicks of Long Island, New York. His doctrines differed from the orthodox Quaker views of Christ and the Scriptures. The Quakers, who early colonized Penn-

sylvania and New Jersey, had long labored for abolition, even in the eighteenth century. They continued their fight against slavery during the nineteenth century and also worked for the welfare of the American Indian.

Many offshoots of the main large Protestant denominations had already been established over the years, so that by the twenty-year period before the Civil War, there were innumerable small splinter sects scattered about in all areas of the country. Minority sects were also having phenomenal growth. The Jews as a minority group had increased their numbers from 4,000 in 1820 to 50,000 by 1850. By this year there were 30 synagogues in the country distributed as follows: New York, 9; Pennsylvania, 7; South Carolina and Ohio both, 3; Connecticut, 2; and one each in Massachusetts, Rhode Island, Virginia, Kentucky, Mississippi, and Louisiana.[5]

The great migration westward of foreign-born continually swelled the ranks of the American Catholic Church, especially along the great basin of the Mississippi River and in the Southwest. The Sisters of Charity were hard at work here in the wilderness, and the Mississippi Valley was dotted with chapels. In the cities

Methodist preaching was plain and direct. A sketch from a religious periodical of 1857.

1849
The Quakers were prejudiced against having portraits taken in the early 1840s; however, by 1849, many prominent Friends had consented to sit for their likenesses. A Quaker costume is illustrated above.

One reason for the growing number of churches was the efforts of women members. An example of this could be noted when the *National Intelligencer,* a Washington, D. C., newspaper, in this same year of 1847 ran a news item for the Ladies of the Congregation of St. Mary's Church, who were giving a May Festival to be held at "Mr. Todd's storeroom on Pennsylvania Avenue between Sixth and Seventh Street." Refreshments of the best quality were promised by the ladies, and fancy articles, children's clothes for summer wear, and religious books were to be on sale. Admission was 12½ cents and included "good music." The public was invited to attend and "aid the German Roman Catholics to finish the beautiful edifice which they have nearly completed on Fifth Street."

The national government in 1848 opened diplomatic relations with the Pope, but the venture did not work out well, ending within twenty years. By 1850, dioceses had been formed in almost every city of any size; in

of St. Louis and New Orleans, the best schools were said to be Catholic. The Catholic Church in the West had many problems. It was difficult to root old religious church forms into a completely new environment, and the mixture of so many nationalities of Irish, French, Spanish, German, Italian, and American made for internal strife. Also, in the eastern cities, Catholics were in trouble. Native Americans were afraid that old-world ideas and the allegiance the Catholics held to the Pope would undermine democracy and the American way. The Catholic Church did not conform to American methods of church administration or popular education. Foreign influence in politics was feared, which resulted in anti-Catholic rioting in several cities in the 1830 and 1840 decades. It did not help matters when the newcomers, especially the Irish and German, criticized American institutions during labor disputes. Secret fraternal and political groups formed and worked actively against the Catholic Church during this period.

Despite their problems and challenges, the church grew at a fantastic rate. The Catholic Almanac for 1847 stated in that year that the number of priests was 834, representing an increase of 91 in that one year; also, there were 812 churches in America, 72 of which had been built that year. In addition to this, there were 577 "stations" visited by the clergy in districts which at that time were without a formal place to worship.[6]

1858   *Courtesy Herb Peck, Jr.*
Sisters of Charity were hard at work helping to establish new chapels and schools in the American wilderness, especially along the Mississippi Valley and in the southwest, where many foreign-born Catholics settled in large numbers.

this year, the Catholics were ahead of all others as a single denominational body. John Gilmary Shea, church historian, estimated church membership grew from 244,500 in 1820 to 1,000,000 in 1840, and to 1,726,470 in 1850. By 1860 it held about 3,000,000 members.

An important change in America's religious pattern was the rise of new religious groups, mostly communistic in nature. Americans had already accepted quite tolerantly the Shakers, a small group who had lived in America since 1776. The Shakers, forerunners of modern Spiritualism, believed in Divine healing, spiritual visions, dream prophecy, revelations, and testimonies. They were best known for their practice of celibacy. "Mother Ann," daughter of an English blacksmith and founder of the religious group, was considered to be the female manifestation of Christ. The theology of this denomination was based on the idea of the dualism of God—the creator of male and female "in our

Courtesy The Peale Museum, Baltimore, Md.
A view of Baltimore, about 1851. The Roman Catholic cathedral surmounted by a dome 125 feet high (above left of center) dominated the city skyline in this era. Baltimore was the seat of a Roman Catholic archbishopric and the center of the church in the early days of America. Other religions also had centers in Baltimore. The first known photograph of the city, taken by H. H. Clark.

1850
The symbol of the cross was not often worn by women of the era.

The woodcut, below, illustrates "Shakers near Lebanon, state of New York, their mode of worship." The Shakers were a celibate and communistic sect founded in America by Ann Lee (1736–1784), the daughter of a Manchester (England) blacksmith. Followers of the new religious sect became established in New York, Massachusetts, Connecticut, New Hampshire, and Maine. After a Kentucky revival of 1800– 1801, Shaker societies were founded in Kentucky and Ohio. Shaker songs, dances, and rituals, and their exquisite craftsmanship made the society a distinctive one in American history.

image" showing the bi-sexuality of the creator. In "Mother Ann" it was believed that the promise of the Second Coming had been fulfilled; therefore, marriage was to be done away with. (After the Second Appearance, there was to be no marriage or giving in marriage.) Virtues of the sect were considered to be virgin purity, Christian communism, confession of sin, and separateness from the world. From the two early settlements at Watervliet, near Albany, New York, and Lebanon, New York, grew 19 societies in America by 1843. The years 1837 to 1847 were a period of spiritual manifestation among the believers. Children told of visits to cities of the spiritual realm and gave messages from "Mother Ann." The spirits reportedly left in 1847 after first giving a warning.

The Shaker system called for community possession of property. Idleness was not part of their life; they rose early and worked late. There was no privacy—sometimes there were watchtowers on roofs and from two to six persons shared sleeping rooms. Everything was organized and done in groups. Never less than three adults traveled together in the outside world. Committees or bands inspected the "households" of all the societies' groups regularly. Children lived apart under the watchful eyes of caretakers. Character building and useful arts, such as manual training, were stressed, but it was not all work nor as cheerless as it might seem for the young ones, for need for childhood fun was recognized.

The society gained high respect in America because of its absolute cleanliness and industry. It also provided refuge for the poor and needy, much of their money being used for such purposes. An editor of a well-known magazine visited the Shaker village of Lebanon, New York, in the late 1850s, during the month of February. His first impression was that of a great, clean, ugly house opposite a clean, large church. The word office was plainly printed above the door of the house. Directly inside, behind the front door, was a white marble sink, which suggested water and hinted of cleanliness. Before the doors of the inside rooms were trim Shaker mats but no carpets. In the office the only furniture was straight-backed chairs with plaited straw seats; some had cushions. A clean iron stove, placed in the middle of the room, provided heat. The walls were plain white plaster; no mirrors were seen, only a black wooden frame that held a copy of rhymes in praise of punctuality! A glance in the bedrooms showed crisp white curtains and shining floors, burnished doors and simple iron stoves. The only books about the place were some dry-looking treatises on Shaker Theology. These thrifty people had no time or taste for study, and education was

not fostered by the society. Trade and essentials for their welfare were the basic instructions.

An old Shaker gentleman with long, homespun coat and broad-brimmed hat and two Shaker women dressed in slim, scant skirts, severe caps, and neckerchiefs led the editor into a work shop that contained delicate baskets, white table mats, floor mats, and beautifully crafted rocking chairs of cherry, maple, and butternut. It was the editor's opinion that Shakers were very shrewd in the prices of their goods, were good neighbors, sober, industrious, domestic, and successful. He noted, too, that they ate little meat, chiefly vegetables and fruits. Although admiring their qualities, the editor noted that their numbers were decreasing, that most were recruited from the poorhouses, from which they took children, "molding them and telling them if they ventured beyond Shaker bounds the earth will yawn and swallow them."[7] He was much impressed with the sweetness, simplicity, neatness, and cheerfulness of the sisters. He ended in the final note that he felt there was a glint of yearning in their eyes as they looked into his.

Indeed, their generosity to the poor, the expansion of their property, higher taxes, and the lack of interest shown by the young people led to their decline. They numbered in 1852, before their gradual decline, 6,000

1857

Many women of this period entered freely into church activities, which included, in some cases, ministry to the poor, prison reforms, and anti-slavery work.

members, with eighteen branches and fifty-eight "families." Of this number, 1,417 members were in the West. Their distinctive and expressive songs, dances and rituals, and their superb craftsmanship made an indelible mark on the American scene.

Other communistic ventures were tried in America. All failed, some more quickly than others. In 1826 an English social reformer, Robert Owen, tried a self-contained community in New Harmony, Indiana. After a trial of two years and cost of $200,000 it failed completely. Brook Farm, founded in 1841 and visited by the Transcendentalists, lasted only until 1847. Oneida Community in New York State, established in 1848 by Alfred Noyes and which practiced the unorthodox complex marriage, lasted many years and was reorganized in 1881 as a stock company. It was estimated that between 1840 and 1850 there were more than forty communistic group projects.

A new religious group destined to play an important historical part in American history was the beginning and migration of the Mormons. The Mormons or the "Church of Jesus Christ of Latter-Day Saints" was founded by Joseph Smith of Manchester, New York, in 1830, and after 1848, was largely concentrated about Salt Lake City, Utah.

Joseph Smith, like his parents and grandparents before him, believed in visions and revelations. He claimed in 1823 that the angel Moroni appeared to him three times and told him that the Bible of the Western continent, a supplement to the New Testament, was buried in a hill called Cumorah. Smith said that on September 22, 1827, he dug up on a hill near Manchester a stone box in which there was a volume six inches thick, made of thin gold plates eight by seven inches, and fastened together with three gold rings. Along with the gold book, Smith claimed he found a breastplate of gold and a pair of supernatural spectacles consisting of two crystals set in a silver bow and called "Urim and Thummim." By aid of these, the mystic characters on the gold plates could be read. No one actually saw the plates, and it was said after the printing of the Book of Mormon in 1830 in Palmyra, New York, that the angel Moroni took them away. The newly printed book professed Joseph Smith to be God's prophet and gave the history of America from its first settlement by a colony of "Jaredites" down to the year 5 A.D.

In the early 1830s the migration to Missouri had begun; and from the very first, the native Missourians were hostile to the new group. Between the wranglings of the Mormons themselves and the hostility of the outsiders, it reached the point of civil war. After having trouble with the state militia, the followers, numbering 15,000, crossed over to Illinois. Because of the oncoming Presidential election of 1840, the politicians in Illinois welcomed the religious group. The Mormons founded the city of Nauvoo and obtained a state charter (December, 1840) that made the city practically independent of state control and gave Smith nearly unlimited civil power.

The Book of Mormon had forbidden polygamy, but there was a conditional clause. From letters written back East in 1842, it was known that Smith had taught "strange doctrines"—a plurality of Gods, a plurality of living wives, and unconditional sealing up to eternal life against all sins save the shedding blood of innocents. Many of the early followers were uneasy; they had suffered much in their wanderings and had been devout in their new faith. Those who did not believe the new teachings were cut off from the church. On July 12, 1843, Smith had a revelation expressly establishing and approving polygamy; although the revelation was not published officially until 1852, it was well-known in Nauvoo.

Determined to put an end to the new trend their religion was taking, a few dissenters, a Dr. R. D. Foster, whose wife Smith had taken a liking to, William Law and Wilson Law, wealthy Canadian members, and Sylvester Emmons, a member of the church council, set up a newspaper at the cost of $600 called the *Expositor*. It published only one copy, June 7, 1844, in which Smith's views on polygamy were exposed. Joseph Smith and his brother Hyrum Smith denied the revelation and destroyed the printing office. The publishers fled for their lives. An ensuing general uprising against the Mormons resulted, and Joseph and Hyrum were arrested on a charge of treason, June 25, 1844, and were put in jail. Two days later a mob broke into the prison and shot and killed the brothers.

Brigham Young, a former Vermont painter and glazier, who had been a member since 1832, then took over as leader and the migration to Salt Lake City was not long in coming. A temple built by the Mormons at Nauvoo was dedicated on May 1, 1846, but was soon offered for sale at very low terms by the migrating Mormons who made their headquarters at Voree, Wisconsin.[8] The first migration arrived in Salt Lake City in September, 1847; before the close of 1848, its population numbered about 5,000. The city was not prosperous at first, but the California Gold Rush in 1849 made it a depot and outfitting place for those California bound.

Mormon missionary work abroad brought in large groups of foreign immigrants to increase their numbers. There must **have** been unrest, for numbers of dissatisfied Mormons left for California. The New York *Evening Post,* July 29, 1852, noted that "several large trains of Mormons from Salt Lake City, dissatisfied with Deseret, reached Carson Valley Saturday with about 600 head of cattle. They had renounced their religion and had decided to settle permanently in Cali-

fornia." The news item also mentioned that "Brigham Young had left Salt Lake City with one hundred men in search of a settlement, bringing with him two or three hundred thousand dollars. His real aim, to be out of the way when the new Governor comes. All speak hardest terms of him." (A continuing and defiant attitude of the Mormons toward authority had led to

1851   *Courtesy the California Historical Society,*
                                                                San Francisco

Salt Lake City, 1851
Founded in 1847 by the Mormons, Salt Lake City became a stopover for the California-bound gold seekers in 1849. The population of the city in 1849 was about 5,000 and by 1860 the residents numbered 8,236. An artist-daguerreian, J. Wesley Jones, went westward in 1850 and by the following year was believed to have taken about 1,500 daguerreotypes of the Rockies and the Great Plains to the Missouri River. Sketches and paintings were made from many of his daguerreotypes, as above.

Courtesy Library of Congress
Brigham Young, above, became the leader of the Mormons after the death of Joseph Smith. He led the Mormons westward and founded Salt Lake City.

a hostile relationship with the United States government.)

In 1855, according to the British Agency, there were 4,425 immigrants to Salt Lake City. An attempt was made by the Mormons to cut down expenses, and proper provision was not made for transportation for these travelers from abroad. Hand carts and push carts only were provided for the difficult trip from Iowa City to Utah. One party of four hundred lost one-sixth of their number in a winter trek across the plains, from exhaustion and starvation. These simple folk and many others that migrated to the religious city endured unbelievable hardships because of their great faith in their new belief.

A Mormon "Reformation" had begun in 1856, one of which was "blood atonement . . . cutting people off from the earth . . . is to save them, not destroy them." Many outrages were committed by a Mormon band of desperadoes who called themselves "wolf hunters." Claims were made of killings of those planning to go to California. The blackest day for the Mormon Church history was the "Mountain Meadow Massacre" of September, 1857, when a band of white men and Indians fell on more than 100 disarmed overland travelers, killing all but a few children. The United States, sickened by the atrocity, blamed the Mormons; the Mormons in turn blamed the Indians. Twenty years

later John D. Lee, once a founder with Joseph Smith and Brigham Young, was executed for the crime. However, the crime could not be blamed on one man alone. The blame remained obscure. Almost a century later a historian came to the belief that scattered families (seventy-nine) beyond Cedar City, being outnumbered by Indians, joined forces with them—the Indians, wanting the loot and horses of the massacred party. By the year 1860 the Mormons' problems were many, and their struggles would continue through the century to have a great influence on the saga of the West.

Another very interesting sect of this period was called the Millerites, named after their leader, William Miller (1782–1849). Miller had been a recruiting officer at the beginning of the War of 1812, was promoted to Captain, and retired in 1815. An atheist, Miller became a Baptist, and after studying the Bible for two years, he became a Second Adventist. As leader of this movement, he lectured and argued from 1831 onward that a Bible passage, Daniel 8:13–14, predicted the date of March 21, 1843, as the end of the world, when the resurrection and judgment were to take place.

The dire prediction caused great excitement; many disposed of their properties; suicides and insanity were reported. One Millerite, clad in ascension robes, climbed a tree and attempted to fly to heaven. As a result, he broke his neck. When the end failed to come in 1843, Miller blamed it on an error of following Hebrew instead of Roman chronology. The date

"I thought the Methodist indefatigable at camp meetings, but these people can beat 'em hollow," so said a New York reporter after covering the Millerite meetings at Newark, New Jersey, 1842. The tent pictured above was 120 feet in diameter, about 50 feet high at the peak, and it could seat between 3,000 and 4,000 people.

was then set as October 22, 1844. On the evening of that date it was estimated that 50,000 people waited in their white muslin robes on house tops and on hills. The end did not come, but that did not discourage the fast-growing movement. The date was now set for October 23, 1847. The movement now included populous masses in the north. The fanatical group was in full force in Philadelphia. Some communities, one of which was Concord, New Hampshire, were entirely enveloped in the movement. In Boston white robes were offered for sale for the ascension. Some New Yorkers passed the twenty-third and twenty-fourth waiting for the trumpet of the angel. In the most public part of Boston a huge "shantie" had been built to house from two to three thousand people. On the night of the long-awaited event a great throng robed in white passed the night in prayer, singing:

> I'm all in white, my soul is clear.
> I'm going up, nought keeps me here.

The huge room was gaily decked with flowers, lighted by seven-branched candlesticks, and hung with Hebrew texts. The night passed, morning came, and no one "went up." The society became bankrupt, and the hall they had built became a theatre. The "Millerites," however, were the forerunners of a strong Second Adventist movement.

Many unusual men of the cloth were active in this period of history. One of these was Christopher Pearce Cranch, born in Alexandria, Virginia. After receiving

The leader of the Millerite movement, William Miller, had predicted the end of the world on March 21, 1843. The end failed to come on the fixed date. Miller was lampooned in many newspapers and broadsides, as shown above.

his degree in 1832 from Columbia College, he went on to Cambridge, Massachusetts, and the Theological School. During his stay there he became a frequent visitor to Brook Farm, where he imparted to the old farm and its homely furnishings his own mellow charm. His rich baritone voice vibrated throughout the rooms. He did his own accompaniment with guitar or piano. His entertainment there was not limited just to musical instruments or singing; he gave poetry readings and was a master of ventriloquism, imitating all the sounds of nature and mechanical devices.[9] The tall, graceful Cranch, however, was most remembered for his comical cartoon drawings and delightful caricatures, which he was apt to draw anywhere on his travels. He preached in many churches throughout New England and Virginia, his manner of preaching depending upon his audience. To the simple and sometimes rough farmers, he gave the plain, practical sermons they liked. The Virginians wanted doctrinal and controversial preaching. During all of his travels, he liked preaching in Richmond, Virginia, the best. The versatile Cranch received attention also as a poet, on May 25, 1840, when he delivered a poem celebrating the two-hundredth anniversary of the incorporated town of Quincy at the "First Church There." Besides his other poetry, in 1853 he composed a poem for Jenny Lind, "Farewell to America."

Perhaps the most articulate and certainly the most famous preacher of this era was Henry Ward Beecher (1813–1887) of the famous Beecher family. After graduating from Amherst College, he began his career in the ministry. His fluent, extemporaneous style of speaking was unconventional. He was a master of words, but it was not this alone. He was an artist at impersonating, and to this was added strong intellectual views, sympathy, and an energetic enthusiasm. He attracted people who never went to church.

His keen interest in men rather than books was shown in 1844 when he was preacher to the frontier town of Indianapolis. There he wrote "Seven Lectures to Young Men" after becoming acquainted at first hand with the temptations and evils surrounding a frontier town. In 1847 he accepted a pastorate at "Plymouth Congregational," a newly organized church in Brooklyn, New York. It was from this point forward that Beecher made the pulpit a national platform and became a national leader. "Cross the Fulton Ferry and follow the crowd" was the stock answer on how to find Mr. Beecher's church in Brooklyn. The famed church, "Plymouth," was a large white building. Inside there was a gallery on both sides and an organ loft and choir just behind the pulpit. Four long windows on each side of the building lightened the interior. The plan of the edifice gave the congregation an unobstructed view of the speaker platform from every part of the church; there were no columns. The decor was very plain— white walls and no ornamentation, suggestive of the cold barns and New England Meeting Houses of early New England.[10] Nevertheless, it seemed cheerful and comfortable. At Beecher's church, seats were usually filled an hour before services, and the windows resembled bee hives with all the faces looking in from the outside.

Henry Beecher stood as a moderate on the slavery issue, although he was always anti-slavery. His leadership inspired patriotism in the North, and he was instrumental in forming public opinion on various national issues of the day.

Beecher and most of the outstanding ministers of the era used an evangelistic technique of preaching that had been very successful in reaching the masses of the people. From the early days of the Methodist "circuit rider," methods of evangelistic preaching had evolved, and during the nineteenth century a successful technique was developed by the hard-working clergy in both frontier and city. The evangelistic style of religion had won for America the admiration of Europe, which was astounded by the religious growth in America. These evangelistic ministers, stemming from voluntary and democratic churches and communities, had founded colleges and organizations, and they had joined wholeheartedly in humanitarian reforms that influenced many outside their church domains.

Piety had become the watchword with these ministers and church laymen. While many worked on the frontiers, others tackled the problems of social conditions in the city, brought on by industry and immigration. For example, in September 1856, the New York Sunday School Union asked churches of all denominations if they would found mission Sunday Schools throughout the poor sections of the city and visit homes and study conditions of the area. The scheme caught fire and by the next spring 2,000 workers, in teams of two for each block, covered the city with weekly visits to those outside church membership.[11] A great deal of tangible help was given in this manner to the unfortunate, and on an individual basis. Other cities and communities adopted the idea and found it workable. The following year, concurrent with the Panic of 1857, a great religious revival followed. During this period the Methodists, Baptists, Congregationalists, and "New School" Presbyterians instigated noon prayer meetings, which took root in the American cities. Other denominations were affected by the sweeping movement, even Episcopalians and Unitarians. A new concern for the common man had become an integral part of the era's religion.

1856

Ministers had to maintain a style of living equally as good as their parishioners and were expected to have an overall knowledge of current affairs, literature, arts, and sciences. While the national average for salaries for preachers was $500 a year, many prominent city clergymen made upwards of $2,000 annually.

During 1851 the Young Men's Christian Association, first founded in London in 1844, was started in Boston. By 1861 there were 200 branches in the United States for the purpose of helping uprooted young men. The society provided prayer meetings, Bible classes, mission schools, libraries, reading rooms, and lecture courses.

It was evident at the close of the 1850 decade that American religion had experienced a profound change. Much had been accomplished; the revamping job was well on its way. Education had been furthered; all of the main denominations had built colleges. A great number of churches had been built. The arts had benefited, church music had been composed, paintings reflected the era's religion. Most important of all was the meeting of problems head-on in humanitarian reform. A great melting pot of religion had been accomplished. Religion in the era—despite its bickering, despite its short-comings—had recognized, and was molding a pattern to fit, the needs of a new age.

Sunday schools helped to supplement home religious training for the child. The Methodists had instituted the Sunday school about 1790 and by 1850 it had become an accepted part of Sunday worship.

In 1852 over 700,000 copies of Bibles and Testaments were printed in this imposing building in New York City. In the pleasant, well-lighted rooms on the sixth floor, 300 women were employed binding and stitching Bibles. A good Bible sold for twenty-five cents. This scene was engraved from a daguerreotype, 1853.

THE

FLOATING CHURCH OF OUR SAVIOUR.

REV. B. C. C. PARKER, PASTOR.

The floating church of our Saviour for Seamen, now permanently moored at the foot of Pike-street, New-York, on the East river, of which an engraving is here presented, was finished and consecrated to the service of God on the 19th of February, 1844. It was constructed by Charles M. Simonson for the Young Men's Church Missionary Society of the City of New-York. It is 70 feet long and 30 feet wide, and will comfortably seat 500 persons. It has an end gallery, in which is an organ. A beautiful Baptismal Font of white marble, in the exact shape of the capstan of a ship, surmounted by a shell of exquisite workmanship, chiseled from the same block with the shaft, was a gift of St. Marks' Church in the Bowery. It stands in front of the chancel rail; the top of the communion table is a marble slab, and the Ten Commandments are placed on the panels on each side in the recess over it. An anchor, in gold, painted on the back ground between these panels, rests upon the Bible and Prayer-Book. The edifice is built on a broad deck 76 by 36, covering two boats of 80 tons each, placed ten feet apart to prevent careening when the congregation might happen to be unequally distributed on either side. The spire contains a bell, and the top of the flag-staff is about 70 feet from the deck. Divine service is regularly performed on Sundays, commencing in the morning at half past 10 o'clock, and in the afternoon at 3 o'clock. The motion of the water is scarcely felt more than in an edifice on land, the location being in the midst of the shipping on the East River, but out of the reach of the winds, ice, and tides.

150

An ad from "The Citizens and Strangers Pictorial and Business Directory" for the city of New York, 1853.

8
Education

Historians generally agree that education is the product of the social order in which it is developed. Therefore, it is necessary to understand the social, political, and economic structure of all the competing sections of America—East, South, and West—from 1830–1860, in order to comprehend the emergence, during these years, of a growing nationwide educational system that would bring new opportunities in all levels of education to the common man.

In the East, where industry had taken root, the farmers and small merchants, born of an agrarian society, were struggling with industrial capitalists. The South had created a social order distinctly its own, owing in part to the increased demand from northern mill owners for cotton. The plantation, worked by slaves, experienced a revival as southerners moved into the cotton belt to share in the booming economy. The West was settled mostly by small farmers, democratic men without formal class distinctions. The western economy was greatly influenced by the new transportation and invention of machinery and it would become increasingly linked with the East.

Social upheavals were taking place in all of these sectional areas, some because of the great westward migration and the movement of population to the cities, which left behind broken family groups and abandoned farms. Meanwhile, the old religion was loosening its grip in the new changing social order. The heavy influx of immigrants coming into the country and the exploitation of labor by industry were creating problems of poverty, crime, and delinquency seldom seen in the former agrarian society. These new forces abroad in the land and the social and economic changes they wrought threw a heavy load on all established public institutions, which were found inadequate to cope with the new situation.

It became crystal clear to the intelligent citizen, whether political leader, social leader, or business man, that something must be done if the country was to continue with strong leadership and if the reins of the newly expanding industry were to be guided in the right direction. Education, it was believed, must provide the answer. The young people could be taught to respect law and authority, labor would produce more efficiently, poverty and crime would abate. Education would also tend to reduce class distinction, and the status of the working man would be improved.

Politicians could see signs of disaster building up on the changing American scene. When the right to vote was given to parents who could not provide a means of education for their offspring, then the state must play a new role and take measures to provide an educational program designed to meet the new political and social conditions; however, supporting the state would have to be the task of every American, and shaping public opinion to support the new educational measures calling for taxation would not be an easy undertaking.

After the Revolutionary War a large national domain was formed out of land that would be future states. Congress in 1785 adopted a survey in which the lands were laid out in townships six miles square, and each township was divided into sections one mile square. The sections of every township were numbered 1–36, the 16th section being reserved for the support of education. On July 13, 1787, an "Ordinance for the Government of the Territory of the United States North West of the River Ohio," was passed. The lands covered in this ordinance were the states of Ohio, Indiana, Illinois, Michigan and the eastern side of Minnesota. The following statement was included in the act: "Religion, morality, and knowledge being necessary to good government and the happiness of mankind, schools and the means of education shall forever be encouraged." The funds received from the sale and lease of these lands formed the greater part of public school endowment to the states created out of this northwest territory. Every state admitted to the union before 1848 reserved section number 16 in every township of public land for schools. After 1848 all new states reserved number 16 and number 36 in every township, with the exception of three southwestern states which, being very dry and arid, received four sections.[1] These and other grants became a great aid to education, especially to the western states, and a basic pattern was thereby established for the older states to follow, to set aside lands and begin to build permanent funds for education.

Education up to 1840 was a hodgepodge of varieties and procedures as it drifted toward state support and control.

New England traditionally set the example for education in America, yet as late as 1840 only one half of the children were given a free education. If parents could afford to pay for their children's education they were expected to do so. The New England figure was

Mount Holyoke was the site of the famous seminary for girls. Mary Lyon, female educator, furthered the idea of a permanent school for training young women of moderate means and giving them the best in education. In 1836 she secured $27,000 in small subscriptions, ranging from six cents to one thousand dollars. Her dream came true with the opening of Mount Holyoke Female Seminary in 1837.

higher than the Middle States or West, which stood one-seventh and one-sixth, respectively.[2] New England and New York State let districts levy taxes to help support their schools, but their main income came from rate bills that were charged to the parents, the rate depending upon the number of children attending school. By 1840 other states followed with the district school system. Among them were Ohio, Illinois, Indiana, Tennessee, Kentucky, and North Carolina. The district school system was considered democracy in purest form and it had taken root politically. Rules for these school systems were greatly varied as to taxes, curricula, teachers, and textbooks. There was no uniformity among states, their rules and taxes varying greatly. State revenues were very small and were sometimes derived from fines and forfeitures, fees and indirect taxes from various sources. Philanthropic societies, church organizations, and churches aided and supported education.

The early school was not expected to prepare a child fully for his life's work. The home and group environ-ment were supposed to play an important role in conjunction with the school in educating the child. A typical early school would be a small roughly clapboarded structure located close to a highway. The school children were crowded on benches that faced steep sloping shelves, or they sat at desks that were fastened to the walls on three sides of the room. The schoolmaster's high desk and a wood-burning stove would furnish the fourth side of the room. As many as 100 pupils attended school in a one-room building under the guidance of a teacher not always professionally prepared for the task. In rural areas the long, flat, cherrywood ruler was the teacher's baton of command. The ruler served a double purpose; it ruled the good boy's copy books and it wielded its authority on the bad boy's person. The old adage "spare the rod and spoil the child" was kept in mind always in the schoolhouse. But the image of the despotic schoolmaster or schoolmistress gradually began to fade when the new ideas from state and city began creeping in.

The census of 1840 showed that 16,000 students were attending 173 universities and colleges, 164,000 were attending 3,200 academies and grammar schools, and there were 1,845,000 children in attendance in the 47,000 primary schools throughout the country. Also by 1840 a few high schools were established in New York, Vermont, Maine, Pennsylvania, South Carolina, and Connecticut. There were many factors to overcome before converting the American public to the idea of free schooling. The poor were generally apathetic, while the wealthy and the middle-class society could afford private schools for their children. Some citizens feared that the rights of the individual would be invaded and that education would bring a weakening of religion. Others were afraid of a new class equalization that education might bring. A strong argument heard against education was that the states could not stand the financial drain involved in providing free schooling for the masses. The arguments for education, however, sounded more feasible than the arguments against, and many influential men, politicians, and numerous interested groups were drawn into its cause. Hundreds of organizations, all with the purpose of promoting free schools, were active all over the country. Two of these organizations were outstanding. One was "The Western Academic Institute and Board of Education" founded by Albert Pickett; it was reorganized and became known as the "Western Literary Institute and College of Professional Teachers," in 1832. Under the guidance of such educators as Samuel Lewis, Calvin Stowe, and Lyman Beecher, the Society grew rapidly and in a period of three years it had groups established in Ohio,

1855
Many educators led state-wide campaigns for more and bet-ter education to fit their individual state needs.

1850

The early schoolhouse was often a rough clapboard structure located close to a highway. In rural areas a hundred pupils might attend school in a one-room building under the guidance of a teacher not always professionally prepared for the task. Basic subjects taught by the grammar school were reading, writing, arithmetic, grammar, geography, and history.

Indiana, Illinois, Missouri, Kentucky, Tennessee, Mississippi, and Louisiana. By 1840 it embraced all states except those of New England, New York, New Jersey, Delaware, and Maryland. The work of this institute had a tremendous effect on furthering education in the West.[3]

The American Lyceum, the better known of the organizations, had its beginning in the town of Millbury, Massachusetts, in 1826. A voluntary group, it was composed of farmers and mechanics who gathered together weekly to discuss subjects of general public interest, and members would contribute essays, give lectures, or have public debates on current topics. Any public discussion was encouraged. Meanwhile, a national lyceum was formed in 1831, and by 1832 there were reported to be, besides many state and county lyceums, 900 formed in

1855

The old adage "spare the rod and spoil the child" was always kept in mind in the schoolhouse.

towns throughout the country. By 1839 more than 3,000 had been organized. All of these groups sought to stimulate and improve existing education and to be an aid to the Boards of Education. Some of the societies paid well-known lecturers to address their meetings, and it was evident that wherever a lyceum was organized the public interest in education was aroused. These societies created a common foundation for the country to join hands in a unified cause. Thoughts and opinions could be exchanged and debated. At state conventions, which were held until 1839, new plans and ideas, and needs and defects of education were brought forward for the American people to examine; free schooling was urged. Local lyceums flourished until the Civil War.

Journals and newspapers were used nationwide as mediums to arouse the public interest in education and to point out the need for better schools at all levels. They also advocated more and better education for girls, more libraries, and better trained teachers. Also the growing need for infant schools and mechanic institutes was stressed in their editorials.

Another influence instrumental in improving and shaping the educational system in America was the reports coming in from many Americans traveling abroad in Europe. The travelers particularly noted the excellence of the school system in Prussia, and their reports were widely publicized.

Labor was demanding free education for the masses. Seth Luther, a spokesman for Labor in Boston said, "In our review, we have seen a large body of human

1858

A more general educational program for girls was needed in this era. Journals, newspapers, and public lyceums sought to promote public interest in the project.

beings ruined by a neglect of education, rendered miserable in the extreme, and incapable of self government; and this by the grinding of the rich on the faces of the poor, through the operation of cotton and other machinery." The agitation of labor did much for the cause for education.

Educational leaders had become busy on the home front. One of these pioneers was James G. Carter. After graduating from Harvard in 1820, Carter taught school, wrote textbooks, and essays, and did articles for the

Boston Transcript. His attitude on education is expressed in his "Letters to Hon. William Prescott, L.L.D. on the Free Schools of New England." He wrote, "The success of our schools depends as much on the principles by which they are governed, and the school books, as on the personal and literary qualifications of the instructor." This was in 1824. Carter's work paved the way for the public school revival that took place in Massachusetts and made Horace Mann's road a much smoother one when he became the great leader for public education in America.

Courtesy Library of Congress
Horace Mann, above, believed that nothing could more benefit mankind morally, intellectually, and materially than education. His campaigns for school reform led to a better educational system in America.

Horace Mann had the needed leadership qualities and the energy to put his reforms over. In 1837 he became secretary of a newly appointed board of education in Massachusetts and began the work that would bring him national fame. He disclosed to the public defects of the school system—the poorly qualified school committees, badly trained teachers, absenteeism in the schools—and also brought out the need for more and better libraries. Horace Mann traveled extensively campaigning for better education. In 1843 he visited Europe at his own expense to study the educational methods abroad. He was elected to Congress in 1848 and served until 1853, when he accepted the Presidency of Antioch College, Ohio. Mann's outspoken criticisms of the district school system, his tireless work in trying to extend state supervision of schools, and the resulting controversies, gave to education a greater impetus than the influence of any other man. He revolutionized the common school system of Massachusetts and, indirectly,

that of other states. Horace Mann firmly believed that nothing could benefit mankind morally, intellectually, and materially more than education.

A contemporary of Horace Mann who was working for the better supervision of schools in New England was Henry Barnard. After graduating from Yale in 1830, Barnard entered law and politics in Connecticut. In 1838 he introduced a bill to provide better supervision of schools; it was passed unanimously by the legislature. This bill created a State Board of Commissioners of Common Schools. Barnard became its first secretary. He also founded and edited the Connecticut Common School Journal and established the first teachers' institute. After four years of hard work, Barnard's office was voted out by enemies of public education in the legislature. Rhode Island, seeing an opportunity to get an experienced leader in the educational field, called in Barnard to reorganize their state school system, which was floundering badly. A strenuous campaign was launched by Barnard, and as a result, a school

1854
The standard average wage for female teachers was nineteen dollars a month. However, at a first-class school it was possible for a woman to earn a salary of fifty dollars.

law with teeth was passed in 1845. Barnard, as the State Commissioner of public schools (1845–1849), put this law into operation before he resigned in 1849. After considering several offers he accepted in 1851 a position as principal of a newly organized normal school (New Britain). He resigned in 1855 because of failing health and devoted his time to writing. Among other writings, he produced between 1855–1882 a large work of 32 volumes, each with over 800 pages, on all phases of education.

In the South, an outstanding leader, Calvin Wiley, was arousing the public. After graduating from the University of North Carolina in 1840, he was admitted to the bar in the following year. For ten years Wiley practiced law and edited the *Oxford Mercury;* he was elected to the state legislature in 1850. While in the legislature he made it possible for a superintendent of common schools to be chosen for a two-year term. Calvin Wiley was chosen as the first superintendent. He began office in 1853 and remained until the end of the Civil War. During his term as superintendent he reorganized and improved the schools and created public interest in the southern states by traveling and making speeches, and by editing the *North Carolina Journal of Education.* He also wrote other important works in his field.

In the West, Indiana needed able leadership to overcome its illiteracy problem and was fortunate in having a New Hampshire-born educator, Caleb Mills. A graduate of Dartmouth College and Andover Theological Seminary, Mills took time from his teaching at Wabash College to exert a great influence in the State of Indiana for more than 25 years, helping to develop a good public school system in that state. In 1846 he published the first of a series of six annual publications, "Addresses to the Legislatures." The sixth of these annuals urging reforms was published by the order of the legislature and was circulated around the state. School laws enacted reflected his advanced thinking on education. Mills was State Superintendent of Public Instruction from 1854–1856 and later was given the honor of being named "Father of the Common Schools of Indiana."

Reformers were not limited to just these few. Other states had similar educators who led campaigns to fit their individual state needs. Some of the men who should be noted were Calvin Stowe, Samuel Lewis, and Samuel Galloway of Ohio. Ninian W. Edwards of Illinois; John D. Pierce and Isaac E. Crary of Michigan; Robert J. Breckinridge of Kentucky; and John Swett of California.[4]

Secondary schools in America in this period were of three categories: the Latin school, the academy, and the high school. The Latin grammar school was the oldest

1843

As late as 1840 only one half of the children were given a free education. In 1850 the Middle Atlantic States had 1639 private academies. Regulation jackets were required at many of these schools.

established secondary school in America and stressed Latin and mathematics. Restricted in its curriculum, it had a difficult time adjusting to new ideas and would gradually lose out in competition to the academy and high school. Academies, dating back to 1750, had grown very rapidly and were so numerous between 1830–1860 that hardly a community was without one. These were largely independent schools and most were small in size. The academy drew the middle-class patron; it provided practical training as well as college preparatory. Institute, seminary, or college were the names given the academy. In spite of some state grants and subsidies, for these institutions were mostly controlled by religious or private means and were tuition schools; they would be replaced by the public school as the century progressed.

An interesting example of the academy was the Fellenberg School, which opened at Windsor, Connecticut, in 1824. Its curriculum offered English, Latin, Greek, arithmetic, bookkeeping, geography, algebra, surveying, navigation, natural philosophy, history, rhetoric, logic, botany, chemistry, and mineralogy. The school had a farm attached to it, so that students could observe daily the various mechanics of farming. If the student was planning a vocation in agriculture, a course of lectures was provided to acquaint him with the new

1848
Oratory was encouraged for gifted students.

scientific improvements and practice in farming.[5] The academy was not a great success, and it was surmised that the yearly tuition of $150, and the fact the academy made a promise that drudgery by the students would be avoided, were probably factors in its failure.

As the public elementary school program expanded and improved, the growing middle-class demanded a program of continuing higher education. The first real effort to establish high schools by legislation was enactment of a law by the Massachusetts legislature in 1827 requiring that a high school be established in all areas of 500 or more families. Also, when towns or districts had 4,000 inhabitants, Latin and Greek were added to the courses. New Hampshire, Maine, and Vermont soon followed this procedure. By 1860 high schools were founded not only in New England but in the large cities—New York, Philadelphia, Baltimore, Portland, Chicago, Mobile, San Francisco, New Orleans, and Louisville. Also there were many academies for girls that were doing well financially. There were no public schools for girls in some areas. The public demand for such a facility was shown when a Boston public high

school was planned for 120 girls between ages eleven and fifteen. It was opened in 1826 with 133 girls, aged 12–15, who were accepted from about 300 applicants. The following year none of the girls were ready to leave and 427 new applicants were clamoring for admission. The enrollment by then was limited to ages 14–16 years of age. In a few months the school was discontinued to solve its problem of being overpopular, but public demand led to its reopening. Usually high schools were not separate for girls; the trend was to have "female departments." This was a step toward coeducation. From the first public high school, started in Boston in 1821, the list grew and by 1860 there were 321 throughout the country. More than half of this number, 167, were found in Massachusetts, New York, and Ohio. As high schools were urban institutions, there were few in the West and South.

On the college level, education in 1840 was to have a period of dramatic growth. The early colleges were of religious origin of various denominations. As society needed new halls of learning, the states sought to establish new institutions or revamp the older ones, making them subject to control by the legislatures rather than the religious denominations. There was resistance to this; early in the nineteenth century the New Hampshire legislature tried to change the charter of Dartmouth College. This ended in a United States Supreme Court decision declaring the New Hampshire legislation unconstitutional. After this decision the various church denominations established colleges without fear of state interference. The desire of the churches to have their denominations represented in the various states led to a rapid expansion of colleges. They were supported by student fees, gifts from communities in which they were founded, and funds raised by church conferences.

Some states had already established colleges, such as the University of North Carolina in 1795 and the University of Georgia in 1801. Virginia established her state university in 1825, and in the West colleges were generally state controlled. Even so, until the beginning of the Civil War, there were only 17 state college institutions. These were supported by tuition, legislative appropriations, and land endowments.[6]

The basic college courses of the era were Latin, Greek, and mathematics. The courses were gradually expanded to include the sciences, history, political economy, and modern languages, among others. The new industrial trend in the nation led many students to become interested in science. This had an influence on increased scientific and technological training programs. Leading in this type of training was Rensselaer Poly-

O.C. SEMINARY.   CAZENOVIA, N.Y.

H.E. PEASE, ALBANY.

Courtesy New York State Library, Albany, N.Y.
The Oneida Conference Seminary was founded in 1831.
In 1868 its name changed to Central New York Conference
Seminary and it again changed in 1873 to Cazenovia Semi-
nary. In the twentieth century it became Cazenovia Junior
College.

1850
. . . At some of the best schools girls were kept out of school
two thirds of the time for social reasons.

technic Institute, founded in 1824; others followed. Yale established Sheffield Scientific School in 1846; the year following, the Lawrence Scientific School was founded at Harvard. Dartmouth followed in 1851 with the Chandler School of Science. Before 1860, Michigan started an Agricultural and Industrial College. Science became firmly entrenched in the schools; also medical and law schools were being founded. Many of the old established schools took on a new look.

Before 1860 much progress toward education for girls had been made. The "Ladies' Departments" in the academies and high schools had provided some higher education, and a large number of seminaries and 60 colleges for women had been established, although not all had the power to grant degrees. One female college in Mississippi was reported to have been given the power to grant degrees in March, 1838. Newspaper editorials sometimes ridiculed the granting of degrees for women. Meanwhile, women educators were busy. Emma Willard secured $4,000 in funds in 1820 and founded Troy Seminary in 1821. Another remarkable woman named Mary Lyon, born on a farm in Franklin County, Massachusetts, began teaching at 17 and furthered her education by earning money from spinning and weaving. She taught in district schools and conducted informal normal schools, and from 1822–24 was assistant principal of Sanderson Academy. Eager to understand science, she studied chemistry and natural science with

1858

Students of O. C. Seminary
The girls shown above were students of Oneida Conference
Seminary, Cazenovia, New York. The daguerreotype was
taken March 13, 1858, by a Mr. Weld.

A year after Oberlin College Institute was chartered in 1834, the First Ladies' Hall was completed. The building (above) was of frame construction, thirty-eight feet by eighty, and was three stories high. It had a wing of two stories on each end, extending toward the south. The upper story and the flights of stairs were given to young men; the remainder, except for certain rights in the dining room and parlor, were given to the Steward's family and young women.

Edward Hitchcock, the geologist. Her interest in education led her to the idea of a permanent school for training young women, one that would put the best in education within reach of students of moderate means. In 1836 she secured $27,000 in small subscriptions ranging from six cents to one thousand dollars, to establish such a school. Her dream was realized in 1837 when Mount Holyoke Female Seminary opened. She headed the school until her death in 1849.

The first experimental college of the day and the first American college to adopt coeducation was Oberlin. It was also a pioneer in the coeducation of the white and black races. Oberlin was founded in the wild swamps of northern Ohio by the Reverend John S. Shepherd. It was chartered Oberlin College Institute in 1834 and the name Oberlin College was adopted in 1850. Oberlin experimented with new ideas. It embraced the fad of Graham's Vegetarianism, thus outlawing meat from the commons. The main center of the "peace movement" beyond the Appalachians was found here. Also, the largest local chapter of the American Moral Reform Society in the West had its home in Oberlin.

Interesting in Oberlin's early life was the admitting from Lane Seminary of 40 defecting students, four-fifths of the student body, in 1835. Lane Seminary, situated in the northeastern part of Cincinnati, had for its president Lyman Beecher. The faculty and the students fought a bitter contest against Lane's Board of Trustees, who forbade the discussion of anti-slavery in the seminary. Theodore Weld, an abolitionist, and many other faculty members and students left and went to Oberlin.

Oberlin combined in one institution four different departments of education: a preparatory school, a female seminary, a theological school, and a college.[7] In the early years of Oberlin's history all students were required to help, either in manual labor, agricultural, mechanical, or domestic work. The first teacher's training course in the West is believed to have been started there in 1846. Liberal in its curriculum, the college substituted English literature and Hebrew for some of the old standby Latin and Greek courses. Oberlin abolished all grades, ranks, and honors. Young women taking the Ladies' (Seminary) course were admitted to classes with men. There was some disagreement as to the advisability of this mixing of the sexes from the very beginning. John Morgan, professor of New Testament Literature, wrote to Theodore Weld (then at Lane Seminary), "The mixing of young men and women together strikes me as not at all judicious." Ten years later the problem still existed. A report on "Educating the Sexes Together," was prepared by a committee made up of two professors and the wife of the president of the college. The contents revealed that certain evils were recognized. The tendency was for the boys and girls to spend too much time together, often resulting in early marriage. The idea of coeducation did not sit well in other areas of the country and stirred up quite a controversy. Four Oberlin females were admitted in 1837 to a full classical course and to candidacy for a baccalaureate degree. Attendance at some regular college courses was required of the young ladies as part of their special ladies' course. The principal of the "Ladies' Department" was Mrs. Alice Welsh Cowles. Her brother-in-law, who was a faculty member at Oberlin, was reported to have been dismissed because he did not approve of joint education of the sexes and did not like some of the experimental ideas permitted there. Education became more firmly rooted for women as time went on. After 1858, the young women of the college were allowed to read their own graduation exercises; formerly they had had to remain silent at the college graduations. Mary Jane Patterson, a Negro, in 1862 received an A.B. degree from Oberlin College, and was the first Negro woman in America to complete a regular college course. She went on to teach in a Negro high school in Washington, D.C.

In the period before the Civil War, Oberlin became a focus of anti-slavery and underground railroad activity.

In 1858 a runaway slave named Littlejohn was taken at Oberlin by a United States Marshal, but was rescued at Wallington by several anti-slavery men, among whom was Professor Henry Peck of Oberlin College, who was arrested and imprisoned for several months. This resulted in a famous fugitive case. The village itself became a station of the underground railway and an important center for anti-slavery sentiment.

Courtesy New York State Library, Albany, N.Y.
This lithograph shows Albany Normal School as it appeared in 1850. The school was established by the New York State Legislature in 1844. Its rapid growth made it necessary to move to larger quarters by 1850. Albany Normal School was the first of its kind in America to require a high school diploma for entrance; it also had the distinction of being the first institute to train teachers on the college level. An unusual feature in connection with the establishment was an Experimental School that had 88 pupils, younger children. The senior class of the normal school were employed alternately, eight at a time, under the direction of one of the teachers, to instruct the young students. The school changed its name in 1890 to New York State Normal College and again in 1914, when it became New York State College for Teachers.

1850   Faculty of the Albany Normal School
George R. Perkins, A.M., Principal, and Mathematics
William F. Phelps, Experimental School
Darwin G. Eaton, Mathematics
Sumner C. Webb, Arithmetic
Silas T. Bowen, Grammar and Mathematics
William W. Clark, Nature and Chemistry
Truman H. Bowen, Vocal Music
Elizabeth C. Hance, Reading and Geography
Ann Marie Ostrom, Drawing, etc.

Other coeducational colleges began. In 1853 Antioch College, under Horace Mann's leadership, began its experiment. Genesee College (later Syracuse University) was coeducational from its founding in 1850. The University of Iowa opened in 1856 as coeducational. These were the important early colleges to set the trend.

Teachers' training schools and the normal school movement began to provide teachers for the expanding education in all categories. In some cases the increased demand for teachers lowered standards. A basic knowledge of subjects and ability to maintain order in a classroom were not enough. Teachers had to be better qualified. Teachers' training schools began in the 1820s. The first state normal school to open in America was at

Lexington, Massachusetts, in July, 1839. A second school followed in the autumn of the same year at Barre; a third opened at Bridgewater in 1840.

Normal schools suffered much opposition. Teachers around the countryside were suspicious and considered this a reflection on their teaching. Academies opposed them and opponents of the publc school system feared them.

A typical example of progressive education of the day was the establishment of Albany Normal School by the New York State Legislature in 1844. It opened its doors at 119 State Street, Albany, New York. The student body, half of which was girls, grew to approximately 350 by 1849, making it necessary to expand and move to larger quarters at the corner of Lodge and Howard Street.

Certain rules and procedures were evident in the early coeducational school. The girls occupied the front half of the classrooms, the boys the rear. The entrances were separate. Some infringements of the rules were noted. A boy was expelled in 1850 on the charge that he repeatedly visited the girls' dormitories after 6 P.M.

The Albany Normal School was the first of its kind in the nation to require a high school diploma for entrance requirement. Horace Mann said of the school, "New York through her normal school is carrying forward public education more rapidly than any other state in the union."

The only normal school in the state of New York until 1864, it was the educational Mecca of New York State teachers and carried the heaviest load until 1889. In 1890 the name was changed to New York State Normal College. It changed again in 1914 to New York State College for Teachers. The school had the distinction of being the first institute to train teachers on the college level.

Whether training of teachers took place in academies or normal schools, their curriculum was completely academic, although sometimes there were included courses in school management or principles of teaching. Training varied in length of time, most courses being three years, although a few schools admitted students for just a few weeks. Graduates, after training, often went West to teach and many times this was considered a missionary venture. The number of normal schools by 1860 stood at twelve established in nine states. In addition, six private normal schools were founded and St. Louis had started the first city normal school.

School enrollment made remarkable gains in the northwestern states, and smaller but substantial gains in the South. Most of these states, with two or three exceptions, doubled or tripled their enrollment during the 20-year period of 1840–1860.[8]

1851
Teachers had gained prestige in the 1840–1860 era and were considered second only to the clergy. This man's fraternity key is clearly visible. The first college fraternity was Phi Beta Kappa, founded in 1776, and it was still an exclusive institution for men in 1860. By 1840 many honorary societies had been founded.

A great shifting took place from 1830–1860 from private to public schools. Several normal schools were established, curriculums were expanded, all levels of education were developing, and there was more administrative control. Statesmen and politicians all over the country were instrumental in making legislative provisions. Schools also were becoming centers of more social activity. The district school was brought under a mild form of state supervision by the control of funds by the state. The district could refuse or accept the conditions the state offered, but the tendency was to accept the needed funds.

Cubberley, in his book, *Public Education in United States*, comments on progress in education in this era. "By the close of the second quarter of the nineteenth century, certainly by 1860, we find the American public school system fully established, in principle at least, in all our Northern States. Much yet remained to be done to carry into full effect what had been established in principle, but everywhere democracy had won its fight, and the American public school, supported by general taxation, freed from the pauper-school taint, free and equally open to all, under the direction of representatives of the people, free from sectarian control, and complete from the primary school through the high school, and in the Western States through the University as well, may be considered as established permanently in American public policy."[9]

As with any great undertaking, getting started is not enough; ironing out the problems and carrying out the laws are an endless process, one requiring great patience. Problems of education, both political and social, would have to be worked out. Teachers, who had gained much prestige and were considered socially and intellectually to be second only to the clergy were often overworked, their health sometimes impaired. An editor of *Harper's Monthly Magazine,* a well-known periodical of the day, visited some schools in 1860 and noted the poor health of many of the boys and girls. Many looked pale and puny; all were subject to colds; and absenteeism was evident. The long sessions, six hours as compared with the former two-hour sessions,

1849
Some observers felt that in the frenzy for better education, the students were being pushed too fast. The longer hours of study were taking a toll on health. Many looked pale and puny; all were subject to colds. Absenteeism was much in evidence.

were taking their toll on health. The short recess did not give much time for rest or refreshment. The editor expressed his feeling that scholars of ten and twelve years old could safely give six or eight hours to a wisely rounded program of school studies, but when it went beyond ten hours, and midnight found the young ones still burning their oil lamps, the result was deplorable. Were the children being pushed too soon in this frenzy for education? Every community shared this problem. Was it better to go back to the old school system of shorter hours than to sacrifice health and common sense for book learning? Would it be better to keep the young ones in school a year or two longer?[10] Then too, in the rigorous routine, the dull pupils were often discouraged and the gifted overworked! Worse still, study was often combined with social display. At some of the best schools girls were kept out of school two-thirds of the time for social reasons.

An indifferent attitude toward education now took an about-face to a new danger of too much meddling. In many small communities suspicious and sensitive parents often interfered with instruction and supervision, and in the larger communities political and sectarian questions and the election of school inspectors or commissioners instigated feuds. The editor of the above-mentioned monthly periodical advised a conservative attitude and made suggestions for appointing school committees by popular vote and by the common council of the city involved. Thus grievances could be checked and schools kept under the jurisdiction of the people.

The new widespread attitude toward education led to the establishment of libraries throughout the country. By 1847 the United States had 236 public libraries.[11] A movement was in progress in Boston in 1847 for a free public library; $30,000 was being raised.[12] Philadelphia had an apprentice library with a female department. During 1847–1848 there were 7,648 books loaned to females, of whom 250 were listed in the library as members.[13] In addition to public libraries there were numerous Historical Society libraries.

Of great importance to American learning was the establishing of the Smithsonian Institution, founded by an Act of Congress, August 10, 1846. The institution came into being by the bequest of an Englishman named James Smithson. It is believed Smithson, a British chemist and mineralogist must have heard of a plan by Joel Barlow for a national institution of learning in Washington, D. C., in accordance with the wishes of George Washington's farewell address of 1796. Smithson's estate was left to his nephew Henry James Hungerford, with the stipulation that if Hungerford should die without issue, the entire estate would go to the creation of

1848

Education at the college level from 1840 onward was in a period of dramatic growth. The distinguished group of men shown above is probably part of a college graduating class. Numerous scrolls rest on the floor (foreground). A daguerreotype from the South.

"Smithsonian Institution," the purpose being to increase and diffuse knowledge among men. The Board of Regents in December 1846 elected Joseph Henry, professor of natural philosophy at the College of New Jersey (Princeton), as the first secretary and director of the institution. He carried out the wishes of the founder to increase and diffuse knowledge in his capacity as director, from 1846 until his death in 1878. Its organization was primarily owing to him.

Congress, recognizing the need for training and educating the military, passed a bill signed by President Jefferson on March 16, 1802. This bill established a permanent military school, administered by the Corps of Engineers. It was started at West Point, New York, on the Hudson River. The sole purpose of the academy was to train military officers.

A beginning of a naval training center for the United States Government was delayed because of the general feeling that men should be trained at sea. Between 1821 and 1837 some makeshift schools were established at several navy yards, where midshipmen on leave could study and take examinations with a hope for promotion. In 1827 a recommendation for a naval school almost went through missing by just one vote. A petition of protest from officers of the *Constitution* and the *Vandalia* in 1836, some articles written by Mathew Maury in 1840–1841, and recommendations from Secretaries of Navy kept the issue of a naval school alive. George Bancroft, appointed Secretary of Navy by President Polk, also a diplomat and historian, set up a school without asking Congress for money and, although a civilian himself, he talked two naval boards into accepting Annapolis as a site—a site that occupied more than 200 acres on the southern bank of the Severn River. He secured the transfer of Fort Severn in Annapolis from the Army and brought to the site about 40 midshipmen and seven schoolmasters already serving the Navy. Commander Franklin Buchanan, named superintendent, opened the naval school October 10, 1845. Within the year the superintendent and some of the midshipmen left to fight in the Mexican War. The next superintendent failed to maintain discipline. Complaints were heard from the local townsfolk on questionable behavior. This condition did not last, for a new curriculum and a strict code of regulations were put into effect July 1, 1850, when Commander Cornelius K. Stribling took over as new superintendent. The name was then changed from Naval School to United States Naval Academy. Practice cruises began in 1851. The historic frigate *Constitution* was stationed there and was

The United States Military Academy at West Point was the focus for military education in the era, particularly after the successful Mexican War. A sketch from Gleason's Pictorial, *1852.*

used as a training ship. A great naval training center had been established.

The West had expanded education as rapidly as possible; it was a large undertaking to build an educational foundation from nothing. The western states realized that only by knowledge and communication of ideas could they hope to compete with the East and South in affairs of national government and business.

In the South education had risen at an incredible pace, especially during the last ten to twenty years before the Civil War. During 1850–60, 11,000 students were enrolled in colleges of all of the cotton states, while in the state of Massachusetts, with half as many white people as in all the cotton states, there were only 1,733 college students. The income of all the higher institutions of the lower South in 1860 was $708,000, a 100 percent increase over the 1850 figures.[14] Although the South's expenditure on education during these years was higher than in any other part of the country, its enrollment per free pupil was lower than the rest. The political leaders of the South were aware that they must have the loyalty and beliefs of all the southern people in their social philosophies in order to keep the South a strong power in the national government, and they hoped that education was the answer.

The East, in defending its long established leadership in the field of education, had hastened to revive the old, and to cement the new foundations for learning.

Looking back in retrospect to more than a century ago, the middle-class society in that era deserves a tribute. Without its wholehearted support and agreement these vast changes in the educational field certainly could not have taken place in America.

SUNNYSIDE,
THE RESIDENCE OF
WASHINGTON IRVING.

9

The Arts

Native art had made its way into the average American home by the 1840–1860 era. Some of the early ladies' magazines, and later monthly periodicals, contained novels and poems written by many of the great literary men of the day: Edgar Allan Poe, James Fenimore Cooper, and Henry Wadsworth Longfellow, among others. For illustrations, the periodicals used lithographs, some beautifully colored, of various artistic subjects and scenes, which were sandwiched between literature, poetry, and the latest ladies' fashions. Monthly periodicals such as *Harper's* in 1850, *Putnam's* in 1853, and the *Atlantic Monthly* in 1857, stressed not only the arts but politics, religion, and social opinion.

The widespread interest abroad in America from the 1830s onward, in literature, native painting, architecture, and music, would reach the masses by 1840–1860. America was creating a character of its own, developing its own art forms. This massive array of talent in the art field had not been seen, before or since this age, on such a wide, concentrated scale.

At first American literature belonged culturally to New York, then to Boston, Cambridge, and Concord. The beloved writer of the age with the people was Washington Irving. An easy-going friendly man, his writings reflected his love of America and nature. James Fenimore Cooper, dramatic story teller, brought the exciting frontier life into the lives of Americans. William Cullen Bryant, a champion of reforms, gave stature to American journalism. Edgar Allan Poe reflected the quest for something new in his romantic writings and poetry. Nathaniel Hawthorne wrote as a moralist, with great emphasis on the past. Herman Melville produced his classic and symbolic *Moby Dick*, the great sea adventure. Richard Henry Dana wrote the great classic *Two Years Before the Mast* from notes taken on his two-year voyage to California, and Walt Whitman contributed *Leaves of Grass*, which was considered by Emerson to be the most extraordinary piece of wit and wisdom that America had yet produced.

The Cambridge writers and poets, Henry Wadsworth Longfellow, James Russell Lowell, Oliver Wendell Holmes, and John Greenleaf Whittier were all contributing, all idealizing and trying to represent the whole aspect of human life and its surroundings through the medium of poetry.

America's great philosophers of the era, Ralph Waldo Emerson and Henry David Thoreau, in their writing portrayed an intellectual searching, bringing into play nature and all of its philosophical undertones, creating a philosophy seemingly of utter simplicity yet deeply profound.

Ralph Waldo Emerson (1803–1882) born in Boston, Massachusetts, was the son of a Unitarian clergyman. He was brought up with a strict moral code of discipline and a lively respect for hard work. He graduated from Harvard in 1821. During college and in later life, his personality showed a certain reserve, modified with a serenity and charm that appealed to all men. Four years after graduation Emerson entered the Divinity school in Cambridge to prepare for preaching the Unitarian doctrines. His early sermons were simple, direct, considered rather unconventional, but nevertheless they charmed his audience. His conviction that the Lord's supper was not intended by Christ to be a permanent

Washington Allston, unique among artists, was also a poet. In 1844, William H. Dougal, aged 22, engraved the above to illustrate Allston's poem "The Paint King."

among the American people. Although Emerson was a central figure among the Transcendentalists, he was a moderate. A practical man as well as idealistic, he discarded any doctrine that he felt was without value. In his lectures he entreated his audience to have absolute self-reliance and used such inspirational messages as, "Cast conformity behind you, and acquaint men at first hand with Deity." His lectures, varied and wide in scope, delivered with a compelling, musical voice and expressive face, brought intellectual stimulation to American men and women. The lectures were not confined to Boston but were given all over the country, in towns and cities, colleges and small country lyceums.

Emerson's essays were an outgrowth of his lectures, and they were taken from his manuscripts with one exception, the volume *Nature* in 1836. The influence Emerson wielded through these mediums gave to men new hope and optimism; it incited in them a spirit of self-reliance and a seeking for a goal in life, one of man's basic needs.

Henry David Thoreau (1817–1862), America's great naturalist and philosopher, did not receive recognition

1853
The work of American artists in this era reflected the mood of the country and its people. An artist posed in his smock.

sacrament, and his statement that he wished to continue the sacrament as a simple ceremony of remembrance, led to a disagreement among his parishioners. With considerable regret he left his church but continued to preach until 1847. However, he did not take charge of another parish. Emerson believed that every man had worth, and a spark of the divine. His hope was to guide and strengthen the inner life of man. He became interested in the philosophies of the ancients and also became interested in those of Coleridge, Swedenborg, and Carlyle. During a trip abroad in 1832 he met Carlyle and made a lasting friendship with him.

After returning from England in 1833 he began a career of lecturing that would bring him not only great fame but would make him a very powerful leader

eyes of a naturalist. It was in 1845 that he made his famous experiment at Walden Pond. With his own hands he built a hut, furnished it, and lived there in utmost simplicity, close to nature, for two years. Thoreau liked simplicity in life, whether with people or surroundings. He had small interest in reform, church, public doings, government, or a career. He felt that possessions, or the usual mechanical contraptions of civilization, made man a slave with little time left for thought. In the book considered his best, *Walden, or Life in the Woods,* he wrote, "But lo! men have become the tools of their tools."

1856

Walt Whitman

The cheerful, optimistic, and informal poet associated habitually with the common people—working men of all kinds. He liked to wear open shirts, wide brimmed hats, and comfortable denims. Whitman worked during the years 1851–1854 building and selling small houses in Brooklyn. He did considerable writing during this period. The idea for his famous Leaves of Grass *probably germinated during the years 1853–1855, when he spent his time between carpentering and his poems. In the summer of 1855 the first edition of* Leaves of Grass *appeared—a small quarto of 94 pages. It did not attract much attention until Emerson said this work was "the most extraordinary piece of wit and wisdom that America has yet contributed."*

from many of his contemporaries. Early in life Thoreau was deeply interested in nature. At the age of twelve he made a collection for the great naturalist, Agassiz. After college he became a schoolmaster for a while; later his principal occupation was surveying, which worked in very well with his love of nature, for as he surveyed the land he studied his surroundings with the

1841

The portrait (above) is believed to be an early daguerreotype taken of Henry David Thoreau when he was a schoolmaster for a brief period. Thoreau had become acquainted with nature as a child, when he drove his mother's cow to pasture; streams and meadows became well known to him. After he left schoolmastering, Thoreau became a lecturer and author as well as naturalist and often made a living by surveying. His famous experiment at Walden Pond, where he lived in Spartan simplicity, resulted in the book Walden; or Life in the Woods. *In his book he expounded a philosophy based on nature. The daguerreotype was taken by John Plumbe Jr., Boston.*

Thoreau and Emerson became close friends, exchanging thoughts and philosophies, learning much from each other. Thoreau became a Transcendentalist but did not lose his individuality in so doing. As society became more complex, he grew in stature as a philosopher. One hundred years later his words took on a special meaning, giving pause and having a quieting effect, waking man to the realization that he is a slave to time and clutter. In the twentieth century India would gain freedom, partly because its leader Gandhi had been influenced by the reading of Thoreau's essay "Civil Disobedience" while in jail for civil disobedience. Thoreau did not feel that lesser men in politics and government could best judge his "pursuit of happiness" as set forth in the Constitution.

Many of the literary men of the day who were interested in Transcendentalism visited Brook Farm, a utopian communistic experiment that was based on the idea of reducing labor to a minimum, thus saving time for mental and spiritual development. All members were to share any profit from their combined labors, with the added attraction of freedom from competitive industry. The farm, founded by George Ripley, was located on a tract of land in West Roxbury, Massachusetts. It opened in the summer of 1841 with 20 members. In September of that year the Institute of Agriculture and Education was founded and formed into an unincorporated joint stock company. Most of the farm's income was derived from this school. In 1844, because of the influence of Fourier's doctrines, which were modified by the socialist Albert Brisbane, the plan of the community was changed to a "Fourierist Phalanx." A weekly journal, *Harbinger,* was published, to which many noted writers contributed. Charles Anderson Dana, one of the trustees of Brook Farm and headwaiter when it changed, wrote for and managed the new publication. In 1846 the community buildings were burned and in 1847 the experiment was abandoned.

Some of the well-known figures who visited the farm and who were indirectly connected with the experiment although never regular members, were Ralph Waldo Emerson, Amos Bronson Alcott, Orestes A. Brownson, Theodore Parker and William Henry Channing, Margaret Fuller, and Elizabeth Palmer Peabody. Principal members of the farm, besides Ripley and Dana, were Nathaniel Hawthorne, John S. Dwight, Minot Pratt, George Partridge Bradford, and Warren Burton.

While the literary men were more or less in a concentrated area, artists with their brushes could be found everywhere in the country; some were on westward expeditions, capturing the frontier landscapes and painting the images of Indians; some were in the mining camps in California; others were in cities and many were recording the unspoiled eastern rural countryside. The romantic eyes of the primitive painters were busily putting on canvas everyday life and people as they saw them. A British art critic, Anna Brownell Jameson, who had made a trip to America in 1837–1838, wrote of the swarms of artists she saw everywhere in the country. She noted the imagination and originality of the painters and, although she expressed the opinion that a great proportion of the artists were "outrageously bad," there was, she said, too much genius in America to produce "mediocrity."[1]

The eighteenth century had seen the emergence of many notable native-born painters, among them John Singleton Copley, James Claypoole, and Benjamin West. By the 1820s art had come of age in America, having passed through several stages of development. The solitary portraits, historical scenes, and religious subjects

1857

Artists with their brushes could be found everywhere in the country; some were on westward expeditions, some were in the mining camps, others were recording the unspoiled countryside of the East.

1844
Landscape painting in America came into great popularity through the guidance and influence of Asher B. Durand, above (attributed). In the 1830s Durand abandoned the engraving profession for painting; he became a portrait artist of note and was commissioned to do portraits of presidents. After a trip to Europe in 1840, Durand was convinced that his own realism in painting had merit and from then onward he turned to landscape scenes. One of the founders of the National Academy of Design, Durand served as its president from 1846–1861.

by many well-known artists of the early nineteenth century were slowly becoming eclipsed by a new group of landscape and genre painters.

Environmental forces played a great part in this change and in influencing art; the westward expansion, the literature of the day, political and industrial changes were all factors. While there was some European influence on American painters, and some went abroad to study, the artists used fundamentally their own form and improvised. The native art reflected the mood of the country and the current great interest in nature.

Some native artists, such as Allston, Vanderlyn, Morse, and Neagle did an occasional landscape, but it was as a side line. The three men to bring landscape painting to notice were Thomas Doughty and Thomas Cole, shortly followed by Asher B. Durand. The landscape

came into full attention as an art under the influence of Asher B. Durand (1796–1886), who would later be named the father of the "Hudson River School." A son of a watchmaker and farmer from New Jersey, Durand spent his childhood on the farm, living close to nature. As a young man he was apprenticed to an engraver and became so skillful that he came to the attention of Trumbull, a historical painter who had long sought a capable man to reproduce an engraving of his famous painting "Declaration of Independence." Durand was 24 years old at the time and completed the project in three years. Durand's fine work on this project placed him at the top of the engraving profession, a profession that came into great importance when Jackson closed the Bank of United States, as local banks then needed the services of engravers to print bank notes. This in-

1855

The above ambrotypes are copies of the early nineteenth-century paintings believed to have been the work of a New England primitive painter, Zedekiah Belknap or Abraham G. D. Tuthill. Both of the men were itinerant artists who traveled the backwoods of New England painting rural subjects. Belknap and Tuthill were active during the first part of the nineteenth century. A note in the rear of the daguerreotype case identifies the subjects as William Walter Smith and wife of Meriden, New Hampshire.

creased the engraving field and later many of these men turned to painting.

In the 1830s Durand abandoned engraving and became a portrait artist of considerable note. His realistic subjects were basically of black and white design, the faces yellowish, creating a theatrical effect that gained him considerable popularity. He was commissioned to do portraits of presidents. In 1834 he did a portrait of ex-president Madison, painted by the request of George P. Morris, Esquire. In 1835 he did portraits of Andrew Jackson and John Quincy Adams. Also in that year he did a historical scene "The Capture of Major Andre."[2] He became associated with Thomas Cole and went with him in 1836 to the Catskill Mountains, but the two artists looked at nature differently, and Durand felt rather disappointed with his first attempts at landscape painting. He sailed for Europe in 1840 and viewed the works of various European artists. This trip helped to create in his mind his own realistic vision of art, and when he returned to America he concentrated on landscapes, which the Americans loved for their quiet, serene beauty and which captured nature so realistically. After Cole's death, Durand became the leader in American painting. He was President of the National Academy of Design from 1846–1861. Also he published serials in the *Crayon,* an art publication, during 1855 and 1856, as well as other writings. His view on original native art was expressed as follows: "Americans could in accordance with the principles of self government, boldly originate a high and independent style based on our own resources."

Other landscape artists of note in this era were Frederick Church (1826–1900), a pupil of Cole, who made a debut at the National Academy in 1845 when nineteen. In his paintings he placed emphasis on light, realism, and accurate detail. John Frederick Kensett (1816–1872) expressed the nature theme and was a leader among the new generation of painters.

John James Audubon, a naturalist and artist of realism, at the age of 50 in 1840 entered the second greatest project of his life (the first was birds) drawing the likenesses and recording the habits of American mammals. The resulting book, "The Viviparous Quadrupeds of North America," was published between 1845–1848.

America's western historian on canvas of this era was George Caleb Bingham (1811–1879). Born in Virginia, he moved to Missouri when eight years old. He studied a short while at the Pennsylvania Academy of Fine Arts in Philadelphia in 1837–1838. When he returned to Missouri in 1844, he did an amazing and original work, "The Fur Traders Descending the Missouri." His paintings were in wide use for illustrations depicting frontier life. Other frontier and Indian painters of note were: George Catlin, Karl Bodmer, Alfred Miller, Seth Eastman, Charles Deas, and John Mix Stanley.

Henry Inman (1801–1846) was looked upon as the leading portrait painter of the period. He was in New York except for the years 1831–1834, which he spent in Philadelphia. His depiction of portrait subjects on canvas reflected his own pleasant personality. When his works were sold after his death in 1846, a few genre canvases were found among the many portraits.

A fresh, varied school of genre painting emerged. An outstanding genre artist was William Sidney Mount (1807–1868), who turned from religious subjects to nature and rural life. Also many illustrators were contributing both amusing and factual portrayals of American life.

The most controversial artist of the era was William Page (1811–1885). An original and experimental painter, he held to the view that painting should be based on sculpture. On this outmoded view, he stood alone. He preferred dark, rich pictures when the trend was to lighten color. He strongly believed that art should do more than reflect nature. His "Cupid and Psyche" showed him to be the most sensual artist of his time. The painting was banned from the National Academy.

The greatest influence in bringing art to the public and in creating a great demand that would benefit the painter was the founding of art unions. There were several in the country after 1840, in New York, Philadelphia, Boston, Newark, and Cincinnati.[3] They were organized in the form of lotteries or raffles similar to that of the Irish Sweepstakes, and tickets went into every state and territory. It all began in 1838 when not many paintings were being sold by an artists' cooperative known as Apollo Gallery (later, American Art Union) in New York. Taking the idea from Germany, which had originated it, the gallery had the public subscribe $5.00 a year per member, and in return they would receive engravings of original paintings. At the end of the year, lucky winners at a drawing would receive the originals. This became the most famous of all the art unions that encouraged native American art and was a turnabout from the American Academy, which had been founded in 1803 by a group of leading New York families who had tried to bring imported art to America.

A great influence on art in this era was the coming of the camera. When many of the prominent artists saw the results of Daguerre's photographs, they felt, as one artist declared, "Painting is dead from this day." Others, like Samuel Morse, referred to the daguerreotype enthusiastically and said "Rembrandt perfected."

1847

The Golden Portrait

Many early photographers were also artists or had studied the art principles of posing, lighting, and proportion. Some daguerreians experimented in bringing color to the portrait by emulating miniature paintings and often created beautiful portraits like the one shown above. Daguerreotype by the daguerreian-artist Lorenzo G. Chase, Boston.

Experts one hundred years later would agree that no subsequent photographic process could achieve more brilliance and rendering of detail than the original daguerreotype, and although the range was not as great as the more modern paper print, intermediate tones were well shown, the daguerreotype was not flat, and top and side lighting had been almost immediately adopted.[4]

In the early 1840s pessimistic artists, as well as the optimistic ones, enthusiastically embraced the photo-realistic daguerreotype as not only an art in itself but an invaluable and revolutionary aid to the painter with his brush. No longer would he have to depend completely on his sketchbook for proportions; for the first time he had an exact mechanical reproduction to guide him in producing his painting.

The Draper-Morse improvements, combined with the reduction of exposure time by 1841, made it possible

1849

An example of an unknown painting preserved for posterity by daguerreotypists of the era.

for the daguerreotype to enter its natural field, that of the portrait. Miniature painters, so popular before 1840, were put out of business almost completely; however, many of the artists turned to the photography industry. As the era progressed, because an artist was able to produce a much larger rendition of his subject on canvas than could be captured by camera, he was assured of continued success in his field. Photography was limited in size, the popular, average size being 2¾ inch by 3¼ inch; the largest daguerreotype plate 13½ by 16½, was difficult, rare, and expensive.

If the daguerreotype had an effect on art, so did art have an effect on the daguerreotype. The approach of the daguerreotypist was identical to that of an artist with a subject to record. The small cadre of pioneer photographers, many former artists themselves, would stand out prominently, using the accepted traditional art form as a guide to lighting, proportions, subject posing, and facial expressions. Many of the devices that were used to bring out the subject's character had been inspired by the great art masters.[5]

No sharp line would be drawn between art and photography until the Civil War, when photography would begin emerging on its own path. Future art critics would declare that the daguerreotype, with its photo-realistic approach, influenced the school of impressionists through the camera's gift of "instantaneous-

make popular the works of landscape and genre artists.

Chemistry was to play an important role. The year 1856 provided a new landmark in painting. To supplement or replace the usual simple earth and vegetable pigments, a new array of chemical paints came into being with the discovery of the first coal tar color, mauve, by an English chemist, Perkin. This product created new and bolder reds and purples. Mauve was soon followed by magenta and cobalt violet in 1859, and cobalt yellow about 1861. Later, the paintings of the French Impressionists furnished examples of the use of these colors.

A small but active group of sculptors was busy in America in the 1830–1850 period. Many of the artists worked in marble abroad in art centers of Italy. Among the best known were Horatio Greenbough, Hiram Powers, Thomas Crawford, Randolph Rogers, and Harriet Hosmer. Because of the decline of the neoclassical style of art and the fact that many of the works were lacking in popular appeal, they did not gain widespread acceptance. The only work that received great attention here and in Europe was Hiram Powers' "The Greek Slave," which was successfully displayed in New York City.

Meanwhile, in architecture, the Grecian style had been used extensively and with considerable success. The 1830s had ushered in an era of Greek Revival, featuring the great white columns that were used in Greek temples. The acceptance of the Grecian style of construction that dominated the American scene from the 1820s through the 1840s, as no other style had before or since, was in part because Greek architecture was a symbol of liberty. Builders' Guides written by early

1852
Another unknown painting preserved for posterity.

ness," the "candid" life views in the world of art.

Also, adding impetus to the art field were collectors such as Philip Hone, and many professional men and merchants who, by their interest, created a demand for art. The artist-illustrator and engraver did much to

An architectural drawing from a sketch of 1849.

architects also promoted the style's popularity. The country's most famous architect to take up the Greek Revival style was Robert Mills (1781–1855) of Charleston, South Carolina. He was the architect and engineer in charge during the 1830s, when United States Government buildings in Washington took on an air of simplicity, built now in this Greek traditional style. Mills's attitude on style can be best summed up from a statement written by him in an unfinished essay. "Go back as the Greeks did to the source of all art forms in nature . . . study your country's tastes and requirements and make classic ground here for your art."[6]

By the 1840s it became the fad for the up-and-coming young architects to attack the Greek mode as un-American. A new leader in the field, Andrew Jackson Downing (1815–1852), landscape architect from Newburgh, New York, wrote in 1841 a "Treatise on the Theory and Practice of Landscape Gardening, Adapted to North

Andrew Jackson Downing, celebrated landscape architect of Newburgh, New York, contributed to the American scene with his landscape designs of the public gardens near the Capitol, and the landscaping of the White House and the Smithsonian Institution.

America." He said that a Greek temple form was perfect for a public building, but not for private dwellings. He furthered this idea in a book the following year, *Cottage Residences.* Architecture plan books were advertised in 1847 for the price of 50 cents, showing eight separate homes and floor plans for the middle-class home buyer or builder.

A clever argument was used by the opposition that it was more "Christian" to have a Gothic style of architecture than the "Pagan" Greek. No American could refute the statement. The new Gothic revival sweeping the country showed off the new wealth in spectacular Oriental domes and turrets. The Gothic style began as a fad in 1799 for a brief period, and started regaining its popularity in the 1830s and 1840s under the architectural leaders, Downing and Davis. Orson Squire Fowler, promoter of the Octagon house, reasoned that Gothic style was not good for the ordinary people. Others joined in with the complaints that Gothic was pretentious, nonconformist, and artificial; furthermore, it had no roots in American tradition. Fowler, who tired of phrenology and turned to architecture, wrote a book entitled, *A Home for All; or, the Gravel Wall and Octagon Mode of Building,* published in 1849. His book created a flurry of octagon buildings about the country, not only homes but schools, churches, and other public buildings. Fowler's idea was to reject the past and take a pattern from nature, whose form was mostly spherical, and to produce a home that was economical, functional, and healthy. Although conceived with the idea of simplicity, many of these structures were elaborate. The design lost its popular appeal after a few years. However, in Wisconsin for instance, the octagon houses, still standing over 100 years later, proved to be not only the most elaborate but the most successful, architecturally, and the best preserved of all old houses.

A new type of intellectual architect, men who were also connoisseurs of art, had come into the field by the 1850s. They mixed styles on the same buildings so that a completely Gothic structure in every detail was rare. (A striking example of Gothic architecture is the old building of the Smithsonian Institution in Washington, D. C.)

Alexander Jackson Davis, a contemporary of Downing, designed country cottages of a more practical nature; however, the two men were good collaborators. Among Downing's great contributions to America were his landscape designs of public gardens near the Capitol and the landscaping of the White House and the Smithsonian Institution. He was well known in America and England as a horticultural authority. He lost his life in a boating accident aboard the *Henry Clay* before he

1847   *Courtesy Miss Josephine Cobb*
As the era progressed, affluence was sometimes reflected in repairs and alterations of homes. The large house in Lebanon, New Hampshire (above), had used the rear wing for storage and as a stable in the 1840 decade. See page 170 for same house in the 1850s.

was able to see many of his ideas come to life in the completion of Central Park, New York.

Another architectural trend destined to play an important part in American style during the nineteenth century was the "Italian Villa." A variant of Gothic, it was less ostentatious and in the mid-century the most flexible. The "villa" found a place in the country as well as the city, especially after lawn mowers were invented in the 1840s. In the 1850s the "Italianate" was the nearest thing to a national style. When these homes, with their creamy walls with dark trim, were set off by lush green shrubbery, they expressed the elegance of the age.

The Italianate was the only trend adaptable for experimentation, and so it became the vehicle of expression in American architecture, from the transition of a highly individual society to a more complex era coming after the Civil War.

The outhouses in vogue in the latter part of the nineteenth century represented a decline in sanitation in America. The fad for sanitation and properly ventilated homes in the 1850s disappeared in the Civil War era. Porcelain night pots and fear of night air held sway from 1870 until the twentieth century, and progress in the field of health thus suffered a considerable setback. In the early 1840s the English started developing high-pressure municipal water systems. This development started a series of improvements on water closet designs by enterprising inventors. The English patent office issued many new patents on these. By 1850, Ameri-

1856   *Courtesy Miss Josephine Cobb*
The Lebanon home shown left after it had been remodeled and repainted. The old rear wing had been converted into living quarters, sash and dormers had been added, and a new building constructed at the end of the wing. The modern fence completed the aura of prosperity.

1855   *Courtesy Time-Out Antiques, N.Y.C.*
An interest in horticulture, the art and science of cultivating garden plants for utilitarian or for decorative purposes, was widespread in this era. The large house (above) illustrates the contemporary trend toward Gothic architecture.

cans were busy copying the latest English water closet and were incorporating its design for use in spacious indoor bathrooms. Plan books issued by architects showed a sink, bathtub, and water closet compactly arranged in a room about 8 by 10 in size. Plans showed that this new room could be used for modestly priced homes as well as the more costly residences. Architects, aware of health problems, cautioned people to keep their cesspools covered at all times, as the open sewer bred disease. The home designer was able to place his bathroom on the second floor if desired, by a system of new pipes and fittings that carried the high pressure water to the upstairs room. Copper bathroom fixtures entered the faddist field in 1857 and had become the rage by 1858. A lithograph of the era showed a bath-room of George Vanderbilt's entitled "New York Bath-room" and the accompanying notation suggested that the sanitary fixtures should be made of porcelain. A self-stopping faucet, invented by George and William Gee, was widely used by 1848. According to an advertisement in a New York City newspaper, the faucet worked very simply "just press down the knob on the top of the faucet, no wasted water."

Other improvements in the home for middle-class Americans were experiencing a transitional trend in this period. Women were demanding built-in kitchen cabinets and wealthy women were asking for doors on their built-ins. For winter comfort a central heating furnace system, complete with fresh air return pipes, was commonplace in home construction. The system was so well laid out that heat emitted to each room could be controlled with floor hot air registers.

To overcome summer heat, one home designer advocated a double roof, one roof to be six inches higher than the first one, with vents to admit cool air placed in the soffit; other vents placed in the peak of the roof would discharge the hot air, thus keeping the home always cool.[7] Air conditioning was available to the very rich through an elaborate system, utilizing cool water atomized with air and blown by a fan through pipes to the various rooms to be cooled.

The building industry had the use of improved materials in this era. A steam-treating process to preserve lumber from rot and decay was used in 1846. This process, called "Kyanizing," would be used as a wood-preserving method for more than a century. Also the use of steam enabled the lumber industry to speed lumber drying through the use of kilns. Roller-type cutting machinery produced veneers that made plywood available for the first time in the home building industry. New wood-cutting machinery made millwork patterns for trimming doorways and baseboards more orna-

1857   *Courtesy Time-Out Antiques, N.Y.C.*
The outlook for the building industry was changing in the 1840–1860 era. For the first time modest homes for the masses were being erected in great numbers.

mental. Expert scroll sawyers were adding gingerbread designs, and were thus instrumental in making elaborate house exteriors on a mass-producing basis. All of these contributing factors, plus many more, were changing the home building picture in America. Modest homes for the masses were fast becoming a reality in the days before the Civil War!

As mechanical methods became prevalent, the creative master cabinet-makers would disappear and in their place would come workers making reproductions, usually using a publication, "The Cabinet Maker's Assistant," written by a Baltimore architect, John Hall, in 1840. As the decade from 1840 progressed, more and more cabinet-type work was done in factories in all major cities and towns throughout the country. Thousands of chairs were turned out in the 1840s and 1850s. The number of men engaged in cabinet work and in making chairs gained, according to census records from 1810–1850, from 1,000 men to an estimated 37,359. The art of cabinet-making degenerated when factories were run by businessmen and not artists.

1855
Cabinet-making became less of an art when factories were operated by business men and not artists. Tools pictured include brace and bit, mitre saw, mallet, and wood chisel.

If the American home was elaborate, the new hotels being built were like palaces. Famous watering places like the United States Hotel, Atlantic City (shown above), were popular with the wealthy and middle-class American.

Mass production of furnishings had already begun in the 1830s, which brought to the modest home owner a variety of inexpensive furnishings. The list included carpets, chairs, wallpapers, and curtain materials. In 1844 the first wallpaper printing machine was imported from England. Also in 1844, Erastus B. Bigelow invented a power loom for making ingrain carpets, and in 1848 he produced a loom to make Brussels and tapestry carpets, which made possible brightly colored designs to cover American floors. After 1840 factory-made furniture and upholstery skyrocketed from a $7,000,000 business to a $28,000,000 one in a 20-year span. With the mass production of household furnishings there began a new home decorating drift toward the elaborate.

If the American home was elaborate, the new hotels being built were palaces. The first palatial hotel built in the country was the Tremont Hotel in Boston. It opened with great fanfare on October 16, 1829. Nothing had ever been seen like it anywhere in the world and every city now wanted such a hotel. The designer, Isaiah Rogers, son of a shipbuilder from Massachusetts, had incorporated plumbing in the structure, and also a system of speaking tubes running from the desk in the office to various suites and rooms. He included a reading room that would contain books and publications from all over the United States. Rogers's designs had formality and dignity. After designing the Astor Hotel for John Jacob Astor, he traveled South and West, leaving in his wake many elegant hotels. He stood by the Grecian style of architecture that made him famous even into the 1860s.

Hotel building started America on a golden binge. Even in San Francisco during the gold rush days, the saloons and gambling houses were big and plush, the decor contrasting sharply with the motley group of miners always in evidence. In cost and lavishness, the St. Nicholas Hotel in New York, opening in 1853, outdid them all, costing more than a million dollars to build. Its curtains were reported to have cost $700 each and the gold embroidered drapes $1,000. The ceilings were 22 feet high. The rugs were Turkish, and gold leaf was used profusely throughout.

The new sweeping-forward movement of native arts, literature, painting, and architecture, also included music and the theatre. The highly individualistic eighteenth-century New England psalm singing was fast becoming outmoded after the turn of the nineteenth century, although native hymnody turned westward to the frontier and southward to rural areas where being old-fashioned was still acceptable. Later, in the twentieth century, many of these old tunes would experience a revival. Ironically, a New Englander would become responsible for infiltrating, on a wide scale, America's native music with a somewhat imitative quality, echoing European compositions. However, the coming leader in American music would, because of an uncanny talent for organization and a businesslike approach, bring music to the masses through the medium of public school instruction and church music. The influence of Lowell Mason (1792–1872) would dominate the country's music scene for sixty years.

In addition to introducing singing classes to the public school, Mason founded teacher training institutes for future music teachers. He organized music conventions in different areas of the country, and in the new liberal arts colleges of the West he established theoretical and practical music courses. Lowell Mason at the age of twenty moved from his New England home to Savannah, Georgia, where he worked in a bank and became choirmaster and organist of a local church. Meanwhile, he studied harmony and composition under a German musician named Abel. In 1822 his first collection of musical compositions, including some of his own tunes, was published. In 1827 Mason moved to Boston and was soon elected president of the "Handel and Haydn Music Society," and became the organist of Lyman Beecher's church. A prominent leader by this time in music circles, he founded the Boston Academy of Music in 1832, and by 1838 succeeded in having music accepted as an essential part of the public school system. His lecturing talents made him a widely recognized authority in music, and in 1855 New York University conferred on him a distinctive tribute, an honorary degree in music. Mason's "musical collections," most of which were made into tunebooks, sold in such quantities that he became wealthy. Among his own compositions, the best known are the hymns "My Faith Looks up to Thee" and "Nearer my God to Thee."

Boston was not the only center for musical compositions that were being produced for the masses. Philadelphia had become an important publishing center for both vocal and instrumental music of all kinds. The ever-increasing popularity of the pianoforte and other musical instruments created a favorable climate in this era for young American composers. Piano music with vocal arrangement was often composed for such monthly periodicals as *Godey's Lady's Book*. Ballads, marches, and polkas were favorite selections for publication. One of the young Philadelphia ballad composers, Septimus Winner (1827–1902), had become very popular under the name "Alice Hawthorne." He earned his living as a teacher, having students for a variety of instruments. He opened a music store and publishing house in 1847.

A Group of Musicians of the Era

1857

1860

Included among his 200 volumes of music were music instruction books composed for 23 different instruments. His most famous song was "Listen to the Mocking Bird."

Now that America as a nation was becoming more musical, groups of native musicians toured the country, playing to large receptive audiences, and no matter what the quality of the entertainment provided, at least their performances stimulated an interest in music in many towns and villages throughout the land.

Perhaps the best known of the itinerant musicians were the prominent Hutchinson family, the "good old-fashioned singers." Beginning with their first concert in 1839 at a Baptist meetinghouse in Milford, New Hampshire, the eleven sons and two daughters of Jesse Hutchinson had given, by 1843, a number of successful concerts in Boston and elsewhere. Much of their music was of local New England composition and included melodramatic songs such as "The Grave of Bonaparte," temperance songs, and old-fashioned revival tunes. The singing group toured England and Ireland in 1845, and later traveled about America. The family was instrumental in bringing music to the everyday kind of people who liked and understood their kind of music.

1856

1858

Minstrel performers and amateur rural singers enjoyed great popularity in America. The minstrel idea had its beginning back in 1820, when white men imitated the southern Negro plantation worker by blackening their faces. A minstrel show emerged from this experimenting and was often called Ethiopian Opera. The musical show added amusing repartee, dances, speeches, and jokes. The "black face" performers wore striped pants, swallowtail coats, white gloves, and collars that were several sizes too large. The first black-face song combined with a dance act was written by Thomas Rice, better known as "Daddy" or "Jim Crow." His short piece was written to impersonate an old deformed Negro named Jim Crow. It became an immediate sensation and popularized the minstrel shows in the late 1830s and the early 1840s. From then on the minstrel show became a part of American life.

The best remembered and the most beloved ballads and minstrel music from this era were composed by Stephen Foster (1826–1864). He was born in Lawrenceville, near Pittsburgh, Pennsylvania. His first song was

1856　　　　　*Courtesy Time-Out Antiques, N.Y.C.*
Women, more than men, began using the newly invented accordion. Amateur musicians often provided welcome musical entertainment for those who could not afford professional concerts.

1846

An Unknown Composer
With the popularity of the piano and other musical instruments for home entertainment, young composers found a ready market for their music.

written at thirteen, "Try to Find the Picture." At fourteen he wrote a composition, "The Tioga Waltz," while attending school at Athens; it was composed for four flutes and was performed at the Athens Academy commencement. He published his first ballad, "Open Thy Lattice, Love" in 1844. He left home in 1846 and joined his brother in Cincinnati and worked for him as a bookkeeper for two years. Before coming home he had composed "Oh! Susannah." Its first performance was given at Andrew's "Eagle Ice Cream Saloon" in Pittsburgh in 1848, and it was then taken over the following year by Christy's minstrels. This song brought the country together in spirit; it was on the lips of pioneers going West and became the theme song of the gold miner. Whenever people gathered the song was sung. Foster's song "Old Folks at Home," later widely known by the title "Swanee River," was first published under the name E. P. Christy of Christy Minstrels in 1851. It was not until the song became known as "Swanee River" and had become tremendously popular in both America and England that the true identify of the composer, Stephen Foster, became public.

It was an enigma how Stephen Foster was able to capture essence of the South when his only known trip there was to New Orleans in 1852. Some of his other

1845   *Courtesy Time-Oue Antiques, N.Y.C.*
Music was one of the arts most encouraged for young women. Social gatherings often featured the singing of ballads with a guitar accompaniment.

1853

Unknown Musician
The two great pianists of the age were William Mason and Louis Moreau Gottschalk. Mason composed and played music of popular appeal, besides doing concert work. Gottschalk became an internationally famous concert artist. He was the first American composer to recognize the value of American music. Both men were born the same year, 1829.

well-known songs were "Nelly was a Lady," 1849, "Camptown Races," 1850, "Massa's in de Cold, Cold Ground," 1852, "My Old Kentucky Home," 1853, "Old Dog Tray," 1853, "Jeanie with the Light Brown Hair," 1854, "Old Black Joe," 1860. In 1860 Foster moved with his family to New York. He found it difficult to keep a job and tried to earn a living selling songs. He began drinking very heavily and died, after a fall, in Bellevue Hospital Charity Ward on June 13, 1864.

America was not without talented piano concert artists and composers. Otto Dresel performed a series of chamber concerts in Boston and was considered by many to be one of the most accomplished pianists in the country in this era.[8] In Philadelphia, the prominent music publisher, Edward L. Walker, gave a series of piano concerts during 1849, and the music editor of *Godey's Lady's Book* (Philadelphia) wrote that he was one of the best living performers and also said if Walker were "to go incognito to Europe and return with a

mustachio and imperial, and an unpronounceable name, he would make a fortune in a year."[9] From Boston, a young pianist and composer, William Mason (1829–1908), youngest son of Lowell Mason, became nationally known. He was a teacher in addition to giving concerts and composing music for the piano and cello. America's first internationally known concert pianist and composer was Louis Moreau Gottschalk. He was born in New Orleans in 1829, the son of a Creole mother and English father. In 1842 he went abroad for study and to further develop his musical genius. By 1847, he had made a debut in Sedan, France, and in 1849, Paris. In early 1853, he returned to the United States and gave a premiere piano recital at Niblo's in New York City. The music editor of *Putnam's Monthly Magazine* described his performance: "He has such wild exuberance, such capricious facility, such prodigious power and rapidity." After his New York concert, he toured about the country creating a sensation, especially among the women, with his dark and delicate handsomeness and romantic music. He later lived in Cuba from 1859–1862 and toured the Caribbean Islands, composing and giving concerts. Gottschalk was one of the first American composers to recognize the importance of native American music.

Another champion of native music was William Henry Fry (1813–1864), composer, music critic, and journalist. He was the first native composer to have a grand opera publicly performed. "Leonora" was presented on June 4, 1845, in Philadelphia, at the Chestnut Street Theatre. Thirteen years later it was revived in New York. From 1846 until 1852, Fry was abroad as a correspondent to the New York *Tribune* and other newspapers. After returning to New York in 1852, he became an editorial writer and music editor for the *Tribune*. In this capacity he was able to support native composers and American music. Fry began a series of musical lectures in the Metropolitan Hall, New York, on November 30, 1852. For the era, his lectures were a most remarkable music event. The scope presented in the ten lecture series was widely varied, and it provided a historical, aesthetic, scientific, and critical review of music. The program included "good" solo singers, orchestra, and a chorus of 200 voices. The concert-lectures were aimed at instruction and were not presented especially to please the audience. This is probably the reason that the audience gradually declined near the end of the lecture series. However, his lectures and criticisms that America and its institutions ignored native American music and composers and that an "American school" should be founded were well accepted, considering this age of European influence on American music. The editor of *Putnam's Monthly Magazine* wrote of Fry's lectures: "his course has not only made its mark upon the musical season in New York, but upon the musical history of the country."

A young American composer, George Frederick Bristow (1825–1898), violinist for the esteemed New York Philharmonic Society (founded in 1842), came to public attention when he left the society in 1852 because it did not play the works of American composers. In the early summer of 1855, Bristow was the first American conductor to be at the head of an operatic orchestra— it was the English opera troupe of Miss Louisa Pyne, then playing at the New York Academy of Music.[10] On September 27, 1855, an opera, "Rip van Winkle," composed by Bristow, was given at "Niblo's" and ran four weeks. A music editor of the day reviewed Bristow's opera with some reservations, although he praised the second act: "but the second act contains the substance of the composition, and its songs of love and the camp are fresh, well marked, and delightful."[11] The following year Bristow was reunited with the New York Philharmonic Society and on March 1, 1856, the orchestra performed his "Second Symphony in D Minor." Later, other compositions by Bristow were performed.

Two excellent journals of music history and criticisms of the contemporary music and performances of the period were: *Dwight's Journal of Music* and *Willis's*

1848   *Courtesy Time-Out Antiques, N.Y.C.*
A boy with a flute.

Musical World and Times. The former was published in Boston, the other in New York.

Notwithstanding isolated American achievements, both the opera and the theatre from the early 1840s were dominated by European artists and other players. Performances given by famous foreign stars were offered to prosperous Americans at prices ranging, usually, from fifty cents to three dollars a seat. Like the native troupes of musicians, the talented Europeans played their longest engagements in the larger cities and many toured the South and a few traveled westward.

Some resistance was met in New England to amusements of a theatrical or dramatic nature. In Connecticut a presentation of a Shakespearian play was subject to fine and imprisonment. In Massachusetts, Shakespearian plays could be given under a special license and fee, but were not allowed to run on Saturday or Sunday. Every theatre, opera house, and circus in New York paid a yearly fee to the city to be used for a public charity.[12] Some adverse comment about the theatre was made in New York City during the 1840s on moral grounds. Much editorializing was done in newspapers on the evils of the theatre. In 1844, the famous journalist N. P. Willis, in commenting on the critics of

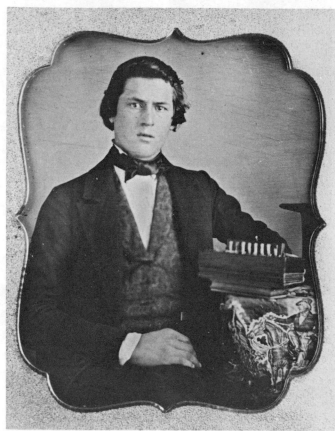

1855
A popular musical instrument of the era (above). Probably a variation of the concertina, the forerunner of the accordion.

both drama and literature, said that the public was tired of having its taste interpreted and expressed by one man's pen.

In New York, where all of the European stars eventually migrated, the theatrical business was controlled almost completely by Englishmen until about 1854. The reason for this was probably that a distinctive American theatre had not yet developed. The indifference on the part of the public at times to the drama often reflected a lack of interest in foreign performers and foreign productions. A walk inside most of the theatres was like stepping into London, which most of the stage scenery represented. Despite an occasional native performer or play written by an American, it was but a grain of sand to the total theatrical picture. The parade of stars, dancers, opera troupes, and touring

orchestras from Europe from 1840 was seemingly endless, and they were greeted mostly (except for drama) by receptive audiences; but by 1854 the public was becoming somewhat disgruntled with the "starring system." However, the big names made the theatre proprietors wealthy. Some of the actors and actresses made large fortunes, and a few managers became millionaires. Men of capital in the era were not averse to investing money in the theatrical business.

Of all the stars from abroad to come to America, the arrival in 1850 of Jenny Lind, Swedish opera star, stirred the greatest interest among the American people. She reached New York on September 1, 1850, and was greeted by more than 20,000 people on the wharf when she landed. Crowds waited along the streets to see her pass. Her first concert was given at Castle Gardens, New York, on the evening of the twelfth. This was followed

1855   *Courtesy Miss Josephine Cobb*
Success on the stage could bring immediate fame and fortune. A typical young actor is shown above.

Opera, music, drama, and public exhibitions were presented in the large hall of Castle Gardens, New York City. It was here that Jenny Lind, the famous Swedish opera star, made her debut in America.

rapidly by five other concerts held at the same place. The number of people attending each appearance was estimated to have been at least 7,000. The first night's receipts were about $30,000, of which she immediately gave $10,000 to several worthy charities in New York City.[13] Competition was strong for the first ticket to each concert in every city in which she sang. In New York it sold for $250, in Boston, $625, in Providence, $650, and in Philadelphia, $625.[14]

Another European performer to capture the hearts of the Americans in the era was Ole Bull, a Norwegian, known as the most brilliant violinist of his time. His first of five tours in America began in 1843. The great musician was called "the St. Peter of the heaven of stringed instruments."

The earliest American play performed in the 1840–1860 era was "Jack Cade," written by Robert T. Conrad. It played at the New York Park Theatre, May 24, 1841. The starring role was performed by Edwin Forrest, a famous American actor. Probably the most outstanding native play of the era was written by Anna Cora Mowatt, a New Yorker. It was a comic satire on society titled *Fashion* and was presented at the Park Theatre on March 26, 1845. Three months later the young and pretty playwright made her debut as an actress in the stage role of "Pauline" in the popular English play *The Lady of Lyons.* After this success, she became a star of influence both at home and abroad. Another native playwright, George Henry Boker, wrote poetic tragedy. His play "Calaynos" was performed in 1848 and another, "Anne Boleyn," in 1850. The most successful play during the 1850s, from a financial standpoint, was *Uncle Tom's Cabin,* which had been dramatized by George L. Aiken from Harriet Beecher Stowe's book. Opening at the Chatham Street Theatre, New York, on July 18, 1853, it ran for 325 nights. The original version consisted of six acts, eight tableaux, and thirty scenes. The drama had little merit, the dialogue was religious, but it was American in tone and the actors were native. A version of *Uncle Tom's Cabin* adapted to southern tastes ran for a long time in the theatre attached to Barnum's Museum. An American comedy founded on a French story was written by John Brougham (also an actor) and was performed in the fall of 1855 at Wallack's Lyceum Theatre, an elegant little house that played English comedy and domestic dramas as its chief attractions. A native of New York, Mrs. Sidney F. Bateman, wrote a play, *Self,* somewhat similar to *Fashion,* and it played at Burton's Chambers Street Theatre on October 27, 1856.

Some of the notable American stage personalities of the age were: Louisa Lane (Mrs. John Drew), Charlotte Cushman, Edward L. Davenport, Edwin Forrest, and Edwin Booth. American dancers included: George Washington Smith, Mary Anne Lee, Julia Turnbull, and Augusta Maywood.

The arts in this era were memorable in that they were improvising, originating, and adding to the basics, keeping pace with the moods and needs of the people. In striving to appeal to the masses, artists must have penetrated the shell of indifference and planted seeds of culture that would continue to grow. Man was made aware as never before of the beauty of nature by the literature he read, the paintings he saw, by the lectures and music he heard. A freshness and naturalness in art evolved that went very well with the American way. and to counterbalance this naturalness was the elaborate ornateness that the materialistic society offered. It made a pleasing balance on the art scales that would serve as a challenge to future American arts.

Section III

PROGRESSIVE AMERICA

10
Inventions and Theoretical Discoveries

No historian has successfully explained the cause of the tremendous surge of scientific invention in the period of 1840–1860. The bright men of the day, regardless of their formal education or financial status, had a mental common denominator—an inquiring and imaginative mind. This was true in all fields of endeavor. The inventor's ability to combine the abstract with the practical was outstanding in this era.

This golden age of invention resulted in far more than a series of patented workable inventions, operating in a practical manner, for the benefit of those people then alive. For every practical invention, there were tenfold that number of theories too far advanced in conception to take a practical form in that age. For example, Joseph Henry succeeded, in 1840, in transmitting the first electric radio wave impulse. Lack of supporting mechanical discoveries would leave future generations to explore the vast field of air communications. With this period of history as a background, it is no wonder that Jules Verne's imaginative writings reflected the broad horizon of the day, and the prophetic visions portrayed in his stories would continue to astonish the later generations.

The field of communications and man's ability to transmit news quickly received its first great impetus with the invention of Samuel F. B. Morse's newly perfected telegraph in the early 1840s. So rapidly did his invention spread that the telegraph pole, with its multiple wires, became a familiar city sight within a few years. At the time of the Mexican War, the leading American cities had already been joined together by the telegraph, thus it helped to relay fresh news from the war front. Wire communications with Europe were established in 1858 when the first partially successful transatlantic cable had been completed. As new uses for the telegraph were found, the horizon widened. The fire alarm telegraph system became a reality in 1852 and was patented in 1857 by Farmer and Channing. The theory of police protection through the use of an alarm system telegraph was being developed.[1] Central bureaus, using the telegraph for gathering and dispersing data, were being established. The Smithsonian Institute, through Joseph Henry's insistence, had established a central point at the institute for gathering information on weather data. It was Matthew F. Maury who envisioned a use for the weather data. Maury was a man of definite convictions and an outstanding theorist. His character was described by his contemporaries as pompous, obstinate, petty, visionary, great! Many of the theories he propounded were for the benefit of all mankind; many became vast new fields for future study and exploration.

One of Maury's visions in the late 1850s was to organize a farmer's agricultural weather bureau. The proposed bureau would notify farmers in advance of storms or disturbances that might affect their crops. To complete the proposal, he suggested that the weather data gathered by the Smithsonian be sent by telegraphic bulletins to sections of the country that might be affected by expected stormy weather. Cooperating jointly, in this field of weather theory, Joseph Henry foresaw gathering data and Matthew Maury foresaw distribution through communications of accumulated facts to the various interested fields. "Physical geography makes the whole world kin," Maury later wrote.

However, Matthew Maury's outstanding talents were

Courtesy The Peale Museum, Baltimore, Md.
A famous Baltimore locomotive inventor, Ross Winans,
built a new conception for water travel in 1858 (above). It
was a surface ship and made one round trip to Norfolk, but
proved impractical for future use.

in the field of Oceanography. In his book *The Physical Geography of the Sea,* two of his broad and astounding theories were described in his chapters "The Basin of the Atlantic" and "The Depths of the Oceans." Another chapter "Influence of the Gulf Stream upon Climates" was best summed up in an 1873 quotation regarding his work: "Truth emerges out of error rather than out of chaos," explaining that while Maury's theories might not have been correct in detail, they were correct and valid theories to be inherited by future generations for completion of the correcting details. Maury also advanced the theory that "the inhabitants of the oceans are as much the creatures of climate as are those of dry land."

While many of the ideas set forth by Maury would remain untested in this era, other Americans of this age were beginning to explore the vast underwater world by physical means. Underwater treasure hunts were gaining widespread interest. In the summer of 1849,

a group of young men from Boston organized a party to recover the treasure reputed to be aboard the English brig *Plumper.* His Majesty's ship had been sunk in 1812 about 44 miles up the coast from Eastport, Maine. The treasure hunters had information that the ship had gone down off a cliff in 60 feet of water at a point between Depper Harbor and Point Lepreau (Canada). After locating the wreck, the diving party used an apparatus made of "india-rubber," probably designed by one of the divers for this expedition. An air tube connected the recovery boat and the diver's apparatus. Air was forced down through the tube by a small steam-engine pump. Information had placed the amount of money aboard the *Plumper* when she sank at £74,000. The treasure party, despite summer storms and high tides, were able to recover about $2,000 by August. Most of the salvaged coins found were of silver, although some of the treasure was gold.[2]

Other Americans were being attracted toward the

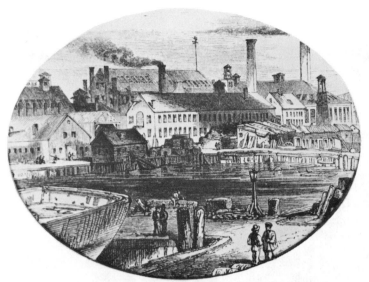

A view of the Novelty Iron Works from the East River, New York City. The Novelty Works was a huge plant for constructing steamships, from the drawing board to completion. In 1848, the company employed 600 men and had an average weekly payroll of $5,400. By 1851, the working force grew to 1,000 to 1,200 men.

development of a practical submarine as a way to explore the underseas. The idea of a submarine was not new when L. Alexander announced, jointly with the American Institute, that he had at last perfected a diving ship in 1852. Mr. Alexander stated that the express purpose of his submarine would be to study and explore the bottoms of rivers, lakes, and harbors, to recover from sunken vessels, or, anticipating a future use, to mine the underwater gold fields. Further, he projected that it would be used to lay underwater wires for the telegraph. A successful descent was made off

Castle Garden (New York Harbor) on October 28, 1852, when a depth of 35 feet was reached. On the dive, the ship carried a crew of seven men, who brought up specimens of rock from the river bottom as proof of their achievement. Later, Alexander made public the construction details of his submarine; it included a fresh air system, designed to provide air for up to seven hours for a crew of six men. A system of compressed air valves equalized the cabin pressure with that of the water. This feature made it possible to open the underside hatch for exploration and close observation of the sea bottom. The cigar-shaped craft was 30 feet long and 10 feet wide. It was powered by a screw propeller and had a system of compressed air pumps, which raised or lowered the submarine.[3]

Ships, boats, yachts, rowboats, and their accompanying accessories all came in for their share of improvements, particularly in the 1850s. The steam-powered screw-driven boat was fast becoming an accepted fact in this era. But already men were seeking to make the screw propeller obsolete. In 1847, a new advanced idea was proposed; it was called a "Fumic Propeller." The simple device consisted of a pipe extended through the stern of a boat; heated air was forced through the pipe by means of a bellows, thus driving the craft forward— a forerunner of jet propulsion. The quest for an unsinkable boat or lifeboat had its school of adherents. Probably the best unsinkable lifeboat was the one displayed by Charles Goodyear at the Crystal Palace Exhibition in London, 1851.[4] His portable boat was made of "india-rubber" and had air chambers on each side for buoyancy. Also, among the multitude of inventions for unsinkable boats, there were many made of wood or iron. Leaders in patents issued for boating accessories were

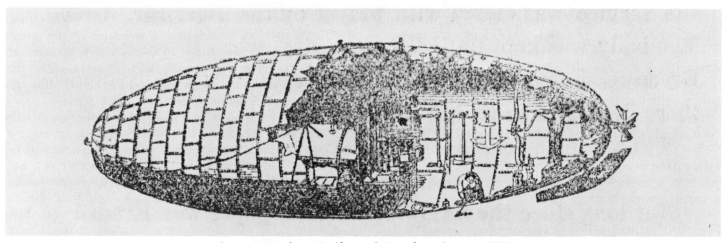

A cutaway view of Alexander's submarine of 1852.

Inventions and improvements had made the marine steam engine capable of driving large ships. The drawing above shows the engine-room of the Humboldt, a new Atlantic steamer in 1851.

life jackets, preservers, and improvements on the breeches buoy.

Professor Moses G. Farmer may have gained recognition through the invention of a fire alarm system, but as a dreamer of the future he had few equals. Back in 1847, he had constructed a miniature electric train consisting of two cars. The "engine car" had self-sustaining batteries and a built-in motor to run the train. In portraying his vision, he pictured a future rail travel by means of electricity as the motivating power, one that would be universally adopted. Later, Professor Farmer, in the year 1859, managed to wire a house for electric lighting, using incandescent lamps for the light. Thomas A. Edison would perfect this working theory at a later date in history.

Many Americans were thinking in terms of personal or family transportation. In its issue of October 2, 1845, Rufus Porter, editor of the newly established *Scientific American* printed a lithograph of his proposed "steam carriage" for the common road. In detail it showed a

steam engine built on the rear of a large four-wheel open carriage. Two bench-type seats were placed on the forward part of the chassis. The operator-driver could steer the vehicle by means of a lever connected with the front wheels. The pictured automobile was forecast as "the common man's transportation by 1850." Small details as to who would feed wood fuel to the steam engine or where the fuel supply would be placed on the vehicle were not made clear. Nevertheless, the theory for private automotive travel did exist, although it would not become a reality for many years.

Patents for railroad improvements made up a substantial portion of the total patents issued during the 1840–1860 period of American history. Lasting and renowned rail inventions were patented in this era. For example, William Howe patented his truss frame bridge in 1840 and on July 16, 1842, John A. Roebling's patent for his "stranded wire rope cable" was issued. This ingenious cable would make the long suspension bridge a reality. In 1842, and within a few days of each other,

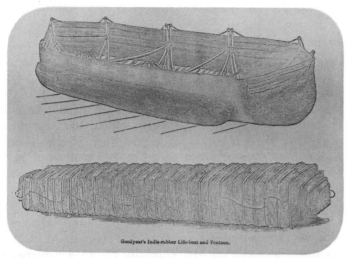

Goodyear's India-rubber Life-boat and Pontoon.

Charles Goodyear (1800–1860), from his original process to vulcanize rubber, was issued more than 60 patents for its various applications and uses. Above is a sketch of his exhibit at the International Exhibition, Crystal Palace, London, 1851.

"The common man's transportation by 1850." A drawing from the Scientific American *of October 2, 1845.*

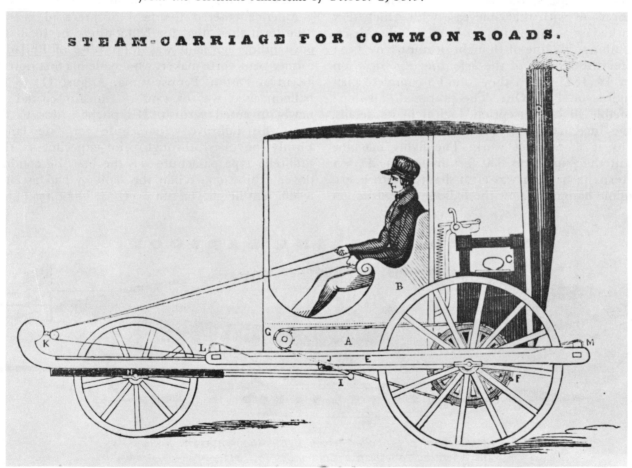

STEAM-CARRIAGE FOR COMMON ROADS.

R. L. Stevens and M. W. Baldwin patented their famous locomotives. John H. Tims of Newark, New Jersey, patented what would become a standard of rail equipment, his bearing and oil box for railroad cars in 1844. Car couplings, seat chairs, rail wheels, devices for clearing the right-of-way—all were being steadily improved. The story of the many rail innovations was that by 1860 the American public was using the finest railroads in the world and had far outdistanced Europe in this field.

Man's quest to ascend from the earth and to travel by air transportation was not new in 1840. Earlier, in 1804, J. L. Gay-Lussac, under the auspices of the French Academy of Science, had risen to a height of almost 23,000 feet, using a balloon for the ascension. No one had yet invented a practical means to propel a balloon through the air, but in 1836, two Englishmen ascending in "The Great Nassau" balloon had made an incredible journey of 500 miles in eighteen hours, using air currents as the propellent.

After the discovery of hydrogen gas, many extravagant projects dazzled and bewildered the minds of men. Many envisioned that the time was not far distant when men would be embarking on a trip to the moon or to Mercury, Venus, Mars, the asteroids, or some of the other planets—all with the same ease with which they now embarked on a ship bound for France, Italy, Africa, or China. Along this line of thought, it must have been thrilling for the readers of the *Scientific American* on September 18, 1845, when they found a complete plan for a dirigible on Page One. The proposed "air-ship" was reasonable in its conception, logical in its details, and to the imagination of the reader, there was no reason why it should not work. The flying machine pictured in the paper was 350 feet in length, 35 feet in diameter; the balloon was cigar-shaped, with a spacious gondola hanging below the balloon. Construction

details proposed that the balloon section be made of a strong linen cloth and filled with hydrogen gas for buoyancy. Two jet-like pipes for the exhaust of the steam engines extended from the rear of the gondola. A sixteen foot spiral fan wheel powered by the engines drove the craft forward. The inventor, Rufus Porter, claimed it could attain a speed of 100 miles per hour. He also proposed mooring the lighter-than-air craft to a mast 100 feet above the ground. No record exists of whether the proposed dirigible was constructed; presumably it never left the drawing board. However, some work was done on a power-driven balloon in 1849. Its purpose was to speed gold miners to California at 200 miles per hour. While its projected use was popular, it, too, was not completed. Mr. John Wise, in telling of its failure in 1850, said: "Had these projectors gone on from their miniature model, to the erection of one capable of carrying one or two persons, in order to prove its practicability on a larger scale, there might have been reason to believe that they harbored an idea of its general usefulness." But the dream of air transportation by dirigible would remain unsatisfied until Count Zeppelin constructed his Zeppelin IV in 1908, and even then it would resemble the 1845 version.

America entered the field of practical aeronautics (the term then used for ballooning) in 1838. Its first outstanding aeronaut was John Wise of Philadelphia, former pianoforte maker, who made his first noteworthy ascent at Easton, Pennsylvania, August 11, 1838. The balloon used was of cambric muslin coated with a newly invented varnish. His purpose was to demonstrate his improved "parachute for safe landings." Firmly convinced, through prior experiments, that the umbrella type parachute was the best, he conducted a novel exhibition. When the balloon had ascended to a sufficient height, he put overboard first a cat and then

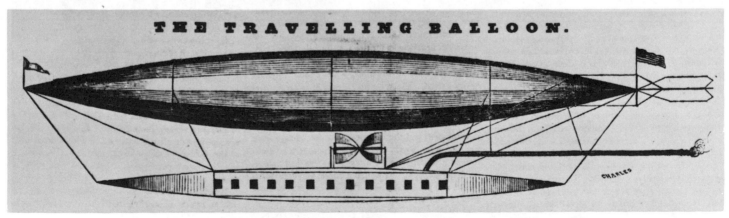

A sketch of a propeller driven lighter-than-air craft. From the Scientific American *of September 18, 1845.*

Aerial View of Boston, 1860

Professor Samuel A. King, cooperating with James W. Black, a photographer, took this remarkable view of Boston from a balloon. King, like John Wise, was one of the pioneer aeronauts experimenting in "ballooning" in this era.

a dog, each of which parachuted safely to earth. The results of this successful trial caused Mr. Wise to proclaim loudly that in the fall of the same year he would explode an ascended balloon, and, with the remains of the balloon, he would parachute to earth. He did go through with his project and, while it was not nearly so dramatic as formerly claimed, he did make a safe landing.

In the years following 1838, Mr. Wise became a world figure in aeronautics. He developed a theory that the prevailing winds above the earth's surface blew at a rate of 20 to 60 miles per hour, depending on the elevation. In early 1843 he proposed a transatlantic aerial trip carrying a crew of three men. The envisioned balloon would have a gondola car shaped like a sea boat and would include portable masts in case of balloon failure. John Wise petitioned Congress for financial support, and in his petition he expanded his pro-

posals to include a trip around the world. The projected trip would cross Europe and China, dispatching airmail along the route. He would then reenter the United States, coming in over Oregon territory and ending at Washington City. He estimated that it would take from 30 to 40 days for the world trip. His petition was turned over to the committee of naval affairs, who did not make a report—deeming the entire scheme of doubtful practicability and safety.[5] In the years following 1843, Wise became an increasingly prominent figure in aeronautics. In 1851, he suggested bombing from an airship, and in 1859, he had the satisfaction of carrying airmail on the longest balloon flight in the nineteenth century, a distance of 1,120 miles, making a record not broken until 1900.

In this era there were developments in other fields of science concerning the heavens. In the weighty realm of abstract mathematical science, Benjamin Peirce, expounder of theories pertaining to the universe, was the first American to gain international recognition as both mathematician and astronomer. His original and creative works brought a definite respect, for the first time, from the intellectual elite and academies of Europe. As early as 1843, Peirce's mathematical calculations, created by a new form of binary arithmetic, clarified certain astronomical problems. In 1846, he challenged the Frenchman, Leverrier, discoverer of the planet Neptune. Mathematically, Peirce proved the Frenchman wrong. Much later, calculations proved them both wrong! Peirce taught mathematics at Harvard College for almost fifty years. In 1853, he advanced the theory that science and the Bible have equal authority, but each in its own sphere. Thus, in a way, he somewhat put aside the tremendous academic controversy raging in this era over the Darwin theory and the adherents of Darwinism.

Photography, too, made its contribution to astronomy. John A. Whipple of Boston exhibited his daguerreotype of the moon at the Crystal Palace fair at London in 1851. It was the first example of a magnified celestial body and had been taken through the telescope at the Cambridge (U. S.) Observatory. The diameter of the image was $4\frac{7}{8}$ inches, nearly twice the size of any former impressions. The cost of the daguerreotype, including the instrument that made it possible, was reputed to be $25,000. After the fair, Whipple went on and projected a 13-inch diameter of the moon on a daguerreotype.[6]

If America in the 1840–1860 period be generally separated into large fields of endeavor, it would be found that agriculture and general industry would be the twin giants—each competing for the labor talent available

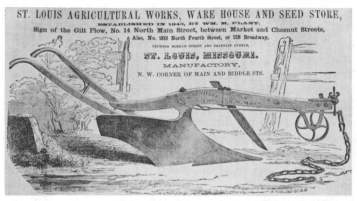

ST. LOUIS AGRICULTURAL WORKS, WARE HOUSE AND SEED STORE,
ESTABLISHED IN 1842, BY WM. M. PLANT.
Sign of the Gilt Plow, No. 14 North Main Street, between Market and Chesnut Streets,
Also, No. 203 North Fourth Street, or 218 Broadway,
BETWEEN MORGAN STREET AND FRANKLIN AVENUE,
ST. LOUIS, MISSOURI.
MANUFACTORY,
N. W. CORNER OF MAIN AND BIDDLE STS.

Courtesy the Georgia Historical Society
An advertisement from the Southern Pictorial Advertiser,
*1858, showing one of the "Deep Tiller" plows being offered
to the farmer.*

in the era. Agriculture was advancing rapidly and its progress was far more than just the employment of mechanical inventions or their improvement. Much of the increased food production could be attributed to the efforts of the individual farmer. Many farmers, like their contemporaries in other fields, had inquiring minds and were busy experimenting not only with developing new hybrids but also with devising new fertilizing methods to increase plant growth.

The American Institute held a fair annually in New York City. Because of its great size and its range of fields, it could be considered as a measure of the nation's growth. Typical of these fairs was the one that opened in October, 1852. Here the production examples of 24 states were displayed. Competitive showings included: farm livestock, produce, flower offerings, agricultural implements and manufactures, and mechanics' art. At each section new items were proudly displayed and talked about. Vegetables and fruits, more than any other category, presented new and often startling varieties and strains. At one of the many booths C. W. Forbush of Massachusetts exhibited a "Peach Blow Potatoe" weighing 17½ ounces—grown from a sprout and not planted in the usual manner, he said. And Mr. J. P. Girand, Jr., at another booth, had on display two new varieties of hybrid corn; he called them "The Golden Spike" and "The Golden Sioux." The Golden Spike was an eight-row corn, averaging from 10 to 13 inches per ear. A new apple strain, "Sherwood's Wax Apple," was shown by L. W. Annan of New York City. A high degree of interest was created by a display of artificial, or as it was called, "Composition Model" fruit, displayed by Mr. Townsend Glover. It had been so faithfully created and copied that many of the viewers were deluded into believing that they had seen natural fruit;

a decayed spot, here and there, helped to complete the illusion. Mr. Glover would not reveal the nature of his new composition fruit but stated flatly that "they were not made of wax."[7]

The name of John Jay Mapes dominated the agricultural section of the fair. Mapes, a man of multiple talents and interests, had invented back in 1832 a sugar-refining system; its principles were used throughout the entire nineteenth century. After 1832, he became a chemical analytic expert on beer and wine and contributed improvements on the then-current distilling methods. Between 1835 and 1838, Mapes became a professor of chemistry and natural philosophy of colors at the National Academy of Design in New York City. He had gained the chair through recognition as an amateur painter and as an experimenter with pigments of colors. Switching to a related field in 1840, he edited the *American Repertory of Arts, Sciences and Manufacturers* until 1843, when he became an associate editor of the *Journal of the Franklin Institute*. Through his recognized abilities, he became president of the Mechanics' Institute, New York, in 1845. In 1847 he became vice-president of the American Institute. Turning back to his interest in agriculture, he bought a "worn-out" farm just south of Newark, New Jersey, in 1847. By 1852, working out his ideas and theories, he had created a model farm, and it had become an unofficial national headquarters for agriculture, particularly in the field of agricultural chemistry and experiments in fertilization and subsoil plowing. Mapes, throughout the 1850s, became the country's leading agriculturist and discoverer of the first synthetic fertilizer—"superphosphate of lime" which he finally patented in 1859. He again turned to writing in 1863, when he founded and edited *The Working Farmer*. John Mapes passed on in 1866, and it was then that astute Horace Greeley observed: "Few men have delivered more addresses at agricultural fairs, or have done more lasting good by them. Certainly American agriculture owes as much to him as to any man who lives or has ever lived." So it was not surprising, even at the 1852 fair, that the opinions and judgments of Mapes were the dominating factors of the American Institute reports in the agricultural field. (One item of minor interest in the Institute's report of 1852 stated that experiments on the effect of electricity on plants had proved of no value.) [8]

Many items of interest displayed at the 1852 exhibition were not only for the farmer's interest but also for the consumer public. One entry was a watering pot with two outlets on the spout. The roses (stoppers) for the two outlets, one of which had a hole, were interchangeable—a convenient way to water indoor plants. Fowler's patented "self-rising flour," a bread-rising compound, was shown in detail. Among the miscellaneous items was a patented covering to preserve hams on a long voyage.

In 1850 more than 118 million acres of improved farm land was in operation, and, in addition, there were 184 million acres of unimproved land that was used for farm purposes. Approximately 4,000,000 people were engaged in the cultivation of land. The estimated worth of implements and machinery on the farms was $151,- 569,675. The tendency toward agricultural mechaniza- tion had been one of steady expansion, so by the start of this era it is not surprising to find a rush of creative talent bent on devising new farm machinery. The story of the development of the reaper began in 1833 when the first patent was issued to Obed Hassey of Ohio, soon followed by Cyrus H. McCormick's patented reaper in 1834. From the offset, keen competition had caused each man repeatedly to improve his machine. By 1845, McCormick had perfected his reaper to such a degree that it had gained widespread farmer acceptance. A

Courtesy The Peale Museum, Baltimore, Md.
The port of Baltimore about 1851. The observatory, above, center, flew a house flag to alert the merchants of the city that a ship had safely arrived. Baltimore became a center for the importation of raw materials necessary to manufacture the "new type fertilizers."

description by the *Chicago Journal* in that year de- scribed the reaper machine as being pulled by two horses, with a boy to drive. A man was seated on the side of the machine, and it was his task to rake off the wheat in bunches ready for binding. But the real heart of the reaper was in its cutting action. A series of curved

fingers at intervals along the blade held the stalks of grain for the sawing action of the vibrating knife. With the McCormick reaper of 1845, it was claimed that between 15 and 20 acres of wheat could be cut in a single day! Hussey, too, had improved his machine and he and McCormick shared a market in which thousands of machines were being sold each year. By 1850, fac- tory production of McCormick's reaper had reached 1,600 machines and further expansion was necessary because he had just signed a contract with England to supply 500 machines for its next harvest season. Later, McCormick made one other major improvement to his now-famous reaper: he added the patented endless belt conveyor to his machine in 1858. Threshing and win- nowing machines, grain separators, improvements in mills for grinding grains—all were being developed and patented in large numbers. George Westinghouse, of Schoharie, New York, patented a threshing and win- nowing machine of merit in 1844. Rakes, shovels, wheel- barrows, cultivators, and plows, made of wrought iron, were all helping the farmer ease his burden. Farm wagons, used to spread manure on the fields, were being steadily improved. Improved hay presses, cotton presses, and machines for preparing tobacco for pressing were being offered the farm market. In the year 1844 alone, six patents were issued for cotton presses. And for the farmer's wife, new cheese presses and butter churns were being developed to lighten the chore of producing foods on the farm. John L. Mason's jar was the solution to preserve fresh fruits and vegetables in 1857. One di- rect result of increased agricultural efficiency was that, by 1850, farmers were rapidly becoming an affluent sec- tion of American society. A typical section of the na- tion's farm belt was that of central New Jersey in 1850. The United States census for this year showed the aver- age farmer of Mercer County to have a net worth of $17,500, considerably more than his city brother.

Production and speed were the bywords of industrial expansion in this new age of the steam engine. The broad horizon of mechanical invention gave license to American ingenuity. Machines began to replace men; still, manpower shortages were acute despite European immigration. Labor-saving devices were in great de- mand. The cycle to an industrial giant had begun! From the tinkering Yankee to the profound thinker and those of like bent, all found a ready and eager mar- ket for their inventions and gadgets. And in industry, as in other fields, there were men not ready to com- promise their vision of the future with that of ready fame and fortune. One visionary felt that the use of electricity to replace steam power must come. The pro- pounder of this theory was Professor Charles Grafton

Prior inventions for preserving foods, such as Arthur's patented can (above), were made obsolete when Mason introduced his easy method of canning in 1857.

Page. He stated in 1850: "There can be no further doubt as to the application of this power as a substitute for steam." To support his theory, Professor Page exhibited an electro-magnetic engine of between four and

1849
An unknown machinist holding a calibrated rosewood rule.

five horsepower at the Smithsonian Institute in 1850. Batteries had been used to supply electricity, and the entire apparatus, including motor and engine, measured three cubic feet and weighed about one ton. Page's machine had a reciprocating type of engine, which had a two-foot stroke and a capable output of 80 strokes a minute. To demonstrate its effectiveness as a practical machine, the professor had attached a 10-inch circular saw blade to its power head, and it had been able to cut up to 1¼ inch boards. Financially, he proved that the machine could compete with steam, that for every three pounds of zinc it consumed per day, it would produce one horsepower.[9] The story of Page's struggle with the electric motor had been a long one. As an early pioneer in the field of electricity, he had experimented with the induction coil, and by 1837 he had developed a successful one. Page, again like many of his contemporaries, had been a man whose fields of interest were many and wide—electricity, medicine, chemistry, and rose culture —all had challenged his talent. An acknowledgment of his ability had come with his appointment as one of two patent examiners in 1841. Still experimenting, he made his first small-scale reciprocating electro-magnetic motor in 1846. Congress made an appropriation in 1849 for Page to continue his work in this field. The one-ton unit he displayed at the Smithsonian had been completed in early 1850, and in 1851 he built a second motor—a twin to the first. To test his theory that electric power could replace steam, he constructed a locomotive to carry his two one-ton motors. The locomotive attained the speed of 19 miles per hour on a five-mile test run. The results of the test had proved that electricity could be used for power; however, it had also pointed out that batteries were incapable of providing electricity for sustained operation, and it would be left for future generations to explore the self-sustaining electric vehicle.

Steam power had come of age and improvements for a more efficient steam engine were being explored; the smaller details necessary for the refinement of the steam engine were being developed. A new valve-regulating system to control the steam was patented by George H. Corliss in 1849. Patent reissues on his original system came in 1851 and 1859. Meanwhile, Corliss had founded his own steam engine works in Providence, Rhode Island. He said his engine ran with 25 percent more efficiency than those of other makers. To back up his claim, he offered a unique sales presentation. His steam engines were sold on consignment; his price was a fixed percentage for the life of the machine, based on the cost of the fuel saved.

Other inventors used a different approach to improve the steam engine. They felt that a better method

1856
Water power was harnessed by New England towns for the manufacture of its many products. The river at Saco, Maine (above), fell about 55 feet and provided the community with excellent water power. Ambrotype by A. R. Davis.

for the condensation of steam might be the answer. The use of Pirsson's Double Vacuum Steam Condenser, so it was claimed, reduced fuel costs.[10] And for the ship's steam engine, the problem of converting salt water to fresh remained only partially solved in this era.

In general, to harness a steam engine's power and to utilize its energy for the machinery it would operate, a connecting link was necessary. The system used by industry in this age was a belt and a pulley, or a series of them, to link the power engine with one or more machines. The endless belt was made of leather and the specialty trade producing it was searching for an improvement on the quality of the leather. Hides were imported from Argentina, Mexico, and England. Time tests, in terms of percentages of weights gained, and ex-

periments with oak and hemlock were being made in the process of tanning. The efforts by the trade in this era produced a better endless belt—one with enough quality to become a standard for many years to come.

The problem of producing sheet metal—gold, silver, copper, and other metals—of uniform thickness and quality had become an urgent one in the early 1840s. Heavy cast steel rollers with conventional cogs had been a partial solution but variations were still occurring. The answer to improved sheet metal production was a simple one; Blake and Johnson of Waterbury, Massachusetts, invented and manufactured pairs of rollers in which the cogs, instead of being parallel to the shaft, were "spiral form angular" to insure a steadiness when rolling sheets of metal.

The connecting link between the power source and the machine was the "pulley and belt."

At the great exhibition held in London's Crystal Palace in 1851, the water pump displayed by the American, James Gwynne, probably excited but very little interest in the average sightseer. Invented and patented by Gwynne, it was a radical departure from earlier pumps then in use. It was a centrifugal pump, and it had a potential of pumping up to 100,000 gallons of water per minute.[11] The invention brought an immediate change to fire fighting techniques in the 1850s. The pump's principles would make possible a solution for future large drainage problems and would be instrumental in the construction of future large water and steam turbines.

Gold mining in California created a new demand for industrial products. By the mid-1850s the solitary miner was almost a thing of the past; big business had moved in and with it technical skill and machinery for mining and mass-producing gold. Hydraulic and other methods for mining ore in large quantities were introduced. To keep pace with the large volume of ore, an immediate market opened for a more efficient rock-crushing machine. One of the most effective machines for rock crushing was invented by John W. Cochran. It was made to pulverize gold, and also iron, zinc, copper, and lead ores. Cochran's machine used a steam-driven band for power and could perfectly pulverize in excess of 7,000 pounds of raw materials per hour. His invention made obsolete the stamping-type machine that had been previously used.

The magic word "steel" emerged in this era. William Kelly, a Pittsburgh dry goods merchant, experimented independently, although along the same line of inquiry as Bessemer of England, and he was able to demonstrate his first successful steel furnace at Johnstown, Pennsylvania, in 1851. He patented his new process for making steel on June 23, 1857. In the ensuing years, a controversy developed between the Kelly and Bessemer interests as to the priority of patent rights. The dispute was established in Kelly's favor, and eventually the two interests merged, making possible the large steel industry of the future.

American manufacturers of woodworking machines were eclipsing the Europeans in this era. J. A. Fay's tenoning machine (1840) had replaced hand labor for

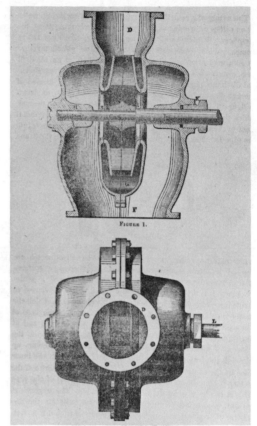

Three cutaway drawings illustrating the interior of "Gwynne's Centrifugal Balance Pump." The Gwynne pump revolutionized fire-fighting techniques.

1857   *Courtesy Time-Out Antiques, N.Y.C.*
*The solitary miner had given way to large mining operations,
as illustrated above. It is probably a scene of Murderer's Bar,
a bend in the middle fork of the American River in Placer
County, California. It was here that one of the earliest attempts was made to turn the course of a large river to explore the bottom for gold. The company at Murderer's Bar
was owned by 75 men and employed 200 workmen in the
dry season. The bulwarks diverting the river were washed
away in the rainy season and the river would then go back
to its original bed. The next dry season the works would be
reconstructed and new gold, washed down by the river,
would be found. Financially, the operation at Murderer's
Bar was highly successful.*

making a mortise and tenon joint with wood. A result
of Fay's invention was that the use of the tongue and
groove joint became widespread by the 1850 decade in
the manufacture of many small wooden items and was
a standard procedure in milling lumber. Two patents,
Greenleaf and Cole's (U. S. pat., 1493) and Dresser's

(U. S. pat., 1758), for cutting veneers were also issued
in 1840. Dresser's patent was a rotary cutter to peel a
veneer from logs, thus insuring the conservation of fine
woods and a foundation for a future plywood industry.
Although the idea of a band saw was not new, the first
practical and workable one was invented by Lemuel

Cochran's Quartz-crushing Machine.

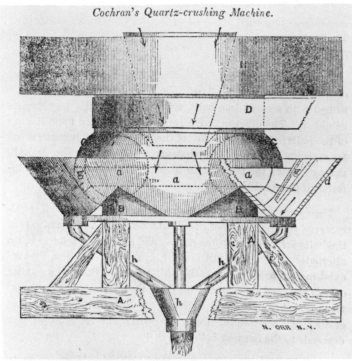

Mr. John W. Cochran of New York City claimed that his new machine was particularly effective in the granulation of gold-bearing quartz.

The dovetailing machine, above, was one of the many varied and useful inventions devised by Ari Davis, who was one of America's most prolific inventors during this era.

Hedge in 1849. The first wood milling machine was invented by F. W. Howe; it was manufactured and marketed by Robbins and Lawrence of Windsor, Vermont, and became world famous. By the early 1850s the Americans had gone beyond simple basic improvements and were producing relatively sophisticated woodworking machines like the one invented by Ari Davis titled "Dovetailing Machine." This machine, with its numbered saws and clamps, could mitre wood corners and insert metal reinforcings in the mitred joints—its principal use was in making wood picture frames.[12]

Perhaps in this American age of discoveries, no single item of small personal convenience received more inventive effort than the clock. Not discounting improvements made to the conventional clock in all shapes, sizes, and forms, two new and unique varieties were introduced. One was an electric clock powered by batteries, which was displayed proudly by its inventor, William Bond of Boston, in 1851, at the Crystal Palace, London. The other was a specialty clock marketed by J. H. Hawes of Ithaca, New York, in that same year, called a "Counting House Calendar Clock." Each of the two models Hawes had invented gave the time of the day, the name of the day, and the date of the month and year, all at a glance.

The invention of the "safety elevator" by Elisha

Graves Otis would change the architecture of cities; future planners would construct tall buildings. Otis demonstrated his first successful full-size elevator at the American Institute's fair in 1854. In his sensational exhibition, he raised his safety elevator to some height and deliberately cut the ropes supporting the elevator to illustrate his effective invention. In 1861, he patented a steam-power-operated safety elevator.

During the first half of the nineteenth century, America had made tremendous strides in mass education, and as a result, with more and more people able to read, the demand for newspapers had increased. A swift new method of newspaper printing to replace the old flat bed system was an urgent need by 1840. The first step in the quest for a more rapid printing process came in 1841, when Delcambre and Young invented a machine for type-composing, a forerunner to the many type-

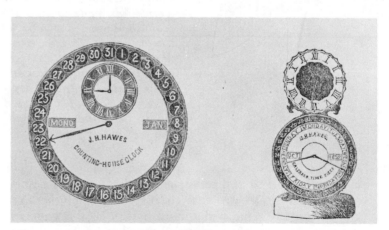

The American Institute awarded the Hawes clock a gold medal in 1852. The clockmaker claimed "no changing or winding during the year."

setting machines to follow. The other complementary part to quicker newspaper production came in 1846, when Robert M. Hoe patented his rotary or "Lightning" press. The "Hoe Type Revolving Machine" was the first to use securely fastened type on a large central cylinder fixed horizontally. Hoe's original machine also became the basic invention for innumerable future improvements, which would provide ever-faster and more accurate newsprinting for the public.

Personal comforts, a new experience to each generation, took on a fresh outlook in the 1840–1860 era. A widening circle of demand was created by the ever-increasing numbers of middle-class Americans who were now looking for longer life, better health, and greater creature comforts in daily living. Ways to achieve all of these were being investigated by men of this Utopian age. A milestone had been reached in 1840 when henceforth the field of dentistry would separate from that of

1857

A Rural Industrial Town
From the drawing board to the finished product, new inventions were entering the commercial market from the many small rural industrial towns throughout America.

general medicine. Health booklets for oral hygiene were being issued by the professional dentists, urging people to brush their teeth one or more times a day—"the best time [was] after each meal." The two cleaning agents recommended were the bark of the wild cherry tree or a compound of orris-root, prepared chalk, and magnesia.[13] The new scientific art of dentistry gained prestige in this era in the field of anaesthetics when Dr. Horace Wells, a dentist, discovered laughing gas (nitrous oxide) in 1844. Following Dr. Wells's success, another dentist, Dr. W. T. G. Morton of Boston, was the first to use ether as an anaesthetic. These discoveries opened a new era for surgery. The use of chloroform soon followed. By 1850, so widespread had become the use of anaesthetics that the popular monthly magazines were critically comparing the odors and aftereffects of ether and chloroform. The use of dentures was perfected in about 1846–1847 by a Dr. John Allen of New York City, and was improved in 1855 by Charles Goodyear, who thought of vulcanized caoutchouc as a denture base.

The traditional peg leg was being outmoded by the development of artificial arms and legs made of cork. The art of plastic surgery (nose) was being practiced in Cincinnati, Ohio, in 1845. For the sensitive bald man, a number of wig improvements began with William Dowell's patented wig in December, 1842, and for the ladies there were patented preparations for cleansing dandruff and beautifying the human hair. Contraceptives, too, were being patented by various inventors—J. Jennings patented a pessary in January, 1843, and in July of that year a pessary and uterine supporter were recorded.

Humor was often mixed with the Utopian inventions. One was the "Victorian Pap Spoon." The humorist declared "it would feed the babies, serves as a baby jumper, rocks the cradle, draws the baby's wagon, plays with the poodle, takes paregoric, and washes out diapers. As a nursery assistant it is indispensable." But help for the mother was not all humor, for in 1851 an automatic rocking cradle was patented. It had a canopy top and a gentle rocking motion to lull the baby to sleep. Mothers had a real helper on the market just a few years before, one of the greatest inventions of the era—a simple safety pin! Another simple long-lasting product of the age was Hyman Lipman's patent of 1857—the first pencil with an eraser. The quest for the fountain pen began, with its first patent issued on September 9, 1843.

The handmade clothing for the male, which had held sway through the ages, was losing out to style and ready-made factory-produced garments. "Seamless cloth"

for male clothing was offered to the consumer by 1851. Methods to improve waterproofing of garments had begun with Thomas Roger's patent in 1841. Shoe manufacturers commenced packaging pairs of shoes in cartons and boxes in the 1840s. This helped to outmode the traditional shoe that would fit either foot. By the 1850s, pairs of shoes were commonplace. The fad of the era was a novelty shoe of "india-rubber" made possible through Charles Goodyear's invention.

Comforts for the home—improvements to save time and chores, mechanical inventions to lighten the upkeep of a house—were not overlooked. The appliance most essential in the home was the cooking stove, and its need for improvement was reflected in the 1844 patent records that showed 27 patented cooking stoves; of the 27, only one was not for home use; it was a railway cook stove. New fuels were causing a change in home illumination. The age of whale oil was fast disappearing under the onslaught of the often-patentable hydro-

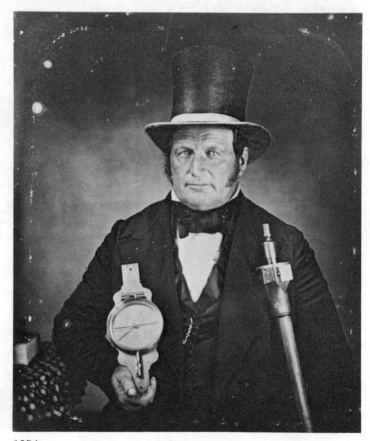

1854

Two patents were issued for the surveyor's compass in the era 1840–1860. The unknown surveyor, above, is holding a surveyor's compass made by R. Patton, New York (left) and a plain Jacob's staff (right).

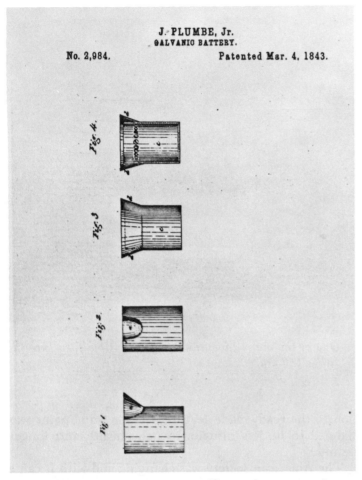

J. PLUMBE, Jr.
GALVANIC BATTERY.

No. 2,984.   Patented Mar. 4, 1843.

John Plumbe, Jr., a man of multiple talents, was also an inventor. While he did not invent the galvanic battery, he patented the improvement illustrated above. For its use, see below. A Plumbe advertisement from an Albany city directory of 1843.

carbon fuels. New lamps and lights to meet lighting styles were being devised. Also, illuminating gas was exacting its toll in the competitive market. The first gas meter was patented by C. F. Brown in June of 1842, opening the way for home gas lights. A patented washing machine in 1843 was designed as a labor-saving device for the housewife. As a further help, Chaffee patented in 1852 a drying machine for clothes, which was hand-geared and used centrifugal force. Public baths had long been common in the cities, but the era of home bathing for the "every-day man" began when Warren patented his portable bath in 1840. Several new models of shower baths made an appearance in 1843. The new *Scientific American* in 1846 highly recommended "Locke's Portable Shower Bath," which was complete with heat. The fashion for private home baths and showers was part of life's picture in 1850. The cast iron bathtub was introduced in 1853, a forerunner to the future built-in home bath, and it became a harbinger of intense competition between the copper and the cast iron tub in the latter part of the nineteenth century.

Gadgets for the kitchen were being turned out in uncommon numbers—apple peelers, butter churns, and cheese presses, in that order, were the leaders. The first mechanical refrigerator was invented in 1851, foreshadowing a future use in the home. For the housewife's convenience in shopping, Benjamin T. Babbitt was first to package soap powder in 1844, and this was followed by Dwight and Church's baking soda in 1846. William Colgate, New York City, won a gold medal for the best "pearl starch" at the American Institute's fair in 1852. A new home ice cream freezer was in use by 1851.

The first murmur of a mechanical sewing machine came when Elias Howe patented his invention in 1846. With its great discovery came a wild rush of novice sewing-machine makers bent on capturing the market, both the industrial trade and the home. In the years following Howe's patent issue, infringements became commonplace, and it was not until 1854 that the rights to the key parts of the sewing machine were finally decided in his favor. When Howe died in 1867, it was estimated that he had realized in excess of $2,000,000 on his invention, thus reflecting the immense size of the industry he had created. The promotion of the sewing machine for use in the home mirrored the success story of Isaac M. Singer. His advertising approach had appealed to the woman in the home and by 1852 he had become the leading sewing-machine manufacturer; he had further been awarded the prize medal of the American Institute.

Home furnishings were not neglected. In March, 1840, a rocking chair had been patented, followed by a

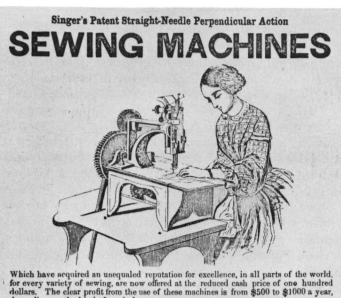

An advertisement from The Illinois and Missouri State Directory, *1854.*

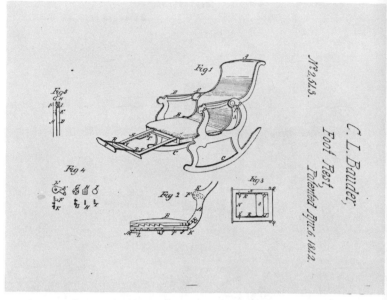

One of the many inventions for convertible furniture in the 1840–1860 era.

"tilting chair" in August of that year. Bauder patented a rocking chair with a footrest in 1842. (This may have led to the first dental chair in 1848.) Carpets for the home, within the reach of the general public's pocketbook, had been the result of Erastus B. Bigelow's invention for weaving Wilton and Brussels carpets.

New paints for maintaining the home had been introduced. A leader was "Brown's Metallic Zinc Paint," a ready-mixed paint aimed at replacing the "White Lead" paint that had to be mixed on the job. In addition to the ready-made feature, the new zinc paint was claimed to be less injurious to the health and longer lasting.[14]

The American society was changing and with it came new buying habits. The specialty store, selling one line of merchandise, had a new competitive threat—the large department store that stocked a wide variety of items, attractively displayed. By 1850 the largest department store in the world was A. T. Stewart and Company, New York City. Stewart's "Marble Palace," called the second most beautiful building in the city, fronted on Broadway and occupied an entire block; it was five stories high and all of its displays provided glamor for the shopper. In Philadelphia, it was L. J. Levy and Company, Chestnut Street—the "Stewart's" of the Quaker City. Like its New York counterpart, Levy and Company had glittering plate-glass windows, but it outdid the Stewart store when it added "a throng of pretty girls who were stationed behind the counters." Each department in Levy's had its own attendants; eighty-four persons were employed in all. To transact a sale, a saleslady marked the price of the purchase on a piece of paper, then struck a bell to call a little boy who took the sales slip and money to the cashier and returned with the change. On the main floor of Levy's a broad staircase led to a gallery above. Below the main floor ran a "ware-room" for storage of boxes and bales. The entire store was illuminated by gas lights, with some special lighting provided for the fitting rooms.[15]

1850   *Courtesy Time-Out Antiques, N.Y.C.*
With the increasing importance of the textile and carpet industries during the era, the weaver was in great demand.

Arts and art crafts were not without their share of inventions and innovations. Those practicing the newly invented "art of Daguerreotyping" had become a firmly established trade group in the first few years of the 1840s. The daguerreotype needed one ingredient to successfully compete with painting—color! The quest for color began almost with photography itself, and in the 1840s many methods and some inventions were publicized. It was the story of Levi L. Hill's search for a photographic image in natural color that became the most important photography news of the era. His startling and interesting announcement that he had succeeded in producing a daguerreotype in color came in *The Magic Buff,* a technical photography manual, in November, 1850. Hill wrote: "Several years of experimentation have led us to the discovery of some remarkable facts in reference to the process of daguerreotyping in colors of nature. For instance, we can produce blue, red, violet and orange on one plate, at one and the same time."

All over the country, newspapers eagerly publicized this great discovery. Daguerreotype sales slumped. The public was waiting to have portraits captured in color!

Efforts were made by the photographic industry to have Hill make his process public, but he patiently explained that while his process was complete, he was still having trouble producing yellows satisfactorily. He also wanted adequate compensation (the U.S. Patent Office was unable to issue a patent to protect Hill's discovery).

By March 21, 1851, Hill had produced 40 specimens of his daguerreotypes in color, three of which he described in detail: "A view, containing a red house, green grass and foliage, the wood color of trees, several cows of different shades of red and brindle, colored garments on the clothesline, blue sky and faint blue atmosphere intervening between the camera, and the distant mountains very delicately spread over the picture as if by the hand of a fairy artist"; the second was "A sunset scene, in which the play of colors on the clouds is impressed a truthfulness and gorgeous beauty which I cannot describe"; the third description related to portraits, "Several portraits, in which I have the true complexion of the skin, the rosy cheeks and lips, blue and hazel eyes, auburn, brown and sandy hair, and every color of drapery." Hill also wrote, "I have a most exquisite type of my little girl (one year old) taken in the act of crying, the plate not having been exposed a full second. At the same time my light required 15 seconds for a daguerreotype. The picture has caught the expression perfectly, both of the eye and the whole face. On one cheek is seen a bright-tear-drop, and the color showing through it much deeper than the surrounding parts; which latter, I suppose is owing to the refractive action of the fluid."

As time went on Hill still did not reveal his process for "hillotypes" to the public—"the invisible goblins of the yellows" were continuing to be troublesome. But many prominent daguerreotypists and artists of the brush visited Hill at his home in the Catskill Mountains and many became enthusiastic adherents of Hill's color process.

Among some of the hillotypes seen and described by Hill's visitors and Hill included: Portraits of living persons, various plates of colored prints, copies of paintings, a rose bush, a blackberry bush, Hill's daughter posed on a trunk, a large color lithograph of the village of Prattsville, New York, and a laboring man with sunburned face, blue eyes, auburn hair, red-flannel shirt, and red and blue cravat.

As time went on and Hill would not make his process public, some of the photography world pronounced him

Levi L. Hill conducted his experiments with color photography at his mountain home located just a few miles away from the famous Mountain House in the wild country of the Catskill Mountains. James Smillie engraved the above scene from a painting by George Harvey.

a fraud. Realizing that he would need backing in order to verify his claim, Hill sought the eye-witness testimony of America's leading inventor, Samuel F. B. Morse, who was also a pioneer daguerreotypist and a capable portrait painter. Morse, a man of recognized integrity, visited Hill in September 1852, viewed his process, and was convinced. One of the hillotypes seen by Morse was of a bird of varied plumage, taken in two seconds, which "showed conclusively that the blues, yellows, and reds were distinctively given and fixed." In another letter to Hill, published in the *New York Times*, October 26, 1852, Morse wrote, "It gives me great pleasure to testify from ocular demonstrations, to the reality of your discovery of a process for fixing the colors of the camera

obscura image . . . whoever builds must build on your foundation."

Hill continued working on his discovery, despite personal difficulties, until about 1855, when he asked, through the medium of the press, that the daguerreians who might still be interested write him regarding his heliochromatic process. He also said he was still having trouble with the yellows. When Hill finally published a book, *A Treatise on Heliochromy,* the interest in color daguerreotypes was as dead as the method itself—other photography methods were becoming popular. The making of a hillotype was explained in detail in Hill's book. Chemical instructions were included in his formula. Hill first cleaned his plate with great care and

era and exposed, a developer was then used to bring out the latent color images. The plate was then fixed and finished by first immersing in a solution, then rinsing and drying. A polish was applied with a soft buckskin, if desired.

Hill frankly stated that he could not chemically explain how he produced color photographs. The only explanation he made in reference to the preparation of plates was "on this one thing, molecular arrangement—the whole phenomenon of coloration depends." Morse said, in referring to Hill's process, "It must be in the hands of no ordinary man, but will require the production of the perfect picture, the taste, the skill, the feeling of thorough and accomplished artists." In Europe, Becquerel and Niepce de St. Victor, working along similar lines, had produced photographs in color but had not been able to make the color permanent.

Levi Hill, after nine long years of experimenting with dangerous chemicals and fumes, and after failing to receive recognition or honor for his labors in the photography world, left the field of photography in 1856.[16]

1852
Samuel Morse wrote of "the beauty of the flesh tints . . ." when describing a hillotype of Hill's daughter. Mary Hill, seated on an oval trunk, above.

then electrotyped it in a chemical solution until it assumed a deep blue. Next, exposure to a series of separate chemicals and compounds resulted in the plate's turning a bright pink color. From there, diffused light, heat, and more chemical reaction produced a light bluish cast to the plate. The plate was then placed in a jar of chlorine gas until it turned a faint yellow. If kept in total darkness, the plate would be ready, when wanted, for use. To render the plate sensitive, it was necessary to immerse it in a special solution until it appeared almost black (candlelight was suggested for this operation), and then, after being rinsed by water and dried, at that point it would reproduce colors by prolonged exposure to the image. The plate was then placed in a "quickner" solution to reduce the exposure time necessary. To increase the strength and brilliancy of the picture, the plate could be heated until it assumed a red or it could be exposed to the action of orange rays of light. After the plate was placed in a cam-

1852
A country boy photographed by Levi L. Hill.

1853

"Invisible goblins of the new photogenic process"; so said Hill when describing his efforts to reproduce the colors of nature. Color failures must have been frequent.

Critchlow of Florence, Massachusetts. Each man, working independently of the other, succeeded in producing a workable plastic to fill the need for a new kind of a daguerreotype case.[17] It was Peck who first patented a plastic daguerreotype case in 1854. The two men had created the first widespread commercial use for plastic, and each had contributed to the founding of a new native art. The molds used for the new plastic designs in deep relief were produced by the best artist die-engravers of the day.

While Stephen Foster was carving a tradition for American music in the 1840–1860 era, inventors were seeking to improve or design new musical instruments. Many of the new instruments were made for use in the home. In 1852, H. B. Horton and Company exhibited their "Melo-Pean," a compact home organ for the family. It was a keyboard instrument operated by a simple and easy blowing apparatus. In tones, it combined the playing qualities of the organ with those of the piano and violin. It was smaller than a piano and could fit into the most modest of homes. Another instrument,

If photography had left Hill unrewarded, he found his recognition in a new field of chemical exploration. He continued to experiment with chemicals and in 1858 he patented an "Improvement in the Manufacture of Burning Fluids." The following year he patented a "Hydrocarbon Vapor Apparatus." Other patent issues followed until his death in early 1865. During his lifetime Hill had shown multiple talents so common with the era; he had been a minister, author, daguerreian, a student of art, and finally an inventor.

After the discovery of photography, there was a direct need for a miniature case to protect the delicate silvered image of the daguerreotype. The traditional leather-covered wood frame case used by miniature painters had proved a ready-made product for the new daguerreian art. Because of the heavy demand for miniature cases, new materials and designs were investigated. Experiments were made in the early 1850s with thermoplastics for molding a new style of case, both by Samuel Peck of New Haven, Connecticut, and by Alfred

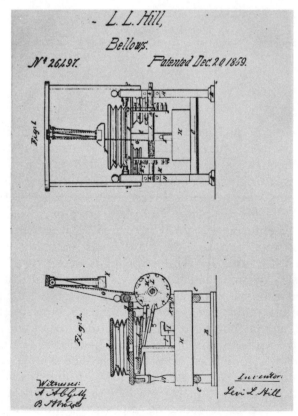

Levi L. Hill's patent for vaporizing hydrocarbons.

A souvenir of the Crystal Palace, New York City, where the Great Exhibition of 1853–1854 was held. Objects of art as well as new inventions were displayed.

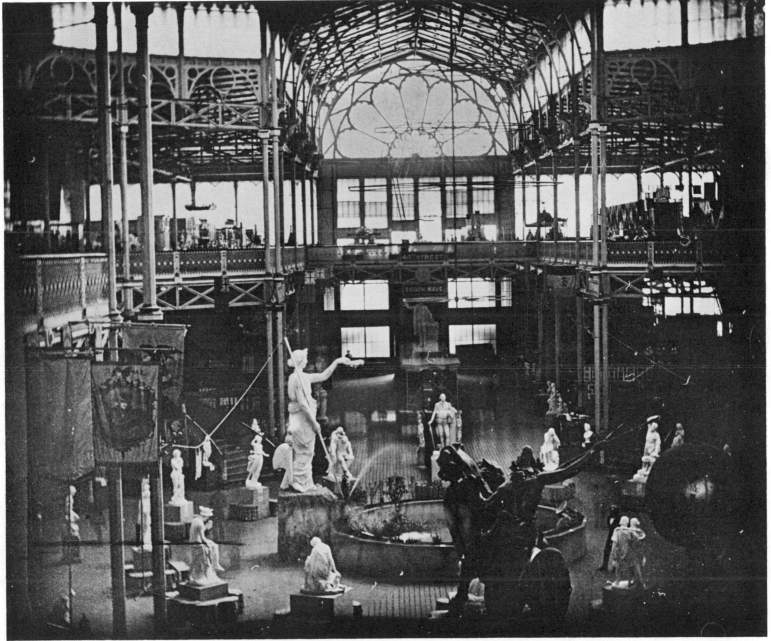

1853
An interior view of the Crystal Palace, New York City, sometimes called the House of Glass. It was the scene of an international exhibition of Art, Industry, and Invention in 1853. The throngs of visitors could see the greatest assembly of sculpture in America, as well as the many wonders of the new inventions.

The miniature case shown above was molded from a thermoplastic composition. It was patented (1854) and manufactured by Samuel Peck and Company of New Haven, Connecticut.

produced so many inventive "men of parts." Some claimed that the inventive surge had come from the patent law of 1838, which, in setting up the "principles of search," had provided and encouraged inventors with a new measure of protection. But, no matter what the answer might have been, it had been a great and busy period in America's history.

1856   Courtesy Time-Out Antiques, N.Y.C.
The young boy with the accordion (above) is one of the many to enjoy the invention of the musical instrument by Anthony Faas.

which would become famous, was the accordion, invented by Anthony Faas in 1854.

The avalanche of ideas, theories, and inventions that were the gauge of the era 1840–1860, provided future America with many of its basic tools of greatness. Many theories and ideas were swept away when the nation and its inventive effort were diverted to the turmoil of democracy's failure—the Civil War. As the era drew to a close in 1861, those then living could ponder why a small nation, in its challenge for world leadership, had

11

Transportation

Innovations and speed in transportation in the 1840 and 1850 decades gradually transformed America into an industrial nation. The country's first fast clipper ships roamed the high seas, reigning supreme. And great American steamship lines were formed, featuring speed and ease of travel. Scores of colorful side-wheelers dotted inland rivers and canals; these, connected with stage-coach lines, linked American cities. Railroads, still primitive in the 1840s but ever expanding, spread their networks of lines deeper into virgin lands. The clumsy yet reliable Conestoga wagons, "Prairie Schooners," suited for rough terrains and turnpikes, were abroad in the land in great numbers. Such was the overall pattern of America's network of transportation in the 1840–1860 era.

America gained greatly in prestige on the sea in the 1840s. John W. Griffiths, a young naval architect, created a new marine design that changed a ship's traditional blunt bow to a sharp one that would cut easily through oncoming waves, and the hull was designed for minimum water resistance and maximum sail area. On Washington's Birthday, in 1845, America's first clipper ship of Griffith's innovation, *Rainbow,* a 750 ton vessel, was launched from the shipyard of Smith and Dimon, New York. Her first round trip took seven months and seventeen days, two weeks of that time spent in China ports. With this record, the American clipper ship had almost succeeded in cutting in half the speed of the round trip from the east coast of the United States. Formerly, upwards of a year had been needed.

The opening of four China ports to foreign trade had unquestionably hastened the building of American clipper ships. The Treaty of Nanking, providing that "all nations should be on equal footing," was signed by China and Great Britain in 1842. The United States also signed the treaty ratifying the Nanking document, and in addition negotiated certain separate concessions with the Chinese. Henceforth, much of the premium high-priced cargo left China in the faster American vessels. By the fall of 1845, America had 44 ships and two barques carrying on trade with China on a regular basis.

England, more than any other country, felt the effects of clipper competition and, faced with a merchant marine disaster, opened her ports to ships of all nations. In 1849 Great Britain repealed its Monopolistic Navigation Act. As a result a frenzy of competition began among American shipbuilders to produce the finest and fastest ships afloat. The builders were often given carte blanche as to costs so that ships could be built without delay. Going freight rates for some of these fast sailing vessels in November, 1851, were one dollar per cubic foot for ordinary cargo and double that for fine goods. The slower sailing competitors had to take freight at a half or five-eighths of a dollar.[1] An example of how a quick fortune could be made on one successful voyage is furnished by *The White Cloud,* a fast sailing ship of 1,200 tons, which left the Pacific with a freight of $70,000. The cost of building the ship was $90,000; barring accidents, her trip could clear the whole cost to her owners by the time she was a year old.[2] (The capacity of these lighter vessels was one-fifth less than that of those of the same tonnage employed as sailing packets between the United States and London or Liverpool.) When in 1850 the new two-decked American clipper ship *Oriental* came up the Thames River looking for business, local merchants flocked aboard and promptly chartered her for a run to Hong Kong at a rate of $29.30 per ton, which was almost twice the sum paid for a British ship for the same run. The *Oriental* proved her worth by making the trip in 97 days, and brought back a cargo of perishable tea for the English market. English boat builders confronted with such competition worked feverishly and launched a fleet of clippers by the mid-1850s. Although the English clippers were not so fast as their American counterparts, they were of stouter design and carried more cargo. En-

gland could now offer effective competition to the American clipper, which had dominated the China trade for almost ten years.

The American clipper ship was in its zenith in the early 1850s. A typical route, especially after gold was discovered in California, ran from New York City or Boston to San Francisco, carrying West Coast-bound passengers at $160 a head and merchandise at $60 a ton. (Most clippers during this period carried about a 2,000-ton burden.) In this period steam navigation could offer little competition on the seas, for the clipper carried no fuel but took advantage of the great planetary winds on their long hauls, sometimes achieving a speed of 18 miles per hour.

Eleanor and Mabel Van Alstyne Collection,
Smithsonian Institution
The America, *a Hudson River side-paddle-wheel towboat, began commuting between New York City and Albany in the 1850s, and it was one of the many river steamers painted by James Bard (above). In 1852, about 1,150 first-class river steamers were in operation in the United States.*

1848   *Courtesy Time-Out Antiques, N.Y.C.*
Coastal cities were often buffeted by storms. A disaster scene invariably attracted sightseers, as above. Unidentified port city.

America also challenged Great Britain on the ocean by building great transatlantic steamships. The first of England's subsidized luxury ships was the *Great Western,* which made its maiden voyage to America in 1839. This magnificent ship heralded huge steamships of iron to come.

Edward Knight Collins, whose American sailing packets had dominated the transatlantic run, concentrated all of his efforts, after Britain's *Great Western* was launched, on building a steamship line. Collins named his new steamers after the seas—*Atlantic, Pacific, Arctic,* *Baltic,* and *Adriatic.* The first of his line, the *Atlantic,* left New York on April 27, 1850, and arrived in the Mersey, a river in the northwest of England, on May 10, making the passage in about thirteen days. The voyage suffered two accidents: the bursting of a condenser and the discovery of a weakness of the floats or boards on the paddle-wheels. About two days had been lost. (Before the year was out, it made the passage directly in ten days and sixteen hours.)

During a 19-day layover of the *Atlantic* in Liverpool, the ship was open to visitors on payment of sixpence

1859

Sailing boats, such as the one pictured above, served as a basic transportation link for America's smaller coastal towns. An early Melainotype.

each, the money to be turned over to a local Institution for the Blind. One of these English visitors vividly described the historic ship:

She is undoubtedly clumsy; the three masts are low, the funnel is short and dumpy, there is no bowsprit, and her sides are painted black, relieved only by one long streak of dark red. Her length between the perpendiculars—that is, the length of her keel—is 276 feet; breadth (exclusive of paddleboxes), 45; thus keeping up the proportion, as old as Noah's ark, of six feet of length to one of breadth. The stern is rounded, having in the centre the American eagle, clasping the starred and striped shield, but no other device. The figurehead is of colossal dimensions, intended, say some, for Neptune; others say Wordsworth; and some old wags assert that it is the proprietor of the ship blowing his own trumpet. . . . Like all the other Atlantic steamers, the run of the deck is almost a straight line. Around the

the saloons contain beautifully-finished emblems of each of the states in the Union. . . . The cabin windows are of beautifully-painted glass, embellished with the arms of New York, and other cities in the States. . . . The general effect is that of chasteness and a certain kind of solidity. There is not much gilding, the colors used are not gaudy, and there is a degree of elegant comfort about the saloons that is sometimes wanting amid splendid fittings. There is a ladies drawing-room near the chief saloon full of every luxury. The berths are about 150 in number, leading out, as usual, from the saloons. The most novel feature about them is the "Wedding berths," wider and more handsomely furnished than the others, intended for such newly-married couples as wish to spend the first fortnight of the honeymoon on the Atlantic. . . . The machinery which propels the ship consists of two engines, each of 500 horse-power. . . . Such cylinders, and shafts, and pistons, and beams are, I believe, unrivaled in the world. There are four boilers, each heated by eight furnaces, in two rows of four each. The consumption of coal is about fifty tons every twenty-four hours. . . . In the engine-room is a long box with five compartments, each communicating with a wire fastened like a bell-pull to the side of the paddle-box. funnel, and between the paddleboxes, is a long wooden house, and another is placed at the stern. These contain the state-rooms of the captain and officers; and in a cluster are to be found the kitchen, the pastry-room, and the barber's shop. The two former are, like similar establishments, replete with every convenience, having even a French *maître de cuisine*; but the latter is quite unique. It is fitted up with all necessary apparatus—with glass-cases containing perfumery, etc; and in the centre is "the barber's chair." This is a comfortable, well stuffed seat, with an inclined back. In front is a stuffed trestle, on which to rest feet and legs; and behind is a little stuffed apparatus like a crutch, on which to rest the head. These are movable, so as to suit people of all sizes. . . . The house at the stern contains a smoking-room, and a small apartment completely sheltered from the weather for the steersman. The smoking-room communicates with the cabin below, so that, after dinner . . . enjoy the weed of old Virginia in perfection. . . . Proceeding below, we come to the great saloon, 67 feet long, and the dining-saloon, 60 feet long, each being 20 feet broad, and divided from each other by the steward's pantry. This pantry is more like a silversmith's shop, the sides being lined with glass-cases stored with beautifully-burnished plate; crockery of every description, well secured, is seen in great quantities. . . . Above the tables in the dining-saloon are suspended racks, cut to receive decanters, glasses, etc. so that they can be immediately placed on the table without the risk attendant on carrying them from place to place. The two saloons are fitted up in a very superior manner: rose, satin, and olive are the principal woods that have been used, and some of the tables are beautifully variegated marble, with metal supporters. The carpets are very rich, and the coverings of the sofas, chairs, etc. are of the same superior quality. The panels around

These handles are marked respectively, "ahead," "slow," "fast," "back," and "hook-on;" and whenever one is pulled, a printed card with the corresponding signal appears in the box opposite the engineer, who has to act accordingly. There is thus no noise of human voices on board this ship: the helmsman steers by his bells, the engineer works by the telegraph, and the steward waits by the annunciator.[8]

The observant English visitor, while inspecting the *Atlantic,* was impressed with the shell-shaped "spittoons," brightly painted in sea-colors—a reminder of the popular American custom of "chewing." He noticed, too, that the American way of having ladies leave the ship before the men did not meet favor with English women.

The *Atlantic,* first of her line, was the most fortunate of the three ocean-named vessels. In 1854 the *Arctic* was lost off Newfoundland; in 1856 the *Pacific* disappeared without a trace. With increasing loss of patronage, the ill-fated Collins Line, which had had such a promising beginning, went out of business by 1858.

Meanwhile, America led the world in inland naviga-

The Anson Northup *provided the connecting link between St. Paul and the Selkirk Settlement in Canada. To provide this service the boat had been dismantled at the Crow Wing River, Minnesota, (a tributary of the Mississippi), and transported overland by horse and ox-drawn sleighs in the late winter of 1858. It was reassembled on the banks of the Red River where it was put to use carrying people and supplies to the Canadian settlement.*

1853   *Courtesy the Missouri Historical Society,*
                                                    St. Louis
Steam navigation brought a rapid increase in population and
wealth to the city of St. Louis. Its population grew from
6,000 in 1832 to about 63,000 by 1849, and in the 1850s it
expanded even more rapidly. For example, in 1854 new
building construction, excluding houses, totaled 1,254, and
at a cost of $3,811,000. A daguerreotype, above, of the St.
Louis levee.

tion. The colorful paddle-wheeled river steamboat was the major carrier of people and goods in its golden years of 1840–1860. From 1820 onward it had become longer and faster, was more ornamental, and it stressed the comfort that the American traveler demanded. Most of these riverboats were inexpensively built, with mechanical equipment often of the cheapest quality, especially boilers and engines; the average life of paddle-wheels was from four to five years. Mechanical failures, coupled with the sporting mettle shown by the captains of these boats, often proved a fatal combination. Insurance rates reflected the mania for speed. Rates on cargoes ran one and three-quarter percent from New Orleans up river the first 200 miles, after which it jumped to four percent of the cargo's value.

New Orleans in 1840 was the fourth port in the world; its exports were far greater than imports. Lordly paddle-wheelers of New Orleans swept downstream at ten to twelve miles per hour and upstream at six, their holds always filled to capacity. On downstream trips they were laden with cotton—a first step en route to Europe or New England. Upstream, they carried cargoes from eastern seaboard ports to meet the increasing demand of incoming settlers. Their passengers included emigrants and traders, as this transportation was the cheapest available travel.

One voyager in the 1840s described western steamboats, traveling from New Orleans up the Mississippi, as very different from those of the North:

> They comprise an upper and lower world. The first consists of a long saloon, as it is termed, sustained by pillars resting on the lower deck, some eight or ten feet high, extending nearly the whole length of the vessel, and carpeted and handsomely decorated. On each side of the saloon is a row of state-rooms, each containing two berths, and the little articles required in a bedchamber. By courtesy of our captain, I was permitted to have one of these to myself, which added greatly to the comfort of my voyage. These little rooms have each a half glass door, which opens on a gallery running all round the boat, with only the interruption of the wheel-house, outside of which is a door of Venetian blinds, which being thrown open, you can sit in your room and see every object on one side of the river. Above is a platform, called, I think, the hurricane deck, which, being greatly elevated above the river, affords a view in all directions, bounded only by the windings of the stream and the deep forests skirting its margins. The appearance of these boats is singularly picturesque, and as they are on the high pressure principle, they announce their approach by a repetition of explosions resembling the firing of cannon at a distance. . . . In the lower region of these floating castles, will generally be found a good number of broadhorns or flats, who, having disposed of cargo and boat at New Orleans, are making tracks homewards,

as fast and as cheaply as possible. For this purpose, they make some kind of agreement with the captain, "to work their passage"—in nautical phrase—and find themselves, paying some trifle. . . . They never visit the saloon, though they will sometimes ascend to the hurricane deck, and may be seen a great part of the day reclining on a soft plank, or a cotton bag, which is considered a great luxury. . . . They are nowise particular in their dress; eschew shaving; and though never obtrusive, there is a good, honest republican air of independence about them which is peculiarly offensive to John Bull travelers. . . . They are like singed cats, much better than they look, and there is not one of them but can tell you a great deal you never knew before. . . .[4]

An entertaining part of a traveler's voyage up the Mississippi by paddle-wheel was to watch the process of taking on wood from the bank, which occurred at intervals of every 20 to 30 miles. As there were no pines along the river, ash and cottonwood were used for fuel. Wood was furnished by enterprising folk who, without leave of anybody, built a hut along the river and cut

1847
The blinds seen in the background of this rare daguerreotype scene suggest that it was probably taken aboard a riverboat. The costume also implies boat travel.

away at convenient wood. Wood was piled along the river bank, where a boat could come alongside; there were no wharves. Once the boat was fast, all of the men on the lower region of the vessel formed a procession and went back and forth to the woodpile, all the while cracking jokes and enjoying the chore.

Delays and accidents were frequent along the river routes. One disgruntled traveler, wearing a small coonskin cap, made his feelings known after the paddlewheeler hit a log. He set his saddlebags and "pocketbook" down in front of one of the officers and announced that he would make the rest of the trip by land. When encouraged to wait for repairs, he replied, "No . . . this is the last time I ever mean to put my foot in one of these etarnal contrivances. I have been five times run high and dry on a sandbank, four times snagged, three times sawyered [tree down in river],

and twice blown up sky-high [boiler explosion]. I calculate I have given these creturs a pretty fair trial, and darn my breeches if I ever trust my carcase in one again. Take care of my plunder; I will call for it at St. Louis." So saying, he stalked off into the forest.

A universal practice in this western world of Mississippi River travel was "whittling." If a man had a knife and stick, he could defy time and all of the ordinary incidents of traveling. A riverboat captain, after he had fastened his vessel to a post in some little town along the river, would sometimes chat with a native; each with his knife and stick whiled away the time, deep in some mysterious conversation. The passion for speed that marked the northern people was not evident in the southwestern world.

Tales were told of daguerreotypists' having flatboat galleries on the principal rivers, some fitted up with

THE TRAVELER'S HOME.

The above is a westward-bound traveler's sketch of a place at which he stopped for food. Most pioneers, whenever possible, foraged for and cooked their own meat, fish, and fowl to augment their usual fare of bread and fried salt pork. A few hotels and inns were available along the country's turnpikes for the less hardy travelers. An average charge was one dollar a day for man and his horse, with lunch provided.

skylights, chemical rooms, and reception rooms. When they were not busy photographing, they passed the time in hunting and fishing. One daguerreotypist spent three years on a 65-foot boat, which carried as extras a good cook and musical instruments. Also traveling the rivers of the Midwest were showboats of various kinds, bringing entertainment, some of good quality, most of bad, to the rugged frontier settlers.

In the 1850s travel on the Mississippi became faster as well as more elaborate. The best side-wheelers catered to rich celebrating planters and suave gamblers, who wished to travel amid luxurious surroundings and excellent personal service. The *Eclipse,* the most ornamental packet of the 1850s, advertised 48 bridal chambers, and it featured a three-hundred-foot saloon, the last word in opulent luxury.

Steamship lines made regular runs on the Great Lakes, Hudson River, and Chesapeake Bay. In fact, all large rivers along which cities had been built were utilized and were heavy with boat traffic. In the New York area alone over 2,000,000 passengers traveled on three main steamboat routes during the year ending July, 1851. Also, thousands of excursionists traveled to nearby beaches, camp meetings, and other resort areas.

In the early 1850s Americans began eying a trade route on the Pacific side of South America. The British had held a ten-year monopoly on the 21 ports between Valparaiso, Chile, and Panama, and the agreement had expired.[5] The South American Republics along the route quickly opened their ports to the many California-bound ships, and American steamers were welcomed to compete with the English for local freight and passenger trade.

Enterprising stagecoach lines formed the connecting link between the inland waterways and the villages and towns. A typical example was a daily coach line running between Norfolk, Virginia, and Elizabeth City, North Carolina. After making connections with a

The wealthy young man in this era was proud of driving a fast rig. Buggies were built for speed; seats were richly padded with leather, and comfort was assured by "springing" the seat with two cylindrical bars.

steamer at Norfolk, the stagecoach followed the Dismal Swamp Canal towpath for most of its journey. Fourteen miles from the northern end of the canal, the State Line was reached, which was also a stopover for dinner. The State Line was marked by an inscribed stone that bisected a little tavern standing between the two states. The landlord lived and voted in North Carolina and entertained his visitors in the Old Dominion State. Many of his guests were honeymooners, for the isolated stagecoach route was a favorite with newlyweds until the railroad weakened its popularity. The travelers, after a hearty dinner, resumed their journey to Elizabeth City, a beautiful little village at the end of the stagecoach line.

Stagecoach lines were established wherever a need

The ferry shown above carried passengers across the river free of charge. The enterprising citizens of Anoka, Minnesota, appealed to the ferryman to do his share in helping pioneers of the great Northwest exploring expeditions.

existed. In 1850 a regular line of stages began to run monthly between Independence, Missouri, and Santa Fé, New Mexico—an important step toward the settlement of the West. Each coach carried eight people, and was made watertight so that it could be used as a boat in crossing streams.[6] For fast travel on post roads the famous custom-built Concord coaches were reliable and widely used. During Gold Rush days Concord coaches sped westward, usually covering about a hundred miles a day. It was necessary to change their six-horse teams every 12 to 15 miles. Over rough roads this fast mode of travel brought loud complaints from hardy travelers.

For pioneers moving West, the Conestoga type of wagons—the "Prairie Schooner," as it was later named—were used. These big canvas-covered wagons had wide tires and were built for rough travel; their weight was about 3,000 pounds and they usually carried about three tons; they also had brakes and skids for downhill grades and carried tools for needed repairs. The westward-bound Conestoga wagons generally were pulled by ten oxen, usually of the Illinois or Missouri variety. The animals were adapted to forage the trails and their average speed was about 17 miles a day. Two main routes were used by the westward pioneer—the northern route, or Oregon Trail, from Missouri or Iowa, following the Platte River and then across to Fort Laramie, traveling north and on to Oregon or south to California. The southern route, or Santa Fé Trail, went from St. Louis to Independence, then across Kansas to Santa Fé, and onward.

River crossings were forded or crossed by ferries. *The Emigrant's Guide to California,* by Joseph H. Ware, published in 1849, described the "Papan's" ferry thus:

> At the Kansas crossing, distance 100 miles, you will find a ferry owned by two Indians (French Kaws) . The charge for crossing is one dollar for a wagon; horses or loose stock you can swim across. About ten miles above there is a mission station by the M. E. Church where any blacksmith work can be done, which accidents have made necessary.

The ferry was not always in the same place. As the river changed it would move to whatever banks made the best landings. The ferryboat was a crude affair, made of hand-hewn logs, with a guide rope to keep it in place. The current helped it across, but most of the power was furnished by sweeps and poles in the hands of the ferrymen and the passengers, who usually had to work, even though they paid their fare across. By 1856 the Papan's ferry had improved, according to an old-time native who had crossed the Kansas River on the ferry during that year. It now had a flatboat large

The prototype locomotive had emerged by 1860. Its development made American railroads the world leader in this era. A carte de visite of #22, Rhode Island Locomotive Works, above.

1853
"Big box, little box, bandbox, bundle" was a favorite expression of men to describe lady travelers on the railroads in this era.

enough to carry a wagon and two yoke of oxen and had a strong cable wire that stretched across the river. The old native described the crossing as quicker and safer than the one on the Missouri River.[7]

Although steamboats and Prairie Schooners provided needed transportation to the West, not a foot of railroad track had been laid west of the Mississippi at the dawning of 1850. Meanwhile, railroad transportation had been gaining steadily in the eastern states. The first regularly scheduled passenger train, "Best Friend of Charleston," South Carolina, made its first trip December 25, 1830. From this beginning, rail transportation spread, and by 1840 it covered the eastern part of the country with a series of short independent railroad lines. These generally ran between large cities and the nearest body of navigable water, where boat transportation took over.

Railroad stock promoters advertised safety features for the early railroad, ranging from a horseman with a red flag leading the train, to the provision of a railroad car next to the train engine, furnished with cotton bales to protect passengers from an unexpected explosion. Sometime in the 1840s the first whistle was added to a locomotive, and its earsplitting shriek gave adequate warning. The Americans built the first locomotive with enclosed candlelight reflector headlights in 1840. In this period from 1840, the passenger car assumed its standard center aisle with seats on both sides. Sleeping cars were in operation, but they consisted of crudely renovated day coaches, providing little comfort. (In 1858 George Pullman began to experiment and designed a railroad car with comfortable sleeping arrangements.)

Early iron horses ran about ten miles an hour, but within a short time railroads increased their speed, and the need for safety became a paramount factor. No standard group of safety rules existed; each railroad established its own rules. The *Scientific American* from 1845 onward began a crusade of analyzing every train wreck and advertised that there was a lack of safety equipment. Almost every issue of the paper furnished factual descriptions of one or more wrecks in America. Undoubtedly this crusade helped. State legislation had come about in the 1840s but it was feeble and mostly confined to laws regulating construction details. Although at first states participated in railroad building, most states by about 1850 had passed laws prohibiting state railroad ventures. In the 1850s more and more railroads adopted a system of displaying red flags and red lanterns to guide the engineer over a perilous course. Also, speed limits were put in force under certain dangerous conditions. However, these conditions continued and it was not until 1862 that Congress, feeling an overwhelming need for regulation, passed the first Railroad Act. Such news items as the follow-

1856   *Courtesy Time-Out Antiques, N.Y.C.*
Weymouth, Massachusetts
*The use of oxen for pulling heavy loads was widespread, not
only for the freighting business but by industry and agriculture. Oxen were easier to train if "well mated." The driver
for his part had to have "coolness of temper" and to "teach
the oxen to respond to motion not voice." An average team
could plod 2 miles an hour for a 7- to 8-hour day.*

ing of June, 1859, may have been instrumental in its passage:

A man called M'Laughlin has been tried at Chicago, Illinois, on the accusation of causing trains of cars of Galena and Chicago Railroad to be thrown from the tracks. From what has been disclosed it is apparent there is a league of villains in the West banded together for the purpose of murder, theft and arson. Women as well as men belong to the gang which has branches in Chicago, Cleve-

land, Buffalo and all lake cities. Causing railroad accidents is one of their favorite deeds.

At last, in the 1850s, the need for a railroad to run from the Atlantic to the Pacific coast was given serious consideration and surveys for suitable routes were undertaken by government topographical engineers. The political parties at their national conventions in 1856 made this issue a part of their platforms, but a railroad spanning the continent was not completed

1859   *Courtesy Miss Josephine Cobb*
*The above oxen worked on a Maine farm. They were also
hired out for heavy haulage at the local Portland Harbor.*

until 1869, when the Union Pacific, building from the Missouri River at Omaha, met the Central Pacific, which built from San Francisco eastward.

Local freight transportation depended on wagons in localities where water transportation was not available. Depending on conditions, these wagons were towed by horses, oxen, or mules. The "Allegheny Conestoga" wagon could usually cover 20 to 25 miles a day if horses were used.[8] Even in the winter these versatile wagons were utilized by removing the wheels and substituting sled runners, enabling the horses to pull their loads at a greater speed.

Some horse-drawn wagons were fitted up by enterprising tradesmen and other itinerant merchants. Like the tin peddlers, photographers roamed the pikes of the East in their wagons, visiting small villages. In the West

they toured the mining camps. One very elaborate wagon was seen not far from Syracuse, New York, and was reported to be 28 feet long, 11 feet wide, and 9 feet high. It had a skylight and was tastefully furnished.

As cities grew, so did the variety of vehicles on their streets. Leading the way in city passenger transportation was the heavy-wheeled horse-drawn omnibus. New York City, by 1835, had over 100 of these conveyances, mostly independently owned.[9] New omnibuses seen on New York City streets in 1844 were described as having "a costliness and splendour that would have done for a *sovereign's* carriage in the golden age. Claret bodies, silver-plated hubs and yellow wheels, cut velvet linings and cushions, and all to tempt the once unconsidered sixpence to get up and ride!"

The omnibus driver had a reputation of being "fast,

ca. 1860   Courtesy Time-Out Antiques, N.Y.C.
The horse-drawn sleigh was used not only in America but
in Russia and the Scandinavian countries for a conveyance
when roads became snowbound.

reckless and accident prone." Racing, however, could be prevented by pulling the "check-string," which was always obeyed. "Terrified ladies who chance to have no fancy for riding races in Broadway should be reminded of this leather preservative."

The horse-railway coach made its appearance on the American scene in 1832 in New York, running on a track between Prince and Fourteenth. The coaches were obviously patterned after the steam engine "De Witt Clinton," and were mounted on iron wheels. The cars were drawn by horses over rails laid in the middle of the street. The lines had been extended to other avenues by the early 1850s. New Orleans soon adopted the street railway, and Boston received attention in the news in 1857 with its "Metropolitan Horse Railroad."[10] Street railways were in operation in Pittsburgh, Cincinnati, and Chicago by 1859. Hacking cabs were abroad

on city streets. New York City in 1855 issued a total of 601 hack licenses. Private carriages, however, were the mainstay of the wealthier members of society. In the winter horse-drawn sleighs were popular in the city as well as in rural areas. Sturdily built carts used in business enterprises added to the enormousness of city traffic.

Transportation in the 20-year span before 1860 brought about great social change in an expanding nation. Accelerated travel helped to spread religion, education, and the arts. Most important, increased transportation led to the growth of settlements in remote areas. Inland navigation hastened the new industrial revolution. Railroad short lines served small communities well by bringing in needed goods and passenger service. Transportation networks by 1860 would open up almost all of America for future expansion.

12
The Enterprising

American salesmanship for promoting new ideas would begin to emerge in this era as a definite way of life in the United States. The census statistics of 1840 show 117,000 Americans engaged in commercial pursuits. No record exists of the number of salesmen who sold the products of the day.

The newspapers of the 1840s and 1850s show glowing written descriptions of products for sale. More often than not, fantastic properties were claimed in the advertisements. There were no laws enacted to control fraudulent advertising. Honest ethical competition was best typified by the traveling salesman, selling to the rural consumer. This purveyor of wares and gossip considered 1,000 percent his normal profit markup. However, in the course of making a sale to a shrewd buyer, he would often cut his profit to 500 percent, thus winning a friend as well as an eager buyer. In this period, demand and salesmanship would determine the selling price of an article, not a markup based on a fixed percentage of the wholesale cost.

The enterprising traveling salesman was fundamentally a wanderer, an adventurer in the age of adventure. The drivers of these wagons full of nicely displayed merchandise came from all walks of life; there were ministers' sons, prosperous farm boys, and, if the rumor of the day was correct, they might even have included Bronson Alcott, the philosopher. Many avid gossipers claimed that the itinerant merchant of the open road haunted low taverns, drank far too much, and frequented rough gatherings. His now faded image was that of a lean, wiry fellow who told dirty jokes with a straight face to the menfolk, showed the farmer's wife

the latest in fashions, and, of a summer's night, to a susceptible farmer's daughter of weak virtue possibly displayed a measure of irresistable romantic charm. His stock of trade goods ran from clocks to bolts of cloth. Wheeling and dealing equally for cash or barter, his summer jaunts took him on the byroads from Vermont to Savannah, Georgia.

The enterprising were spreading American inventions and mechanical ability all over the world. The Czar of all the Russias decided, in 1847, to construct a railroad from Moscow to St. Petersburg. The American firm of Harrison, Winans and Eastwick, of Baltimore, Maryland, received the contract. Besides bestowing the honor of building a foreign nation's railroad system, the contract stipulated 162 locomotives of 25 tons each, 2,500 freight cars, 70 regular passenger cars having eight wheels each, and, presumably for the Czar, two passenger cars, 80 feet long with 16 wheels each. The 400 miles of double track was in operation in 1850. Trains ran on a regular schedule and at an average speed of 30 miles per hour. The Americans, at the height of the railroad's construction, had employed almost 2,000 workmen and had also secured an additional contract to maintain the railroad for the next twelve years.[1]

American private enterprise, mostly consisting of railroad stock companies operating short lines, had made the puffing locomotive commonplace in the American scene by the mid 1840s. Back in 1836 the first dream of a transcontinental railroad stretching from Maine to Oregon was conceived. The dreamer was John Plumbe, Jr., surveyor, author, professor of the art of daguerreo-

1850

The Tin Peddler

*America's first traveling salesman meandered along the high-
ways and byways from Vermont to Savannah, Georgia. His
shrewd dealings with merchandise that covered everything
from buttons and bows to pots and pans won for him the
name "Sam Slick" in American folklore. The nattily dressed
charmer of the farmer's daughter became notorious from
coast to coast.*

typing, and first large promoter of photography. Mr. Plumbe was born in Wales in 1809. In appearance, he had the traditional black hair and blue eyes of the Welsh people. He had emigrated to America as a young fellow and by the age of 23 had become superintendent of a railroad running between Richmond, Virginia, and Roanoke Rapids, North Carolina. Sometime in the year 1836 he had envisioned continuous railroad transportation between the Atlantic and Pacific oceans. In the two years following 1836 he must have had some success in selling Congress his grand idea, for in 1838 Congress granted him $2,000 to survey a railroad route between Milwaukee and Sinipee, Wisconsin. This partial success must have been gratifying, for in one link of his original proposed transcontinental railroad he had envisioned a route between Lake Michigan and the Missouri River. By 1860 this route would be called the southern route to the West. After completing the Milwaukee-Sinipee survey, he returned to Washington.

For the next three years, he besieged Congress for additional grants to pursue his grand dream. Plumbe said, "I was laughed at for a madman," and by 1841 he was forced to take up the new art of daguerreotyping. All of his private capital had been exhausted on surveys and in trying to convince Congress of the feasibility of his dream.

It is not known who taught Mr. Plumbe the art of daguerreotyping or where he learned it, but in March 1841 there appeared in *The Boston Observer,* a daily newspaper, the following advertisement:

Mr. Plumbe, Professor of Photography, having at length succeeded in so far improving his apparatus, as to be enabled to produce a perfect photographic miniature in any weather, and consequently, without using direct rays of the sun, proposes to instruct a limited number of gentlemen in the beautiful art, who will be furnished with complete sets of improved patented apparatus, by means of which any one may be enabled to take a likeness in an ordinary room, *without opening a window* or requiring any peculiar adjustment of light. Hitherto it has been generally supposed that sunshine and an open window

1854   *Courtesy Time-Out Antiques, N.Y.C.*
The instrument of American expansion—the surveyor.

were indispensable to the production of Daguerreo miniatures, but an important improvement just perfected proves this a mistake. The new apparatus costs only one-half the price of the other and furnishes the ability of its possessor the security of independence in a profession as honorable, interesting and agreeable as any other, by the expenditure of a mere trifle and a few days application. Can any other pursuit in life present the same advantage in furnishing the means of gentlemanly support, not to say fortune. Miniatures taken in beautiful style—terms $3.00—Daguerreo Rooms, Harrington Museum, 75 Court St.

By May of that year, revising the same advertisement, he called his establishment the "United States Photographic Institute."

From this flourishing beginning, Mr. Plumbe would become photography's first large-scale sales promoter. The years 1840–1841 saw most pioneer daguerreotypists appealing to the leading citizens only to have their likeness captured. Unlike his competitors, Plumbe realized that "the vast horizon of photography lay in photographing the mass of common people." Later in 1841, according to other advertisements, he had expanded his field and reduced his price for a miniature likeness to $1.00, including the case. Plumbe believed in advertising and by 1843 he had opened two additional "Plumbe Daguerrian Parlors," one in New York City and one in Washington, D. C. Unlike other pioneers, Plumbe stamped his name in the miniature cases, thus assuring himself of additional publicity. The year 1846 saw Mr. Plumbe the owner of a chain of eleven daguerreian parlors, including one in Liverpool, England, and one in Paris. In addition, he had a "Plumbe National Daguerrian Depot" in New York City, a manufacturing and wholesale outlet of photographic apparatus. His vast enterprises employed 500 people. This same year saw him add a new invention in his line; he called it the "Plumbeotype." It consisted, so he claimed, of a process whereby a daguerreotype likeness could be transferred to paper. That same year he entered the publishing field with his first (perhaps only) issue of a newspaper called *The Plumbeian.* By 1847 author Plumbe, using the name "National Publishing Company, Philadelphia, Pennsylvania," began publishing sheet music and also issuing a magazine called *The National Plumbeotype Gallery,* consisting of reproductions of prominent Americans of the day. In this venture, Plumbe realized the sales value of promoting a nationwide formation of literary clubs devoted to his offerings, and as an added inducement to form the clubs, he offered premiums to the founders. His monthly magazine *Pictorial Works of the National Plumbeotype Gallery, New Series* offered 313 portraits and a port-

1844

The daguerreotype above was taken by John Plumbe, Jr., Boston, who was America's first large-scale promoter of photography. Plumbe took up the art of photography after exhausting his own private capital on surveys for railroad routes that he had envisioned from the Atlantic to the Pacific. The man shown above was probably born about 1750.

folio for $15 per year, with additional subscriptions reducing the price.

PLUMBE DAGUERRIAN GALLERY
OF
PATENT COLORED PHOTOGRAPHS,

Corner of State and Market-streets, Douw's Buildings, Albany.

Corner of Court and Brattle-streets, ⎱
  and 123 Washington street, ...⎰ *Boston.*
Corner of Murray-street and Broadway, *New-York.*
No. 173 Chesnut-street,.............. *Philadelphia.*
Broadway,....................... *Saratoga Springs.*
Corner of Calvert and Baltimore-streets, *Baltimore.*

Constituting the oldest and most extensive establishment of the kind in the world, and containing upwards of a thousand pictures. Admittance free.

The proprietor has lately discovered and patented an entirely new process, by means of which he is now enabled to produce *Colored Photographs,* the superiority of which is so great as to defy all attempts at competition. The patent right being secured, the price of those beautiful COLORED PORTRAITS has been reduced to THREE DOLLARS, and a duplicate gratis, being only half the usual charge for the old style of likenesses.

.*. Patent Rights, Apparatus, and Instruction supplied at a moderate charge.

An advertisement by John Plumbe, Jr. in the 1843 Albany city directory.

From his beginning in 1841, Plumbe had varied his advertising. Sometimes he offered something for nothing, as in this quotation from an 1846 newspaper: "The gallery and lounge is free, frequented by the elite of the city who find it an agreeable resting place." Other times his advertisements boasted of his "having been awarded eight medals by the institutes in Massachusetts, New York, Pennsylvania and Ohio for the most beautiful colored daguerreotypes and best apparatus ever exhibited."

Toward the latter part of 1847, Plumbe commenced selling his daguerreian parlors to his individual operators in the various cities. The empire had grown too large. "His agents had stole him blind," wrote Marcus Root in a short biography of Plumbe written in 1864.

Plumbe had not forgotten his dream. Besides, in 1848 he had witnessed the old number one of the Galena and Chicago Railroad smoke her way into Chicago, the first link on the transcontinental railroad. The next year saw him in California, after he had made a preliminary survey of the southern route to the West at his own expense. Back in Washington that year, he entered a bitter controversy with Asa Whitney, who advocated a northern railroad route. In 1853, Congress authorized the first coast-to-coast railroad route survey. Plumbe's fight with Whitney and Congress continued until finally, on the morning of May 29, 1857, despondent, he locked himself in a room in his brother's house at Dubuque, Iowa, and committed suicide by cutting his throat with a razor.

The pattern of promotion and advertising pioneered by John Plumbe was copied not only by photography but by other fields as well. Successful Mathew Brady and Jessie Whitehurst, both photographers, would gain in the 1850s worldwide fame through the same basic type of promotion.

The immense number of advertisements, symbolic of American enterprise, showed in statistics; an American newspaper in 1848 showed 1,200 to 1,400 advertisements as compared with a London newspaper carrying 800 for the same period.[2] The Americans were out to sell, not only at home, but abroad. If the American railroad locomotive was being exported to Europe in large numbers, so too was the lowly broom, for in 1844, Troy, Wisconsin, had exported 80,000 brooms for the English market.[3]

Money and money circulation in this period were interesting and complicated. The confliction between hard money and soft money was great. The United States Government pursued a policy of hard money and only specie (coinage) was recognized as legal tender. In 1840 the United States Government accepted only

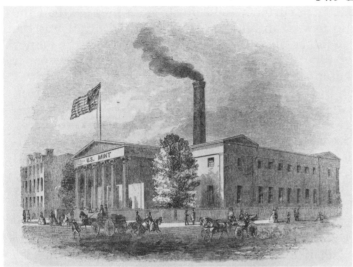

United States Mint, Philadelphia
The two-story building built of marble and completely fire-proof was located between Thirteenth and Fourteenth streets on Chestnut. The most valuable coinage during the era was made in 1851 with 24,985,716 pieces, including 147,672 half cents, altogether worth $49,258,058.

specie for the payment of taxes and revenue from the sale of public lands. A bill to establish an independent treasury department was passed this same year, and while this law was repealed two years later, the department was reinstated in 1846 and thereafter became a permanent part of the federal government. Prior to 1840 the old "Second United States Bank" had served as a treasury collection depot, but in 1836 the Government in Washington had withdrawn its support and thereby caused its political and financial destruction. In the four years following 1836, the government had placed its revenues in various state banks, oftentimes selected by political patronage. Thus, with the treasury building a reality, the United States would henceforth guard the tax revenues in the government vaults in Washington.

Hard money, throughout the 1840–1860 period, was in short supply. The manufacture of specie by the United States Government could not keep pace with the exploding population. British, Spanish, Mexican, and French coins, in that order of popularity, were widely circulated all over the country. Both foreign and domestic coins of good standing were accepted as legal tender. Also, the bimetallic (gold and silver) character of American coins added complications to the history of money in this era. For with the discovery of gold in California, the supply of silver coins, particularly the smaller denominations, became short. These shortages caused railroad companies to pay a

premium to obtain change for their ticket offices. Often prices quoted in newspaper advertisements were in terms of the English shilling. The shilling, the Spanish dollar, and the Mexican dollar were in widespread use, particularly during the forties. American coins were well manufactured and of a reliable full weight. This added further to the general specie shortage, for American coins drifted out of the country and into the hands of foreign speculators. A Congressional act of March 1849, introduced the gold Double Eagle (twenty dollars), a large coin ($1\frac{5}{16}''$ diameter), and at the same time it caused to be issued a tiny one dollar gold piece. This came about because of the scarcity of the silver dollar coin at that time. The golden Double Eagle became a symbol of American wealth to the world, and presumably it was exported on a large scale. In the gold rush era, private companies manufactured and circulated gold coins, generally a fifty dollar gold piece. In 1853 Congress debased the coinage by the introduction of substandard content of metal and in 1857 legis-

1855
A banker's dignity often depended on a tall beaver hat and a cutaway coat. The number of banks grew rapidly in the United States, from 1,000 in 1840 to 2,000 by 1860.

lation was finally enacted canceling the legal tender status of all foreign coins.

The thought of the people on the national scale, in 1840, was that, ideally, a free banking system was best equipped with the resources necessary to meet the rapidly expanding country's need for capital. It was the duty of the various states, so held the Federal Government of this era, to regulate and to issue charters to the banking industry. Soft money in this period was not a new thing. Back in 1838, feeling the effects of the banking panic of 1837, the New York State legislature passed the first American legislation regulating the banking industry. While not a comprehensive law, for the first time in any state it clearly defined certain qualifications and conditions to be met before a bank could issue paper currency, oftentimes called bank notes. Louisiana, by 1842, had passed stringent laws to protect the interest of bank depositors. As the years passed, other states reluctantly followed Louisiana's lead and passed banking legislation. Not until the election of Lincoln and the Civil War would the need be felt for Federal banking regulation. Generally speaking, during the forties in the several states, anyone could establish a bank and issue paper currency with or without a state charter. State charters were a mere formality and easy to obtain.

In 1846 it was estimated that paper bank notes had a circulation of 100 million dollars. In the early forties, Michigan passed a banking law requiring that 30 percent of a bank's capital be in specie and be kept on hand in a bank's vault. The state employed inspectors to enforce the law and to make regular inspections of the bank vaults. But some professional solidarity must have existed among the Michigan banks for, as it worked out, they made evasion of the law an easy thing. Apparently the same bag of coins was transferred from one bank to another, for it became an adage that "when the inspector came in the front door, the coins came in the back door." This was repeated throughout the circuit, with the reserve hard money moving just a little more quickly than the inspectors. Another popular evasion of the law was revealed when a suspicious inspector had a box marked "Specie" broken open. Its contents revealed lead and tenpenny nails.[4]

New York was gradually becoming the banking center of the country, especially so with the establishment of a New York State Banking Department in 1851. A booklet known as a "bank note detector," issued weekly, described each bank note in circulation, gave the value of the note, and stated if a counterfeit was in circulation. Counterfeiting, as well as defunct bank notes, was a constant source of danger to the general public. Dirty bank note currency held much more prestige than the crisp new clean ones, and most desired of all was the note full of pin holes, for this indicated that the money had been in the hands of many banks. A newspaper joke appearing in 1846 was reported as follows: "A dog was seen to pick up a bank note on State Street, Boston, on Saturday—but [he] dropped it instantly with a growl. He then put his paw on it and tore it to pieces. Examining the torn pieces proved the bill to be counterfeit."[5] This newspaper article went on to prove that even dogs could be trained to spot counterfeit currency.

The rapid growth of banks, 1,000 in 1840 to nearly 2,000 in 1860, reflected more than anything else the great scarcity of capital in the United States. This shortage of capital must have been particularly galling to the imaginative and ethical enterprising men of the day who realized the tremendous economic potentiality in the development of the nation's resources. In the North, however, the bank expansion represented a growing richness of a financially stable middle class of citizens.

The boom atmosphere of the era in the banking industry was also connected with the issuance of stock, and the stock market. If the age of the free-swinging soft money currency ended with the Civil War, not so the stock market. The stock market had become firmly fixed in the American way of life. Before 1840, stock manipulation was generally confined to the wealthy, but in this expanding period it would become part of the enterprising middle-class method of income. Railroad stock, which played a prominent part in the American rail expansion, began with the first issue for the Mohawk

1859
A successful transaction.

ca. 1855   *Courtesy Northampton (Massachusetts)*
Historical Society
The State Bank at Conway, Massachusetts
In the era, independent banking systems were thought to
best serve the country's expanding financial needs.

and Hudson Railroad Company in 1830.[6] Millions of dollars would be issued for the newly forming railroad companies. By 1838, the New York Exchange Board had 175 millions of listed securities, mostly railroads, canals, and turnpikes.[7] In the mid-1830s, a great fever of land speculation seized the country. Everyone bought and sold land at ever-increasing prices. The collapse of land prices in 1837 contributed greatly to the bank

Courtesy Library of Congress
New York gradually became the banking center of the country in this era. A stereograph view of Wall Street, New York, above, taken about 1856 by Frederick and William Langenheim. The large dome, upper right, is the roof of the Merchant's Exchange Building.

panic of that year. After the panic, speculation decreased but expanding transportation demands remained. With the need for a stock center, the New York Exchange Board would play an increasingly important part in providing that service.

Before 1842 the Exchange Board had temporarily occupied a hayloft. It secured rooms in the Merchants Exchange Building in 1842. The Board had telegraphic communications installed in the early 1840s and thus it was that New York City was greatly aided in becoming the national securities center. It had long since surpassed Philadelphia as a stock center. The recovery from the 1837 panic was long. The membership of the Stock Exchange Board had grown to 75 brokers by 1848. Both morning and afternoon sessions were held. Shares also were sold after hours, in front of the exchange building. No records exist, but something like 5,000 shares probably changed hands daily in the 1840s. The Board's receipts for the year 1848 were $10,396, expenditures $9,317, surplus $1,079.[8] A breakdown of the outstanding securities in the country shows that they were in excess of $1,178 million. Of this figure, $111 million of the total were state issues; furthermore, of that total, 18 percent was owned by foreign investors.

In the early 1850s money became plentiful and the public flocked to the "Board's" rooms. So great was the speculation in this period that an "outside board sprang up with even more brokers than the regular exchange."[9] The new board leased quarters below the regular exchange and constant communications were maintained between the two markets. Banks aided the early 50s' speculative craze with a liberal hand. For example, brokers were known to deposit $1,500 cash and immediately draw checks of $100,000 to $300,000, which were promptly certified. Historians claim that the twelve-month period ending June 1853 has never been equaled in prosperity. In the latter part of this year the picture suddenly darkened. London sold American securities, banks called in loans, deposits fell. In late 1853 it was said that "Wall Street was as somber as a plague-ridden city, with brokers flitting in and out like ghosts." The Exchange Board almost ceased to exist.

By the summer of 1855, prosperity had returned, money was as plentiful as ever, crops were excellent, railroad earnings were high, and speculation was again profitable. The year 1857 saw the big bank panic of the period; the bottom dropped out. Erie Railroad stock fell from 64 to 18; New York Central from 95 to 53. An irresponsible banking system had again created chaos in the nation's economic organizations. The Exchange Board showed marked strength in this panic,

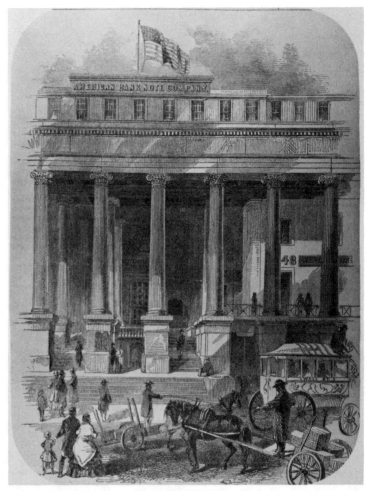

The Merchants' Exchange, New York
As banks increased in numbers, the demand for distinctive bank notes grew. In 1858 the leading bank note companies, nine in number, united into an Association, "American Bank Note Company." They conducted their business of making superior bank notes within this imposing building on Wall Street.

and although its securities showed a sharp drop, it still had a market. The unlisted securities were unmarketable, by contrast. The desirability for a seat on the Exchange was greatly increased in 1858, but the Board was in no mood for new members. Interestingly, it had become an exclusive Club, a situation of which its members were proud. The members had adopted the standard dress of silk hats and swallow-tail coats during business hours. It had become a genteel business as well as a profitable one. The entry of young men was frowned upon. To this end, entry fees were raised to $1,000 which hard fact kept many young men from joining even if they were able to overcome the hurdle of five blackballs, which would reject their membership. As one perceptive broker of the day observed "The

1858
Many successful father-and-son financial dynasties were being founded in this period. Large-scale manipulation of money in America's future history would to some extent result from this beginning.

mendous growth of the express companies in the United States. Their growth, from inception to a large substantial industry, all within a period of 15 years, was owing solely to the astute efforts of the pioneer expressmen in the field of private enterprise. Historians disagree as to who founded the first express company and exactly when it came into being. The idea of a private concern's carrying goods, valuables, and money safely from one destination to another was strictly an American innovation, and probably the first express company was founded in the mid-1830s. By 1840, William F. Harnden offered weekly express service between Boston and New York City. He soon added Albany, New York, to his regular schedule. Tracing the path of the westward expansion of the express companies, Pomeroy and Company of Buffalo commenced its Albany to Buffalo service in 1841. Henry Wells, new manager of Pomeroy and

old fellows were united together in a mutual admiration league and fought the young men tooth and nail, contesting every inch of the ground when a young man sought entrance to their sacred circle."[10]

The volume of speculation showed a substantial increase in the late 50s. In one month of 1856 it reached 1,000,000 shares. For one day in 1857 its volume was 71,000. The Exchange Board in 1856 had raised its annual dues to $50. In this era speculation had had its day and Jacob Little typified the great bear operator of the period. Mr. Little had won and lost four fortunes, but in 1856 he was caught short with 100,000 shares of Erie Railroad stock. He lost ten million dollars, for he had sold short too soon! He never recovered. The pattern and system of stock speculation developed during this era, laying the groundwork that would be exploited so fully by the industrial pirates in the latter part of the century!

A history of the enterprising in this era would not be complete without recounting the story of the tre-

1851
By the mid 1850s the American express companies had established their new industry by crisscrossing the entire country with their service. On western routes, guards were placed to watch and defend valuable express shipments.

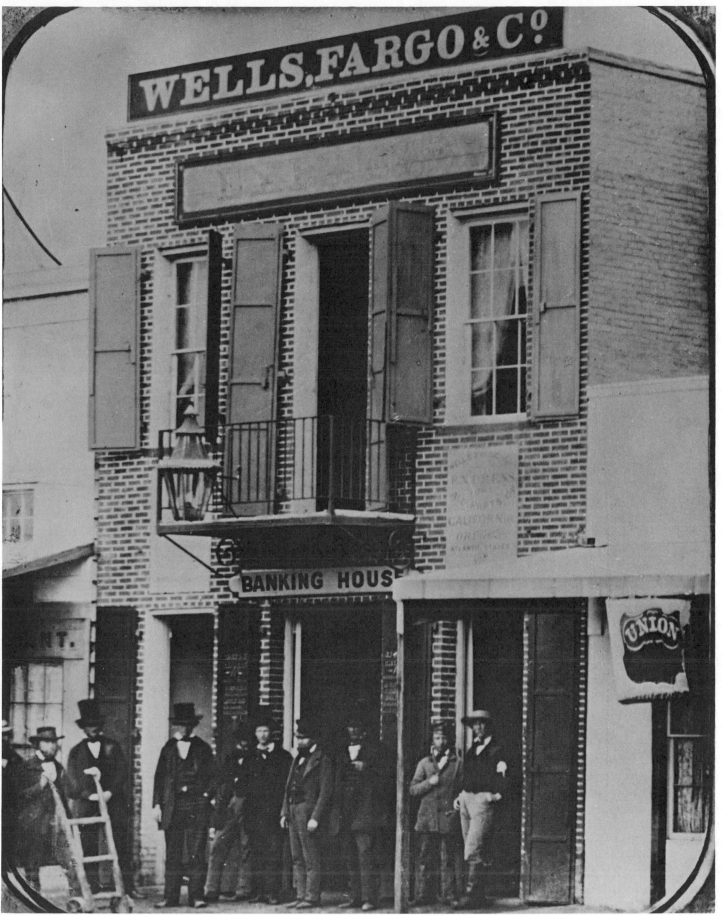

1852   *Courtesy Wells Fargo Bank History Room,*
                                    San Francisco
The Wells Fargo Express Company, by the time this daguer-
reotype was taken, had broken the near monopoly enjoyed
by the Adams Company in transporting gold shipments to
the East.

Company, made the historic first trip. He left Albany carrying a bag of gold, silver, and currency that was consigned to the businessmen of Buffalo. Alternately, he rode on trains and connecting stagecoach lines, the entire trip taking him three nights and two days to complete. In the following few years Pomeroy's business boomed, mostly because of Henry Wells's astute management. With the Pomeroy and Company's success assured, Wells looked around for other related services to add to the normal express business. In 1845, he decided to add a mail service from Buffalo to New York City in competition with the government. He printed a series of six-cent stamps, his price for this mail service. As can be imagined, the United States Government was busy with legal indictments to prevent an intrusion on their monopoly. Until this time, the United States Post Office's price on a letter mailed from Buffalo to New York had been 25 cents. The outcome of this uneven competitive situation was that the government cut its price to below that which the express company could operate. The end result of this unexpected competition from private enterprise was that in 1848, the United States Post Office Department began issuing stamps and put into effect a uniform postal rate of three cents for the first three hundred miles and ten cents for longer distances.

The expanding express business looked very bright, and in 1844 Henry Wells had entered into a partnership with William G. Fargo and Daniel Dunning to open an express line between Buffalo and Detroit. In 1845, with the name changed to Western Express, they extended the service to Chicago, Cincinnati, and St. Louis. Express company competition, fierce and rough, had sprung up all over the country, and by 1848 Adams and Company had reached St. Louis from New York City by way of Baltimore, Washington, and Cincinnati. By 1852, Wells and Fargo had merged with other competing companies to form the American Express Company. Immediately after the merger, Wells and Fargo proposed that the newly formed company extend its operation westward from St. Louis to California. Adams and Company had already extended its operation into the gold fields of California and was reaping a lion's share of the express shipments to the east. However, it was Wells and Fargo formed as a separate company, not the American Express, that finally broke the Adams monopoly. The arrangement made was that Wells, Fargo Express Company would carry express east from California to the Missouri River and the American Express would then carry it from there to the East and New York City.

The trials and tribulation of the new express companies in the early 50s were many, ranging from losing $50,000 in specie with the sinking of the steamer *Atlantic* between Buffalo and Detroit, to the acceptance for shipment of a box allegedly containing $50,000 in specie destined for the United States Treasury, which, when opened at its New York City destination, was found to contain only lead bullets. Both claims were promptly paid by the express companies involved.

Stage coach routes were springing up, carrying the United States mails to the far reaches of the rapidly developing West, and with the establishment of stage coach routes, express company service was also extended. On the western routes, Wells Fargo Company placed guards to watch and defend valuable express shipments. These guards became the world-famous "Wells Fargo Guards" in the latter part of the nineteenth century.

By the mid-50s the express companies had established their new industry solidly by crisscrossing the entire country with their services. Two words described their creed—"Reliability and Responsibility." In the East oftentimes their guards wore black silk hats and black broadcloth coats and usually drove dark blue wagons with scarlet wheels.

Thus, in this era, through enterprise and demand, a whole new industry had been born. It had spread its services to include the delivery of money, jewelry, goods, packages, presents, and daguerreotypes. In addition, it offered a C.O.D. system of delivery that enabled merchants to ship their merchandise collect.

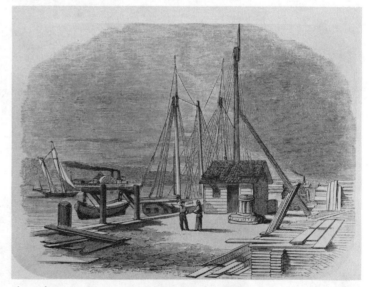

America made great strides in the field of communication after the telegraph was introduced by Samuel Morse. The above illustrates the service wires for the American Telegraph Company at Fifteenth Street, New York City, in the late 1850s.

1851   *Courtesy Time-Out Antiques, N.Y.C.*
*The more enterprising town blacksmith included placing
iron rims on wheels and maintenance of wagons and carriages as a part of his business. In the shoeing of a horse, the
smith was an expert who knew when a corn should be pared
and he had a delicate skill in making sure that the shoe fit
well and did not come in contact with the horny sole. A
typical blacksmith's shop above; to the far left, the rear of an
itinerant daguerreotypist's wagon.*

Many enduring newspapers were established by the enterprising in this period. The *Chicago Tribune* in 1847, the St. Louis *Post-Dispatch* in 1851, and the New York *Times* in 1851, are but a few of the great newspapers that came into print at this time. Horace Greeley reached national fame through his New York *Tribune*, which he started in 1841. The illustrated weekly newspapers, *Frank Leslie's Illustrated,* 1855, and *Harper's Weekly,* 1856, would gain great fame in the Civil War to come. Generally in this day, newspapers reserved their first page for advertisements consisting of many small ones rather than a few large. The second page usually had a very opinionated editorial on national political questions. News was conveyed in chatty columns of printed matter rather than under separate subject headings. Society judged a man by the newspaper he bought and he was frowned upon if he did not provide at least one paper a day for his family to read.

Competition was great among the leading dailies, with the reporters' personal coverage paramount. Also, the electric telegraph had brought faster news transmission. Competitive newspapers often arranged ingenious methods for speeding the news stories. Newspaper prestige often hinged on being first with the latest news. For example, a weekly boat would arrive with European news. On the boat there would be agents aboard representing two or more competing newspapers, bringing the latest news from Europe. One paper had arranged for its agent to throw the news story ashore to a waiting foot-messenger, who would in turn run to a mounted messenger, who would speed it to the nearest telegraph office. Despite this apparently speedy method, another competing editor devised a more ingenious scheme. He arranged for his agent on the boat to shoot his story ashore with a bow and arrow into the waiting hands of his land messenger, who in turn raced to the nearby telegraph office and, presumably, tied up the telegraphic wire by transmitting the first news of Europe—the first to reach the printed page.[11]

Through the many enterprising Americans of the day, the country gained in substance and, through this increased substance, added new members to the rapidly increasing middle-class segment of society.

13
The War with Mexico

For the people of Texas, the years that were often referred to as the "Dark Ages" began when Santa Anna overthrew the Mexican Federal Constitution in 1834 and established a dictatorship. His action brought to a head the smouldering differences that had grown up over the years prior to 1834. Before 1822, there had been three Anglo-American military expeditions invading the Mexican state of Texas. All three had been failures. It was estimated in 1821 that there were 4,000 Americans living under the Mexican banner. By 1830 the Anglo-American population figure had grown to 20,000. This sudden influx of settlers so alarmed the Mexican authorities in 1830 that they passed in that year a federal decree prohibiting further immigration from the United States. Although the incoming Texas-Americans had been allowed to live in peace and with a measure of self-government, there were also other events, in the era before 1834, whereby the relationship had become strained. In their resistance to the Santa Anna dictatorship, the Anglo-Texans formed a convention of representatives from the Texas communities under the direction of Stephen F. Austin in 1835. Not desiring autonomy, the delegates rejected a movement to create an independent state of Texas; instead, they issued a recommendation for a union with the other Mexican states to reestablish the Mexican Federal Constitution. However, the convention did institute a provisional government and created a militia army to be under the command of Sam Houston. Alarmed at what appeared to be open rebellion, Santa Anna moved firmly to suppress the revolt by promptly invading

Texas. Fate had it that he would win a costly victory at the Alamo in March of 1836. This was offset by his inglorious defeat in the later battle of San Jacinto, where he was captured by the Texans. This quickly led to the establishment of the Republic of Texas in that same year. The independent state of Texas was recognized officially by the United States, Great Britain, France, and Belgium in 1837. With the formation of the Republic of Texas, a blending of Spanish cultural influences and Anglo-American habits became a reality. Texan law and order became a compromise of the Spanish jurisprudence system and English common law. Settlers from the southern states now began pouring into Texas and in many ways started a revival of American habits and customs.

A description of Texas in the years 1841 and 1842 was given by a self-styled immigrant merchant from the United States. When he wrote of his recollections of the first years in his newly adopted home, he stated that his vocation was "selling rags, and other odds, ends, and variorum." In his general description of Texas, he said that the "country was very sparsely populated and the residents were about as queer kettle of fish as could be found anywhere." There was little or no money and anyone having six bits was termed "a real whale." Under the general category of groceries fell a varied array of merchandise, such as sugar, coffee, and brogans; all of these items were strictly cash articles. The prices he quoted on basic food items were: beef and pork, one to two cents a pound; a whole venison ham, fifteen to twenty-five cents apiece; eggs, five cents a dozen; butter,

Courtesy Library of Congress
Military Plaza, San Antonio, ca. 1852–1853, above, where
the Mexican General Santa Anna gained a costly victory over
the Texas defenders at the Alamo, March, 1836.

six and a quarter to ten cents a pound. Coffee was in short supply and a great luxury to the old Texans. They drank it half a dozen times a day, straight black, and "strong enough to float an iron wedge." Coffee was bought by the dollar's worth, and a quantity for that amount "would generally fill a pillow slip with the beans." The merchant went on to describe the Texas winters of 1841 and 1842 as being so mild that "the leaves on the peach trees were pushed off by the buds in the following spring."[1]

By 1844 the stage had been set for the gathering black clouds of war. One strong factor was the large immigration of Americans whose blood-ties bound them intimately with the destiny of the United States, particularly the southern states. Another was the fact that the government of Mexico had not recognized the Republic of Texas, nor had it any intention of doing so. Mexico had built a large army, a well-trained army steeped in the traditional Euorpean tactics of the day. The government had imported from Europe trained military instructors to help build it. Santa Anna, always in the background, had steadily applied pressure for a strong Mexico.

The year 1845 was one of political change in Mexico. Paredes was elected President, a man dedicated to upholding Mexico's national rights and honor against the

1848   *Courtesy Library of Congress*
*The battle of San Jacinto on April 21, 1836, proved an over-
whelming victory for Sam Houston (above) and his revenge-
seeking Texas army. Nearly all of Santa Anna's army was
killed, wounded, or taken prisoner; the General was captured the following day.*

United States. Texas had petitioned in 1844 for annexation by the United States, and had been rejected
by the Senate in Washington. In 1845, sentiment had
changed and on March 1, the acquisition of Texas was
sanctioned by a joint resolution of the United States
Congress. The terms of the resolution provided that
Texas would become a state on the 22nd of December,
1845, but it was not until February 16, 1846 that the
American flag was first raised over the state capital
of Texas.

In faithfulness to a pledge, early in 1845, the Mexican
government announced that "if the United States an-
nexes Texas, it will be considered an act of war."

To the eye of the observer, the United States was
unprepared for war. Its small standing army led by West
Point graduates was, as yet, untried on the field of
battle, its tactics yet untested. The idea of a United

States military school had first been proposed by George
Washington, but it was not until 1802, with a student
body of ten men, that West Point was formally opened.
In the years following 1802, the academy slowly expanded. Its men had fought in the War of 1812 and in
the later Florida-Indian wars with distinction, but the
real test would come in the war with Mexico. The
premise that the academy was a wise investment seemed
still in the trial-and-error stage to most Americans in
the spring of 1845. Furthermore, it was apparent to the
discerning eye that neither President Polk nor Congress anticipated the war to come, despite the bad feelings with Mexico that had grown over the immediately
preceding years. The vast consequences and responsibilities of war might remain an enigma to the Washington politicians of 1845, but they practically invited it
when they passed the resolution to admit Texas as a
state. The war was underway before the officials of the
United States government were aware that hostilities
had commenced. It was not until the spring of 1846

1847   *Courtesy Herb Peck, Jr.*
*American uniforms varied greatly in the Mexican War vol-
unteer regiments. The private soldier in the regular army
wore a plain blue uniform.*

Courtesy West Point Museum Collections,
United States Military Academy
A view of West Point, about 1840, as seen across the river
from the Ferry Landing at Garrison, New York. A lithograph.

that President Polk belatedly issued a call for volunteers, some 65,000 in number. Also, the regular army was authorized to increase its strength to 25,000 men.

Throughout the year 1845, the United States had contended that the presumptive border between Mexico and Texas would be the Rio Grande River. However, Mexican nationals and troops were occupying much of the territory close to the river.

Washington had sent General Zachary Taylor and 4,000 men to Corpus Christi, Texas, with instructions to secure the border at the Rio Grande. On March 8,

1846, in pursuance of his orders, General Taylor left Corpus Christi to begin his rendezvous with destiny. His blue-clad men, flags proudly displayed by the leading regiment, had as their objective Point Isabel, near the mouth of the Rio Grande. The plan of attack showed good timing and thought. After a seventeen-day march overland, the General and his army seized Point Isabel; that same day of March 25, the navy's supply ships had entered the harbor. The Mexican garrison had fled across the Rio Grande without a fight. The first step toward establishment of the border had been accomplished without bloodshed. The capture of Point Isabel had secured a permanent supply depot for future operations by the General. Taylor moved with speed and decision and on the 29th of March, after he had advanced his army up the Rio Grande's north bank to a point opposite the Mexican city of Matamoros, he began building a defensive fortification on the American side of the river. The name "Fort Texas" was short-lived, for upon the death of Major Jacob Brown a few days later, the stronghold was renamed "Fort Brown."

The construction of an American fort opposite Matamoros and the prior capture of Point Isabel caused an immediate reaction in Mexico. On April 11, General Pedro de Ampudia, a veteran of the north Mexican wars, arrived to assume command of the Mexican army, which was now assembled at Matamoros. He was replaced two weeks later by another veteran of the Texas wars, General Mariano Arista. The new commander produced action immediately, and on April 25 a large detachment of Mexican cavalry defeated and captured an American scouting party of 63 men commanded by Seth Thorton. To Mexico went the honor of winning the first engagement. Arista's basic plan of strategy was to disrupt and cut the American army's supply line to Fort Brown from their base at Point Isabel. The Taylor countermove to meet the Mexican threat was to take his army back to Point Isabel after leaving a garrison under Major Brown in the now almost-completed fort. In one stroke, like a smooth craftsman of war, Taylor had consolidated his position and had secured his army's supply line and had left the Mexican foe to dash its strength against the fort in futile day and night assaults.

General Taylor, after having received light reinforcements and a secured supply base in his rear, moved out of Point Isabel toward the beleaguered fort on the 7th of May. The battle-seeking Mexican army had meanwhile moved across the river to Palo Alto, astride the Fort Brown-Point Isabel road, thus isolating the fort completely. In the bright afternoon sun of May 8th, at Palo Alto, the American army under General Taylor met and defeated a Mexican army of three times its number in the opening battle of the war.

It was at Palo Alto that many of the future Civil War leaders and heroes saw blood for the first time. Lieutenant George G. Meade, one of the three Topographical Engineers on Taylor's staff, who would win fame at the battle of Gettysburg in the years to come, was personally commended in the general's report of the battle. And the American soldier learned that the Mexican warrior carried his food rations in a compart-

Fort Brown, opposite Matamoros, was the key to Taylor's strategy in his movements leading to the battle of Palo Alto.

ment in his tall leather hat. Also, the Mexican overcoat, which served as a blanket by night, must be worn during the day, no matter how hot the weather. The Mexican army, which the Taylor forces had soundly beaten, had created fear among the American soldiers just a few days before. The Americans had listened to eye-witness reports of the Mexican encampment near Matamoros. It had been described to them as having all the splendor in the tradition of Europe's finest

The invading American army, expanded by raw recruits, was forced to teach its men the military arts almost on the eve of a battle. European observers felt that the ill-trained Americans would fall easy prey to the well-drilled and equipped Mexican army.

armies. The headquarters of Arista, commanding general, had been a great bell-shaped tent of multi-colored stripes, giving it an "almost holy day appearance." The tent had been centered in the encampment, with properly and meticulously dressed officers holding post outside. Five hundred saddles for mules were attractively arranged near the general's tent and also nearby were military bands playing patriotic airs so necessary for a martial display. In contrast with the plain tent of General Taylor and his two blue chests that served as his desk, the Mexican general had brought to his camp beautiful furniture, services of silver, and many highly decorated chests. Amid these splendors, General Arista held his court while old "Rough and Ready" Taylor kept his lonely vigil outside a tent placed in the shade of an old gnarled tree. Only the shade and the tree marked his superior rank in the American camp. The General wore no gold braid, and his plain, wrinkled blue uniform, like his soldiers', was his symbol to the American military fraternity.

On the next day, May 9, General Arista's regrouped army again faced the Americans at a place a little closer to Fort Brown, known as Resaca de Palma. The result of the ensuing battle was a victory for the Americans and a complete rout of the now-disintegrating Mexican force. The army that General Arista had reported as numbering 6,800 Mexican regulars, plus Canale's rancheros and other irregular units, probably brought the total Mexican strength to about 9,000 men before the battle of Palo Alto. By nightfall of May 9th, the relief of Fort Brown was assured.

1847
The Mexican boy (above) wears the type of military hat used by the Mexican soldier.

On May 8, 1846, at Palo Alto, the Americans under General Taylor met and defeated a Mexican army three times its number in the opening battle of the war.

Congress, upon receiving the news of the first bloodshed, declared war on Mexico on May 11, 1846. Six days later, General Taylor and his army occupied the Mexican town of Matamoros. To the jubilant victors belonged the spoils of war left behind by the fleeing enemy. Eight pieces of field artillery complete with shot and accessories, four hundred English Tower muskets, five hundred saddles, and mules, wagons, horses, and even oxen were part of the booty. The weary American troops fell heir to the finer things in life—tobacco, cigars, playing cards. In addition to this, they found approximately $500,000 worth of stores when they opened the Mexican government's warehouse in Matamoros.[2] Taylor and his army had become national heroes overnight.

Throughout the rest of May, Taylor pondered his next move. Reinforcements of volunteer troops were rapidly adding to his army. Washington's communiqués and instructions were many; rumors were even more plentiful. General Winfield Scott had been appointed the general in charge of the war campaign, and, as the rumor ran, was coming to take charge of operations in northern Mexico. Whatever thoughts Taylor had, whatever dread he might have felt of the spit and polish of a command under Scott, he remained silent, bided his time, marshaled his forces, and in the first week of June began a slow advance toward the city of Monterey. Moving up along the south bank of the Rio Grande, he captured the city of Reynosa. There Taylor remained in camp six weeks while awaiting additional reinforcements and supplies. Toward the middle of August, he was convinced that his provisions were adequate and that his army, now some 6,000 men, could defeat any Mexican force. Once again the old general began to move with speed and certainty. On September 17th he had captured Marín, the last stepping stone along the road to Monterey. He approached the outskirts of his objective two days later. Monterey was a flourishing

Mexican city of 15,000 inhabitants and the Mexicans, under the crafty General Ampudia, had placed the strongly fortified city in a complete state of defense. The city was manned by 7,000 Mexican troops of the line and 3,000 irregulars; all were supplied with ammunition and equipment. To quote General Scott when he described the American victory in Monterey, "three glorious days that followed, saw the Americans moving with almost textbook precision." The moves he spoke of were, first, a brilliant flanking maneuver under General W. J. Worth that had captured the most important key fort in the rear of the city's defenses. Second, Taylor's series of frontal assaults, by means of which he had maintained steady pressure on the Mexican defenders, gaining ground slowly until the attackers, by the third day, were fighting their way along the city streets of Monterey. These and other strategic moves

The capture of Point Isabel by General Taylor gave the Americans a supply base. The sketch above shows American reinforcements landing at Point Isabel.

by the Americans left General Ampudia little choice but to ask for quarter. The resulting treaty, unique for two opposing generals to effect, granted a general armistice of hostilities for a period of eight weeks. Other terms of the treaty yielded to the American large quantities of military equipment, which included 25 pieces of artillery and a vast store of ammunition.[3] General Taylor, when news of the victorious battle reached the American public, was once again reaffirmed as the hero of the nation, this time with political overtones, much to the alarmed vexation of many Washington politicians. On September 26 "Old Rough and Ready" had to issue an order prohibiting intoxicants in or near the American encampment; his hard-fighting, triumphant soldiers had overcelebrated their victory. The price of the battle of Monterey had been 500 American lives and twice that number of Mexicans.

The government at Washington, in October 1846, had decided that a major offensive should be mounted to bring the conquest of Mexico to completion. The plan of attack was to capture the port city of Vera Cruz, and then march overland and end with invasion of Mexico City. The planners felt that, with the fall of the Mexican capital, the war would speedily have a successful conclusion. To this end, General Winfield Scott was appointed to lead the expedition. General Taylor, hurt and crestfallen because he had not received the command of the Vera Cruz expedition, refrained from making a public statement condemning the Washington decision. Also, he had received definite orders that he should not advance further into northern Mexico.

After he issued the command confirming Taylor's restricted movements, Scott began transferring a substantial number of Taylor's veterans to the projected Vera Cruz expedition. A dispatch of the American plan to attack Vera Cruz and orders to reduce Taylor's army fell by chance into the hands of Santa Anna.

Santa Anna was striving for full command of the Mexican war effort. He, always wily and astute, and with the knowledge of the American plans in his possession, saw a glorious day ahead for both himself and Mexico. His plan of attack was sound; he would first destroy the now-weakened Taylor army in northern Mexico, and would then return to Vera Cruz at the head of a victorious and exuberant army to meet and defeat General Scott's military force.

Meanwhile, other American campaigns, other armed prongs, were reaching out, covering and conquering the territories outside of Mexico proper. General John E. Wool's expedition was one of the many; his ultimate objective had been the capture of Chihuahua, a major city in northwestern Mexico. There was no reason to

Coe Collection of Western Americana
Yale University, New Haven, Conn.
The Virginia Regiment Entering Calle Real
The Mississippi and Virginia volunteers were among the more reliable units in the Taylor army.

believe that his venture would not have been successful, but when his fighting men reached the Rio Grande, he received an intelligence report that indicated that Santa Anna had been preparing a force to destroy Taylor's army. Wool's decisive action characterized the American officers of the day; he promptly diverted his command and by the end of December 1846, he had reinforced Taylor with his detachment. These additional troops would spell the difference between victory and defeat to General Taylor in the days to come.

The Taylor army numbered some 5,000 men in early January 1847. By January 8, Taylor had advanced to the Mexican town of Agua Nueva, well beyond Saltillo and Monterey, somewhat in defiance of his orders not to advance further than Monterey.

Santa Anna, begging the influential, bluffing the reluctant, and glorifying patriotism, had managed to put together a Mexican army of some 20,000 to 25,000 men for his plan of victory. On February 2, 1847, his army started northward on its three-week march to surprise and destroy the enemy. As an added precaution, he had left behind a well-fortified city of Vera Cruz.

Persistent rumor, always ahead of an oncoming Mexican army, alerted General Taylor to the danger of his position. Acting with his usual precision, he dispatched his best scout, Ben McCulloch, a former Texas Ranger, to spy on Santa Anna's army. McCulloch returned with a detailed report on the foe's strength, equipment, and weakness. Withdrawing here, fortifying there, deftly

Coe Collection of Western Americana
Yale University, New Haven, Conn.
General John E. Wool's defection from his original objective
would spell the difference between victory and defeat for
General Taylor's forces. General Wool, a veteran of the War
of 1812, was breveted major general for his services at Buena
Vista.

moving his force, Taylor lived up to his name "Rough and Ready." Santa Anna saw a well-placed American army when contact was first made. Taylor had chosen the battlefield, not Santa Anna. The site selected by the Americans was a pass between two mountain hills, about two miles in front of the ranch of Buena Vista. The valley in front of the pass selected was about three miles across; the surface was very irregular, dotted with hills and ravines and cut up with deep arroyos, all bounded by lofty mountains. The main road to the ranch ran along the course of a very deep arroyo. On the right of the road, gullies extended to the mountains; on the left, a steep ascent rose to the spurs of the mountains. Perhaps remembering the classic battle of Ther-

A sketch showing Ben McCulloch, Taylor's best scout and a former Texas Ranger, questioning a Mexican deserter. At Buena Vista it was McCulloch who alerted Taylor to the danger of the approaching Mexican army.

mopylae and how the Spartans had held off Xerxes and his Persian army, Taylor arranged his force at the pass, the portal that Santa Anna must capture if the American army was to be destroyed. General Wool had placed his artillery in such order as to command the main road to Saltillo, the road leading to the pass. The other American units were placed astride the road and beyond to the left, extended in battle array in front of the pass.

On February 22, between the hours of ten and eleven in the morning, the Mexicans first sighted the entrenched Americans. Santa Anna halted his troops and, in the custom of the day, politely demanded that the Americans surrender. General Taylor just as politely declined. Hostilities began with a Mexican attack on the American left wing about 3 P.M. of the same day. Inconclusive fighting lasted until sunset, when the Mexicans withdrew for the night.

On February 23, beginning with sunrise and lasting all through the daylight hours, the Mexicans launched a series of determined frontal attacks on the American position. Santa Anna's first move on that morning was a massed direct assault against Taylor's left wing. This vicious charge marked the supreme effort by the determined Mexicans; success was nearly within their grasp and only the arrival of the Mississippi regiment that Taylor had brought up from Saltillo saved the American left from being overrun. The accurate and unexpected firing power of the Mississippians proved devastating; it broke the charge of the oncoming Mexicans, causing heavy loss to their already bleeding ranks. Other fierce Mexican charges against the American left fol-

lowed, all ending with failure. By afternoon of that day, General Taylor, feeling perhaps undue confidence, launched a counter-attack with three of his regiments. In the fighting that followed, these units were badly hurt and forced to fall back on their original prepared positions. However, one result of the American assault was a shift of strategy by Santa Anna. Late in the afternoon he decided to launch what would prove to be his last large attack, one on the center of the American position. The well-placed American artillery cut bloody rows in the Mexican ranks and the ensuing carnage resulted in complete defeat for the attacking units.

The confidence and dreams of a quick, overwhelming victory were fast disappearing from the Mexican scheme, and under the cover of night, by early morning of the 24th the Mexican army had slipped away from the field of battle. Only with the rising sun, on that morning, did the Americans discover that the enemy had fled. Official orders and exhaustion prevented any pursuit of Santa Anna. The Taylor-led army had suffered 267 killed and 456 wounded, and had soundly beaten a Mexican army four times its number.[4] The battle of Buena Vista firmly established the American position in northwestern Mexico. The Mexican defeat removed any plans for recapturing the American-occupied territories outside of Mexico proper; the hope for reannexation of Texas was gone forever.

The Americans had long assumed that with the capture of the Mexican capital, Mexico would be brought to bay. In the early spring of 1847, events were moving rapidly to realize the American ambition to capture

A lithograph picturing one of the many futile charges made by the Mexican army during the Battle of Buena Vista.

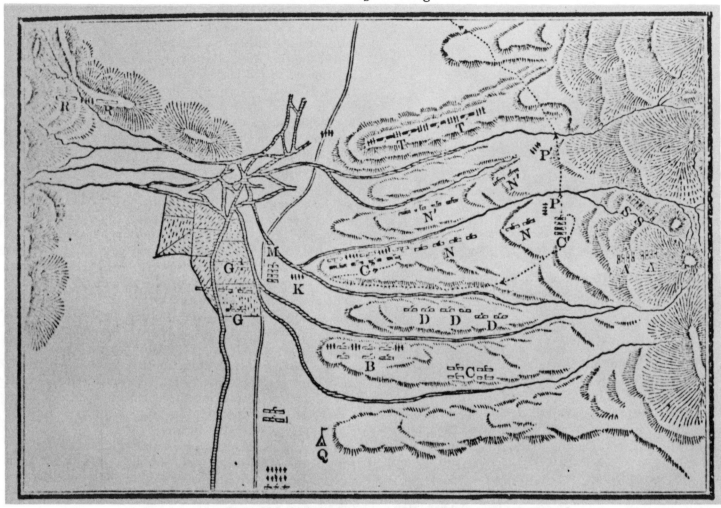

The old map (above) of Buena Vista illustrates the effective disposition of American forces under General Taylor. Letters A through N represent the location of the Mexican army in the various stages of their attack. The main body of Taylor's army (T) is well protected on both flanks by Bragg's battery and the Kentucky volunteers (R), and the American skirmishers (SS).

Mexico City. General Winfield Scott, now firmly in charge of the final American effort, began an amphibious operation to capture the city of Vera Cruz, which was located on the Mexican seacoast at a point nearest, by land, to Mexico City. Hernando Cortez and his little band of courageous Spaniards had set the pattern for the conquest of the Mexican capital when they had marched inland from the sea in 1519. Scott's route was roughly that of Cortez and would be equally successful.

Back in February, the Americans had sent two warships to sound out the Vera Cruz defenses. A Mexican eyewitness described the ships as "Full of officers bent on gaining information as to the weaknesses of the city's fortifications." Hence it came as no surprise to the Vera

Cruz citizens when, in early March, a large American fleet and army transports led by the flagship Mississippi appeared off the city.[5] Probing for Mexican weakness, a United States steam warship engaged the forts in heavy gunfire on March 6th. Two days later, the Americans began pouring troops ashore to the north and south of the city, the objective being to encircle and isolate the town. Methodically, Scott's men began the encirclement, to compress the city in a ring of steel. Helpless, and with a measure of hopelessness, the Vera Cruz garrison of 3,000 men watched the American maneuver. Some resistance, however, was met with from the Mexican guerrillas operating outside the city. After surrounding Vera Cruz, the Americans began the emplacement

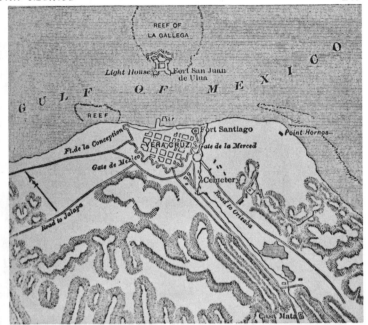

Like Cortez, the Americans made Vera Cruz the first step in the capture of Mexico City. The Americans landed men to the north and south of the city and encircled it with a ring of steel, thus rendering the Mexican fort in the harbor useless.

General Winfield Scott (above, carte de visite, 1861) was twice given a gold medal by Congress. His military record began in 1807. Breveted a major general in the War of 1812, he served in the Indian wars that followed. As a senior officer, he commanded the American invasion of Mexico in 1847. After capturing Vera Cruz (March 29, 1847), victory followed victory, culminating in the capture of Mexico City (September 14, 1847). Its occupation virtually ended the war with Mexico.

of their artillery so skillfully as to leave no doubt that the destruction of the city could only be a matter of time. By March 22 the Americans had completed all of their preparations for the siege of the city, and at 2 P.M. on that day they gave the Mexican defenders just two hours to surrender. The request was rejected by the Mexicans and promptly at 4 P.M. the emplaced artillery began shelling the central plaza of the city. On March 25 the United States warships moved in to attack the fortresses that defended the city from the sea. The ships shelled the forts for about three hours, but on meeting stiff resistance were withdrawn. Rations within the city had long been in short supply, and even in normal times were not abundant. Misery and suffering were fast be-

coming the daily routine of the Vera Cruz Mexicans.

Before dawn on March 27, the consul for England, France, Spain, Prussia, and the Hanseatic cities, went out to the American camp to ask for permission to evacuate all foreign residents and the Mexican women and children trapped in the beleaguered city. Scott refused the request and further stated that, beginning at 7 A.M., the shelling of the city would be on a far heavier scale. The end of the Mexican resistance came quickly, and on March 29, at the head of his army, Scott entered the city to accept its surrender. The town had suffered the ravages of an estimated 6,700 projectiles with a total weight of 463,000 pounds of metal.[6]

Scott, with his total force of 25,000 men, had had a surplus of power to effect the capture of Vera Cruz and had meanwhile dispatched part of his force to secure his flanks. He had sent General Quitman's brigade with a naval force to capture the neighboring town of Alvarado to the south of Vera Cruz. On the same day he had sent another force, under General Twigg, to capture the National Bridge on the road to Jalapa, a two-day march north of Vera Cruz. Both Twigg and Quitman had been successful in capturing their objectives and, with the fall of Vera Cruz, Scott had secured his military position both to the north and south, and at very little cost to his army. The gateway for the capture of Mexico

Perry commanding, to capture the Mexican port of Tuxpan. Tuxpan was located about halfway up the Mexican coast, northward toward the United States. Its capture at the cost of 17 sailors killed or wounded secured for the Americans the eastern Mexican coast north of Vera Cruz.

Meanwhile, the Mexican War effort had taken on a new look of determination. The Mexican newspapers were appealing to the citizens to take heart, that all was not yet lost. A Mexico City paper printed "Can it be possible that among 8 million Mexicans, we cannot find a sufficient number of patriots and determined men who will resist the enemy that is invading our soil without the least regard to our rights?" This change in Mexican attitude was reflected in an American report, which said: "At first the prisoners (during the fighting at Vera Cruz) they had captured seemed cheerful but after the battle of Cerro Gordo, the prisoners were silent and sad." By April General Santa Anna had seized complete control of the Mexican military endeavors. He had gathered together a considerable force and was determined to attack the Americans near Jalapa. Strategically there were several points in his favor; Santa Anna was a native of Jalapa and knew the terrain well; also, if he succeeded in beating the Americans, he would have them confined to the seacoast towns beyond the National Bridge. He had left Mexico City at the head of his army

1842

Lieutenant George G. Meade

Among the Taylor and Scott armies, many young officers would gain, later, their measure of fame in the Civil War yet to come. Meade served in the Mexican War as a courier at Palo Alto and Resaca de la Palma and was officially commended by Taylor. At Monterey, he was attached to General W. J. Worth's staff. In his report Worth wrote: "I am indebted as in many other respects, to the intelligent zeal and gallantry of Lieutenant Meade—Engineers. . . . (Bvt. First Lieut. Sept. 23, 1846 for Gallant Conduct in the several Conflicts at Monterey, Mexico)." At Vera Cruz Meade served on the personal staff of General R. Paterson, who, in his report of March 14, 1847, to General Scott, named "Lieut. George Meade, Top'l Engs." as ". . . exposed to a severe fire and rendering valuable service." The above daguerreotype is dated June, 1842, a month following his reappointment as Second Lieutenant, Topographical Engineers, in the United States army.

City had been opened; the road overland was yet to come.

In April Scott, after consolidating his position at Vera Cruz, dispatched a naval force of 15 vessels, Commodore

A sketch of a camp kitchen during the Mexican War.

and by early April had encamped at Cerro Gordo, using his own hacienda as his headquarters. The countryside around Cerro Gordo was hilly, and was described by one of the invading Americans as "a paradise on earth."

General Scott moved out from Vera Cruz, marched northward along the Jalapa Road, across the already secured National Bridge, and on April 18 met the entrenched enemy at Cerro Gordo. In the short hour-and-a-half battle that followed, the Americans quickly captured the Mexican hill fortifications at what they described as a heavy loss to themselves. Ironically, one of the captured hills overlooked the Santa Anna hacienda, and the Americans were able to turn around the captured Mexican guns and begin shelling the Mexican headquarters. Surprised at the turn of events, the wily old general Santa Anna lost no time in fleeing back to Mexico City, leaving General de Vega and four other Mexican generals to their fate of being captured by the Americans.

From Cerro Gordo on, step by step, victory by victory, the American army moved toward the Mexican capital during the late spring and summer of 1847. Its progress was best told by its author, General Scott, in his summary of the operations of the valley of Mexico when he wrote, "Leaving as we all feared . . . inadequate garrisons at Vera Cruz, Perote and Puebla—with much larger hospitals and being obliged, most reluctantly, from the same cause (general paucity of numbers) to abandon Jalapa, we marched (Aug. 7-10) from Puebla with only 10,738 rank and file. This number includes the garrison of Jalapa and the 2,429 brought up by Brig. Gen. Pierce on Aug. 6th. At Contreras, Cherubusco, etc. (Aug. 20) we had but 8,407 men engaged—after deducting the garrison of San Augustin, (our general depot) the intermediate sick and the dead at Molinos del Rey (Sept. 8) but 3 brigades with some cavalry and artillery—making in all 3,251 men were in the battle, in two days (Sept. 12 and 13) our whole operating force, after deducting again the recent killed, wounded or sick, together with the garrison of Mixcoac

Courtesy Library of Congress
General Scott's military ability was accompanied by a love of
pomp and ceremony. He was affectionately called "old fuss
and feathers." The above lithograph drawn in about 1850,
illustrates his "Entrance into Mexico."

(the then general depot) and that of Tacubaya was but 7,180; and finally, after deducting the new garrison at Chapultepec, with the killed and wounded of the two days, we took possession (Sept. 14) of this great capital with less than 6,000 men. The army as always opposed by three and a half times its number."[7]

In statistical summation, the Americans had lost more than 40 percent of their effective force in a little over one month. Their loss, excluding men left for garrison duty, had been 2,703 officers and men, killed, wounded, or missing. Furthermore, the American army had killed or wounded 7,000 Mexicans, taken 3,730 prisoners, including 13 generals, captured 75 pieces of ordnance, 20,000 small arms, and an immense quantity of ammunition. Nevertheless, it had been disease and not battle casualties that consistently thinned the American ranks from the original landing force of 25,000 men at Vera Cruz. As one American soldier declared in his reminiscences of the Mexican campaign: "An army surgeon had little practical sense except when extracting bullets from dead soldiers or ordering one buried."[8]

On the afternoon of September 13, a deputation from the Mexican city Ayantamiento reached General Scott's headquarters. The group informed the American general that the government of Mexico and its army of about 20,000 men had fled the capital. An armistice agreement was quickly reached, one point being that the Americans would restore law and order to the new chaotic conditions within the city by establishing both

1852
America's military might began dressing up after the successful Mexican War, and the regular army offered a career for the young enlisted man. The "stove pipe" head gear (shown above) held by these noncommissioned officers was topped by a pompon of red, white, and blue feathers. On rainy and windy days the costly feathers had to be removed from the caps.

Coe Collection of Western Americana
Yale University, New Haven, Conn.
Webster's Battery at Minon's Pass
The highly maneuverable American artillery and its accurate marksmanship easily outclassed their foe—the Mexican artillery.

a Mexican police force and a military police from the American occupying troops under the command of General Quitman.

Throughout the day of September 14 the American force literally fought their way through the city, oftentimes from rooftop to rooftop, until, by nightfall, control of the city became a reality. Some of the lawless conditions had been caused by the releasing of 2,000 convicts from the city prisons. This had been the Mexican government's last defiant gesture before fleeing the city.

Later lithographers, in portraying the American army's triumphant entry into Mexico City, would show the army to be garbed in immaculate bright blue uniforms, would depict fresh and clear-eyed men with beautiful banners flying. The eyewitnesses of the entry painted a truer picture when they told of faded and often nondescript blue uniforms, tattered regimental and American flags, and tired horses, and above all this, the proud air of a victorious army somewhat resembling the weatherbeaten stout band of conquistadores under Cortez who had entered the same capital centuries before.

The American war-planners had been right. The fall of the Mexican capital signaled the virtual end of the war. Santa Anna was deprived of his command; the often well-equipped Mexican army was no more. A Treaty of Peace was agreed upon and signed into being on February 2, 1848. One of the more important provisions of the treaty gave the United States a clear title to the areas of Texas, New Mexico, and the occupied portions of California. In exchange for these territories, the United States would pay Mexico $15,000,000.

By 1848 the Americans had emerged as a world military power. Their innovations in military theories had been utilized and proved on the field of battle. Their investment in a military school had worked well. From the very onset of hostilities with Mexico, the superiority of American military tactics was apparent. European observers of the war had returned to their native states with new notions of military strategy. However, it was their criticism rather than their new-found knowledge that received wide publicity throughout Europe. Criticized or not, the Mexican War had been the most successful war the United States had ever waged and it firmly established the Americans as a world power.

Section IV

THE PEOPLE OF AMERICA

14
Love and Marriage

Marriage represented to a woman of this young republic social position and security. Marriage and family for a man was a definite social asset if he conformed to society's image of father and husband. Choice of wife for an ambitious man was of utmost importance to enhance his prestige. He sought a woman who could play the role of a lady and supply the necessary social graces and cultural atmosphere to his household. Also it helped if a future wife could take a leading role in church and welfare work. Men of all stations in life shared this view of womankind; miners were heard to remark after making a rich strike, "Thank God, now my wife can be a lady!"

This male viewpoint made it necessary for a woman to be well versed in the art of housewifery, to read extensively, and to have a lively interest in the arts, especially music. The ideal of woman created from the social order of the day enabled her to be placed on a pedestal by all men. "True ladies" were in great demand and a woman catered to this universal male image of her, in outward appearance at least.

Foreign visitors looked askance on the American male's attitude toward woman and roundly denounced the American woman as reading much but having few ideas of her own, and insisted that she tried to imitate the aristocratic manners of Europe. History belies the former criticism. Although some segments of American society undoubtedly carried the ladylike theme to extremes, such as restrictive exercise and uselessness, it is unlikely if this had nationwide acceptance, especially in the extensive rural and frontier areas in America.

The educated and well-bred woman was found very helpful in the West, forming school classes and cultural circles; on a nation-wide basis women worked in a quiet way for better education and other social reforms. Photography of the 1840–1860 period refutes the idea that these women were pale, pinched, subservient, or sexless. Instead are found vitality, beauty, and a certain attractive dignity.

It was also important for the woman of this age to make a suitable marriage, for laws were generally not favorable to widows left in poor circumstances or to divorcées. The courts, not wanting to have public charges on their hands, usually saw that the widow had "necessaries" prior to any claim on her late husband's estate; however, if the widow was left penniless, she would become a public charge or be at the mercy of her relatives. Since employment was not plentiful for women of this era, marriage and preparation for marriage formed a serious consideration.

Although most marriages stemmed from a romantic origin and courtship, it was also common practice to marry for convenience, money, social position, or a combination of these. Many novels of this period show this custom. Laws varied in the states as to woman's property rights after marriage; most of them took from her all rights and responsibilities. Some states were making an effort to correct this situation. In Alabama in 1848 a law was passed to create a separate estate for a woman, but generally speaking, a married woman needed a third party or trustee to handle her affairs. It was a common custom, if a man married a well-to-do woman,

1842

A fine home and charming family were achievements esteemed in all communities. Gracious manners and hospitality were cultivated. Visitors were welcomed in an age when communications were still in infancy. The scene above was one of the earliest photographs to be taken of a modest home in America.

for a family lawyer to draw up a contract prior to the marriage ceremony, designating the woman's wishes in regard to the dispersing of her money or property in the event that she died before her husband or if she wished certain rights of her estate to be retained.

Marriage laws in 1855 were as varied as were interpretations of what was the law of the land. The old common law still held sway in some areas, where it had not been superseded by statute marriage laws. The old common law was a civil ceremony or contract.[1] Three factors only were needed: the ability to contract the mar-

riage, willingness, and proof of contract. This agreement was made before witnesses and was considered a valid marriage. In America the sacredness of the marriage institution was widely recognized and public sentiment generally supported a marriage with religious overtones, performed by a clergyman.

Many of the old marriage customs were carried over to America from England, Scotland, and Wales. The old English ceremony of sprinkling wheat over the head of the bride was practiced. Anglo-Saxon marriage parties, usually attended by music, feasting, and dancing, were

1854

. . . The ideal of woman created from the social order of the day enabled her to be placed on a pedestal by all men. . . . Photograph by Jeremiah Gurney, New York.

customs adopted by American brides. Also prevalent was the custom of the wedding cake and ring, handed down from remote antiquity. The wedding ring, which was worn on the fourth finger of the left hand, came from the ancient belief that a small artery ran from the finger to the heart. It was a common belief in England that the wedding ring signified eternity and purity (because the ring had no end and was made of virgin gold.

The Golden Wedding, also called "Golden Bridal" and originating in Germany, was widely celebrated but was not so romantic a custom in America as in the German version. A marriage of sixty years was a rare event because of the high mortality rate after the age of seventy. An interesting celebration of a sixtieth wedding anniversary took place at East Hampton, Massachusetts, on January 14, 1856. The aged couple were Mr. and Mrs. Wright. It was a cold, icy day and the

festivities were planned for six in the evening. Four of the five sons of the couple came for the gala event, the absent one being in Wisconsin. A few well-loved neighbors came to wish the Wrights well. The special guest of the evening was the minister who had wed them, the Reverend Dr. Williston, still spry at ninety-three. He blessed the couple in the name of the Lord. Also present and adding further zest to the gathering were four of the original wedding guests. The eldest son of the honored couple, a well-known former principal of the Williston Seminary, gave a speech expressing the gratitude that the young of the community felt toward the elderly couple and made pleasant general remarks applauding the aged. Music was a part of the evening's entertainment. All hearts were thrilled to hear the old-time tunes, "St. Martins," "Lenox," "Majesty," and "Greenville." One of the songs sung was composed expressly for the occasion. At nine o'clock the guests took leave of the happy couple. (This was the usual hour for country festivities to end.)

In the transitional period between a rural and an industrial America, the family remained large. The age for getting married depended usually on the section of the country. In the South and West girls married very young, and it was not uncommon for a woman of twenty-three to be a widow for the second time. Nor was it rare in these areas to find double or triple divorces. Sometimes it was reason enough for a woman to be free of her marriage bond if she could show the judge some moral danger; for instance, if her husband was a gambler, drank too much, or was too lazy to support the children. Alimony was given in some instances. In New England the marriage ages were different, and frequently women married men old enough to be their fathers.

Many of the middle-class society, including prosperous farmers, had servants. Often a widowed relative, young cousin, or newly arrived immigrant in need of a home came to live in the household, thus freeing the mother for careful training of children and other timely pursuits. Actually the running of these spacious, often formal homes called for considerable ingenuity and talent.

Foreigners visiting the American family were shocked and appalled by the perpetual tumult and revolt in the nursery, by the children's talking back and having bad manners early in childhood. The observers noted that a boy could talk politics before he was in knee breeches. The American parent argued back that a child's spirit must not be broken. The great debate went on: to spoil or not to spoil children.

Lectures and books on rearing children, marriage, and

birth control were immensely popular and books were printed and sold by the thousands. Orson Squire Fowler, noted phrenologist, wrote many of these books and added the interesting theory that a good mother had a large head and an unmotherly one had a small one! There were good parents and bad parents; no in-between.

Responsible parents were expected to teach their child at an early age to be industrious. Little ones were kept out of mischief by such chores as making patch-work quilts, knitting socks, making feather fans, picking berries and flowers. The son in a rural area was taught the rudiments of farming; in the city, a trade. Girls in all areas were taught the household arts. At home, rules of good health were observed early because of prevalent disease, also the home was expected to encourage the

Arts and Sciences. The school was to cultivate the intellect and science again was stressed. At the higher level of education the student was expected not only to become a bookworm but to be practical and wise. The parent was advised to educate the child in a three-pronged manner, physically, mentally, and morally, the latter the most important. Above all, in rearing a child a good disposition was to be cultivated, religion being the helping partner. The bad parent was one who was indulgent, neglectful of education, health, and religion.[2] Parents were continually warned by newspapers, books, periodicals, church, and lectures that if they did not provide an ideal home standard and good example the child would grow up to lead a miserable, unhappy life, a direct result of poor upbringing.

While the majority of American families held to this

1841
An outdoor daguerreotype of an affectionate couple.

1852
A new custom began in this era—the portrait of the newly-wed through the eye of the camera.

1853
For casual wear, large checkered "pantaloons" were in style.
A great variety of sport caps were offered; the one pictured
above was covered with oilcloth.

1855
Attractive headdresses were often worn, made of flowers
ribbons woven with other materials. Furred cloaks were
fashion.

1856
An example of a fashionable riding habit.

1850

The Bowtie Portrait

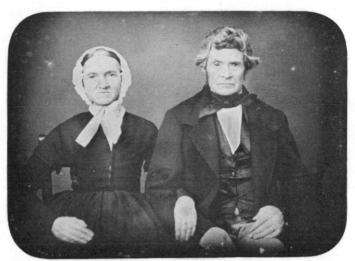

1851

In America the sacredness of marriage was widely recognized. When a couple reached "the golden wedding anniversary" it became a community affair.

1848

The Lock of Hair

Most marriages originated from a romantic courtship. Sentimental tokens were many.

1853
The pride in marriage and children during this era is well illustrated above.

1857
Foreigners visiting the American family were shocked and appalled by the perpetual tumult and revolt in the nursery.

As social graces were important in this age, parties were frequent for the young ones of wealthy and middle-class families. Music, dancing, and refreshments provided much of the entertainment.

1845 Courtesy Time-Out Antiques, N.Y.C.
Books and pleasant home surroundings for children were encouraged in this era.

1858
Religion was the helping partner in the rearing of a child.

1857
Newspapers advised parents to join in with childhood games and warned fathers to beware of "gain and fame."

1856
Lectures and books on rearing children, marriage, and birth control were immensely popular and sold by the thousands.

traditional pattern of marriage and family, a few experimenters in society were embarked in "free love" society movements. One of these experiments that became moderately successful was based on communistic principles, including the unorthodox principle of "complex marriage." The founder of this unusual community was John Humphrey Noyes (1811–1886). He was born in Brattleboro, Vermont, of good parentage. His mother was an aunt of Rutherford B. Hayes, later president of the United States. Noyes was graduated from Dartmouth in 1830 at age nineteen. He continued studying law for a year and then after being converted in a revival, his interests turned toward the ministry. After a year of theology at Andover, he studied for another year and a half at Yale. By 1833 he was licensed to preach by the New Haven Association. His unorthodox views of present salvation from sin resulted in the withdrawal of his license in February, 1834, and he was thereafter called a "Perfectionist." In 1836, he returned to his father's home in Putney, Vermont, where he founded a Bible school. His ideas brought him many disciples, one of whom he married in 1838. In 1843, Noyes and his followers formed the Putney Corporation or "Association of Perfectionists." This was the forerunner of the famed Oneida Community, which was founded on the basis of common property ownership, and held radical religious and social concepts. It

1854

Visitors from abroad mistakenly believed that American parents showed tenderness with their children only in early infancy.

1858

An argument went on in the American home, to spoil or not to spoil children. It was generally decided that a child's will must not be broken.

naturally created considerable opposition from churches and the Vermont people.

On October 25, 1847, Noyes was arrested in Putney and charged with adultery. The case came before the grand jury, charges were preferred, and Noyes left the state, forfeiting bail. He accepted the invitation of Jonathan Burt and others to settle near Oneida, Madison County, New York, and in 1848 the Oneida Community was founded.

Noyes had edited a great deal of material concerning the perfectionist doctrines: from 1838–1843, *The Witness;* 1843–1846, *The Perfectionist;* 1846–1847, *Spiritual Magazine;* followed by the *Oneida Circular* in 1851–1854. A letter written by him in Ithaca, New York, addressed to David Harrison of Meriden, Connecticut, became the well-known "Battle Axe Letter." It got into the hands of dissenters, who exposed excerpts of the letter's contents relating to doctrines of complex marriage, much to the annoyance of Noyes. Some of the letter's disclosures were published in Philadelphia: when

An evening social gathering in the great family hall and meeting place of the Oneida Community, illustrated by the above lithograph.

the will of God is done on Earth as it is in Heaven there will be no marriage; the marriage supper of the Lamb is a feast at which every dish is free to every guest; in a holy community there is no more reason why sexual intercourse should be restrained by law, than why eating and drinking should be, and there is little occasion for shame in the one case as in the other. "I call a certain woman my wife, she is yours, she is Christ's and in him she is the bride of All Saints."

The peculiar religion of the community was set forth in the *Oneida Circular*. They called their social system "Bible Communism" and "Complex Marriage," and stressed the fact that they held freedom of love only within their own families. The community was subject to free criticism and male continence. They professed permanency and responsibility of marriage, and free love was not to mean freedom today and leave tomorrow, or freedom to beget children and then desert them.

The lands belonging to the Oneida Community were principally in the town of Lenox, Madison County, New York, which was four miles south of the village of Oneida. The site of 600 acres had once been an Indian reservation, nearly one mile from north to south. Starting capital for the venture was $100,000 for lands and buildings. A few unsuccessful years made the capital dwindle to $40,000. From the first beginning with two couples, Noyes and his wife and a Mr. Cragin and his wife, the community had increased by 1875 to a total of 253 members. Building on the tract consisted of a mansion, tontine, trap shop, silk factory, and Willow Place residence.

The mansion contained offices, a family hall that served for both social doings and a meeting place for members to air complaints. The room contained seats and a stage. Also in the building were an upper sitting room, a small library of 400 volumes, a scanty museum, and ordinary family rooms for the residents. The Tontine, a large brick building, was just a few yards west of the mansion and was connected by an underground passage. Here domestic duties were carried out for the community—cooking, washing, and other chores. The Willow Place community was a small offshoot of the parent organization, located ten miles north and consisting of 19 members.

The business affairs of the community were handled in an orderly manner. Applications, in written form, were made to a finance board for the desired sum of money needed by members and managers of the small businesses. The board considered all applications and furnished the needed funds. A yearly inventory was taken, which was handed in to the general office by the last day of December. The books were then closed. A full financial statement was then issued concerning income and expenses of the community and how the co-operative earnings, if any, would be invested.

At first the community was devoted solely to agriculture and fruit raising, but made little profit. It was not until the manufacture of steel traps, invented by one of the members, Sewall Newhouse, that they began to prosper. This was followed by the manufacture of chains to be used with the traps. Later the community began canning fruits and vegetables. In 1857, the inventoried capital was $67,000. After the first few years the community was accepted in a tentative way as the members gained the reputation of being industrious, hard-working citizens, and their word was considered good. The community was not very much disturbed by the outside world for twenty-five years until measures

A lithograph illustrating the kitchen of the Oneida Community. The cooking and laundry duties were shared equally by the female members of the colony for the entire membership.

toward legislative action were taken by several ecclesiastical bodies in central New York. In 1879 Noyes, seeing the end in sight, suggested to his followers that it would be necessary to defer to public opinion and to abandon the practice of complex marriage. This change was followed by transforming the Oneida community into the incorporated Oneida Community, Limited, a cooperative joint stock company.

A scientific experiment conducted by some chosen Oneida community couples with the idea of race improvement through breeding had led to much public indignation toward the community. Also the curious public had sent reporters in to ask questions of this unique society group. Various stories came to the outside about Noyes's doctrines on sex. One was that it was undesirable for two inexperienced persons to rush into "fellowship" with each other; another doctrine was that he adjured his followers to let their intercourse and relation be as "free as the fowls of the barn yard."[3] Members of the community claimed they had arrived at a degree of perfection which knows no such thing as shame. Reporters also found out when a female came from the hand of Noyes, she was called "Mother."

Many outsiders had long believed that all was not as spiritual or placid as claimed regarding the complex marriage system. Supposedly women were free to reject whomever they wished, but apparently this was not always so. It was rumored that many women were subjected to severe flogging for not complying with the wishes of men. Substantiating these rumors was the case of Sarah H———, who was said to have received brutal treatment. Her brothers interposed and had the ringleaders arrested and brought to trial.[4] At the trial one of the Oneida community women testified that the H——— case was not exceptional and testified to having been forced to have relations with sixty different men in a period of two weeks. This astounding exposé brought forth only a nominal fine to the accused from the dispensers of justice in Madison County.

An interesting phase of the community involved the children. When a child was born it was cared for by the mother until weaned, and then was placed among the other children with the mother caring for the child at night until it was five years old. The children, reportedly very bright, led a wholesome, healthy, and protected life, enjoying games and sports. A children's hour was held from 6:00 to 7:00 o'clock in the evening, with songs and plays enacted. Special school classes gave them a well-rounded education. All was protective until the ages of thirteen or fourteen, when they were indoctrinated into the society by older members.

The costume of Oneida women was distinctive. Their plain dress was a "bloomer-type," with the skirt reaching to the knees, terminating with a close-fitting straight pantalette that reached to the top of the shoe. The upper bodice was vest-like, buttoning high to the throat, its sleeves short and hanging. Hair was cut short and parted in the center. The costume was completed with a straw hat. Men dressed as they pleased.

Noyes based his principle of communism on his interpretation of the New Testament. In his pamphlet "Bible Communism" (1848), he affirmed that the second coming of Christ took place at the close of the Apostolic Age, right after Jerusalem was destroyed. Noyes argued his beliefs, using many New Testament passages, especially ones from the book of John, to illustrate his meanings. He showed that after the second coming and the beginning of Christ's reign upon earth, the true standard of Christian character was sinlessness, which was possible through vital union with Christ; and that all selfishness was to be done away with, both in property and person. Communism, therefore, argued Noyes, was to be established in all relations of life. He firmly disclaimed any connection with "Free Love" societies, saying that their views leaned toward anarchy.

Despite Noyes's attitude toward these free love societies, Oneida community was linked with those who cried abroad in the country that "marriage is doomed."

1846

Parents were expected to teach their child at an early age to be industrious. Popular chores for the little ones were making patchwork quilts, knitting socks, and making feather fans.

Other societies that joined in the hue and cry were Free Lovers, Individual Sovereigns, Berlin Heights, Spiritualists, Advocates of Woman Suffrage, and Friends of Free Divorce, all participating in varying degrees.

The free-love experiment considered the most important after Oneida was Berlin Heights, which was located 45 miles west of Cleveland and 15 miles east of Sandusky, Ohio. Berlin Heights was an offshoot of "Free Lovers," who had their headquarters in New

York and various settlements throughout the country. The experiment began in 1854 under the leadership of Francis Barry, a plausible-sounding extrovert. As soon as the society, composed mostly of Spiritualists, was established in the picturesque Ohio countryside, it started warfare on marriage by lecturing wherever its members could find an audience. Newspapers were set up that advocated their free love doctrines. They expounded such alarming things· as: it was a sin for a

1855   *Courtesy Miss Josephine Cobb*
An awesome panorama of nature, Niagara Falls, the great showpiece of America, attracted sightseers and artists from home and abroad and was a favorite place for honeymooners. The falls were one of the most challenging and popular subjects for the early daguerreian artists.

couple to quarrel; it was not necessary to be married; a couple living together in adultery were just as pure as the legal ones; marriage was a fraud; and so on. In trying so relentlessly to foist their doctrines on the neighboring people, the Free Lovers stirred up considerable resentment, especially among the women. The villagers were sensitive to stares of visitors to the area, who invariably mistook them for "lovers." Town meetings were called and plans and laws were drawn up to combat the group. The villagers were defeated at every turn; always a court of justice would acquit the intruders.[5] The Free Lovers got into politics and formed a Free Love Party, which began to wield an influence by its widely distributed newspapers. Sometimes the newspapers were confiscated and burned by the townsfolk. This only caused more squabbles. One curious villager, later branded a peeping tom, inadvertently brought some peace through his disclosure that he saw some of the Free Lovers of mixed sexes bathing in the nude in a sheltered pond. This stirred the villagers and brought an indignant protest from leaders of the Free Love Society to their own members, following acknowledgment by the guilty group. After this episode the society began to be more discreet. In 1858 a small group of advanced members bought a farm and lived together. Finally the tired villagers gave up the fight and ignored the affair, which ended in a draw.

The effect of the free love propaganda sponsored by the various groups about the country had an influence on American society. In the eyes of many, marriage was stripped of much of its religious character, lowering it to more of a business arrangement. Also, the expressed views of many of the Advocates of Women's Rights were having an effect on the marriage institution. The most important effect that developed from these societies' efforts was that states began granting divorces with permission to marry again for other causes than adultery, and divorce began increasing at a rapid pace. Divorce laws varied greatly in different states—all conceded adultery as grounds; however, in many states desertion was also cause for ending a marriage. The states that had the largest divorce applications were Vermont, Connecticut, and the western states. The most lax in divorce laws was Indiana. By the late 1860s divorces were pushed in New York, many set up by professional perjurers.[6] Such legal innovations were begun as the granting of alimony after divorce for adultery (1853), and new grounds for divorce in "violent scandalous deportment toward the wife." Not valid as grounds, however, was "boisterous, profane or vulgar language." Incompatibility, too, became cause for terminating a marriage. If a wife was turned out of the house by a husband, he was liable for her "necessaries." These laws were all different and confusing; nevertheless, new laws were emerging. It was realized that legislation was sadly out of harmony with the current view of the people.

The marriage institution was foundering badly and would slip in the years during and following the Civil War, but, as with all American institutions, its roots were deep-seated and would withstand increasing pressures, to renew itself later in the century with a surprising vitality.

15
Medicine, Quackery, and Fads

Dr. Oliver Wendell Holmes said in 1860, with great truth, that if all of the medical material then in use was sunk to the bottom of the sea, "it would be all the better for mankind and all the worse for the fishes."

If the American people were making progress in other fields, medicine was slow in keeping pace with its contemporaries in science. Americans seldom lived beyond the age of 70. The extremely high infant mortality brought down statistics for the life expectancy to about 40 years. Although many doctors had a cherished and welcome place in American households, there were many of that profession leaning toward charlatanism and quackery. This tendency was often owing to the patient himself, who preferred being drugged within an inch of his life to taking advice from the doctor to practice a sensible diet or health routine. The people were fascinated by drugs in this era and the more mystic and distasteful they were, the more the public responded. The medical fraternity was aware of the evils within its profession and tried to do something about it.

In the large cities infant mortality was of such magnitude that an investigation was demanded and launched by the medical profession. Nearly one half of the whole number of deaths occurring in large cities were of infants before the age of five. The death toll of children under five years of age rose in a ten-year period in the city of New York, from 4,588 in 1843 to a staggering 12,963 in 1853, an increase of 8,375. Infant mortality for the three-year period of 1854–1856 was 43,109 deaths under five years old.[1] These figures were vastly beyond the proportional increase of the population.

Ironically, in the large cities of the old world, infant mortality had been decreasing for many years. Yet, American statistics showed life duration to be three-and-a-half percent longer in American cities, collectively, than in cities of Europe. The worried doctors checked causes for the infant deaths. They noted that deaths were considerably fewer in rural areas. The usual causes were checked—heredity, blood factors of either parent, unknown agents acting on the mother, accidents. "Still births" were found to be relatively rare if the patient was under a doctor's care, or if she was in a hospital at the time of the birth. Probing, the medical doctors found that abortion had become a murderous trade in many of the large cities. Furthermore, it was tolerated, even protected, by corrupt civil authorities and even newspapers allowed conspicuous advertisements for the abortion trade. These so called "murderers" were well known to police authorities, along with their names, residences, and names of guilty customers and victims. Abortionists had post office boxes loaded down with mail. Prosperous with their fat fees, they drove splendid carriages, promenaded in their fine clothes, and took seats at the opera, despite their having the "blood of slaughtered innocents on their hands," as the angry doctors referred to it.

The medical men decried the fact that fathers would allow their wives to become the unfortunate victims of this hazardous trade. Doctors also found that married couples postponed having children in this manner. Drugs, employment of instruments, and other means were taken to arrest early pregnancy. The medical report stated that much of the infant mortality stemmed from such injury.

*During the 1850s and later, a "haunted house" in Massachu-
setts drew hundreds of onlookers and some professional
mediums. A succession of families moved into the old house,
located not far from the main road between Waltham and
Cambridge, but none could stand the mysterious noises and
strange happenings. Residents told of a ghostly carriage
(above) that clattered into the driveway at midnight; its
occupant rang the bell, then the grating of the front door
lock could be heard, and a rapid footfall. An hour later a
shoveling of dirt and the chopping of an axe sounded from
the cellar. It was said that many years before, a young gov-
erness and an old peddler had mysteriously disappeared; the
noises were attributed to the murder of the former that had
supposedly taken place in the haunted house. An interesting
note: in a vault near the house was later found a luxurious
head of golden brown hair, on which pieces of the scalp still
remained.*

The Doctor
Medicine was slow in keeping pace with the great strides of science in this period. Many of the doctors leaned toward charlatanism and quackery. However, the medical fraternity decided to do something about it, and by the late 1850s there was a trend toward a strong moral code and condemnation of malpractice. Note instruments on table.

1857
A very young infant such as the one pictured above would have little chance for survival in the big cities. Many of the deaths ascribed to colic, dysentery, and other diseases were in reality often caused by deadly nostrums, adulterated milk, and impure foods.

Some abortion cases came to court. In Boston, a Madame Restell was convicted June 22, 1841, for a misdemeanor in producing the miscarriage of Ann Marie Purdy by use of instruments. It was a jury trial; the district attorney spoke for three and a half hours and had both the jury and spectators in tears. As the 1840s progressed, the law would become strict on abortion, a crime almost unheard of a generation before.

The drugging of women in confinement to make it "easier" led to infant deaths. Mismanagement of newborn babies took a heavy toll. The medical men reported that they had found that nurses and ignorant doctors fed and physicked the new born, taking them from the mother's breast and substituting a thousand and one slops, tea, and drugs, and spooning into the young mouths worse compounds than they were ever likely to swallow throughout life, if they survived! They

were given not only molasses, sugar and water, catnip, tea, olive or castor oil, and goose grease, but also salt and water, soot tea, gin sling, and even urine were force into the infant's throat scarcely before it had known an hour's life.

Thousands of these infant deaths were ascribed variously to colic, cholera, diarrhea, dysentery, or convulsions, though the last was often produced by drugging for relief of symptoms that the mother's milk would, if taken earlier, have prevented or cured. Other dangers to the young lives were such nostrums as soothing syrup, Godfrey's Cordial, Jayne's Carminative, or some other vile mixture of molasses and water with added opium and brandy. These sleeping draughts and anodyne nostrums were more deadly to the budding young lives than all of the diseases in infantile existence.

Also to be counted among the causes of infant deaths was housing for the poor in cities. Living quarters were sometimes cellars, shanties, and garrets, with little light and fresh air. Cleanliness, clothing, and heat were often found sadly inadequate. Adulterated milk and impure foods were added to the long list of causes of infant mortality. Slops from distilleries in the cities furnished a cheap food for cows. Milk from cows fed this concoction could destroy an infant's health more quickly than alcohol ever could an adult's. Other adulteratives of milk were chalk and water.[2]

America was shocked at this high rate of infant mortality because only a generation before it was the exception not to be able to raise a large, healthy family, which was considered a social asset.

Medical quackery and false theories of medicine of the day were based on the new system of drugging and on the idea that everyone could be his own doctor. Men pretending to be physicians in all areas of the country added to the unhealthy situation. People purchased a box advertised "specifics," complete with a book of instructions. The poor misguided purchasers had faith in the contents of the box, especially when it concerned infantile diseases. Medicines were advertised as being purely vegetable, not making clear the fact that opium or other dangerous ingredients might be of vegetable extraction.

1856
Fashionable surgeons were found in the large cities, where the hospitals were located. A lucky specialist might earn as much as $40,000 in a year.

1859
In the rural areas away from the city with its high mortality rate, babies were much healthier. A rare daguerreotype of a smiling baby.

After the report on infant mortality was complete, the medical profession put forth in 1857 some ideas they felt should be made into law. They recommended that couples should receive a medical examination by a qualified doctor before marriage; abortion be abolished; slum dwellings erased; medical police be established. Also, they pleaded for the building of more hospitals for children.

An editor of a monthly magazine noted, in 1859, a decided trend for doctors to insist on a strong moral code and condemn malpractice among their profession. He also recognized a need for an organized, disciplined medical organization that would bring offenders before a bar and would give the public a chance to air their grievances. The editor was also of the opinion that more proficient doctors were needed, doctors who would be less literary and philosophical outside their profession and more competent inside it; he further urged a plea for reasonable fees. Tales of fabulous doctors' incomes had circulated throughout the country and certainly no ordinary practice could yield more than half of what was claimed. A lucky specialist might earn $40,000 in a year, but a regular practice would probably bring in half that figure and a young doctor starting out could expect a very small income.[3]

Medical education for women was receiving attention, in spite of the fact that most men felt women were too impulsive and too emotional to do a man's hardest work. A group of men and women in Boston in 1852 must have shared a different opinion, for a number of them subscribed $100 each to purchase from Paris a complete set of anatomical and physiological instruments for a New England Female Medical College.[4]

Medical students observed at lectures were thought by many to be such an untamed, odd-looking, oddly dressed set of youth as was to be seen anywhere! A rivalry among the students existed to see who could sport the shaggiest hair or wear the most astounding hat, coat, or cane. The reputation of medical students in the college communities was poor, to say the least.

The scientific journals in the 1840s printed remedies for all sorts of ills, from mosquito bites to hydrophobia. Any new achievement in medicine or dentistry was duly noted by the journals in a friendly, informal way. They advertised the price of false teeth in 1845 as $1 to $3.50, and the cost for filling decayed teeth with white cement 50 cents. All newsworthy items were given consideration.[5]

One of the health fads in this period, based on medical ideas, was hydropathy, from the Greek, meaning "water cure." The active agents in the treatment were heat and cold, of which water was the vehicle used, although not always the only one. The great majority of patients who sought the "water cure" had incurable disease, or so the patient believed. The "water cure" was introduced in England by Captain Claridge in 1840. His ideas were made popular by his lectures and writings. Soon establishments spread to Germany, France, and America. The treatment consisted of packings, hot and cold, for sweating and cooling; hot air and steam baths; general baths, both hot and cold; sitz, spinal, head and foot baths; compresses, both wet and dry; and rubbings. Calisthenics and gymnastics were widely employed with the treatments. The *Scientific American* on May 6, 1848, noted that a patient went to one of the many "cold water asylums" in Massachusetts. He reportedly weighed 127 pounds on entering the establishment. After five months of treatment he lost 33 pounds of "bad flesh." His comment on leaving was that he felt made over! Doctors interested in science were impressed with the water cure and endorsed it.

One of the "water cure" establishments that had facilities for both summer and winter treatment was located at Lebanon Springs, New York. At their principal cold spring, a large bathing house was built, adapted for summer treatment. The water temperature of this spring was 46 degrees in midsummer. For winter treatment every desired facility was there. A warm spring poured out 16 barrels of water per minute and the temperature never varied from 72 degrees even in coldest weather. This stream coursed its way through the large "plunge" and swimming baths.[6] Sea bathing was also considered both fashionable and healthful at the many seaside summer resorts. Also, "Congress Water," spring water from Saratoga Springs was a fad of the day.

Health fads took to other forms than water. An interest in vegetarianism swept the country, entering homes, colleges, boarding houses, and restaurants. Besides health reasons, the regime was adopted to keep long-staying visitors at a minimum!

The first man to start vegetarianism in America was the Reverend William Metcalfe, who came over from England in 1819. As Pastor of the Bible Christian Church in Kensington, Philadelphia, he advocated the doctrine, and his loyal followers celebrated a 29th anniversary of vegetarianism in 1848. After religious services, the assembly had a dinner prepared by the ladies of the church that was "a delightful exhibition of all delicacies from the vegetable kingdom."[7]

In the early movement of vegetarianism, three men stood out as leaders, Sylvester Graham (1794–1851), Charles Lane, and Amos Bronson Alcott. Graham, a Presbyterian minister, brought the fad into popularity.

1846

Medical students were thought by many to be an untamed, odd-looking lot. . . . A rivalry among students existed to see who could sport the shaggiest hair or wear the most astounding hat, coat, or cane.

1856
Diet and health regimes were a fad in this age. Gymnasiums were available in most cities and "Water Cure" establishments were located in the country for the health faddist who wanted to keep physically fit.

In 1830, he was made general agent of the Pennsylvania Temperance Society. While in this capacity, he studied physiology, diet, and health regimes. In 1830–1831, he lectured on these subjects in New York and Philadelphia and later along the Atlantic seaboard. He strongly advocated bread baked from unbolted whole wheat, coarsely ground, and stipulated that the bread should be twelve hours old before eating. In addition to his strict diet regime of fruits, vegetables, and coarse cereals he also urged hard mattresses, open bedroom windows, cold showers, pure drinking water, and a cheerful atmosphere during meals. Tea, coffee, and alcohol were to be avoided. Graham's creed was that "the human race would be regenerated if one had no meat, nor anything with life in it." Emerson labeled Sylvester Graham as the "poet of bran bread and pumpkins."

Amos Bronson Alcott, diligent reformer and philosopher, proposed a cooperative vegetarian colony. In the winter of 1843–1844, Alcott, Henry Wright, and Charles Lane and his son William, worked out plans for the community to be named "Fruitlands." Lane sank his life savings into a tract of land near the village of Harvard, Massachusetts, and the community opened in June 1844. Its creed was, no flesh, fish, fowl, eggs, milk, cheese, or butter. Poor organizing and radical theories

doomed the project and by January of the following year it was abandoned.

A young vegetarian leader, Henry S. Clubb, projected in 1855 "The Vegetarian Kansas Emigration Company," the idea being to establish a home in the West for vegetarians. The first meeting of the proposed company was held May 16, 1855. Forty-seven people signed up, with a promise of 26 more. An agent was sent to Kansas to look for a suitable location, and when he returned in January 1856, he suggested an Octagon settlement near Fort Scott, on the Neosho River. The headquarters of the company was located at 308 Broadway, New York.

The *New York Tribune* announced in January 1856 that this company now consisted of 50 families, with an aggregate capital stock amounting to about $75,000. These vegetarian shareholders were made up of one-

The fashionable seashore resorts of the era were Newport, Atlantic City, and Cape May. The ladies wore picturesque "bathing dresses" of brilliant colors (red was a favorite) with resplendent borders. One man of the era, in writing of his scarlet and orange bathing outfit, said: "We looked fitter for a dance of witches or a bandit pantomime, than for sober bathers." A sketch from an 1849 periodical.

After 1854

Octagon House
*Octagon houses were a fad in the 1850s. In 1850 Orson
Squire Fowler, a phrenologist who had turned to architecture, proclaimed an Octagon house to be "healthy, functional
and economical." Fowler had published a book entitled,
A Home for all; or the Gravel Wall and Octagon Mode of
Building. It created a flurry of octagon buildings about the
country—not only homes but schools, churches, and other
public buildings. Although conceived in simplicity, most of
the structures were elaborate.*

third farmers, and two-thirds mechanics and professional men. The *Tribune* stressed the fact that these
founders lacked preparation for frontier life.

Clubb decided to organize a second company, thereby
avoiding the limitation of vegetarian membership, that
would otherwise be a sister company. It was called the
Octagon Settlement Company and opened for subscription in February 1856. The promoters of these com-

panies planned a model community that would include
a "water cure" establishment, agricultural college, and
scientific institute. The Octagon plan of settlement for
both companies was unique. Each octagon settlement
was to be four square miles, or 2,560 acres. On this
square of land a full-sized octagon was to be imposed,
whose eight segments were each to be divided into two
farms of 102 acres each. Each of these 16 farms would

front upon the central octagon of 208 acres, which would be used as common pasture and park for the mutual benefit of all. A communal life would result from the farms facing the central octagon. In the center point of the communal octagon, a public building would be built to serve as a store, meeting-house, school, and church. It was in the plans to make four of these octagon villages and combine them into a "city" of 16 square miles, with a square of 584 acres in the center. The center square was to be used for an agricultural college and model farm.

The venture was given widespread publicity in 1856 and late in March of that year a group of pioneers, members of both companies left for the settlement. The emigrants numbered nearly 100 persons, who brought with them 20 head of oxen, five or six horses, and the makings of a grist mill.

After the town of "Neosho City" was laid out, the venture experienced a short boom. Lots bought in May at $40 sold a few days later at $197.50. The majority of emigrants arrived in April, May, and June.[8]

This project that had a seemingly successful begin-

1856
The fad of the "tight-ring curl" was brief.

An advertisement from Peterson's Magazine, *1855.*

ning failed miserably. The planners obviously had made rash promises they could not keep. The establishment had only one plow. The colony was beset with mosquitoes, chills, and fever. The so-called "inexhaustible" springs dried up and crops that were planted by the settlers were raided by Indians. When winter came everyone who could leave did so. Mortality was heavy among children and the elderly. By the spring of 1857 it was just another short-lived utopian dream.

Although tea and coffee were outlawed in many "diet" regimes, more coffee was drunk in America in this era than in any other country in the world. In 1850, the United States imported 144,986,895 pounds of coffee, the value of which was $11,215,099. The amount of coffee consumed by every man, woman, and child in the country would be seven pounds each! An interesting facet of the coffee story in England was that all of their coffee was adulterated with dock root and sold for double the price of United States coffee.[9] American families were advised to buy their own coffee beans and roast and grind them, as much of the coffee sold was adulterated with ground corn and peas.

Americans heard lectures in towns and cities on "Mesmerism and Animal Magnetism." They became interested in the idea that many of their ills and diseases could be cured by this method, which would later in the century be known to the medical profession as hypnosis.

A Viennese physician, Mesmer, brought the doctrine or "animal magnetism" into prominence in the latter part of the 18th century. He claimed there was a magnetic fluid, which he called "animal magnetism," that would cure many diseases and could be imparted to a subject or patient by the practitioner from the movement of hands on or near the face.

In 1778 Mesmer was so swamped with patients and thousands of applications that he was forced to expand and treat "en masse." In order to treat a large number

1845

Americans heard lectures in towns and cities on "Mesmerism and Animal Magnetism." They became interested in the idea that many of their ills and diseases could be cured by this doctrine. It later became known as hypnosis.

at once he devised a method that was called the Baquet. The device was a large oaken tub, 4 by 5 feet in diameter and a foot or more in depth, covered by a wooden lid. Inside were placed bottles full of water set in rows that radiated from the center of the tub, the necks of the bottles in some rows pointing toward the center and others pointing away. All bottles had been already magnetized by Mesmer. Sometimes several rows of bottles were placed one above the other, which supposedly made the Baquet high pressured. Underneath the bottles were layers of powdered glass and iron filings. The tub itself was filled with water and redundant in its entirety thus forming a kind of galvanized cell. To carry out the cell idea, the tub's cover had holes that had iron rods of various lengths passed through, movable and jointed so they could be applied to any part of the body. The patients were seated around the Baquet forming a circle, each having his iron rod. Also a cord fastened to the end of the tub was put around the body of each to form a chain. Sometimes there would be two circles, the second forming a circle by holding hands. Mesmer would be dressed in a lilac robe and he and his handsome assistants walked about the room placing his iron rods at the diseased parts of the subjects. Also, the operators applied their hands. During the treatment, instrumental or piano music was heard. Reactions varied with the patients. Some underwent convulsions; many cures were claimed.

In 1790, a disciple of Mesmer's noted that while a subject was in a state of "magnetic sleep" he could be cured of some diseases and his movements controlled by the "magnetizer," and that, after awaking, the subject could not recall his actions. This was the first time sleep was recognized as a relative factor.

Many years later, in 1831, when the Academy of Medicine in Paris reacted favorably to the Mesmerism doctrine, it suddenly became very popular abroad and in America. The men who practiced this doctrine adhered closely to the theory of a magnetic fluid emanating from the operator to his subject or patient. However, the combination of the practice of Mesmerism with other fads, such as phrenology, astrology, and the belief in the influence of magnets and certain metals applied externally to their subjects, led to much quackery and kept the medical doctors from discovering the true value of hypnotism for the many years it was cloaked in sensationalism.

Spiritualism, a doctrine that swept America and thence overseas to Europe, had its birth, at least in modern form, in New York State in 1848. Mr. and Mrs. J. D. Fox and their daughters, Kate and Margaret, heard unexplained knocking sounds in their home.

Spiritualism, a doctrine that swept America, had its beginning in New York State in 1848 at the home of Mr. and Mrs. J. D. Fox. Their young daughters heard "rappings." Communications were believed to have been established between the "rappers" and the Fox sisters. Newspapers played up the story and the fad took root. Lectures were given about the country to eager audiences.

Nine-year-old Kate discovered she could communicate with the sounds and they would respond with raps. The "rapper" confessed to being the spirit of a murdered peddler. An investigation was made and it was ruled out that the Fox family took part in the rappings. It was further rumored that noises had been heard on occasion in the house before the Foxes had lived there.

Later, when Kate and Margaret went to live with a married sister in Rochester, New York, it was believed that a communication had been established between the Fox sisters and their deceased relatives and also prominent men who had died. Thus, Kate and her sister became the first "mediums." Early communications with spirits were made with raps; one rap would mean no, three would mean yes. More complicated communication would be obtained by pointing to letters of the alphabet and in other ways that were gradually added.

Newspapers played up the story and the new doctrine spread quickly—not only to the curious but to people already interested in mesmerism and phrenology. A well-known clairvoyant, Andrew Jackson Davis, already had followers who believed that information from the world beyond could come from spirits of the dead and could be obtained from people in a hypnotic state. Davis had written a book in 1847, *The Principles of Nature, Her Divine Revelations*. Many of such clairvoyants went along with the new idea of spiritualism and became "mediums" themselves. Spiritual "Circles" sprang up everywhere and many took on a religious tone and became churches. Many "spirit circles" were formed in families.

American mediums visited England in the 1850s. One was Mrs. Hayden of Boston in the winter of 1852–1853, and Daniel Dunglas Home in 1855. All of the important mediums went abroad to hold seances.

The early phenomena of raps and sounds soon gave way to mysterious movements of furniture and other objects, the ringing of bells, and the playing of musical instruments, all without apparent physical cause. Other manifestations were lights, quasi-human voices, the presence in material form of human heads and faces, and ultimately, a complete figure; also "psychography," or direct writing and drawing, "without human intervention." Even photographers got into the act with "spirit photography," or the appearance on photographic plates of human and other forms when no counterpart was visible before the camera. There were several professional photographers (all detected in fraud sooner or later) who made photographs that contained, beside the normal sitter, representations of deceased friends.

Mediums were sometimes used in business. Seth Paine,

1856   *Courtesy Time-Out Antiques, N.Y.C.*
                                   Unknown Chess Players
One of the great chess players of the nineteenth century was an American, Paul Morphy (1837–1884). By the age of twelve he had become an excellent player and a few years later, in 1857, he was the leading American chess player. In 1858 he toured Europe and defeated the best chess players on the Continent. His record promoted in America a pride in this ancient game.

a strong believer in Spiritualism and the establisher of the Bank of the City of Chicago, installed a medium to sit behind a counter and decide which loans should be granted.

By 1850 the famed Fox sisters were giving séances in New York and charging $100 and up. Even Horace Greeley, always ready to accept new ideas, endorsed the new spiritualism movement. Further speeding the movement was the report in 1850 that the family of Doctor Phelps in Stratford, Connecticut, experienced disturbances in their home.

An author of New England lore wrote of a typical lecture given on Spiritualism in the whaling town of New Bedford, Massachusetts. Large, showy placards announced the presence of a young lady who would lecture on "Spiritualism" at the City Hall, admittance free. A great crowd gathered at the large, handsome City Hall, which was brightly lighted by gas. The mixed audience came from all walks of life, from suburban dwellers to sailors just in from the local grog shops. The attractive young woman, dressed in blue, took her place on the platform, accompanied by an elderly white-haired gentleman in the capacity of showman. He announced to the audience that the medium was suffering from a head cold but that she would do her best in

A writer of the era observed that two necessary ingredients were needed for a frolicking chowder party—the opposite sex and demijohns of Old Jamaica. From a sketch of 1849.

addressing the group. Meanwhile, a collection would be taken to meet expenses and would everyone please be generous. Three hats were passed and the sound of clinking three-cent pieces could be heard, along with the heavier sound of coppers. The listening showman obviously had an ear trained to the jingle of all coins. The assembly then had their choice of two subjects, which were: "What are the proofs of the immortality of the soul, as furnished by Science, Scripture, Spiritualism, etc.?" "How do the doctrines of Spiritualism agree with the religion and morality of the Scripture, as taught by Jesus Christ?"

It was decided by the audience that the medium choose her subject. The medium then assumed several attitudes. First, her head would rest on her hand, then here eyes were turned upward, then she smiled and whispered as if with the spirits. Suddenly she arose and said emphatically "God doeth all things well." The address was then given in a studied and fluent manner. The audience was receptive, but the performance was interrupted by outsiders who yelled "Fire!" This trick, obviously played before on such audiences, did not succeed, so next the gas was turned off and the hall was plunged in darkness. The audience laughed but was well behaved. In a few moments the lights were on and the lecture was resumed, but not for long, for the lights again went off. Everyone agreed it advisable to close the performance, as the spirits might be angered.

This performance took place in the late 1850s and was probably typical of such lectures around the country. Much fraud was perpetrated on the public through this sweeping movement, but as long as the public believed they could commune with the dear departed, it would continue to retain its popularity.

1851

With the new widespread interest in spiritualism, even photographers joined the mania with "spirit photography." On photographic plates, human and other forms appeared when no counterpart was visible before the camera. Several professional photographers were detected in the fraud.

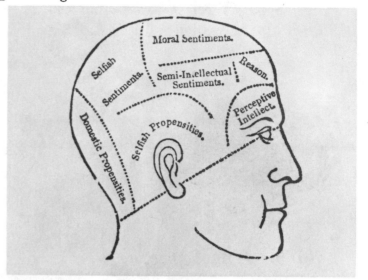

1855

Phrenology, the method of determining man's disposition and character by the study of his skull, had created widespread interest about the country. Heads were even being examined in the schools and prisons. The head shown in the drawing above (left) illustrates how the skull was divided into several main categories called organs or faculties, each with its own name and function.

It was natural, with the interest in science afoot in America in this era, that the doctrines of Phrenology would catch the public fancy. Phrenology was fundamentally a diagnosis of the disposition and character of an individual, determined by study of the shape of his head and skull. Some phrenologists, particulary in Britain, had a system of dividing the skull into 35 sections, which were called organs or faculties, each with its own name and function. Orson Squire Fowler, the American phrenologist who succeeded in interesting a great many of the population of the United States in this so-called science, had a method of dividing the skull into 43 parts, eight more than in Great Britain.

The component faculties of the skull were divided into two large, general groups with subdivisions as follows:

I. Feelings, divided into
    1. Propensities—internal impulses inviting only certain actions
    2. Sentiments—impulses that create emotion as well as activity
        A. Lower—common to man or animals
        B. Higher—proper to man
II. Intellectual faculties
    1. Perceptive faculties
    2. Reflective faculties
An example from the first group of feelings or pro-

pensities, one of nine brain areas in this particular grouping, would be philoprogenitiveness, or love of children. One of the lower-sentiment categories would be self-esteem and one of the higher sentiments would be benevolence.

Phrenology was based on the principle that the brain is the organ of the mind and that the mental powers of man can be analyzed into a definite number of these independent faculties and that each faculty held a definite seat in a region at the surface of the brain; that the size of each could be measured, thus aiding the phrenologist in determining the character of the individual. The correspondence between the outer surface of the skull and the contour of the brain surface was held to be such that the size of these many organs or faculties could be recognized and measured during the examination of the outer surface of the head.

This method of determining man's disposition and character had widespread ramifications around the country. A monthly phrenological journal found its way by the thousands all over the country to eager believers in the new science.

The *Ladies Repository* magazine took up the hue and cry against phrenology by publishing an article denouncing the system. It pointed out that "many a young man has turned from usefulness because a phrenologist said he had no bump for it," and also noted that "parents based education for their children on the premise of Phrenology." Newspapers took up the cudgel against the influence of phrenology. The *New York Observer*, which called phrenologists "Tinkers in Morals and Philosophy," reflected its views in an article published October 17, 1847, as follows:

> The religious and moral community may grieve that the gospel is made of no effect by the introduction of this new mode of reform; but the experiment must be tried. The process is going on in our prisons: It is beginning in our schools; it finds advocates and apologists in our public press; it is becoming the popular theory of the day, and it will be tried, though the ruin of morals, the corruption of minds, and the destruction of souls are the natural and necessary result. The truth of divine wisdom, the experience of ages, the testimony of Christian moralists and philosophers, are all laid aside; while a set of male and female tinkers in philosophy, empirics of a day, without learning or common sense to help or guide them, are allowed to try their experiments on the destiny of immortal men!"

Meanwhile, children's heads were being examined in schools, widespread lectures were being given, and phrenology societies were flourishing. Lectures were given in New York by Orson Fowler on Phrenology and Physiology, and their applications to human im-

1854   *Courtesy Time-Out Antiques, N.Y.C.*
A recurring fad with children—playing with hoops.

provement, self-culture, juvenile education, intellectual discipline, matrimony, or to selections of mate, courtship and married life, the character of woman, and hereditary descent. These subjects were included in a lecture course given at Clinton Hall three nights a week for a three-week period. Also head examinations were given.

Phrenology extended into the business world, into the hiring of young men. An ad in the New York *Weekly Tribune*, March 1, 1847, advertised:

Apprentices wanted, four able bodied young men from sixteen to eighteen years of age, can have an opportunity, by applying to the subscriber of learning the art of moulding in sand for iron castings. They will be required to serve four years and board in my own family. They must pass a phrenological examination, and be approved by Messrs. Fowler and Wells, 131 Nassau Street, N. Y. My business is believed to be a healthy one. They will be allowed the privilege of access to a good Library, the reading of at

1850
The fad of phrenology promoted having pets for children, especially dogs, although birds, cats, and lambs were also suggested. It was believed that by having pets the capacity for love was created and the children would grow up to be affectionate parents.

1849
A little girl's pride, "Calico cat and kittens."

morning with his master and sat on the pew beside him; if his owner missed a Sunday service, he would sit on the pew alone, remaining during the service and departing with the congregation. One Sunday, the dam at the head of the lake gave way and the road was inundated. Very few people attended the church service, but just before the minister began his sermon the poodle came slowly up the aisle, dripping water after a quarter-mile swim.

Legal fights over dogs were going on in the courts. In the month of July 1857, a man shot a dog in Chicago. An immediate suit of trespass ensued. The case was tried in court three times, with victory sometimes for the defendant, sometimes for the plaintiff. In the final trial in the Superior Court of Chicago, James B. Bradwell was counsel for the plaintiff; Robert Hervey, noted leader of St. Andrew's Society, was counsel for the defendant. A description of the trial follows:

It was proved by Mr. Martin, formerly groom for Lord Shurtleff, an English nobleman, that the father and mother

least six weekly newspapers and attendance on a Lyceum. The common wages for Journeymen in this business are from $16 to $35 per month and board.—Jonathan Leonard.

One thing that phrenology did was promote having pets, especially for children. The faculty of philoprogenitiveness, or love of children, could be cultivated, Fowler said, by having pets; favorite birds, dogs, cats, lambs. It was stressed that by cultivating this faculty in children they would grow up to be affectionate parents.[10] Parents were urged to provide their children with suitable toys, such as hobby horses or dolls, as well as live pets.

Pets were widespread in America, as one of the many things expected of a young man in this era was to have the ability to train dogs. According to an animal-training manual of the day, the bulldog was the least intelligent but the most favored as a watchdog! The mastiff was considered the best in strength and intelligence, the pointer and setter best for hunting dogs.[11] The training of dogs was considered an art. An interesting tale of dog obedience was noted by a magazine writer of the day. A poodle went to church each Sunday

1860
A perennial favorite—the hobby horse.

1850
A little girl with Scotch doll. Daguerreotype by H. H. Bart-
lett, Hartford, Connecticut.

the Light Guard Band as carefully and stately as if the fate of worlds depended on each step.

"No, gentlemen, this will not do, for if the logic of my learned friend is true, you would open that vein of his in which courses the blood of kings, and moisten our democratic soil with it before my friend could return to his office.

"No, gentlemen, no such aristocratic man can justify the killing of our noble dog on any such ground.

"We may be forsaken by father, mother, brother, sister, and all our kindred, kicked out of doors, turned loose, upon the wide, wide world but our dog, noble, heoric, faithful, will cling to us with unwavering fidelity till the last faint spark of life dies out!

"But he is dead! and we all ask you, by your verdict to punish his murderer so that he shall remember shooting our dog with sorrow until the last moment of his life."

The outcome of this desperate battle is lost to history, but the moral summation of the tale appears to be the old adage, "Dog is a man's best friend."

Americans in this age were "joiners." Everyone, men

of the plaintiff's dog at one time belonged to said nobleman, and were imported by the witness.

The defendant's counsel wound up his plea as follows:

"Gentlemen of the jury, it is proved that the plaintiff's dog was an aristocrat dog; that he had noble blood coursing through his veins; and having crossed the great water and come to a land of freedom, any good Democrat like my client had a right to open the vein of this aristocratic dog and let the kingly blood flow out. Gentlemen, you cannot find my client guilty for doing to this dog what your fathers of the Revolution did to the aristocratic English. No, gentlemen, never—never!"

The plaintiff's counsel closed in the following way:

"Gentlemen of the jury, the point my learned friend makes in regard to the right to let Americans' blood flow, undoubtedly applies to men as well as dogs; but my friend is the last man to make that point. What! he, who boasts descent from a line of Scottish lords as ancient as the Douglas's, talk of being an enemy to aristocratic blood! Preposterous! Why, gentlemen, we have seen him on holidays, in the St. Andrew's Society, body erect, decorated, not looking right nor left but marching along to the music of

1858
Raising rabbits was an interesting hobby for young boys.
Himalayan rabbits (above) were originally produced by
careful breeding and selection. They usually have all-white
fur with black extremities.

1855

The training of animals in this age was considered an art. One of the many things expected of a young man in this era was to have the ability to train dogs. The mastiff was considered the best in strength and intelligence; the bulldog was favored as a watchdog. The pointer and setter were the hunting dogs.

1855

The Fancy Poodle
In 1846, a fad was abroad in Boston of dyeing the lap dog to match the color of its owner's dress. Pink and blue were the most popular colors.

in particular, belonged to some society or organization. Many fraternal organizations, stemming from the English Friendly Societies, had as a basis a mutual aid plan to benefit their members. This program took a variety of forms, with some groups paying certain amounts of money to their members in case of sickness, accident, or death. It amounted to a mutual insurance plan. Some of the older organizations, of English Friendly Society origin and having masonic characteristics, that were formed in America in this era were: Improved Order of Red Men, founded 1771, reorganized in 1834; Ancient Order of Foresters, 1836; Ancient Order of Hibernians of America, 1836; United Ancient Order of Druids, 1839; Independent Order of Rechabites, 1842; Independent Order of B'nai B'rith, 1843; Order of United American Mechanics, 1845; Independent Order of Free Sons of Israel, 1849; Junior Order of United American Mechanics, 1853. It is to be noted how many of these organizations began just before 1840 and through that decade to the 1850s.

It is estimated that one half of these organizations, many secret, paid benefits of some kind, and that many

of the secret societies had auxiliaries, featuring benefits for members. Many of the popular, secret American fraternal societies had benefit payments as their main objective, such as the Odd Fellows who had 1,392 lodges in the United States by November, 1847. Initiations for the lodge in the year 1846–1847 numbered 32,794 and their total contributing members in America in that year was 118,961. In 1846 retired members of the Odd Fellows received portions of the sum of $302,243.41 in benefits, and total revenue from all of the lodges in the country for the same year was $888,605.07.[12] Surplus money after benefits were paid went to various benevolent ventures. Other fraternal groups with benefits as principal purpose were the Knights of Pythias, Knights of Honor, and Royal Arcanum, among others. Later, trade unions adopted this idea, as would insurance companies.

If some fraternal groups were formed with idealism, as was the order of "Red Men," whose motto was "Freedom, Friendship and Charity," and who outlawed liquor

1850   *Courtesy Time-Out Antiques, N.Y.C.*
*An unknown member of one of the many fraternal orders
of the day. Daguerreotype by Augustus Morand, New York
City.*

in a parlor game, in which he dangled a live snake above
his head. The news spread like wildfire and others
came to be initiated into the secret order. The oath the
new members adopted was:

> Whoever dares our cause reveal
> Shall test the strength of knightly steel;
> And when the torture proves too dull,
> We'll scrape the brains from out his skull
> And place a lamp within the shell
> To light his soul from here to hell.

The first campaign of this new fraternal order was
to conquer Mexico and add it to the southern territory.
This appealed to slavery men, who eagerly joined the
group. It was estimated that at one time there were
60,000 members in the state of Texas alone. The Knights
of the Golden Circle worked their way North with the
onset of the Civil War and by 1861 there were 15,000
members in Indiana. In Illinois members entered politics. After the outbreak of the Civil War, many Democrats of the middle west were opposed to the war policy
and organized members of the "Circle" to be pledged
for peace. The plan would be to overthrow the Lincoln
government in the elections and give Democrats control
of State and Federal governments, which they believed
would bring peace, and the southern states would be
able to come back into the union on their old basis.
"Peace Meetings" were held and arms were purchased
to be used in planned uprisings that would place the
peace party in control of the Federal Government, and
failing this, they would establish a Northwest Con-
federacy. Other plans were to set free confederate prisoners, encourage desertion from Federal Armies, and
prevent enlistments. Members acting as undercover
agents promoted draft riots.

Because of the secrecy involved, facts are uncertain,
but an exposé was written by Felix D. Stedger, a United
States secret agent, who stated that the Knights ordered
the murder of government detectives, plotted train
wrecks (troop trains), and turned Union gold over to
Confederate generals to help the Confederate cause. The
Federal Government moved in with wholesale arrests
and seized arms as well as leaders. The government
finally was able to capture Dr. Bickley and his assistant
Dr. Bowles when, masquerading as Ohio doctors in
Confederate uniforms, they were traveling by train with
Ohio passes. One of the doctors under suspicion got off
the train in Indiana. He was searched and found to be
the Supreme Grand Imperial Potentate, Dr. Bickley.
Bowles was hanged. Bickley was imprisoned. Three other
leaders of the secret order were arrested and sentenced
to death by the military. The sentences were suspended

and political discussions at meetings, other societies were
formed with the express purpose of political action,
especially during the 1840–1860 period.

A sensational, vast secret order of this kind came into
being before the Civil War and lasted for a time during
the war. Although beginning with the name "Knights
of the Golden Circle," it would become known as
"Order of American Knights" in 1863, and "Sons of
Liberty" in 1864. The name "Circle of Honor" was also
used. The main power of the vast organization was in
the North, and it brought into its organization those
who were in sympathy with secession of states and later
conceived the grandiose scheme of a Northwest Con-
federacy, to include the states of Indiana, Ohio, Illinois,
Missouri, Wisconsin, Minnesota, and Michigan.

History believes that this order was conceived in 1854
by a southern surgeon, George Bickley. The primary
objective at the beginning was to rescue Mexico from
barbarism. During a visit to his wife's relatives in
Louisiana, Bickley was said to have initiated his host

until 1866 and the men were later released under a decision of the United States Supreme Court in the famous case Ex parte Milligan. The capture of the organization's ringleaders marked the downfall and end of the Knights of the Golden Circle.

In this era many organizations would stand for a controversial issue, others against. There were masons and anti-masons, anti-slavery organizations and slavery societies. Whatever the issue, there were always two sides of the coin, for and against. In this manner ideas spread, some good, some bad, but communication between men was definitely established.

1846
> *Whoever dares our cause reveal*
> *Shall test the strength of knightly steel;*
> *And when the torture proves too dull,*
> *We'll scrape the brains from out his skull*
> *And place a lamp within the shell*
> *To light his soul from here to hell.*
From the secret initiation rites of the "Knights of the Golden Circle."

1854

Unknown Fraternal Order
Some fraternal groups were formed with idealism, such as the order of "Red Men," whose motto was "Freedom, Friendship and Charity"; other groups were formed as mutual insurance societies and some were joined together for political action, especially during the 1840–1860 period.

16
Fashions

The clothing worn by Americans of the 1840–1860 era reflected the gradual change from a simple agrarian society to the more complex and materialistic society of the 1850 decade.

Classic simplicity highlighted the fashion world of the 1840s. Ornamental accessories provided appropriate stylish accents for women, such as jewelry, gaily trimmed bonnets, colorful beaded bags, and small parasols. Men sported handsome figured, striped, or plain vests and tall beaver hats. Boys were dressed according to their age, little ones in dresses and older boys in jackets and trousers. Tiny tots under five of both sexes wore off-the-shoulder dresses. Girls followed their mothers' styles rather closely. In rural areas of the country, fashions were sometimes several years behind those of the city dweller, and, as clothing was expensive, renovating and "making do" was common practice. As 1850 approached, a new era of fashion would begin. Just as American architecture was leaning toward the ornate, so too would feminine fashions hark back to the middle ages for the elaborate in costuming.[1] Daytime dresses in the 1840s had softly pleated bodices with pleats running from shoulder to waist, ending in a sharp point at the center. Necklines were mostly open; some were V-shaped, some rounded, and they were often finished with a simple ruching of lace or self fabric. Sleeves of these dresses were long and tight. In 1841, the long sleeve began to be finished with an epaulet cap called a jockey, which would remain stylish for many years.[2] A new bodice trend for street dresses appeared in 1842, of revers starting low on the shoulder and coming to a point at center waist. Skirts became very wide and

full in 1845. In the latter 1840s a small flat collar of lace was worn; some were cut square, some were like a surplice; others were worn over a chemisette.

Evening dresses during these years were cut low (off-the-shoulder) and finished with a "bertha" of lace or silk.[3] In 1846, a high-necked evening gown came in to add variety, Tarlatan, a thin, stiff, transparent muslin was a favorite material for dancing frocks, and was popular in plaids as well as plain tints.

Bonnets in 1840 were long and narrow.[4] Shapes changed somewhat during successive years, flaring a little more and becoming rounder about the face. Colorful flowers and plume-like feathers were favorites for trimming. Lacy, coquettish morning caps were widely worn by matrons. Attractive headdresses, using flowers woven throughout with satin ribbons and other materials, were used during these years, especially for evening wear.

Other accessories were dainty mitts or gloves made of lace, which were worn for dress or promenade. Stockings for dress were mostly white, of Scotch thread and silk, often hand embroidered. The sheer silk ones were worn over flesh-colored cashmere. A showier stocking of black mesh was worn over flesh-colored silk. Shoes of the 1840 decade were fragile and dainty. An English visitor in 1833 roundly criticized American women for not wearing boots over their slippers in bad weather; however, it was universally conceded that American women had pretty feet. Shoes came in such fabrics as velvet, satin, and brocade in luscious shades of pink, sky blue, lavender, yellow, and green as well as more sombre colors.[5] Many were ornamented. Boots of kid

1843
Colorful vests were the stylish accent to the male costume. They came in bright colors and rich fabrics; many were made of brocade or satin.

1851
Head coverings were often worn in hot weather to shade the face and shoulders from the sun. Parasols were small and dainty in this period.

1845
The boy's costume above shows the simplicity of the clothing worn by this age group in the 1840s.

1845
The child shown also wears plaid socks.

1845
Fringe was often used for trimming of sleeve epaulets. Skirts became very full and wide in 1845. Curls were popular in this period.

1842
In the early 1840s necklines were mostly open and finished with a simple ruching of lace or self fabric. Dresses had a softly pleated bodice with pleats running from shoulder to waist; sleeves were long and tight.

1846
The print dress was favored among the young women, in soft graceful styles. Gold pens were often worn suspended from a chain worn about the neck.

1858
A portrait by Rufus Anson, prominent Broadway photographer, of a rare daguerreotype in color (above). The quest for color in photography during the 1850s was highly competitive and secretive.

1858
Brandy Legs, a southwestern Indian of the era.

were worn for horseback riding. Jewelry was a popular accessory; brooches at the neck were popular, and earrings. In 1848 bracelets with watches inserted were the rage in the eastern cities.[6]

Hair styles from 1840–1850 were varied. Long curls, always a favorite, continued to be worn. Broad braids and smooth bands of hair parted in the middle were the styles preferred by many. In the early 1840s the ears were frequently displayed. During 1845 and after, the hair was often worn about the head in a coronet braid. By 1849, the hair was worn more distinctly puffed at the sides.[7]

With the arrival of 1850, feminine fashion began its great change. The plain dress gave way to one that was extensively trimmed. The soft pleats disappeared, and a boned stiffness showed up on dress bodices. Glossy materials and silks in new, bolder colors were used. Trimmings included net, looped ribbons, lace, and flowers. Street dresses were now usually high in the neck, some buttoned up to the throat and finished with small

1850
Beginning in 1850 a boned stiffness appeared in dress bodices. Glossy materials and silks in new bolder colors were used. The hair was now often braided in a Grecian knot.

1849
The black dress with its classic simplicity highlighted the fashion world of the 1840s.

collars. The skirts on dresses coming into vogue were much narrower than in the 1840s.[8] Sleeves also underwent a change; they were plain at the shoulder, then gradually widened to just below the elbow, then flared in a chinese or "pagoda" style. A charming vogue was adopted to complete a costume. Dresses were trimmed with fresh flowers and little bouquets were carried in the hand.

Evening gowns of 1850 were made of rich materials, thick brocades, silks, and satins. Trimmings for these were of silk embroidery, and ornaments were of velvet or gold and silver braid appliqué. A typical gown was of plain light blue satin with low-cut bodice and short sleeves. The skirt was trimmed with five narrow flounces of blonde (a silk bobbin lace), which was figured with silver, and each flounce was surmounted by a wreath formed of pearls of various sizes. Some attractive ball gowns were seen in black or white tulle worn over slips of silk or satin. These were richly embroidered with gold or with gold-colored silk. The skirts of these gowns were also flounced.

1853

Street dresses were high in the neck and were worn with small collars.

1853

Ball gowns of the 1850s were made of rich materials—thick brocades, silks, and satins. Bodices were low-cut and had short sleeves. Favorite colors for evening were mauve, amber, pink, lilac, blue, and peach.

1855

An example of a mantelet worn in an off-the-shoulder shawl style. The flowered ribbon on the bonnet made a pleasing accent against the plain color of the costume.

The 1850 bridal gown was beautiful. One creation was composed of a very fine white tarlatan muslin worn over a slip of white silk. The skirt was trimmed with five flounces, which were edged with a one-inch hem. The bodice was worn high at the throat and the neck fullness in both front and back was gathered onto a narrow band that was trimmed with a ruching of lace. The sleeves were demi-long, wide and loose at the ends, finished with a double row of lace. A wreath of orange blossoms was worn about the head with full bouquets falling gracefully at each side. The bridal veil was a scarf of tulle and illusion finished in the same manner as the skirt flounces. Demi-long white kid gloves and white satin shoes completed the outfit.[9]

A jacket called a mantelet came in vogue in this year in a variety of styles. Lace was favored for summer; for cooler days embroidered cloth or velvet, trimmed with chinchilla or sable fur.[10] Cloaks of longer length for cold weather were mostly in dark colors, were loose, and were wadded and quilted all the way through. Embroidered bags were carried.

Parasols were designed for display in the open carriage and came in ice cream colors with white borders edged with embroidered ribbon. Linings were blue or pink. The ordinary promenade parasol was a much more sombre color in blue or dark green, lined with white.

Bonnets were really works of art in this era. An example of a straw hat for 1850 was a broad-brimmed openwork affair trimmed with branches of lilac or fruit. Another pretty bonnet had a very large open-front brim and a small, low, round crown. It was made of lace and was ornamented with pink marabou feathers, sable, and bunches of pink velvet leaves. Another lovely one was constructed of light green fluted ribbon over a plain foundation, waved in front in a vandyked pattern. Many of the summer bonnets were made of white silk, trimmed with lace and ornamented with small bunches of flowers. A carriage bonnet might also be made of velvet trimmed with a feather on each side, and inside the brim velvet flowers and foliage were used to harmonize.

Hair styles had also changed in 1850. The "French twist" was seldom seen now except in the morning; hair was generally braided in a Grecian knot. Young ladies often wore their hair drawn back from the face and knotted behind. Another becoming style was for the front hair to be rolled over a cushion, a loose curl falling behind the ear.[11]

Fashions changed again in 1855. Skirts of ladies' dresses once again became very full and were made elegant with flounces, bordered sometimes with a woven

1850
Long flowing cloaks were worn in cold weather and were wadded and quilted for warmth. Furs were in high fashion.

pattern matching the dress material. Silk dresses that were not flounced were of large plaids or stripes. Light blue, lilac, apple green, stone color, and light brown were the favorite tints. Lace was now used extensively for trimmings. Sleeves remained wider at the bottom than the top; some dresses had undersleeves snug at the wrist, while others had turned-up cuffs. Larger collars were now being worn. Dresses cost anywhere from $18.00 up to $75.00. For $25.00 or $35.00, a very elegant dress could be purchased.[12] At a very exclusive shop in Philadelphia, $100.00 was a common price for a silk gown in 1856.

Ball gowns were often draped, creating a graceful fullness to the bustline. "Berthas" were still popular in a shawl effect. Double and triple skirts were used if the fabric was of very light weight. A typical 1855 ball gown was made of pink crepe combined with Brussels lace. The bodice was done in "shawl" style, trimmed with white lace and a pink bow. The sleeves were short and puffed. The lower part of the skirt consisted of six puffings of crepe, studded by bows of

1850
The beaver hat (center) did not appear often until about 1859. Muffs were popular.

pink satin. Above this were four rows of narrow Brussels lace; above this again were five puffings of crepe, studded with bows, then three rows of lace. Hair was worn back from the face and trimmed with pink flowers.

The skirts were so large now that a woman could hardly walk through a door except sideways. Petticoats were designed to give balloon-like proportions with little weight. They were made of muslin and gored to any needed width. Whalebone was used in a tape casing, but not all around because of the problem of sitting. Corsets were short and not worn over the hips. Every change of style brought a new study for changing the stays in these garments, to be in harmony with the current cut of the gown.[13]

A feminine bathing costume worn for surf bathing was described in a letter dated July 9, 1856. It was written by a young lady staying at a seaside resort: "...you know too, that American women make frights of themselves in their bathing costumes. One had on a pretty Paris rig. Blue and white striped trousers of flannel with lovely fitting blouse and on her head a

piquant little sloping hat, trimmed in some miraculous way so water does not deface them."

Very fancy jackets called mantillas were all the rage in the mid-50s. Materials used were mostly silk and lace, but white muslin was considered "cool" for hot summer days and was worn low on the shoulders, scarf style, and was edged with an embroidered ruffle. Parasols for summer had become very elaborate. They were made of moiré silk, plain or figured, were lined, and had ornamental handles. One of these was fashioned of apricot silk, edged with satin stripes of white and maize. The stick was of wrought ivory with a gilt handle set with imitation emeralds. A large ribbon bow with flowing streamers was the finishing touch. Another dainty parasol was of plain white silk, sprigged all over with small rosebuds and leaves. The edges of the parasol were fringed. The lining was white and the stick was of silver.

The perennial bonnet had been changing shape and by 1855 it was more forward on the head and less open

1856
Fashions changed again in 1855. Skirts once more became very wide and full. Plaids were high style and large collars were worn.

Bonnets of the Era

Matron Caps of the Era

1848

1846

1847

1848

1845

1853

1856

1849

1855

Side view Peterson's, *1855*

1859

Rear view Peterson's, *1855.*

Rear view Peterson's, *1855*

1846
The young man, above, right, wears a riding outfit complete with crop. The daguerreotype was taken at the Plumbe National Daguerreotype Gallery, Boston.

1855
Attractive headdresses were often worn, made of flowers and ribbons woven with other materials. Furred cloaks were high fashion.

1857
Mantillas or fancy jackets were very fashionable and were made of various materials, including taffeta.

1856
An example of a fashionable riding habit.

around the face; the crown sloped less to the back and the front ends of the bonnet met under the chin.[14] Costs for these lavishly trimmed confections varied greatly. In a very exclusive dry goods store in 1856 in Philadelphia, they were advertised as high as $200, whereas a southern girl in Georgia in March 1856 noted in her diary a straw bonnet for $8 and another for $15. In April 1856, she bought a white bonnet for $12.00. The straw bonnet industry had an interesting history. It began in the beautiful little town of Foxborough, Massachusetts, located about 24 miles from Boston, with the establishment of the Union Straw Works in 1853 by the Messrs. O. and E. P. Carpenter. It became the largest manufacturer of straw hats for men and women in both America and Europe.[15]

The mid-1850s saw the revival of the shawl as high style. The selection of a woman's shawl and her way of wearing it, traditionally reflected her true taste. The garment, properly worn, was the "ultra" in femininity and grace, and for practical purposes it had no rival for warmth in an open carriage or a draughty room. The French women were the first to use the "Indian" shawl for feminine appeal. After Napoleon's expedition to Egypt, shawls became the rage in Paris. In India thirty to forty men were employed 18 months to two years to make a single shawl. The wool for these garments came from the Tibet goat. The borders were made in several

pieces, sometimes of ten or 20 sewn together to form a pattern. An Indian shawl could be distinguished from a French or Paisley by these borders. Price for a small one was about $100 and for a double size with deep border $250. Some brought, in the mid-nineteenth century, as high as $1,000 from wealthy buyers.[16] In 1856 in New York, cashmere shawls sold for $300.00 upward. French manufacturers began producing their own lovely, original designs. Also, competing for the shawl market was the China Crape shawl, made of silk, in lovely colors. The foundation of the garment was made in Nanking, then sent to Canton to be embroidered.

In the late 1850s women's dresses now fitted the form more closely. Princess-style dresses with a gored effect were now often seen. Some dress bodies had a surplice look, and the skirt was now in two parts with a tunic effect. Waists of dresses were rounded and collars became smaller. Sleeves had also changed; some had a series of puffs, others were full from the elbow to wrist, many were snug fitting. Cloaks and mantillas were often worn now in full length, made of striped material and trimmed with very large hanging tassels.

An innovation came to women's headgear. Beaver fur hats started appearing quite often in 1859. Heels were now seen on shoes, and stockings were made in colors and in stripes and plaids.

The hair was now arranged on top of the head in heavy braids, wound like a coronet. This coiffure was often worn with a tiara of velvet.

1847
Many shawls came in lovely original designs; some were made of fine wool, others of silk. These garments were considered the "ultra" in femininity and grace.

Men's clothing in the 1840 decade was very close fitting, especially in the coat sleeves. In the early 1840s, the sleeve cuffs were slit and turned up. Coats came in a wide variety for morning wear and sports. The formal tail coat was worn for evening. Patterned coats for daytime were often worn with plain fawn or gray trousers. Sometimes seen were coat, vest, trousers, and tie worn together in various colors, although harmonizing, rather than a matching ensemble. The dark suit was also popular. Coat lapels were very wide and deeply notched during this period. Waists were slim and curved, and gradually lengthened to a long torso by 1850.[17] Overcoats were mostly plain, with velvet collar and large buttons, and were warmly lined with quilted fabric.

Trousers, most of which had hip pockets at the seams, lost their shoe strap during the 1840s, but remained long and close cut at the bottom. Stripes, vertical and horizontal, were now seen; also, plaids were popular along with plain fabrics.

Shirt collars varied during this ten-year period from 1840–1850. In 1840, the choker collar had a shaped tip sewn onto a band so that the collar curved away from

1850

The shawl for practical purposes had no rival for warmth in an open carriage or drafty rooms. A woman's shawl and the way she wore it reflected her taste.

1849

Tarlatan, a stiff, transparent muslin, was a favorite material for dancing frocks and was often seen in plaids. The triangle-part in the hair was stylish in this year.

1858

Off-the-shoulder dresses continued to be worn. Dark lace mitts and jewelry completed the costume. The hair at this date was worn very puffed at the sides.

1859

In 1859 dresses were often elaborately trimmed with ball buttons, cord, and "fancy drop tassels."

1859
In 1859 the bodice was now more relaxed. Ribbons were the current vogue.

1858
A child's cold weather costume.

1848
Overcoats for men were mostly plain; some had velvet collars and were warmly lined with quilted fabric for cool weather. Top hats were very popular and sold for $2.25 upwards in 1843.

1846
An excellent example of outdoor wear for boys. The boy's overcoat, at the left, is patterned after the men's styles. The boy's leggings, on the right, are buttoned on each side. The photograph was taken at Plumbe National Gallery, Boston, Mass.

1849
A young man's pride, the top hat.

the face and the edge turned downward. A stiff standing collar next came in vogue. By 1845–1848 the collar was often worn very low. Ties varied considerably; many were cut of soft silk, often figured in attractive designs. The arrangement of tying the scarf was an art in itself. Many shapes were seen, depending upon the personality of the wearer.

Men's vests were the colorful costume accessories and were fashioned in luxury materials of satin, brocade, and velvet. Jewelry also made a pleasing accent to the costume in the form of scarf pins, studs, and looped neck chains. Changes in men's shoes appeared in the 1840s. Spring heels appeared and shoe colors were black, prunella, and brown.[18] After Goodyear's first patent for rubber in 1844, an industry began for manufacturing rubber shoes, boots for sportswear, and outer shoes. This was a real stride forward in substantial footwear. During the 1840s a shoe fad swept New York and London called the Kemble slipper, named in honor of the popular actress, Fanny Kemble.

Men's fashions did not change drastically on entering the 1850 period. Collars were worn higher and were

A Few Hair Styles from the 1850s

1853

1856

1856

1851

1854

1856

1854

1856   *Courtesy Time-Out Antiques*
A Summer Day in the Park
*The suit with the narrow lapel became fashionable in the
mid-1850s. The cool summer suit of varying style is pictured above. Broad straw hats and low-cut oxfords complete
the costume.*

or low on the neck. Toward 1860 patterns in materials were becoming smaller and coats and trousers wider.

Top hats remained in favor, although other kinds of headgear were seen, depending on the season or regional area. An innovation came in men's footwear in the 1850s, a leather heel with a small protruding insert of rubber. In 1858 a machine invented by Lyman B. Blake for sewing soles and uppers together made for further gains in better and more varied shoes.

Jewelry fads had changed somewhat. Gold watch chains dangled from buttonhole to watch pocket, replacing the neckchain of the 1840s.

Children's fashions early in 1850 varied widely according to age. Little girls wore dresses coming below the knees, with pantalettes just showing. Children aged

1855
This fashionably dressed young man has on a light-colored coat, stylish in the mid-50s. His silk tie is a leaf design; the arrangement of tying the scarf depended on the mood of the wearer.

stiff. Black was a popular suit color and black satin waistcoats were widely worn. White and cream-colored vests, which were rather formal, continued fashionable, especially for summer. The fancy vest also remained.

An interesting fashion for men in this decade was a traveling shawl worn sometimes in place of a topcoat.[19] Coats for travel and sports were in great variety. Coats and trousers usually matched now. Plaid and tweed suits were seen. Topcoats were mostly black, and some were lined in sky-blue, dark green, brown, or gray. Formal overcoats usually had a cape and small velvet collar. After 1855 coats were more squarely cut and lapels became narrower. Cutaway coats were now worn in the morning as well as evening. Buff-colored coats were stylish, and a fashion plate of 1855 featured a brown coat with white trousers for a summer walking costume. Ties and shirt collars continued to vary, high

1853
For casual wear, large checkered "pantaloons" were in style. A great variety of sport caps were offered; the one pictured above was covered with oilcloth.

1846
A rare daguerreotype of a baby in outdoor costume, wearing a fur-trimmed cloak and wide-brimmed hat.

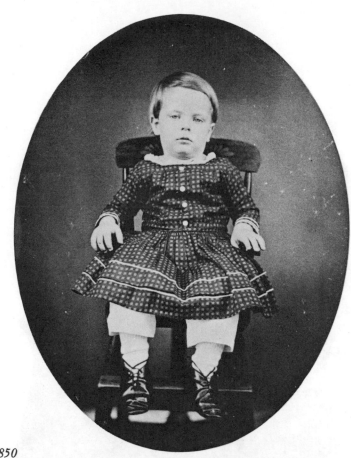

1850
A typical small boy's dress worn over trousers. His shoes are an excellent example of this period. Children's shoes were fragile in all seasons.

1853
Little girls usually wore dresses just below the knee, with pantalettes showing.

1851
Babies were often dressed in dark fabrics. Above, an unusual daguerreotype of a diapered baby.

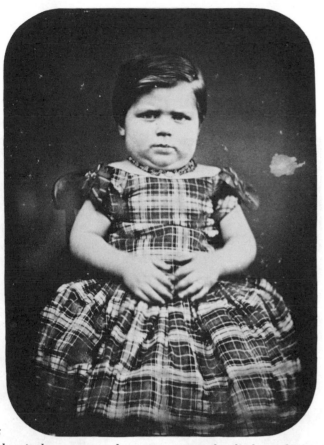

1855
Plaids of the gayest colors were worn by little girls, and short sleeves and full skirts were popular in this year.

1858
From the mid-1850s young girls sometimes wore round black plush hats that were decorated with an ostrich feather.

1846
The simplicity in little girls' dresses in the 1840s is illustrated, above, in identical print costumes. Flowers were often pinned to bodices and children quite often posed holding nosegays.

1857
Little girls' dresses by 1855 and after became very fancy and had trimmings of velvet and other materials.

1853
Little girls' summer dresses in this period were often made of fine white cambric muslin. Short sleeves trimmed with bows were the vogue.

1859
A fashionably dressed boy, above, illustrating the comfortable low-cut shoes and popular toys of the late 1850s.

1847
A variation of the most popular attire for young boys in the era.

A fashionable boy's costume for ages six to seven in this period was a blouse of dark blue cashmere wool trimmed with rows of black velvet. The collar of white, vandyked pattern needlework was worn with a plaid necktie. A helmet cap of black velvet trimmed with black moire silk completed the outfit. A cloak for a small boy was sometimes fashioned of gray cloth trimmed with strips of black velvet put on in points. A frock worn with this would be of gray woolen plaid. A cloth jacket called a "roundabout" was not worn except by boys around nine years old.[20] In the 1850s caps were worn by boys more often than hats.

As the year 1860 approached, all fashions were becoming too elaborate and ungainly. Women's fashions had lost their pretty, romantic charm of former years and colors were becoming drab. Children had an overdressed appearance and men's garments, now made of heavier materials, began to lose their shapely cut and elegance. The style trends seemed to forecast the dreary war years that lay ahead.

1858
This handsomely attired boy illustrates the changing costume of the late 1850s.

five or six had plain bodices, long in the waist and high in the neck, finished by a ruffle or a little collar. Little ones under five had low-cut bodices with short sleeves. Sacque coats that had been worn by girls during the 1840s were by now almost out of use. Deep, round capes were now popular. Boys' overcoats resembled their fathers. Materials and styling for older boys' wear were becoming more elaborate than the plain suits of the 1840s. Dress tunics of plaid wool or velvet were now often worn over trousers.

By 1855 children's clothing was fancy. Flounces were now widely used in girls' dresses. Plain-color silk dresses were often trimmed in black velvet. Plaid dresses had fringed or pinked flounces. Nearly all dresses for over age five were made high in the neck; some had banded long sleeves, others bishop sleeves. Pantalets were worn by girls only to cover the legs. High-fashion cloaks for girls were trimmed with fur or velvet. Bonnets were miniatures of the mothers', minus flowers. Small fur muffs were worn in cool weather.

1852
A fashionable plaid tunic trimmed with black velvet and a crisp white collar.

17
The Reformers

With communications firmly established between men as never before in American history, in this age of so many Utopian dreams it was natural for a multitude of reformers to appear on the scene. As the spotlight focused on local, sectional, or national problems, men were shocked into action. Many reformers who later became powerful and influential leaders of men, developed from local or sectional areas throughout the country; some became fanatical and extreme, others moderate, yet productive. Every town and village aired its cries for and against the new growing and changing issues. These community-minded people were in the process of evaluating the new and reexamining the old social, political, and religious traditions.

Reforms in general were of a diverse nature. North, South, and West were struggling with their own sectional reforms, whether industrial, agricultural, or social. But the important reforms were of national scope—anti-slavery, temperance, Women's Rights. These reforms would become intertwined as time went on. Even before the impact of industry on a predominantly agrarian society was felt, early in the nineteenth century, many reforms were getting underway, and when the church joined hands with the reformer it brought the moral partner he needed. Among the early reform-conscious societies founded were the American Bible Society, 1816; The American Tract Society, 1825; American Sunday School Union, 1825; American Home Missionary Society, 1826; and the American Peace Society, 1828. Great strides were made by 1818, according to John Bristed, who reported in that year: "Missionary and Bible societies have already considerably diminished the ignorance, poverty and vice of our large cities. Many of our most respectable families gratuitously engage in the labor of teaching the Sunday scholars, black and white, old and young."[1]

Universal male suffrage made politics of great interest and importance to the common man. The politician was experiencing a difficult time and was prodded into action not only by the man in the street but by reformers, societies, and churches. In this era of great oratory a receptive audience was assured. Many reformers were clergymen, well educated, respected, and able to sway listeners to a white heat of emotional response on controversial issues. The controversy that gathered momentum in the early 1830s and was destined to sweep away all hope of compromise and calm thinking, and that would set men figuratively and literally at each others' throats, was, of course, slavery.

The anti-slavery movement was well underway from 1830–1840. The American Anti-slavery Society, a militant organization, was founded in December of 1833 by a group of dedicated abolitionists.

A great many of the top leaders of the movement, including Theodore Weld and Henry Stanton, would stem from Lane Seminary, Cincinnati, Ohio, where the slavery question was debated so fiercely that the trustees there issued a policy of silence to preserve peace in this Ohio community. Other colleges in the country that adopted the silent policy because of the public agitation were Harvard, Yale, Princeton, and Amherst.

Theodore Weld had been converted in a western New

1853
Women joined in many reform movements—church work, women's rights, temperance, and anti-slavery, all popular causes of the era.

After the policy of silence on slavery discussion was issued by the Lane trustees, many men, including Theodore Weld, withdrew and transferred to Oberlin College, which was in its infancy. The Tappans immediately endowed the college with several thousand dollars; Charles Grandison Finney came to head the theology department, and Negroes were admitted. In the fall of 1835, Weld returned to Oberlin, after a lecture tour, to train twelve men selected as fine speakers to promote abolition in Ohio. All later became important to the movement; some became agents for the American Anti-slavery Society.

Weld, convinced that he was God's instrument on earth to wipe out human bondage, preached unceasingly. His voice was strong, his oratory eloquent and fiery. He produced a religious-revival effect on his audiences, swaying them to his will. Many prominent men were influenced in this manner. Weld refused to speak in large cities or to take positions of honor or authority, so he remained somewhat obscure. In 1836 he lost his voice and left the lecture platform to edit

York State revival conducted by Charles Grandison Finney. At the revival, he met the liberal Charles Stuart, British anti-slavery leader, who financed his education for the ministry at Oneida Institute. Weld entered Oneida in 1827 and studied there for three years. His religious fervor and persuasive oratory on such subjects as temperance and moral reform caught the interest of Lewis Tappan, one of the wealthy New-York-merchant abolitionist brothers. Tappan was one of the founders of The Society for Promoting Manual Labor in Literary Institutions. The society sent Weld on a lecture tour that encompassed the southern states and the Midwest. One of his instructions was to locate a suitable site for a seminary. It was decided to found Lane Seminary in Cincinnati, in the autumn of 1833. Most of the students at Oneida Institute then transferred to Lane. Cincinnati made a perfect center for debating and testing the slavery question. The city contained more than one third of the 7,500 Negroes in the state of Ohio, three fourths of whom were adult free Negroes. Many were earning money to free others. Cincinnati was also a pro-slavery area.[2]

1853
Many reformers were clergymen who were well educated and able to sway listeners to a white heat of emotional response on controversial issues.

Oberlin College built a one-story building 144 feet long and 24 feet wide to accommodate the anti-slavery students who transferred from Lane Seminary. The outside of the building was battened with "slabs" that retained the bark of the original tree, giving the hall a rustic look.

publications put out by the American Anti-slavery Society. He married Angelina Grimké on May 14, 1838, in Philadelphia. She was also an abolitionist and public speaker, rare for a woman in this era. The daughter of a South Carolina judge, Angelina Grimké and her sister Sarah grew up to hate slavery and became fervent workers in the movement. Three days after her marriage to Weld, Angelina was scheduled to speak at the second National Convention of Anti-slavery Women. The convention was held in Pennsylvania Hall, a newly dedicated building; it was destroyed by a mob immediately after her lecture. Before Theodore Weld retired from public life he wrote several books that wielded considerable influence. One of his books was a shocker. It was written in 1839 and was entitled *American Slavery as It Is.* The book was formed from a collection of extracts taken from southern newspapers. Every appalling incident, atrocity, or flogging concerning a Negro was dug out and expounded by Weld in a moralistic and explosive manner, which incited the abolitionists to a new fever pitch of excitement.

During the 1830s resentment had built up against the anti-slavery agitators, and towns and cities all over the country feared their presence, for it meant mob violence, property destruction, and even death. Abolitionists often feared for their lives; some were mobbed and stoned. As an example of mob violence, in 1834 the Tappan Brothers' store in New York City was mobbed, Lewis Tappan's house was wrecked and his furniture burned in the street.

The most tantalizing, hate-mongering, and dominant personality to emerge in the abolition movement was

William Lloyd Garrison (1805–1879). His unorthodox views on politics, his radical view in favoring the right of women to vote and be part of the movement, and his violent and scathing blasts on churches that condoned slavery brought agitation among the ranks of the more conservative members of the American Anti-slavery party. In Boston in January of 1831, Garrison had founded the *Liberator,* a newspaper that exerted a powerful influence in the North for thirty-five years. The *Liberator* had such an explosive effect on the South that in December of the first year's publication, the legislature of Georgia offered a $5,000 reward for anyone who could cause Garrison to be apprehended and brought to trial. Not a man to be stopped, Garrison made some oft-quoted statements: "I am in earnest"; "I will not equivocate"; "I will not excuse"; "I will not retreat a single inch"; and "I will be heard."

He organized the New England Anti-slavery Society in January, 1832. Already feeling a measure of success, he went abroad in the spring of 1833. He was very well received in England and brought home with him a protest from the British against the American Colonization Society. To add fuel to the already steaming pot of unrest was Garrison's announcement that he had engaged the services of an Englishman, George Thompson, to lecture against American slavery.

Thompson made his appearance the next spring (1834). In the interim mobs had organized to suppress the slavery question and violence began erupting. Thompson had to leave the country secretly in the autumn of 1834, otherwise he might have been killed. An announced lecture for the Women's Anti-slavery

Society of Boston, to be given by him, caused the city of Boston to become emotionally unbalanced. Mobs of "gentlemen of property and good standing" swarmed into the city streets. Missing Thompson, they got to Garrison, stripped off most of his clothes, and dragged him through the streets by a rope. Garrison was rescued with difficulty and put in prison for safety.

Anti-slavery societies were increasing in the North and Midwest and many prominent men joined the cause. By 1835 there were 225 anti-slavery societies; 525 in 1836; 1,006 in 1837; and an estimated 1,406 in 1838.[3] By 1839 there were upward of 100 anti-slavery newspapers, although only a handful of these were of great importance.

Two newspapers, one a daily, the other a weekly, and both under the editorship of Horace Greeley (1811–1872), would have great impact on educating the northern mass of people to new ideas and reforms. Greeley opposed Women's Suffrage but believed in extending employment for women; he opposed theatres, believed in abstinence from liquor, and believed wholeheartedly in the sanctity of marriage. It was as an anti-slavery leader, however, that he was most outstanding. He suffered opposition from all sides. Southern newspapers and speakers denounced him and the abolitionists thought him too conservative.

As a young man Greeley learned his trade in the office of the *Northern Spectator* at East Poultney, Vermont (1826). Here he developed a great interest in politics. The paper went out of business in June 1830. After a stay with his parents, who had moved to a rural spot about 30 miles from Erie, Pennsylvania, where he found but poor prospects for work, he traveled by canal boat to New York, arriving on August 16, 1831. He arrived with his only clothing in a neat pack, fastened on a stick and slung over his shoulders, and with a ten-dollar bill resting in his pocket. His rustic appearance spelled runaway, but he finally got a job and from this poor start moved slowly toward success. In January 1833 he had a brief partnership with a former fellow worker who drowned six months later. His partner's brother-in-law, Jonas Winchester, then joined forces with Greeley and the new partners issued on March 2, 1834, the first copy of the *New Yorker,* a literary weekly and newspaper. It was published for seven years and

Anti-slavery leaders were working everywhere in the country to promote their cause. From a lithograph of 1852.

publication that shaped public opinion in the northwest. In 1837 he became Vice President of the American Slavery Society. His ultimate goal was political action on outlawing slavery. He worked for what he considered the permanent welfare of the Union with regard to the slavery question, rather than the strictly moral issue of emancipation for the Negro. He was nominated for the presidency of the United States by the Liberty Party twice, in 1840 and in 1844. Unfortunately, he had to give up public life in 1845 after a fall from a horse that left him an invalid.

Gerrit Smith, the other leading founder of the Liberty Party, was nominated for the presidency by this organization in 1848 and in 1852. Also in 1848 he was nominated for the presidency by an "Industrial Congress" at Philadelphia and in 1856 by a group called "Land Reformers." Smith managed his father's estate

was popular but not profitable, but from its publication, Greeley came into prominence. During these years he had augmented his income by writing editorials for other publications. With one thousand dollars borrowed from a close friend, he founded *The Tribune* on April 10, 1841. In September of the same year Greeley combined *The New Yorker* and a weekly political campaign paper, *The Log Cabin,* into the *Weekly Tribune.* The daily paper, *The Tribune,* began with 500 subscribers and by the fourth week jumped to 6,000 and by the seventh 11,000. The *Weekly Tribune* at one time during "wild politics" had a circulation of one quarter million. For many years it had from 140,000 to 150,000. Its subscribers, a great many of whom were rural, spanned the northern half of the Union from Maine to Oregon.

By 1840 the American Anti-slavery Society had 250,000 members, had published more than two dozen journals, and had about fifteen state newspapers. The year 1840 brought a new political slant to the cause. The Society had become divided in its approach to reform. Some members believed in moral agitation, others worked for and demanded legislation, while still others such as "Free Soilers" did not believe in immediate abolition. The split or break-away from the parent society by some members resulted in the formation of the political "Liberty Party." The leaders of this group were James Gillespie Birney (1792–1854), Kentucky born and former slave holder, and Gerrit Smith (1797–1874), wealthy New York State philanthropist.

Birney had come into prominence after founding the *Philanthropist* in Cincinnati, Ohio in 1836. It became a

Courtesy Library of Congress
The readers of Horace Greeley's newspaper The Tribune *encompassed the northern part of the country from Maine to Oregon. New ideas and reforms were communicated to the people through this medium. Greeley was anti-slavery and anti-theatre, and was opposed to women's suffrage, although he believed in more employment for women. The early daguerrotype above shows Horace Greeley as a young man.*

1848   *Courtesy The Public Library of Cincinnati*
and Hamilton County, Cincinnati, Ohio
Cincinnati, Ohio

Cincinnati was a city torn by dissension over the slavery issue.
Its industrial interests were often pro-slavery, yet it became
a seat of the abolitionists. It was the home of Lane Seminary,
where the slavery question was debated fiercely in the 1830s,
and it was here that James Birney founded his publication,
Philanthropist. *Harriet Beecher Stowe lived in the city for 16*
years and gathered much of her material for her future book,
Uncle Tom's Cabin. *Dr. Norton S. Townshend was con-*
ductor of his famous "Underground Railroad," which was
active in the city. Illustrated above is part of a panorama of
the Cincinnati waterfront taken in 1848 by daguerreotypists
Charles Fontayne and William Southgate Porter. They used
eight whole-size daguerreotype plates, one of the remarkable
feats of photography during the era.

very successfully. (His father was a partner of John Jacob Astor.) Temperance claimed Gerrit Smith's first interest in reform but he switched to abolition after witnessing an anti-slavery meeting broken up by a mob at Utica, New York, in 1834.

The 1850s would usher in a decade of general public dissension on the slavery question. After the compromise of 1850, of which the Fugitive Slave Law was a part, excitement prevailed in the northern states. The Fugitive Slave Law demanded that runaway slaves be returned to their owners. The first instance in which the law was carried into effect occurred in New York City, where a fugitive named James Hamlet, who had lived in Williamsburg for two years with his family, was taken to Baltimore and restored to his owner. Money was speedily raised by subscription and Hamlet was returned to his family. In Detroit an attempt to arrest a fugitive met with public resistance and the United States troops had to be called out; the Negro was seized but then purchased by voluntary subscription.[4] Large public meetings were held in various towns and cities to protest the law. Its immediate repeal was urged. The unpopularity of the law spurred the northern abolitionists to a new offensive attack. Garrison grimly started attacking the *Constitution*, calling it at one point "a covenant with death and an agreement with hell." He even burned the Constitution at a meeting and proclaimed it a pro-slavery document.

Gerrit Smith often furnished money for legal expenses for those charged with infraction of the Fugitive Slave Law. Petersboro, Smith's home town, was one of the underground railroad stops for escaping slaves on their way to Canada. Also a strong opponent of land monopoly, Smith gave away numerous farms of 50 acres each to indigent families. It is of interest that he experimented unsuccessfully in colonizing tracts of land in New York State with free Negroes. From time to time Smith aided the agitator John Brown with funds and gave him a farm in Essex County, New York. However, it was said, he had no knowledge that his funds were being used to incite slave insurrections. After Brown's raid on Harper's Ferry, Smith suffered a severe nervous breakdown. A moderate reformer, Gerrit Smith took a mild policy toward the South at the close of the war and declared that part of the guilt for slavery was the North's, a statement that caused resentment in most quarters.

The Fugitive Slave Law of 1850 also had its effect on Harriet Beecher Stowe, who moved to Maine after having spent eighteen years in Cincinnati near the "underground railroad." She had accompanied her father, Lyman Beecher, to Lane Seminary, where he was president. She later married a professor there, Calvin Ellis Stowe. In the quiet town of Brunswick, Maine, where her husband was teaching, she wrote *Uncle Tom's Cabin,* the book that would incense the North against the South in an emotional way no other literature had done. It was first published in serial form by *The National Era,* an anti-slavery paper in Washington, D. C. The publication came out in book form on March 20, 1852.

The author-reformer, Harriet Beecher Stowe, above, created a devastating instrument for the abolitionists, Uncle Tom's Cabin. *The Reverend Henry Ward Beecher, above, left, was also an anti-slavery figure in the era. A carte de visite, about 1867.*

The Dred Scott decision in 1856 would cause even further dissension. It was a test case in which the United States Supreme Court declared that the Negro was not entitled to rights as a federal citizen and had no standing in court.

The southerners had not been standing idly by while the northern abolitionists were making headway in the North. Southern states in 1827 had more anti-slavery societies than the North and the cause for colonization of Negroes won the support of many southerners. Many prominent slave-holders had freed their slaves, while others provided freedom in their wills. In 1832 the Virginia Legislature had debated a proposal for a gradual compensatory emancipation of the Negro which would have become effective, ironically, in 1861.

As the northern attacks on slavery became more violent, the South was thrown on the defensive for protection of her economy and for political and moral reasons. In defense, the southerners argued the benefits of the slave system and used quotations from the Bible for moral support. On seeing their long-entrenched power in the federal government unseated, and their economy weakened by threat of immediate emancipation, the southerners' thoughts turned toward secession. Edwin Ruffin, the greatest agricultural reformer of the era, whose writings and prescribed remedies for soil erosion had been highly successful, was interested in more than just soil restoration. He felt that the soil erosion problem had lessened the South's political power and thus put her at the mercy of the northern industrialists. His earnest hope was to restore the South to power and independence. In this belief he preached secession wherever he went. At age seventy, Ruffin fired the first shot of the war at Fort Sumter, South Carolina, and fought for four years. Men such as Ruffin would set the general behavior pattern of southerners who would be willing to fight and die for their traditional way of life.

The temperance movement in America got underway early in the century after an excellent paper was written on the subject in 1804 by a distinguished American doctor and politician, Dr. Benjamin Rush of Philadelphia. He outlined temperance in his text as a question of health. Shortly after, an organized temperance movement began. In 1808 a temperance society was founded at Saratoga, New York. The Massachusetts Society for the Suppression of Intemperance came into being in 1813. These were the early ones. The movement gathered momentum mainly through the influence of churches. In 1826, the American Society for the Promotion of Temperance was founded in Boston and by 1833 there were 6,000 local societies in several states with more than a million members. The campaign was

1856

The central figure in the raging controversy between North and South—the Negro. The Dred Scott decision in 1856 would cause even further dissension throughout the country. Of interest in the above daguerreotype is the tooth hanging from the ribbon. In this age, the tooth often denoted a dentist in advertising.

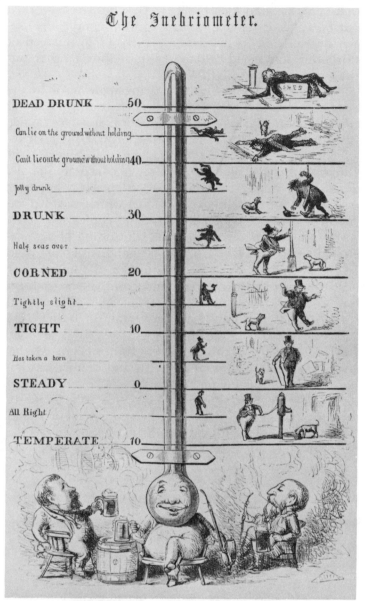

Many well-known Americans took part in the temperance crusades of the 1850s. The greatest temperance festival ever held was at Tripler Hall, New York City, in February, 1852. It was well attended by such notables as General Sam Houston, Horace Mann, the educator, and P. T. Barnum of circus fame. About 1,000 people were seated and after supper a series of speeches was made about the ill effects of alcohol. General Houston made an appropriate talk on the evils of intemperance and made the crowd laugh at his comical anecdotes. The temperance movement was generally supported by the leading publications of the era.

against the use of "spirits" and the pledge of abstinence did not include all alcoholic drinks until 1836. (There were some exceptions.)

In 1840 the "Washington Movement" was started in Baltimore by a group of reformed drunkards. Their activities were carried on by public meetings and from this nucleus many societies were formed, resulting in about a half million people's taking the pledge. After the first early success of the temperance movement, interest lagged and general apathy set in. State legislatures then took over and began introducing laws. New York State passed a law in 1845 prohibiting sale of liquor, but it was repealed in 1847. State prohibition was first introduced in 1846 under agitation in Maine, and by 1851 was adopted there. Other states that had trial prohibition were Vermont in 1852, Connecticut in 1854, New Hampshire in 1855, and later Massachusetts and Rhode Island. States that tried and abandoned the law were Illinois (1851–1853), Indiana (1855–1858), Michigan, Iowa, Nebraska, South Dakota. Some areas had local prohibition in a limited form, known as local vetoes (options). This was an older plan, used by Indiana in 1832 and Georgia in 1833. The system worked out fairly well; its adaptability to local conditions usually outweighed its disadvantages. By 1853, thirteen of thirty-one states had outlawed liquor, but all that was swept away by the Civil War.

Among the various alcoholic drinks consumed by the Americans in the 1840s were: French brandy, London Gin, Monongahela Whisky, Jamaica spirits, Yankee rum, pineapple cider, Philadelphia porter, Ginger champagne, Sling, Toddy, Sangarie, Sherry Cobbler, Mint Julep, Apple-jack, and Ale cocktail (a concoction of ale, ginger and pepper). A note of interest on a porter barrel was the marking of two X's, which meant "too good for common and weak-minded people."

The 1850 census reported the consuming of 42,133,-955 gallons of whiskey, 6,500,000 gallons of rum, and 1,177,924 gallons of beer. The intake of "spirits" per head for every man, woman, and child in the country for 1840 was 2.52 gallons; for 1850, 2.23 gallons; and for 1860, 2.86 gallons. The grand total, including wine and beer for 1840, was 4.17; for 1850, 4.08; and for 1860, 6.43. Much of this figure was liquor exported, but also an appreciable amount of wine and brandy was imported. New England rum was a popular export. When the Reverend John Pierpont made his pilgrimage to the Holy Land, the first object he saw on the wharf at Beirut was a hogshead of New England rum. It was the opinion of many that the above figure on beer con-

After 1856
Tobacco did not escape the reformers. Arguments for and against its use developed into a controversy. Health hazards were pointed out, but as no facts were available, the warnings were ignored by the general public.

sumption was too modest. The capital invested in breweries in 1850 was $4,000,000, with New York and Pennsylvania as the great distilling and beer-making states.

Tobacco did not escape the reformers. It was preached against with some violence, but reportedly the users of tobacco replied to the agitators in temperance language. To quote a reformer's piece of the day against tobacco:

> Tobacco's an outlandish weed,
> Doth in the land strange wonders breed;
> It taints the breath, the blood it dries,
> It burns the head, it blinds the eyes;
> It dries the lungs, scourgeth the lights,
> It numbs the soil, it dulls the sprites;
> It brings a man into a maze,
> And makes him sit for other's gaze.

In 1859 forty different species of tobacco described by botanists were used for tobacco to be smoked, chewed, or snuffed.[5] The health issue of tobacco was constantly brought up, but without facts to substantiate the claims the subject was not debatable.

The widespread interest in temperance and anti-slavery led to the movement of Women's Rights. When Elizabeth Cady Stanton (1815–1912) went to London on her wedding trip in 1840 with her famous abolitionist husband, Henry Brewster Stanton, she met during her stay Mrs. Lucretia Mott, an American delegate who

1858
Some women took care of their own reforms. The Scientific American *reported on July 30, 1846, that an army of about 40 women in Utica, Michigan, armed themselves and proceeded to a bowling alley and demolished the building and all of its apparatus. The building was 80 feet long!*

Brownell Anthony (1820–1906). A writer and an excellent speaker, Miss Anthony strove for complete legal equality of the sexes. She worked closely with Elizabeth Stanton in campaigns for rights of women to vote, own property, get divorced, and wear suitable clothes. It was the dress reform advocated by one member of the movement, Amelia Bloomer, that brought ridicule. This was a mannish type costume fashioned for comfort and was adopted by many of the Women's Rights followers. The movement did not become powerful until after the Civil War.

Although Women's Suffrage was slow in making gains, inroads were being made for employment of women. A catalogue of 1847 listed women now working as makers of gloves, glue, gold and silver leaf, snuff, cigars, trusses, and harnesses; they were also employed as laundresses, stereotypers, leechers (letting of blood), soda room keepers. In 1850 the list grew longer and included makers of men's and boys' clothing and workers in the new industry of manufacture of rubber articles. The year 1849 saw a department store employing female clerks in Philadelphia. The holding of public office by

1852

The Bloomer Costume

A mannish-type costume, designed for comfort, was advocated by Amelia Bloomer, dress reformer. Turkish, bloomer-like trousers were the keynote of the outfit. Many of the Women's Rights followers adopted the costume. Subject (above) is unknown.

had been barred from the World Anti-slavery Convention. (Stanton was also there as an American delegate.) A friendship developed between the women and thereafter both became active in Women's Rights. The Stantons moved from Boston to Seneca Falls, New York, in 1847. The following year Mrs. Stanton circulated a petition to secure passage of a law giving married women property rights. During this same year (1848) Lucretia Mott, Martha C. Wright, and Elizabeth Stanton led the first Women's Rights Convention at Seneca Falls. Other conventions held at Salem and Worcester, Massachusetts, in 1850 were forerunners of annual meetings. Elizabeth Stanton spoke before the New York State Legislature in 1854 on rights of married women and again in 1860 on the subject of drunkenness as grounds for divorce.

An experienced anti-slavery and temperance reformer joined the ranks for Women's Rights in 1854, Susan

ONE OF THE STRONG-MINDED.

A sketch showing a woman dressed in a "Bloomer" costume.

females was virtually nil. The *Nebraska Polladium* on October 31, 1854, noted that the "number of females holding office as postmaster was 128, all unmarried." Amelia Bloomer, dress reformer, saw waitresses in Albany in 1854. By the mid-1850s typesetting was a woman's work. Some female work was dishonest. The *New York Tribune* in 1843 cited pickpockets and counterfeiters.[6]

Crime in general in the 1840s ran the gamut from church ladies' coming before the grand jury for selling lottery tickets at a "Ladies Fair," to bank robberies and murder. Robbers broke in the U.S. patent office in November 1848, and took "considerable valuables." An advertisement run by the patent office offered $1,500 reward. On June 29, 1841, "Hawkeye," the famous burglar of the day, was finally convicted. "Hawkeye," alias William Seal, alias William Thompson, was described as a short, active man 25-30 years old, snugly built. "He is a cad," the paper read; he is an "unlocksmith." The great swindler of the day was Colonel Monroe Edwards.

Blackwell's Island Lunatic Asylum, shown above, was located a short distance from New York City and was accessible by steamboat. A considerable portion of the picturesque grounds was devoted to flower beds, flowering trees, and vegetable plots. Much of the food used at the asylum was grown by the patients. The original building consisted of two wings, forming a right angle with their octagonal center. One wing was occupied by male patients, the other by females. The octagonal center was devoted to offices, parlors, and physicians' apartments. Other buildings were the "Lodge," for violent cases and newcomers, and the "Retreat." Outbuildings were the cook house, stable, blacksmith's forge, paint house, and a dead house.

Typical punishment for crimes were: cheating a tailor of $250 brought the culprit four years and five days;[7] assault and robbery, seven years' hard labor; theft from homes, six months to one year; assault and battery of a constable, three years; stealing a horse and wagon, three years. In Connecticut in 1840 lying was punished by stripes, blasphemy by pillory. The *Clinton Gazette* reported in May 1843, "Friday evening May 22, a crowd assembled to decide the fate of James, accused of inciting the blacks to insurrection. After a vote the hanging group won and James was hung to a mulberry tree." In the West a jury would not convict if it believed the defendant was better than his victim. For debt collection in most parts of the United States, a squire or magistrate who had a small office at town hall issued warrants. (Changes in laws to abolish imprisonment for debt were begun around 1815.) Many debtors or wanted criminals escaped to the West to avoid prosecution.

Quakers from Pennsylvania from the end of the eighteenth century sought to reform the criminal. They believed that help for the living was better than execution for crimes. Prison reform was first begun with Walnut Street Penitentiary, Philadelphia. The idea was to isolate the criminal by placing him in a separate cell, in the belief that this would wean him away from his evil ways and that a cure might follow. No remarkable results were forthcoming. However, this set a precedent and several states followed Pennsylvania's lead. New York built Auburn Penitentiary, following these new principles. The results were deplorable. Many inmates became insane from the complete isolation. Out of this situation a less severe system emerged, called the silent system; the men labored together during the day and were separated at night. This worked out better than the other system but resulted in despotism among the overseers.

In 1831 England was delving into the problem of prisons. English sentiment was strong for confining prisoners in separate cells, one reason being the difficulty in classifying prisoners. A committee set up by the House of Commons in that year was impressed by the superior methods used in America for prison discipline. It was decided by the British to send Mr. W. Crawford on a special mission to study American methods. On his return, in 1834, he presented a lengthy report and many reforms were adopted.

Conditions were far from desirable in American prisons in 1840, but progress was being made. Not until Dorothea Dix appeared on the scene in 1841 would major reforms be accomplished in the prisons and in increased public care of the insane and poor. Miss Dix grew up in the home of her grandmother in Boston.

She taught school for a few years until 1841, when she became interested in the conditions of prisons and poor houses. Her next two years were spent in visiting every such institution in the state of Massachusetts. She looked into the treatment of pauper insane and found to her horror that some were chained in cold, damp rooms in prisons. She also found men imprisoned for a fifty dollar debt, and other sad conditions. By 1847, Dorothea Dix had traveled from Nova Scotia to the Gulf of Mexico and had visited 18 state penitentiaries, 300 county prisons and houses of correction, and over 500 poorhouses. Her hard work brought results. Insane asylums were established in 20 states and also in Nova Scotia and Newfoundland. North Carolina State Hospital for the insane at Raleigh was opened in 1856 as a direct result of her work. In connection with the institution was an epileptic colony.

In 1853 Miss Dix secured better equipment for lifesaving service on Sable Island, Nova Scotia, then called the "graveyard of ships." The following year she secured the passage through Congress of a bill granting the states 12,250,000 acres of public lands to be utilized for the benefit of the insane, deaf, dumb, and blind, but it was vetoed by President Pierce.

After seeing her success turn to failure, Miss Dix went to England for a rest. However, she quickly became interested in conditions of the insane in Scotland and opened the way for many reforms. She was an international figure by then, her work having also extended to other European countries and Japan. At the onset of the Civil War she offered her services to the federal government and was appointed "superintendent of women nurses."

Law books in the 1840s show that many "poor laws" were being passed in the various states to establish care for paupers. Many indigent persons not able to purchase wood or other necessities were helped at these almshouses, usually conducted by the county or state. Some of these establishments had farms attached that were worked by the poor. There were ordinarily no restrictions as to entering or leaving, it being voluntary. Most of the inmates were elderly people, most of whom worked, doing a few chores every day. The men usually worked in the vegetable garden, weather permitting; the women had the duties of washing, ironing, and cooking. South Boston had a very large institution of this sort several stories high. A chapel for Sunday services was provided on each story. The building housed about 200 to 300 paupers and was supported annually with little expense to the community because of the work accomplished by the inmates.

Orphan asylums on this plan did not do well. It was

1845
. . . The problem of old age was recognized in this era and was widespread. . . . The townspeople, churches, county, and state all shared the burden.

Amherst, Massachusetts, recollected the old French war perfectly. From the South came the report from the *Savannah Republican* on March 29, 1849, of the death at Ogeechee of Mrs. Lowrania Thrower, at least 133 years of age. A census taken in 1825 recorded her age at 110. Some accounts made her 137 at death. She had seven children before the Revolution and was a member of the Baptist church for over 100 years.

The problem of old age was recognized in this era, and was widespread. The townspeople, churches, county, and state all shared the burden. The problem would become gradually more acute as foreign immigration was stepped up and the great migration westward contributed to the social breakdown of families.

By 1860 great strides had been made by the reformers in the field of education, with moderate gains in prison reform, care of the poor, the insane, and deaf mutes. Temperance had made headway and Women's Rights

too confining for children and they did not appear to be healthy. The orphan institutions, although established by legislature, were supported wholly by private subscription.

Some interesting reports of the aged were brought to light. The *American Bible Society Record* for May 1849 said that "George Burkhart living in Harlan County, Kentucky was one of the most extraordinary men of his age and oldest man known to be living. 114 Years old, born in Germantown, Pennsylvania. He lived for several years in a hollow sycamore tree of such dimensions as to contain his family, wife and six children, bed, bedding, cooking utensils." (The exploring agent for the American Bible Society found him.) The *Scientific American* of June 9, 1849, reported that a slave who was believed to be 122 years old when he died in

1858
A typical reformer verse from a magazine of the period:
Where the whip is the common master;
Where the strong oppress the weak;
Where the weak upon the weaker
Their petty vengeance wreak . . .

was making steady gains. The slavery question, however, had reached a frenzied impasse. Words were bitter and vindictive in Congress; name-calling was sensational between the North and South. Suddenly the southerner who had been respected and honored as a gentleman a few years before, was, under the same conditions, according to the northerner living licentiously. The North, where the southerner had summered and had often sent his sons to college, was now hated and outlawed. The moderate man North and South was rendered helpless before a movement too strong to fight. This society had been undergoing a tremendous barrage of propaganda, both oral and written, stirring the masses to uncertainty and unrest. The abolitionists had done a remarkable job.

There can be no doubt that the propaganda had overlooked the South's virtues and its contribution to the country as a whole. Some historians almost a century after the Civil War, on looking at the total picture from an unbiased view, began to realize that the South had given a delicate balance to national life, had given a respectability to certain rural social values; most important of all, the South had held back, by her power in the government, a leaning toward consolidation of power in federal government.

The heavy veil of fog that lay over the land in 1860, created by the propaganda of well-meaning but often radical reformers, would obscure the light of reason and strangle this fluid and prosperous society. Democracy would break down and America would enter into a long and tragic Civil War.

18
Obituary

Death was a familiar figure in the household in an age when only the healthy survived. The practical people of the day accepted the inevitable. Death walked with morbidity and sentimentality through the poetry and prose of the era. Epitaphs were long and glowing in their testimonials to the dear departed.

Cholera epidemics were prevalent from 1849–1853, and there were other fatal diseases with no known remedy. Charms, bracelets, and necklaces, plus worthless patent medicines, were the only "solutions" known for these diseases. Sanitation and true medical skill were mere trickles in the sea of demand. Help would come, but not in this age. The people accepted death as God's will, buried their dead, and marched onward.

In this changing period of American history, the physical and mechanical devices of the funeral were undergoing innovations. The fundamental process of disposing of the bodies of the dead grew greatly in ornamentation and elaborateness in this era. Inquisitive and inventive minds were busy devising better products for the burial demand. The American middle-class were being buried with pomp befitting their financial station. The rich man had long held sway with the largest headstone in the cemetery, but his place in the burial yard was being challenged by the stones, tombs, and epitaphs of the growing middle-class. The plain gray slate with its simple inscription had become obsolete. Angels and heavenly designs coupled with flowing verse were helping the souls to the hereafter in splendor.

He Fears Death!
Why I would totter to its gentle arms
As a tired infant to its mother's bosom.
He who knows life, yet fears to die, is mad.[1]

Americans, unlike the Europeans, had an enterprising group of undertakers. "Coffin Stores" displayed their best-grade and most elaborate coffins in front of their establishments. These emporiums were owned and operated by undertakers. On display inside were burial boxes for every pocketbook, ranging from the humble pine box to polished satinwood with solid silver trim. This feature of ready-made coffins was unique; only the American profession of burial men had them; their European counterparts did not standardize their products. In 1844 a Peter Hiram advertised in Columbia County, New York, that he had for sale velvet lined, polished maple coffins for $20 and up.[2] The mortuary business was highly competitive. The coffin was the most expensive single item necessary for purchase by the bereaved, so it was natural for the profession to feature the burial boxes. It was the custom among the more aggressive undertakers to load a wagon full of assorted coffins whenever a tragedy of any magnitude occurred, and head for the scene. For example, when the Hudson River steamer "Henry Clay" exploded and burned in 1852, approximately 70 persons were lost. By the next day a number of undertakers, each with his load of coffins, displayed his wares along the river where the bodies were washing ashore. As the relatives could identify a corpse, they would also transact the coffin purchase on the scene. During the cholera epidemics, so the humor of the day had it, town mayors often appointed undertakers to take the physical measurements of incoming strangers. When a stranger inquired as to the reason, the undertaker would say, "Not a single stranger who has arrived here in the last ten days has lived more than three or four hours, and the Mayor has charged me to prepare coffins in readiness so as soon as your pulse stops

1846

View on Harvard Hill
*The rise of the ornate cemetery in nature's setting began with
the founding of Mt. Auburn, located near Boston, in 1832.
This new conception of burial started a nationwide trend
away from the traditional churchyard plot, and by 1850 the
rural cemetery was commonplace. Engraving by James
Smillie.*

we will have you ready for burial—quick burials are
in the interest of health." Presumably, the incoming
strangers did not linger the necessary time to use the
prepared coffin.

In this era of stock companies and stock manipulation, it is not surprising to find large numbers of "Burial
Companies" organized to provide new cemeteries.
These land-speculating companies paid their stockhold-
ers from ten to 12½ percent profit per annum.[3] Very
few towns were without one or more Burial Companies.
All were busily engaged in selling small burial plots
for the perpetual rest of the dear departed. Firms of
marble dealers were also expanding their stock of fin-

ished products to meet the demand for a sentimental
memory.

Fundamentally, the most essential piece of burial
equipment was the coffin, and to a lesser extent, the
burial case, a popular innovation. In 1840 most coffins
were made of wood or wood products. In 1847 a new
invention would appeal to the undertaker world—that
of the glass coffin. The *Scientific American* in that year
described two new coffins to be offered to the public—
"A coffin of glass or thick plates of china: joined together by a durable cement" and the second, "a wood
case lined with plates of glass, united by a mixture of
fused glass and borax." This newspaper enthusiastically

1848

A Vigil by the Coffin
Death was accepted as God's will.

In 1848 "An air-tight coffin of cast or raised metal" resembling an Egyptian sarcophagus was patented by Almond D. Fisk. Competing metal coffins quickly followed, but "Fisk Metallic Cases" remained the most popular brand in the 1850s. Undertakers were urged to pack evergreen boughs and foliage between the coffin and outside burial case to prevent the casket from banging around when being lowered into the grave. It was also suggested that the undertakers tie the hands of the deceased across the breast if the coffin were very narrow.[6] By 1860 complete burial service was offered. The mortuary advertised hearses, carriages, shrouds, caps, plates, with calls answered day or night. The hearses were special black burial wagons, draped in black and pulled by black horses also draped in black.[7]

Somehow or somewhere in America began a unique innovation—photographing the dead. For the first time

1853

Her hands lie folded on her breast,
Crossed like the cross that gave her rest;
She looks as if some heavenly guest
Had told her that her soul was blest.
                                      Grahams Magazine, *1846*
The traditional hexagon coffin, above, was often used in this era.

endorsed these, for the advantage of the body's being viewed through the glass and also because the sealed casket would enable distant relatives to come and view the mortal remains before being interred. Mr. T. B. Rapp of Philadelphia, Pennsylvania, invented an improved glass coffin in 1852, and he advertised his products to have the following advantages:

> They are made air tight and of sufficient strength to prevent bulging. The durability of glass is well known, and the remains of the departed being entirely protected, decomposition goes on very slowly.[4]

However, back in 1847, chemistry and science were working on the very same problem of decomposition of the mortal remains. In that year, a Mr. James S. Scofield, a chemist of New York, discovered a chemical process for preserving the body after death. Like the adherents of the glass coffin, he had the following advertisement for his embalming fluid:

> The body may be kept any length of time thus permitting the arrival of distant relatives.[5]

A simple rural funeral typical of the early 1840s was the burial of "Little Joe." Little Joseph was eight or nine when he passed on, and, as was the custom of the day, his body was put in a coffin and placed by the open parlor window. Legend had it that "if a coffin was placed by an open window the soul could easily depart." Neighbors, some with babes in arms, would come to view the dead child; the tears flowed. The next day before noon, the family pastor read a simple passage from the Bible to the neighbors assembled in the parlor. After the prayer was finished, the coffin was closed and loaded on the farm wagon. Along the road, following the wagon bearing Little Joe's body, streamed the relatives and friends, some walking and some riding in other wagons, all sad. The procession wound its way to the family burial plot high on the hill. A low stone fence surrounded the area; other, older stones were there, for Little Joe was joining his ancestors. Amid the sounds of the anguished parents and friends, the body was lowered into the open grave. Simple prayers, the final words, consigned "Little Joe" to his final resting place. And there a stone was marked:

1856
Photographers often took portraits of mourners and furnished appropriate black accessories for the occasion, as illustrated above.

the masses of the population were offered a means of preserving an exact image of their dead for posterity. The custom must have begun sometime in the early 1840s. It had no precedence in the history of man; it could not, for photography itself was born in 1839. This innovation was strictly American and was widely practiced by American daguerreotypists. By 1850 it became a lucrative source of income to those specializing in photographing the dead. A competitive charge for this service at the home of the deceased was $75. By comparison a daguerreotype of a living person taken at the studio brought from $1.00 to $5.00, depending on the skill and reputation of the photographer. The custom became so widespread in the 1850s that photographic supply houses offered, as part of their standard stock, framing mats in black, and daguerreotype cases of sentimental design, appropriate for framing the portrait of the dear departed. This recording of an exact moment of history would lead Mathew B. Brady later to photograph his famous battlefield scenes in the Civil War. Probably because of the heavy increase of burials under war conditions, this custom fell into obscurity.

1853
An example of the widespread custom of photographing the dead.

J—— D—— H——, son of —— and ——, Died June 23, 1843, aged eight years, six months and ten days.

> My days on earth, indeed, were few,
> But earth is full of woe;
> And had I staid with Pa and you,
> I must have found it so.

"Little Joe's" simple funeral may be compared with the elaborate funeral of Captain G——— in the late 1850s. This influential man was buried in the style of a great country funeral—New England fashion. Many of the poorer sort were glad of a chance, for once, to enter the grand parlors, to see the marvels with which they were said to be furnished, to look with awe at the brilliant carpets, shining crimson curtains, the pianoforte, the sofa and chairs all cushioned with bright velvet, the mirrors stretching from ceiling to floor, great gilded frames showing richly colored pictures, and the

1849
Legend had it that "if a coffin was placed by an open window, the soul could easily depart."

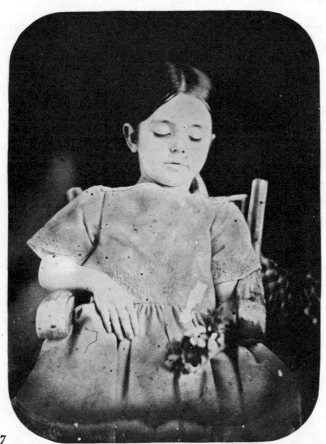

1847
Daguerreotypists advertised that they would take portraits of the deceased in the studio or at home. Occasionally, as in the case of a child, the body was held upright to give a natural effect. See above.

mystery of a hundred knick-knacks, of which none knew the name or use. Country people who came—old men in homespun and old ladies in dim calico—sat on costly seats and pondered, perhaps with a thought of the rich man and Lazarus in the only book they knew, the Bible. Open-mouthed, round eyed urchins stood on softly carpeted stairs; little girls smelled their nosegays of pinks and shyly eyed the unaccustomed splendors. Now and then the children whispered among themselves. For once, the great house was filled. When the clergyman had concluded his remarks and prayer, all guests were invited to view, for the last time, "our dear departed friend." None failed to take advantage of the offer— what a beautiful coffin! Real mahogany, and all lined with white satin! Still and pale the Captain lay for all to look. Afterwards, the lid was screwed down, the coffin lifted by its silvered handles, and the remains were borne, feet foremost, through the handsome hall and down his marble steps, along the shaded walk, never to return. The long procession, the prominent and the relatives in the lead, walked slowly down the path. The bell tolled. The orderly motley line, with the kitchen

1855
. . . My days on earth, indeed, were few.

1844
Professional undertakers always wore gloves.

help in the rear, slowly gathered near the open grave. The bright warm sunlight of a calm June day was all about. With the minister murmuring a prayer, the costly coffin, enclosed in a simple pine box, was slowly lowered into the narrow bed, six feet below the greensward. Thus the Captain was put to rest in the manner of the day.

Beneath the willows which are growing there,
Repose the forms of those once young and fair;
The aged, too, here rest in mystic sleep,
And here the widow often comes to weep.
                    R.I.P.

Source Notes

CHAPTER 1

1. *Seventh Census of the United States,* 1850.
2. Howard Chapelle, *The American Sailing Navy* (New York: 1940), p. 464.
3. John Plumbe, Jr., *The Plumbeian* (1846). The New York Public Library has a copy (uncatalogued) under the title *National Plumbeotype Gallery.*

CHAPTER 2

1. Philarète Chasles, *Anglo-American Literature and Manners* (New York: 1852), p. 286.
2. *Scientific American* (August 28, 1845).
3. *Ibid.* (May 14, 1845).
4. *Ibid.* (July 23, 1846).

CHAPTER 3

1. Goodrich, Charles A., *The Family Tourist* (Philadelphia: J. W. Bradley, 1848), p. 209.
2. *Doggett's Directory,* New York City (1846).
3. *Ibid.*
4. *Scientific American* (July 30, 1846).
5. *Ibid.* (March 11, 1848).
6. *The New-Mirror* (New York: 1844), pp. 104–5.
7. *Harper's Monthly Magazine* 25:318.

CHAPTER 4

1. V. O. Key, Jr., *Southern Politics* (New York: Alfred A. Knopf, 1950), p. 207.
2. Avery Craven, *An Historian and the Civil War* (Chicago: University of Chicago Press, 1964), p. 37.
3. Hodding Carter, *Lower Mississippi* (New York: Rinehart and Company, Inc., 1942), pp. 206–213.
4. Katherine M. Jones, *The Plantation South* (New York: The Bobbs-Merrill Company, 1957), pp. 52–56.
5. Avery Craven, p. 185.
6. *Harper's Monthly Magazine* 29:115–24.
7. *Ibid.,* 35:505–6.
8. *Ibid.,* 25:178.
9. Hodding Carter, pp. 200–210.
10. Langston Hughes and Milton Meltzer, *A Pictorial History of the Negro in America* (New York: Crown Publishers, 1956), p. 68.

CHAPTER 5

1. John McMasters, *The History of the People of the United States, 1841–1850* (New York: D. Appleton and Company, 1910), 7:201.
2. *Ibid.,* 199.
3. *Ibid.,* 226.
4. *Ibid.,* 192.
5. *Bulletin of the Missouri Historical Society* (1953), vol. 10, no. 1, p. 65.
6. *Cleveland Plain Dealer* (newspaper), 1841.
7. *Harper's Monthly Magazine* 21:606.
8. *Ibid.,* 1:276.
9. *Scientific American* (June 30, 1849).
10. *Ibid.*
11. *Ibid.*
12. *The Daguerreian Journal* 11 (1851):308.
13. *Harper's Monthly Magazine* 21:301.

CHAPTER 6

1. United States National Museum. Booklet no. 241, p. 3.
2. *The American Pocket Library* (Philadelphia: 1841), p. 44.
3. *The New-Mirror* 3 (1844):146–49.
4. Orson Squire Fowler, *The American Phrenological Journal* (New York: Fowler and Wells, 1848), p. 335.
5. *Littell's Living Age* 28 (January–March, 1851):516.
6. *Putnam's Monthly Magazine* 3 (1854):19, 20.
7. *Littell's Living Age* 26 (July–September, 1850):492–95.
8. *Putnam's Monthly Magazine* 1 (1853):644–45.
9. *Harper's Monthly Magazine* 13:551, 259.
10. *The Home Circle* (July–December, 1857), p. 494.
11. J. G. Holland, *The Life of Abraham Lincoln* (Springfield, Massachusetts: 1866), p. 168.
12. *Harper's Monthly Magazine* 20:256.
13. *Ibid.,* 832.

CHAPTER 7

1. Katherine M. Jones, *The Plantation South* (New York: The Bobbs-Merrill Company, 1957), p. 188.
2. *Harper's Monthly Magazine* 22:559.
3. *Ibid.,* 20:569.
4. Clifton E. Olmstead, *Religion in America Past and Present* (New Jersey: Prentice-Hall, 1961), p. 73.
5. Edwin Scott Gaustad, *Historical Atlas of Religion in America* (New York: Harper and Row, 1962), p. 145.

6. *The Iris* (newspaper), Binghamton, Broome County, N.Y., February 13, 1847.
7. *Harper's Monthly Magazine* 20:700–702.
8. *The Iris*, February 13, 1847.
9. Leonora Cranch Scott, *The Life and Letters of Christopher Pearse Cranch* (New York: Houghton Mifflin Company, 1917), p. 52.
10. *Harper's Monthly Magazine* 31:126–27.
11. Timothy L. Smith, "Historic Waves of Religious Interest in America." *The Annals of the American Academy of Political and Social Science* 332 (November, 1960):13.

CHAPTER 8

1. Newton Edwards and Herman G. Richey, *The School in the American Social Order* (Cambridge, Massachusetts: The Riverside Press, Houghton Mifflin Company, 1947), p. 239.
2. Carl Russell Fish, *Rise of the Common Man, 1830–1850* (New York: Macmillan Company, 1927), p. 217.
3. Ellwood P. Cubberley, *Public Education in the United States* (Boston: Houghton Mifflin Company, 1934), pp. 169–70.
4. *Ibid.*, 229.
5. *Connecticut Courant* (May 18, 1824: May 17, 1825).
6. Newton Edwards and Herman Richey, p. 404.
7. *The Ohio State Archaeological and Historical Quarterly* (1938) 47:1–7.
8. Herman G. Richey, "Reappraisal of the State School System of the Pre-Civil War Period." *Elementary School Journal* (October, 1940) 41:122–23.
9. Ellwood P. Cubberley, p. 281.
10. *Harper's Monthly Magazine* 20:553.
11. *Scientific American* (November, 1847).
12. *Ibid.* (December, 1847).
13. *Ibid.* (April, 1848).
14. William E. Dodd, *The Cotton Kingdom, A Chronicle of the Old South*, 27. *The Chronicle of American Series* (New Haven: Yale University Press, 1920), pp. 111–15.

CHAPTER 9

1. James T. Flexner, *That Wilder Image* (Boston: Little, Brown and Company, 1962), p. 356.
2. *National Academy of Design Exhibition Record 1826–1860* (New York: New York Historical Society, 1943), p. 135.
3. *Graham's Magazine* (1850), p. 344.
4. Robert Taft, *Photography and the American Scene* (New York: Macmillan Company, 1938), p. 100.
5. Marcus A. Root, *Camera and the Pencil* (Philadelphia, 1864), p. 121.
6. Oliver W. Larkin, *Art and Life in America* (New York: Holt Rinehart and Winston, 1960), p. 166.
7. *Scientific American* (June, 1853).
8. *Putnam's Monthly Magazine* 1 (1853):240.
9. *Godey's Lady's Book* (1849), p. 65.
10. *Putnam's Monthly Magazine* 6 (1855):112.
11. *Ibid.*, 560.
12. *Ibid.*, 3 (1854):142.
13. *Harper's Monthly Magazine* 1:703–4.
14. *Ibid.*, 850.

CHAPTER 10

1. *Ninth Annual Report of the Smithsonian Institution* (1854), pp. 147–55.
2. *Scientific American* (August 4, 1849).
3. *Transactions of the American Institute* (1852), pp. 86–90.
4. *Exposition of 1851 on Industries at Crystal Palace, London*, report (London: 1852), p. 1461 in the United States section.

5. *Harper's Monthly Magazine* 2:323–28.
6. *Humphrey's Journal* 4 (1852):269.
7. *Transactions of the American Institute* (1852), pp. 219–473.
8. *Ibid.*
9. *Harper's Monthly Magazine* 1:564.
10. *Transactions of the American Institute* (1852), p. 74.
11. *Exposition of 1851 on Industries at Crystal Palace, London*, report, p. 1141 in the United States section.
12. *Transactions of the American Institute* (1852), p. 98.
13. *The American Pocket Library* (1841), p. 29.
14. *Transactions of the American Institute* (1852), pp. 129, 130.
15. *Godey's Lady's Book* (1849), p. 469.
16. Floyd and Marion Rinhart, *American Daguerreian Art* (New York: Clarkson N. Potter, Inc., 1967), pp. 60–62.
17. Floyd and Marion Rinhart, *American Miniature Case Art* (Cranbury, New Jersey: A. S. Barnes and Co., 1969), pp. 29–37.

CHAPTER 11

1. *Littell's Living Age* 28 (January–March, 1851):189.
2. *Ibid.*
3. *Harper's Monthly Magazine* 1 (1850):412–14.
4. *Graham's Magazine* 22 (1843):218.
5. *Harper's Monthly Magazine* 1 (1850):851.
6. *Ibid.*, 563.
7. *The Kansas Historical Quarterly*, (vol. 11, no. 4, November, 1933), pp. 365, 366.
8. Clarence P. Horning, *Wheels Across America* (New York: A. S. Barnes and Company, 1959), pp. 33, 34.
9. *Ibid.*, 173.
10. *Ibid.*, 174.

CHAPTER 12

1. *Scientific American* (October, 1852).
2. Philarète P. Chasles, *Anglo-American Literature and Manners* (New York: Scribner 1852), p. 293.
3. *Scientific American* (September 17, 1846).
4. Norman Angell, *The Story of Money* (New York: Garden City Publishing Company, 1929), p. 290.
5. *Scientific American* (July 23, 1846).
6. George L. Leffler, *The Stock Market* (New York: Ronald Press, 1963), p. 85.
7. *Ibid.*, 85.
8. *Ibid.*, 86.
9. *Ibid.*
10. *Ibid.*, 87.
11. Chasles, pp. 293–94.

CHAPTER 13

1. *Harper's Monthly Magazine* 20:126.
2. T. B. Thorpe, *Our Army on the Rio Grande* (Philadelphia: Cary and Hart, 1846), p. 239.
3. *Ibid.*, 202.
4. William Seaton Henry, *Campaign Sketches of the War with Mexico* (New York: Harper Brothers, 1847), p. 322.
5. *National Intelligencer* (May 14, 1847).
6. Alcaraz Ramon, *The Other Side; or, Notes for the History of the War Between Mexico and the United States*, trans. Albert C. Ramsey (New York: John Wiley, 1850), p. 190.
7. John Frost, *Pictorial History of the Mexican War* (1848), p. 594.
8. R. W. Bigham, *California Gold Scenes* (1886), p. 31.

CHAPTER 14

1. *The Family Register, Marriage Rites and Ceremonies* (Columbus, Ohio: L. P. Rail and Company, 1855).
2. The Reverend J. J. Excell, *An Essay on the Family* (Wooster, Ohio: Republican steam book and job office, 1859), p. 212.
3. A. L. Slawson, *Behind the Scenes, Expose of Oneida Community* (Oneida, New York: A. L. Slawson, 1875), p. 68.
4. *Ibid.,* 72.
5. John B. Ellis, *Free Love and its Votaries* (New York: United States Publishing Company, 1870), p. 403.
6. New York *Herald* (December 23, 1869).

CHAPTER 15

1. Merideth Reese (M.D.), *American Medical Gazette,* vol. 8, no. 1, January, 1857, p. 18.
2. *Ibid.*
3. *Harper's Monthly Magazine* 20:840–43.
4. *Scientific American* (March 27, 1852).
5. *Ibid.* (August, 1845).
6. O. S. Fowler, *The American Phrenological Journal* (New York: Fowler and Wells, 1848), p. 359.
7. *Ibid.,* 226.
8. *The Kansas Historical Quarterly* (vol. 11, no. 4, November 1933), pp. 377–85.
9. *Scientific American* (November 22, 1851).
10. Fowler, p. 116.
11. Jesse Haney, *Haney's Art of Training Animals* (New York: Jesse Haney and Company, 1869), p. 68.
12. *Scientific American* (November 13, 1847).

CHAPTER 16

1. *Harper's Monthly Magazine* 1:142.
2. Elizabeth McClellan, *History of American Costume 1607–1870* (New York: Tudor Publishing Company, 1942), pp. 437, 438.
3. *Ibid.*
4. *Ibid.,* 457.
5. R. Turner Wilcox, *The Mode in Footwear* (New York: Charles Scribner's Sons, 1948), p. 136.

6. *Scientific American* (March 18, 1848).
7. McClellan, p. 447.
8. *Harper's Monthly Magazine* 1:142.
9. *Peterson's Magazine* (1850), p. 320.
10. *Ibid.,* 56.
11. *Ibid.,* 176.
12. *Peterson's Magazine* (1855), p. 320.
13. *Ibid.,* 79.
14. *Ibid.,* 256.
15. *Harper's Monthly Magazine* 29:576–84.
16. *Peterson's Magazine* (1855), p. 383.
17. McClellan, p. 801.
18. R. Turner Wilcox, pp. 136, 137.
19. McClellan, p. 599.
20. *Peterson's Magazine* (1855), p. 416.

CHAPTER 17

1. Stowe Persons, *American Minds* (New York: Henry Holt and Company, 1958), p. 415.
2. Dwight L. Dumond, *Anti-slavery* (Ann Arbor: University of Michigan Press, 1961), p. 159.
3. These statistics were given by James Birney at the May meeting of the American Slavery Society in answer to questions of March 8, 1838.
4. *Harper's Monthly Magazine* 1:850.
5. *Ibid.,* 20:183, 186.
6. New York *Tribune* (October 10, 1843).
7. *Boston Daily Advertiser* (August 25, 1841).

CHAPTER 18

1. *Graham's Magazine* (1843), p. 46.
2. Uncle Sam, *Uncle Sam's Peculiarities* (London: John Mortimer, 1844), 1:158.
3. *Ibid.,* 107, 108.
4. *Scientific American* (February 21, 1854).
5. *Ibid.* (November 20, 1847).
6. *Harper's Monthly Magazine* 21:491.
7. New York City directory (1860). (Advertisement)

Selected Bibliography

A Guide to the United States Naval Academy. New York: The Devin, Adair Company, 1941.

Abbot, Charles Greeley, D.S. *Great Inventions.* Vol. 12 of *The Smithsonian Scientific Series.* New York: Smithsonian Series, Inc., 1932.

Albany Annual Register. Albany: E. H. Pease and Company, 1849.

Albany Knickerboker, The (1850)

American Heritage. Vol. 9, no. 1 (December, 1957), pp. 10–113.
Vol. 9, no. 3 (April, 1958), pp. 34–92).

American Pocket Library, The. Philadelphia, 1841.

Andrews, Edward Deming. *The People Called Shakers.* New York: Oxford University Press, 1953.

Angell, Norman. *The Story of Money.* New York: Garden City Publishing Company, 1929.

Appleton's Cyclopaedia of American Biography. Vol. 4. New York: D. Appleton and Company, 1888.

Bakewell, Frederick C. *Great Facts.* New York: D. Appleton and Company, 1859.

Bancroft, Hubert Howe. *Bancroft's Works, History of Mexico.* Vol. 5, 1824–1861. San Francisco: A. L. Bancroft and Company, 1885.

Barnes, Eric Wollencott. *The Lady of Fashion.* New York: Charles Scribner's Sons, 1954.

Beebe, Lucius. *Boston and the Boston Legend.* New York: D. Appleton-Century Company, 1936.

Binkley, Wilfred E. *American Political Parties.* New York: Alfred A. Knopf, Inc., 1964.

Bishop, Joseph B. *Presidential Nominations and Elections.* New York: Charles Scribner's Sons, 1916.

Blessing, Charles W. *Albany Schools and Colleges of Yesterday and Today.* Albany: Fort Orange Press, 1936.

Blum, Catton (ed.). *The National Experience, A History of the United States.* New York: Harcourt, Brace & World, Inc., 1963.

Boston Advertiser (1841)

Brand, Edward D. *Sentimental Years 1836–1860.* New York: D. Appleton-Century, 1934.

Brishop, Joel Prentice. *Law of Married Woman.* Boston: Little, Brown and Company, 1873.

Buchanan, Lamont. *Steel Trails and Iron Horses.* New York: G. P. Putnam's Sons, 1955.

Byron, Edward W. *The Progress of Invention in the Nineteenth Century.* New York: N.P., 1900.

California State Register. Sacramento, California: Langley and Mathews, 1857.

Carlton, Frank Tracy. *Economic Influences upon Educational Progress in the United States 1820–1850.* Madison: University of Wisconsin, 1908.

Carter, Hodding. *Lower Mississippi.* New York: Rinehart and Company, Inc., 1942.

Carvalho, Solomon N. *Incidents of Travel and Adventure in the far West; with Colonel Fremont's last expedition.* New York: Derby & Jackson, 1857.

Cary, Alice. *Married but Not Mated.* New York: Derby and Jackson, 1856.

Chapelle, Howard J. *The History of the American Sailing Navy.* New York: W. W. Norton and Company, Inc., 1949.

Chase, Gilbert. *America's Music.* New York: McGraw-Hill Book Company, 1966.

Chasles, Philarete. *Anglo-American Literature and Manners.* New York: Scribner, 1852.

Clark, Elmer T. *The Small Sects in America.* New York: Abington Press, 1959.

Clarke, John S. *Circus Parade.* New York: Charles Scribner's Sons, 1937.

Cleveland Plain Dealer (1841)

Cobb, Josephine. *Mathew B. Brady's Photographic Gallery in Washington.* Reprint from The Columbia Historical Society Records, Vols. 53–56. Washington, D.C., 1955.

Connecticut Courant (May 18, 1824; May 17, 1825)

Cooley, Donald G. *Modern Medicine.* New York: Franklin Watts, Inc., 1963.

Cord, William H. *A Treatise on the Legal and Equitable Rights of Married Women.* Philadelphia: Kay & brother, 1861.

Cornell, William M. *Honorable Horace Greeley*. Boston: D. Lothrop and Company, 1882.

Cowans, Allen. *Images of American Living*. Philadelphia and New York: J. B. Lippincott Company, 1964.

Craven, Avery. *An Historian and the Civil War*. Chicago and London: The University of Chicago Press, 1964.

Cromwell, Otelia. *Lucretia Mott*. Cambridge, Massachusetts: Harvard University Press, 1958.

Cubberley, Ellwood P. *Public Education in the United States*. Boston: Houghton Mifflin Company, 1934.

Cutler, Carl C. *Greyhounds of the Sea*. New York: Halcyon House, 1930.

Daguerreian Journal, The. New York, 1850–1851. Title changed to *Humphrey's Journal*. New York, 1852–1862.

Davenport, Millia. *The Book of Costume*. 2 vols. New York: Crown Publishers, Inc., 1948.

De Voto, Bernard. *The Year of Decision. 1846.* Boston: Little, Brown & Company, 1943.

Dickens, Charles. *American Notes and Pictures from Italy*. New York: Charles Scribner's Sons, 1934.

Dictionary of American Biography. New York: Charles Scribner's Sons, 1934.

Dodd, William E. *Cotton Kingdom, A Chronicle of the Old South. The Chronicle of American Series*. Vol. 27. New Haven: Yale University Press, 1920.

Doggett, John. *The Great Metropolis for 1846*. Directory.

Doggett's New York City Directory (1841–1845)

Downs, Charles A., The Reverend. *History of Lebanon, New Hampshire, 1761–1887*. Concord: Rumford Printing Company, 1908.

Drury, John. *Historic Midwest Houses*. Minneapolis: University of Minnesota Press, 1947.

Dumond, Dwight Lowell. *Anti-slavery*. Ann Arbor: University of Michigan Press, 1961.

———. *A History of the United States*. New York: Henry Holt and Company, Inc., 1942.

Durant, John and Bettman, Otto. *Pictorial History of American Sports*. New York: A. S. Barnes and Company, Inc., 1952.

——— and Durant, Alice. *History of the American Circus*. New York: A. S. Barnes and Company, Inc., 1957.

Eaton, Clement. *The Growth of Southern Civilization*. New York: Harper and Row, 1961.

Edwards, Newton and Richey, Herman G. *The School in the American Social Order*. Cambridge, Massachusetts: The Riverside Press. Houghton Mifflin Company, 1947.

Ellis, John B. Dr. *Free Love and Its Votaries or American Socialism Unmasked*. New York, Cincinnati, Chicago, St. Louis: United States Publishing Company, 1870.

Encyclopaedia Britannica. 11th ed. New York, 1910.

Ewers, John C. *Artists of the Old West*. New York: Doubleday & Company, Inc., 1965.

Excell, J. J., The Reverend. *An Essay on the Family*. Wooster, Ohio: Republican steam book and job office, 1859.

Fairman, Charles E. *Art and Artists of the Capital of the United States of America*. Washington, D.C.: United States Government Printing Office, 1927.

Family Magazine (1856)

Faulkner, Harold. *American Political and Social History*. New York: F. S. Crofts, 1937.

Ferguson, Charles W. *Fifty Million Brothers*. New York: Farrar and Rinehart, Inc., 1937.

Fish, Carl Russell. *The Rise of the Common Man 1830–1850*. New York: The Macmillan Company, 1927.

Flexner, James Thomas. *That Wilder Image*. Boston: Little, Brown and Company, 1962.

Foght, Harold Waldstein. *The Rural Teacher and His Work*. New York: The Macmillan Company, 1917.

Fowler, Charlotte Weld (Mrs.). *History of Weld Family*. Middletown, Connecticut: Pelton and King, 1879.

Fowler, Orson Squire. *Phrenological Journal*. New York: Fowler and Wells, 1848.

———. *A Home for All; or the Gravel Wall and Octagon Mode of Building*. New York: Fowler and Wells, 1849.

Frost, John. *Pictorial History of Mexico and Mexican War*. Philadelphia: Thomas, Cowperthwait and Company for J. A. Bill, 1848.

Frost, Thomas. *Circus Life and Circus Celebrities*. London: Chatto and Windus, 1881.

Gallaway, John Debo C. E. *The First Transcontinental Railroad*. New York: Simmons Boardman, 1950.

Garner, James W. and Lodge, Henry C. *The History of Nations*. Vol. 24. Philadelphia: John D. Morris and Company, 1906.

Garrison, Charles G., The Honorable. "The Fact of Marriage and the Limits of Divorce." An address given March 2, 1894, Philadelphia.

Gaustad, Edwin Scott. *Historical Atlas of Religion in America*. New York and Evanston, Illinois: Harper and Row, 1962.

Gehlmann, John and Bowman, Mary. *Adventures in American Literature*. New York: Harcourt, Brace and Company, 1958.

Gleason, Harold and Morrocco, Thomas, G. *Music in America*. New York: W. W. Norton & Company, Inc., 1964.

Godey's Lady's Book (1849)

Goodrich, Charles A. *The Family Tourist*. Philadelphia: J. W. Bradley, 1848.

Graham's Magazine (1843–1850)

Graham, Philip. *Showboats*. Austin: University of Texas, 1951.

Groce, George C. and Wallace, David H. *The New York Historical Society's Dictionary of Artists in America 1564–1860*. New Haven: Yale University Press, 1957.

Hahn, Emily. *China Only Yesterday*. New York: Doubleday & Company, Inc., 1963.

Handlin, Oscar. *The Americans*. Boston: Little, Brown and Company, 1963.

Haney's Art of Training Animals. New York: Jesse Haney and Company, 1869.

Harper's Monthly Magazine. Vols. 1–37.

Harper's Weekly Magazine (October 13, 1860)

Hatch, Alden. *American Express*. New York: Doubleday & Company, Inc., 1950.

Hayes, Melvin L. *Mr. Lincoln Runs for President*. New York; The Citadel Press, 1960.

Henry, William Seaton. *Campaign Sketches of the War with Mexico.* New York: Harper and Brothers, 1847.

Hill, Levi L. *A Treatise of Daguerreotype,* Part 4, "The Magic Buff." New York: Lexington, 1850. A copy may be found in the Rare Book Room, Library of Congress.

———. *Treatise in Heliochromy.* New York: Robinson and Caswell, 1856.

Hill, Ralph Nading. *Sidewheeler Saga.* New York: Rinehart and Company, Inc., 1953.

Hills, Chester. *The Builder's Guide.* 2nd rev. ed. Hartford, Connecticut: Case, Tiffany and Burnham, 1847.

Holland, J. G. *The Life of Abraham Lincoln.* Springfield, Massachusetts: The Republican Press, Samuel Bowles and Company, 1866.

Home Circle, The. Nashville, 1857.

Horgan, Paul. *Great River the Rio Grande.* Vol. 11, New York: Rinehart and Company, Inc., 1954.

Horning, Clarence P. *Wheels Across America.* New York: A. S. Barnes and Company, Inc., 1959.

Howard, John Tasker. *Our American Music.* 4th ed. New York: Thomas Y. Crowell Company, 1965.

Hughes, Langston and Meltzer, Milton. *A Pictorial History of the Negro in America.* New York: Crown Publishers, Inc., 1956.

Iris, The. Binghamton, New York, 1847.

Johnston, Johanna. *Runaway to Heaven, The Story of Harriet Beecher Stowe and her Era.* New York: Doubleday & Company, Inc., 1963.

Jones, Katherine M. *The Plantation South.* Indianapolis; New York: The Bobbs-Merrill Company, Inc., 1957.

Kansas Historical Quarterly, The. Vol. 11, no. 4. Topeka, Kansas, November, 1933.

Kemble, Hohn Haskell. *The Panama Route,* 1848–1869. Berkeley: University of California Press, 1943.

Key, V. O., Jr. *Southern Politics.* New York: Alfred A. Knopf, Inc., 1950.

Kingston Journal, The (1850)

Knight, Edgar W. *Education in United States.* Boston: Ginn and Company, 1934.

Kocher, A. L. and Dearstyne, H. *Shadows in Silver.* Charlottesville: University of Virginia Press, 1954.

Kouwenhoven, John A. *The Columbia Historical Portrait of New York.* New York: Doubleday & Company, Inc., 1953.

Krout, John Allen. Gabriel, Ralph H. (ed.). *Annal of American Sports. The Pageant of America.* Vol. 15. New Haven: Yale University Press, 1929.

Larcom, Lucy. *An Idyl of Work.* Boston: Osgood and Company, 1875.

Larkin, John W. *History of American Technology.* New York: The Ronald Press Company, 1956.

Larkin, Oliver W. *Art and Life in America.* New York: Rinehart and Winston, 1960.

Laws of Massachusetts. January Session, 1827. Chapter 143.

Leffler, George L. *The Stock Market.* New York: The Ronald Press Company, 1963.

Letters of Theodore Dwight Weld, Angelina Grimké Weld and Sarah Grimké: 1822–1844. Gilbert Hobbs Barnes and Dwight L. Dumond, eds. New York: D. Appleton-Century Company, 1934.

Life and Battles of John Morrissey. New York: E. James, 1879.

Littell's Living Age. Boston, 1850, 1851.

Lubback, Basil. *The Romance of the Clipper Ships.* London: Hennel Locke Limited, 1848.

Lutkin, Reinhard H. *The First Lincoln Campaign.* Cambridge, Massachusetts: Harvard University Press, 1944.

Lynes, Russell. *The Tastemakers.* New York: Harper and Brothers, 1954.

Mabee, Carleton. *The American Leonardo; A Life of Samuel F. B. Morse.* New York: Alfred A. Knopf, Inc., 1943.

Mansfield, E. D. *The Mexican War, A History of Its Origin.* New York: 1850.

Martin, Thomas. *Copies of Letters from Weld Papers.* Manuscript Division, Library of Congress.

Matheson, Richard. *Faith, Cults, and Sects of America.* New York: The Bobbs-Merrill Company, Inc., 1960.

McClellan, Elizabeth. *History of American Costume, 1607–1870.* New York: Tudor Publishing Company, 1942.

McCoy, Charles A. *Polk and the Presidency.* Austin: University of Texas Press, 1960.

McMasters, John. *History of the People of the United States 1841–1850.* Vol. 7. New York and London: D. Appleton and Company, 1905.

Mead, Sidney E. *The Lively Experiment.* New York and London: Harper and Row, 1963.

Meyer, Robert Jr. *Festivals, U. S. A.* New York: Ives Washburn, Inc., 1950.

Miller, Lillian B. *Patrons and Patriotism.* Chicago and London: University of Chicago Press, 1966.

Missouri Historical Society Quarterly. Vol. 111, no. 3 (March, 1936).

Monroe and Harlan. *Law, 1792–1853.* Vols. 1, 11.

Morrison, N. J. Reverend. *Olivet College and its History.* Lansing, Michigan: John A. Kerr and Company, 1866.

Moses, Montrose J. (ed.). *Representative Plays by American Dramatists.* New York: Benjamin Blom, Inc., 1964. First published 1925.

Mulder, William and Mortensen A. Russell (eds.). *Among the Mormons.* New York: Alfred A. Knopf, Inc., 1958.

National Academy of Design Exhibition Record 1826–1860. Vols. 1, 2. New York: Printed for the New York Historical Society, 1943.

National Intelligencer, The (1847, 1852, 1853)

Nevins, Allen. *Frémont.* New York: Longmans, Green & Company, 1955.

Newhall, Beaumont. *The Daguerreotype in America.* New York: Duell, Sloan and Pearce, 1961.

New Hampshire Annual Register. Concord, New Hampshire: 1855.

New-Mirror, The. New York, 1844.

New York City Directory (1860)

New York *Evening Post* (1852)

New York *Globe and Commercial Advertiser* (1844)

New York *Journal of Commerce* (1852)

New York *Times* (1851–1860)

New York *Tribune* (1843)

Nichol, Frances D. *The Midnight Cry.* Takoma Park, Washington, D.C.: Review and Herald Publishing Association, 1944.

Nichols, Roy F. *The Invention of the American Political Parties.* New York: The Macmillan Company, 1967.

Nourse, Mary A. *The Four Hundred Million.* New York: The Bobbs-Merrill Company, Inc., 1935.

Oberlin Jubilee 1833–1883. Oberlin, Ohio: E. J. Goodrich, 1883.

Ohio State Archaeological and Historical Quarterly, The. Vol. 47. Columbus, Ohio: The Ohio State Archaeological and Historical Society, 1938.

Olmstead, Clifton E. *Religion in America Past and Present.* Englewood Cliffs, New Jersey: Prentice-Hall, Inc., 1961.

O'Reilly, John Boyle. *Ethics of Boxing and Manly Sport.* Boston: Ticknor and Company, 1888.

Peregrine, Bingham. *The Law of Infancy and Coverture.* 2d American from the last London edition. Burlington, Vermont: E. H. Bennett, 1849.

Persons, Stow. *American Minds.* New York: Henry Holt and Company, 1958.

Peterson's Magazine (1850, 1855)

Photographic Art Journal, The. New York, 1851–1854. Title changed to *The Photographic and Fine Art Journal.* New York, 1854–1860.

Plumbe, John Jr. *Sketches of Iowa and Wisconsin.* First published in 1839. Preprinted by the State Historical Society of Iowa, 1948.

———. *Plumbeian.* Philadelphia, 1846. An uncatalogued copy can be found in the New York Public Library, New York City, under title *National Plumbeotype Gallery.*

Podmore, Frank. *From Mesmer to Christian Science.* New Hyde Park, New York: University Books. Reprinted 1963 from 1909 edition.

Pollack, Peter. *The Picture History of Photography.* New York: Harry N. Abrams, Inc., 1958.

Prime, Samuel Iraneaus. *The Life of Samuel F. B. Morse.* New York: D. Appleton and Company, 1875.

Putnam's Monthly Magazine. Vols. 1–7 (1853–1857).

Ramon, Alcaraz. *The Other Side; or, Notes for the History of the War Between Mexico and the United States.* Translated and edited by Albert Ramsey. New York: John Wiley, 1850.

Reese, Merideth D. (M.D.). *The American Medical Gazette.* Vol. 8, no. 1 (January, 1857).

Richardson, E. P. *Painting in America.* New York: Thomas Y. Crowell Company, 1956.

Richey, Herman G. "Reappraisal of the State School System of the Pre-Civil War Period." *Elementary School Journal* 41 (October, 1940).

Rinhart, Floyd and Rinhart, Marion. *American Daguerreian Art.* New York: Clarkson N. Potter, Inc., 1967.

———. *American Miniature Case Art.* Cranbury, New Jersey: A. S. Barnes and Company, Inc., 1968.

———. "An American Way of Death." *Art in America.* Vol. 55, no. 5 (1967), pp. 78–81.

Robinson, Harriet Hanson. *Loom and the Spindle.* Boston: Thomas Crowell and Company, 1898.

Root, Marcus A. *The Camera and the Pencil.* Philadelphia: n p., 1864.

Rowe, Joseph Andrew. *California's Pioneer Circus.* San Francisco: S. Crocker Company, Inc., 1856. Copyrighted 1926.

Sandburg, Carl. *Abraham Lincoln: The Prairie Years and the War Years.* 1 vol. New York: Harcourt, Brace & Company, 1954.

Scientific American (1845–1955).

Schlesinger, Arthur M. *A History of American Life.* New York: The Macmillan Company, 1927.

Scott, Leonora Cranch. *The Life and Letters of Christopher Pearse Cranch.* Boston: Houghton Mifflin Company, 1917.

Seager, Robert. *And Tyler Too, A Biography of John and Julia Tyler.* New York: McGraw-Hill Book Company, 1963.

Sigourney, Lydia H. (Mrs.). *Past Meridian.* 2d edition. Hartford, Connecticut: F. A. Brown, 1857.

Singletary, O. A. *The Mexican War.* Chicago: Chicago University Press, 1960.

Slawson, A. L. *Behind the Scenes, An Exposé of Oneida Community.* Oneida, New York: A. L. Slawson, 1875.

Smith, James Ward and Jamison, A. Leland (eds.). *The Shaping of American Religion.* Princeton, New Jersey: Princeton University Press, 1961.

Smith, Justin H. *The War with Mexico.* New York: Macmillan, 1919.

Smith, Oliver P. *The Domestic Architect.* Buffalo: Phinney, 1854.

Smith, Timothy L. "Historic Waves of Religious Interest in America." *The Annals of the American Academy of Political and Social Science.* Vol. 332. November, 1960.

Smithsonian Institution, Ninth Annual Report. Washington, D.C., 1855.

Stevens, Martin D. and Pendlebury, Jones, Capt. *Sea Lanes.* New York: Minton, Batch and Company, 1935.

Stokes, I. N. Phelps and Haskell, Daniel C. *American Historical Prints, Early Views of American Cities, Etc.* New York: The New York Public Library, 1933.

Strode, Judson. *Jefferson Davis, American Patriot 1808–1861.* New York: Harcourt, Brace and World, Inc., 1955.

Taft, Robert. *Photography and the American Scene.* New York: The Macmillan Company, 1938.

Terry, Walter. *The Dance in America.* New York: Harper and Row, 1956.

Thorpe, T. B. *Our Army on the Rio Grande.* Philadelphia: Carey and Hart, 1846.

———. *Our Army at Monterey.* Philadelphia: Thomas Bangs, 1848.

Towle, George M. *American Society.* London: Chapman and Hall, 1870.

Transactions of the American Institute of the City of New-York, for the Year 1852. Albany, 1853.

Trescott, Paul B. *Financing American Enterprise.* New York: Harper and Row, 1963.

Turner, Frederick Jackson. *The Frontier in American History.* New York: Rinehart and Winston, 1920.

Tyler, Lyon G. *The Letters and Times of the Tylers.* Vol. 11. Richmond, Virginia: Whittet and Shepperson, 1885.

Tyron, Warren S. *A Mirror for Americans.* Vol. 1. *Life in the East.* Chicago: Chicago University Press, 1952.

Uncle Sam. *Uncle Sam and his Peculiarities.* Vols. 1, 11.

London: John Mortimer, 1844.

Vail, R. W. G. *Random Notes on History of the Early American Circus*. Barre, Massachusetts: Barre Gazette, 1956.

Webb, Todd. *The Gold Rush Trail and the Road to Oregon*. New York: Doubleday & Company, Inc., 1963.

Webster, Clarence M. *Town Meeting Country*. New York: Duell, Sloan & Pearce, 1945.

Western Journal and Civilian, The. Vol. 6. St. Louis, 1851.

Wilcox, R. Turner. *The Mode in Footwear*. New York: Charles Scribner's Sons, 1948.

Who Was Who in America. The Historical Volume 1607–1896.

Wilkes, Charles. *United States Exploring Expedition*. Vol. 5. Philadelphia: Lea and Blanchard, 1846.

Williams, George W. *Negro Race in America*. Vol. 11. New York: G. P. Putnam's Sons, 1883.

Williams, F. L. *Matthew Fontaine Maury, Scientist of the Sea*. New Brunswick, New Jersey: Rutgers University Press, 1963.

Willison, George P. *Here They Dug Gold*. New York: Reynal and Hitchcock, 1946. Printed by Cornwall Press, Inc.

Woodson, Carter Godwin. *The Negro in our History*. Washington, D.C.: The Associated Publishers, Inc. 10th rev. ed., Charles H. Wesley (ed.), 1959.

Wright, Lawrence. *Clean and Decent*. New York: The Viking Press, Inc., 1960.

Zernow, William Frank. *Kansas, A History of the Jayhawk State*. Norman, Oklahoma: University of Oklahoma Press, 1957.

Index

Figures in italics refer to page on which illustrations occur.